CLASSICAL MYTHS

IN ENGLISH LITERATURE

―――――

quidquid dicam, aut erit aut non.—HORACE

―――――

CLASSICAL MYTHS

in English Literature

DAN S. NORTON

AND

PETERS RUSHTON

With an Introduction by

Charles Grosvenor Osgood

PRINCETON UNIVERSITY

GREENWOOD PRESS, PUBLISHERS
NEW YORK

PREFACE

No one can understand English literature unless he knows something about classical myths, for our writers from the Middle Ages to the present have used and still use classical myths in their stories and poems. Handbooks of mythology are nothing new; but today, when small Latin and less Greek are taught in our schools and when very few people are able to interpret references to classical myths from their own knowledge of Homer or Virgil or Ovid, a book of this kind is essential to most readers.

In the last hundred years a number of such books have been written, but they do not fully meet the needs of a reader of English literature because they focus on the myths themselves and pay little or no attention to the symbolic use of the myths in English literature. Ours is a new kind of handbook designed to answer the questions that the ordinary reader is likely to ask.

The problem, as we see it, is twofold. First, it is necessary to retell the myths and to retain, as far as is possible in a brief summary, the elements of individual character and concrete situation that give them life. These stories have lasted a long time because they are interesting, and we have tried to keep them that way.

Any handbook must retell the myths, but we believe that our arrangement of the material has special advantages. The reader wants to be able to find without difficulty a particular character or situation (for example, Procrustes or the stratagem of the wooden horse) and also to see this character or situation in its proper context. We have therefore grouped the material around great figures and great actions (Theseus and the Trojan War, for example), but we have arranged the book alphabetically and have provided cross references that make the lesser persons and actions in each large myth easy to locate. (The mechanics are explained in "How to Use This Book.") We hope that in this way we have avoided the shortcomings both of the mere dictionary method, which chops the myth into fragments, and of the method of extended narrative, which gives the texture of the myth but makes the reader search the index for a particular character or situation.

The second part of the problem in this sort of book is to show the relation of the myths to English literature. We are as much concerned with the symbolic value of the myth in English literature as we are with the myth itself. Our aim is to show the typical ways in which each myth has been used by English and American writers. We have not, of course, attempted to collect all the references to classical myths in English literature, nor have we allowed ourselves to become involved with anthropology. Had we done so, our work would fill many volumes and would not serve the purpose for which this book is designed.

Since our intention is to relate the myths to English literature, our guide in dealing with variant forms of the myths has usually been English literary usage rather than classical story. When a myth has variant forms, we are apt to give the versions used by English and American writers and to ignore the other versions.

All the material in this book belongs to Greek, Roman, English, and American writers. But we have particular debts to acknowledge. Professor Charles Grosvenor Osgood in our happy association with him, first as his students and then as his friends, has disappointed us only by not writing this book himself. He has read our manuscript and offered many helpful suggestions, and he has contributed a distinguished introductory essay on the values of Greek myth to later writers. We have made use of his *Classical Mythology of Milton's English Poems* and of a similar work prepared under his direction, Henry Gibbons Lotspeich's *Classical Mythology in the Poetry of Edmund Spenser.* Another scholar to whom we are obligated is Professor Douglas Bush, whose *Mythology and the Renaissance Tradition in English Poetry* and *Mythology and the Romantic Tradition in English Poetry* have been our constant companions. If he glances through this book, he will recognize many of his own ideas. His work, however, is intended for scholars; without his two volumes our job would have been more difficult, but we think that for the common reader our book in the hand is worth two of the Bush.

We owe something to earlier handbooks, but with handbooks one never knows where obligations begin. The writers of a handbook may be indebted to another handbook in the vulgar sense that they have copied whatever it says, but they may also be indebted to other handbooks in the field in a way that is complex and puzzling. Everyone who has examined a number of handbooks on any subject will agree that, no matter whose names appear on the title pages, most of the books seem to have been written by the same gray inexorable force, a force smaller than any individual author and quite inhuman. We have sacrificed hecatombs to this anonymous force in the hope of escaping its influence.

Our special thanks are due to Professor James S. Constantine, who has generously given us the benefit of his knowledge of Greek and Roman literature. He has read the book in manuscript and in proof, and has saved us from many errors and suggested many improvements. He also has advised us on the appropriate forms of classical names. The key to pronunciation and the pronunciations themselves are the work of Professor Archibald A. Hill, whose skill in linguistics is widely known and whose kindness we gratefully acknowledge.

We are thankful to Professor John Canaday for drawing the handsome map that appears as the end papers of the book. Our late colleague Professor Walter Montgomery and Mr. Jack Dalton have assisted us with encouragement and good advice. To Professor Willard Thorp we are indebted for his authorita-

tive article on Priapus, the only article in the book that is not
our own work. Finally, we owe a debt, both culinary and
scholarly, to Kathryn Norton, who has fed us in our labors and
checked our work for us.

Since we do homage to the Muses and the Graces in this book,
it is sad to observe how often they deserted us while we were
writing. And we try not to think what our natural talent for
error may have done with the almost unlimited opportunity for
error offered by our subject matter. At one point we hoped that
we might not be banished from the republic of letters for telling
lies about the gods. But later we realized that this was only half
of our dilemma. It was a mortal—a native of Athens—who wished
to punish men for telling lies about the gods, but the gods themselves sometimes punish men for telling the truth about them (see
SISYPHUS).

D. S. N.
P. R.

ACKNOWLEDGMENTS

The numerous quotations from English and American poets and prose writers are all from standard editions. A complete list seems unnecessary, but we wish to thank the editors and publishers of the numerous editions for which permission to reprint is not required, and we are grateful to the following publishers and editors for permissions to reprint: to Cambridge University Press, for excerpts from Abraham Cowley (in *The English Writings,* ed. A. R. Waller) and from Giles Fletcher (in *Poetical Works of Giles and Phineas Fletcher,* ed. F. S. Boas); to the Clarenden Press, for excerpts from Herrick (in *Poetical Works,* ed. F. W. Moorman), from Keats (in *Poetical Works,* ed. H. W. Garrod), from Lovelace (in *The Poems,* ed. C. H. Wilkinson), and from Marvell (in *The Poems and Letters,* ed. H. M. Margoliouth), and for the sonnet by Thomas Russell, "Suppos'd to Be Written on Lemnos," in *The Oxford Book of Eighteenth Century Verse,* ed. D. N. Smith); to Columbia University Press, for excerpts from Milton (in *The Works,* ed. F. A. Patterson and others); to Ginn and Company, for excerpts from Shakespeare (*The Complete Works,* ed. G. L. Kittredge); to Houghton Mifflin Company, for excerpts from Byron (in *The Complete Poetical Works,* ed. P. E. More), from Chaucer (in *The Complete Works,* ed. F. N. Robinson), and from Wordsworth (in *The Complete Poetical Works,* ed. A. J. George); to the Johns Hopkins Press, for excerpts from Spenser (in *The Works, a Variorum Edition,* ed. Edwin Greenlaw, C. G. Osgood, F. M. Padelford, Ray Heffner, and others); to The Macmillan Company, for excerpts from Tennyson (in *The Works,* ed. Hallam, Lord Tennyson); and to The Ronald Press Company, for excerpts from Pope (in *The Best of Pope,* rev. ed., ed. George Sherburn, copyright 1929 by The Ronald Press Company).

CONTENTS

HOW TO USE THIS BOOK

The material is arranged alphabetically, and the titles of the entries are printed in boldface capital letters—for example, **APOLLO.** There is a separate entry for each important character and situation and for some important places and things.

The entries are of two kinds: articles and cross references. If you look in the A's for Apollo, you will find a long article under his name. But if you look in the M's for Marpessa, you will find under her name a brief statement that she "chose for her lover the mortal Idas instead of the god APOLLO." This refers you to the article on Apollo. In every cross reference the title of the article to which you are referred is printed in lightface capital letters, as the title Apollo is in this example. You can find the story about Marpessa quickly by turning to the article on Apollo and running your eye down the pages until you find Marpessa's name printed in boldface capital and lower-case letters—**Marpessa.** Except that the common nouns are not capitalized, the title of every cross reference appears in this way in the article to which it refers. Usually a cross reference sends you to only one article, but occasionally to two or three.

For the god or mortal who has both Greek and Roman names, we use chiefly the Greek name. Therefore the article on the king of the gods, for example, is found under the name Zeus. But his Roman names are also given in the article (it opens "**ZEUS** (zōōs), or **Jupiter,** or **Jove** . . ."), and in addition these Roman names appear in the J's as cross references to the article. In general, Greek names are used without being identified as Greek, whereas

Roman names are said to be Roman in either the article or the cross reference or both.

There are two obvious exceptions to the rule that the Greek name is preferred: we use Roman names in Roman stories (Hera is Juno in the tale of Aeneas, for example) and in quotations and paraphrases from English literature in which the authors have used Roman names. One further exception of a different kind is that, in accordance with custom, a few personages are referred to chiefly by their English names, and the articles about them appear under the English rather than the Greek titles. The article on the Graces, for example, will be found under that name rather than under the name Charites.

In its own entry, each Greek and Roman name is followed by its pronunciation in parentheses—for example, **ODYSSEUS** (ō·dĭs′o͞os). Thus the Greek name of this hero is pronounced at the beginning of the article about him, but his Roman name, Ulysses, is pronounced in the Ulysses entry, which is a cross reference to the article.

Professor Archibald A. Hill, who is an expert in these matters, has supplied the key to pronunciation and the pronunciations themselves. He joins us in making the following statement.

The pronunciations are for the convenience of readers who have not already decided how they want to pronounce these names. To save space, only one pronunciation is given for each name. We are well aware, however, that most of these names have at least two widely accepted pronunciations, and we have no feeling that the pronunciations used here are better than those not used. We make only one claim for the pronunciations you will find here: they are all acceptable and they are all widely used. Ignore them if you wish, use them if you wish, but never think of them as what Meredith calls "The army of unalterable law."

KEY TO PRONUNCIATION

Symbol	Examples
ā	pace, pay
ă	bat, man, can
ä	arm, pot, pa
à	bath, laugh, can't (This symbol represents a sound that may vary in the Middle West and New England between the ă of bat and the ä of arm.)
ȧ, ė, î, ȯ, û	adjust, silent, perceptible, apron, locust (These five symbols all represent the neutral unstressed vowel. They usually all sound the same, but they may vary slightly and unimportantly in different dialects.)
ē	lease, lea
ĕ	men, bet
ė	silent (The neutral unstressed vowel. See ȧ above.)
ī	height, high
ĭ	pin, hit
î	perceptible (The neutral unstressed vowel. See ȧ above.)
ō	throat, throw
ŏ	wash (This symbol represents a sound that may vary in different dialects between the ä of arm and the õ of awl.)
ô	mourning (This symbol represents a sound that varies in different dialects between the ō of throat and the õ of awl.)
õ	awl, law
ȯ	apron (The neutral unstressed vowel. See ȧ above.)
oi	choice, boy
o͞o	stool, boo
o͝o	bull, book
ou	cowed, cow
ū	beauty, butte, pew
ŭ	cut, cud

û	locust (The neutral unstressed vowel. See *á* above.)
b	*b*ut, a*b*out, ca*b*
ch	*ch*eese, it*ch*y, ea*ch*
d	*d*ay, ra*d*io, ree*d*
f	*ph*ilosophy, *f*oot, rou*gh*
g	*g*eese, a*g*o, ra*g*
h	*h*ome, a*h*a
j	*j*ump, a*g*ent, e*dge*
k	*c*oal, a*c*re, ba*ck*
l	*l*oad, a*ll*ow, poo*l*
m	*m*ean, a*m*ount, tra*m*
n	*n*o, a*n*y, trai*n*
ng	si*ng*, si*ng*er, si*n*k
ngg	li*ng*er
p	*p*at, a*p*athy, ca*p*
r	*r*ace, ca*rr*y, ca*r*
s	*s*eed, cla*ss*y, cla*ss*
sh	*sh*oot, *s*ugar, pa*ss*ionate, cla*sh*
t	*t*able, ca*tt*y, ca*t*
th	*th*row, e*th*er, pa*th*
th	*th*ey, ei*th*er, ba*th*e
v	*v*eil, e*v*ery, sto*v*e
w	*w*in, a*w*ay
y	*y*acht, *y*es
z	*z*oo, bla*z*er, day*s*
zh	mea*s*ure, rou*ge* (unless pronounced with j)

CLASSICAL MYTHS

IN ENGLISH LITERATURE

GREEK MYTH AND THE POETS

Many readers or students of poetry in this latter day undoubtedly consider the use of Greek myth by English poets merely an
annoyance. A poet's references to unfamiliar and rather absurd
tales and persons as if they were known to every reader may serve
to exhibit his erudition, but they are a hindrance to the full
enjoyment of his poetry. Either they interrupt the music until
they can get themselves explained, or they are passed over and
discounted as unintelligible. Or so it may seem.

Earlier poets might have retorted—rather obviously—that when
they sang, the myths were a matter of common knowledge,
common to them and to their audiences. Present-day poets, however, cannot offer this retort because, for some unhappy reason,
the knowledge has ceased to be common. The twilight of the gods
has deepened into almost total darkness.

In the sophisticated Roman days of the Emperor Tiberius
there came an Egyptian sailor to Rome with a tale that on his
voyage he had heard a strange voice off the islands of Paxi calling
on him to proclaim: "The great god Pan is dead!" What if, in
this our more sophisticated day, preoccupied as we are with
science and material things, great Pan really *is* dead?

Yet Pan was still alive to the poet Keats, who prays to him:

> Be thou the unimaginable lodge
> For solitary thinkings; such as dodge
> Conception to the very bourne of heaven,
> Then leave the naked brain: be still the leaven
> That spreading in this dull and clodded earth
> Gives it a touch ethereal—a new birth:
> Be still a symbol of immensity,
> A firmament reflected in a sea;
> An element filling the space between;
> An unknown.

1

And even today, though a witty scholar observes that "there is sufficient evidence that Pan is dead in the almost annual assertions that he is not,"* he still lives in Kenneth Grahame's *Dream Days,* just as Hermes still lives in Housman's *The Merry Guide.*

Certainly, whether or not we believe the gods are dead, what we unluckily have come to call "myth," or, worse, "mythology," is not dead. It can perish only with the human spirit itself, for we are all inveterate makers and partakers of myth. We may have exchanged the glorious Athene for the Powerful Katrinka, or Zeus and Hera for Joe and Vi Green, but we *must* have our mythology.

One bright morning a little boy ran out to play, shouting,

> Sun a-calling, Wind a-calling;
> Coming, Wind! Coming, Sun!

Happy young mythmaker, all unconscious of the primitive, perennial instinct that moved him to song! This is what the learned call animism. It is really myth in its genesis. Who is not at times beguiled or bewitched or baffled or rebuffed by that form of life other than ourselves that we call Nature—so alluring, so evasive, so inscrutable? We instinctively try to break down the barrier, or rend the curtain, by giving her forms like our own—anything to make her more familiar, more friendly, more companionable. But we are like the clumsy, oafish Cyclops on the beach, pining in love for the beautiful, milk-white Galatea (sea foam) leaping and playing beside him. "She flies when thou art wooing her; when thou woo'st not, she pursues thee."†

So would we clothe the mystery in human shape in vain hope of exploring it—sun, moon, stars, night, day, storm, sea, mountain, streams, spring, autumn.

* Douglas Bush, *Mythology and the Romantic Tradition in English Poetry* (Cambridge, Mass.: Harvard University Press, 1937), p. 396.
† Theocritus, *Idyll* 6.

Yet other mysteries confront us, too, more intimate and often more terrifying—the mysteries concerning life and death, and the compelling instincts, such as love, hate, greed, hope, despair, and the sense of justice; and the other mysteries concerning the many activities and occupations that spring from these first mysteries and take possession of us, such as wooing, homemaking, war, arts, government, and reform. These, too, assume human, even divine, shape in man's imagination. Hence in time there is an accumulation that we call a mythology; hence Aphrodite, Ares, Athene, Themis, Prometheus, Orpheus, and Zeus.

All peoples with any trace of civilization have thus tried to cope with the mysteries of Nature and life, sometimes grossly and crudely, to be sure. At first local and scattered, the stories—or the best of them—tended to grow and improve and merge with the growth of a people or nation. Our *good* old stories are a survival of the fittest, that is, of the most beautiful and most expressive myths. The poorer stories fade from man's memory.

As children we wanted our favorite stories repeated always without variation, and this conservative instinct survives in us all. Yet every good storyteller will try to improve his stories every time he tells them, if only with an added or altered detail, or tone of voice, or timing here and there. Between these two unceasing contrary forces, conservative and progressive, each surviving legend has been ground and polished like a bit of quartz in a glacier until it has emerged in perfectly rounded form. Thus the story fit to survive loses nought by the telling, except what is not worth keeping, and through generations of repetition grows refined and charged with accretions of truth from its conveyors until it becomes a myth that man does not willingly let die.

In this matter of polishing, the Greeks of all peoples have been the most successful. Greek myth embodies the genius and wisdom of a most enlightened nation with a vast experience in living—a balance of elements in life both grave and gay. It is charged with high literary potentialities that have been expressed in epic, dramatic, and lyric forms and that are still capable of high expression. Thus the Greeks' endeavor to clothe the mysteries of Nature and life in human form and event—their mythology—has survived not only the Greeks themselves but all tumults of civilization to our own day and has saturated the imagination and poetry of the centuries. And it has survived, not primarily because the stories are beautiful or quaint or entertaining, but because they impart some essence of vital truth. Says Milton:

'Tis not vain or fabulous,
(Though so esteem'd by shallow ignorance)
What the sage poets taught by the Heavenly Muse,
Storied of old in high immortal verse,
Of dire Chimeras and enchanted isles,
And rifted rocks whose entrance leads to Hell,
For such there be, but unbelief is blind.

No doubt in earlier stages of culture people grew up with a belief in the literal truth of these stories. How much they realized of the original truth and the power of mystery that had first inspired the myths, who shall say? But as a nation or people grows more sophisticated and the old literal belief fades, intelligent men still discern the original elements of truth and beauty in the myths and cling to them as vehicles of truths far more compelling and acceptable than mere abstract statements. Indeed, these myths in time become universal symbols.

To the poet, though, whether he is ancient or modern, a myth is not static and fixed. In his mind it takes new root and blooms again. He keeps up the old practice of mythmaking. The story of Circe in Spenser's or in Milton's hands, the stories of Prometheus or Arethusa in Shelley's, of Endymion in Keats's, of Atalanta in Swinburne's, undergo transmutations that to the old intrinsic truth add new significance distilled in the poet's genius. The old legend receives new life from his handling. Thus by the very vitality of its inherent truth and beauty the best of the old lore has survived.

At least it survived until the last hundred years or so. Then the mystery that inspired and clothed the old tales evaporated under the literal sunlight of science, and in the pride of our new knowledge we discarded them as mere superstitions and supercargo. What part, we ask, can they take in the pursuit of science, theoretical or applied, in economics, or in the currently fashionable "social" studies?

Oddly enough, this question is not new. It has been asked in one form or another for hundreds of years. And the answer is always the same, for there is only one. The old myth, even the Nature myth, is primarily concerned with human life—with those eternal aspects of it that will elude scientific scrutiny for ever and baffle us with their mystery. Further, it is concerned with human life in a competent way. The perennial issue between youth and age, between radical and conservative, with all its confusion of folly and wisdom, of suffering and defeat, of wrong and right on both sides, is grandly intrinsic in the story of Prometheus. In Ulysses Tennyson reads the unquenchable and tragic thirst of the human soul for knowledge, and in Prometheus Shelley sees the agony of genius confined in a conventional world—he sees, in fact, his own agony. This habit or instinct of a man steeped in ancient myths to identify his own plight or career with a mythical instance is not uncommon. Milton, composing in his blindness, in one of his grandest passages sees in his own fate the common fate of ancient poets, blind Homer and others more mythical; and in this sense of community with them he is raised to highest utterance:

> nor sometimes forget
> Those other two equalled with me in fate,
> So were I equalled with them in renown,
> Blind Thamyris and blind Maeonides,
> And Tiresias and Phineus, prophets old.
> Then feed on thoughts that voluntary move
> Harmonious numbers.

A story that embodies the composite telling by thousands from generation to generation must gather unto itself a heavy freight of truth refined from the many minds that it has touched. The fiction thus becomes not individual, but communal to a group, to a nation, to the entire world; and though it may vary—must vary—in its meaning to various poets and listeners, it contains an essential and constant soul of truth that is common to all who hear or repeat it.

Dr. Johnson defended quotation from classical authors as making for "community of mind." The phrase applies even more to Greek myth; for it is a medium, refined and assayed, for the use of poets in the traffic of their precious merchandise. It helps to establish, chiefly through poetry and art, not only community of mind but community of imagination, and in fact community in the entire spiritual life of man.

Of course earlier poets were well aware of this community with hearers who had assimilated a knowledge of the old myths almost with their mothers' milk. Most people appropriated their knowledge of Greek myths from reading Ovid and Virgil in school, but we who have put away such reading are more or less disqualified from this community. Hence we need handbooks of mythology. Yet in all times, even in old Greek days, there must have been a use and a demand for such handbooks, because they have been compiled in almost every age, and run, I suspect, into hundreds. Most of them are dull, but when they are pleasantly indited, as by that master of tales, Boccaccio, or by Hawthorne in his *Wonder Book,* or by William Morris in *The Earthly Paradise,* or in the present epitome, qualification for the community becomes most agreeable.

We sometimes speak of a big assignment as a Herculean task or of a brawny football guard as rearing the shoulders of Atlas. Hercules and Atlas are familiar superstandards of prowess and strength, much more telling than mere statistics and physical measurements; for they at once stir and release the imagination and carry it back along the course of an age-old human tradition to a transcendent human being at the other end. Thus Hercules and Atlas have become communal symbols with an invariable value. Certain modern poets have tried arbitrarily to establish their own symbols, valid only in their own verse, but these symbols, by the very limitations of their newness and individual origin, prove weak in contrast to the incalculable power of traditional, communal symbols.

Many are the poets' uses of ancient myth. An obvious one is the simile. A maiden roves free and fearless in the wild places,

> Such as Diana, by the sandy shore
> Of swift Eurotas, or on Cynthus green,
> Where all the nymphs have her unwares forlore,
> Wandreth alone with bow and arrows keen
> To seek her game.

Thus Spenser rounds off a detailed portrait of Belphoebe, clothing it in the traditional and dateless beauty of the mythical instance—an instance that has gathered beauty from use by both Homer and Virgil, and, needless to say, also from the inimitable music of Spenser himself. Milton, too, added his variation. Eve

7

> Like a wood nymph light,
> Oread or Dryad, or of Delia's train,
> Betook her to the groves, but Delia's self
> In gait surpassed and goddess-like deport. . . .
> To Pales or Pomona, thus adorned,
> Likest she seemed, Pomona when she fled
> Vertumnus, or to Ceres in her prime,
> Yet virgin of Proserpina from Jove.

Such clustering of allusive and undeveloped similes is characteristic of late Alexandrian poetry. In the overripe, sophisticated latter days of Greek civilization, when Alexandria had become the center and clearinghouse of Greek literary culture, the well-worn but still cherished myths tended to appear in poetry by allusion, not explicitly, because the reader presumably was familiar with the story and found a certain pleasure in recognizing it by the allusion. Milton, in the autumn of the Renaissance, when the old myths were again a matter of everyday knowledge for the cultivated reader, practiced this same Alexandrian manner of allusion. To us, less familiar with the myths, such allusiveness is often baffling and unenjoyable. Yet, whether or not we recognize the myths, any of us with an ear can appreciate Milton's wizardry in turning them to pure poetic delight. He knew how to weave them into cadences the more enchanting for the very mystery of the allusions. Hear this lovely Alexandrian passage from *Comus*—or, better still, get it by heart, until its perfect music, mingled with its dim, far-off magic hints of old legend, rings daily in your ear:

> Listen and appear to us
> In name of great Oceanus,
> By the earth-shaking Neptune's mace,
> And Tethys' grave majestic pace,
> By hoary Nereus' wrinkled look,

And the Carpathian wizard's hook,
By scaly Triton's winding shell,
And old sooth-saying Glaucus' spell,
By Leucothea's lovely hands,
And her son that rules the strands,
By Thetis' tinsel-slippered feet,
And the songs of Sirens sweet,
By dead Parthenope's dear tomb,
And fair Ligea's golden comb,
Wherewith she sits on diamond rocks,
Sleeking her soft, alluring locks,
By all the Nymphs that nightly dance
Upon thy streams with wily glance,
Rise, rise, and heave thy rosy head
From thy coral-paven bed . . . .

It will not so much matter whether you can explain all the allusions, although the music may haunt you until it drives you by its very enchantment to look them up. But I doubt that you will enjoy the passage much more for your efforts. In either case, you have felt the power of the old myth in the hands of a great artist; such appreciation is perhaps enough both for you and for the poet. In this art of enchantment by musical allusion Milton was the grand master, equaled by none except possibly Virgil; and he practiced it most of his life, in early poems and in some of the finest passages of *Paradise Lost* and *Paradise Regained*.

These, then, are some of the uses of classic myths to the poet. They serve to establish community of mind, of imagination, and of life between him and his hearers. In similes they become standard measures of size, or grace, or beauty, or power, or heroism. They draw us into closer and more sympathetic relation with external Nature by humanizing her and thus generating community of understanding and imagination between poet, listener, and Nature herself. Moreover, they also embody the elements of great moral ideas and values invariable in human life. In the story of Dionysus as god of inspiration, ecstasy, and mysticism, his conflict with the literal myopic common sense of the human majority is highly significant to any man keenly aware of unseen impulses. In the fate of the poet Orpheus, who sang so ravishingly as to draw all Nature after him—

> Such strains as would have won the ear
> Of Pluto to have quite set free
> His half-regained Eurydice,

had he not faltered and looked back—yet who was torn asunder by an infuriate and stupid mob that had no ear for music, a great neglected poet is sure to recognize his own suffering.

> What could the Muse herself that Orpheus bore,
> The Muse herself for her enchanting son,
> Whom universal Nature did lament,
> When by the rout that made the hideous roar
> His gory visage down the stream was sent,
> Down the swift Hebrus to the Lesbian shore.

The struggle of Prometheus for the enlightenment of mankind, with the static paralysis of things as they are, his sufferings, his ultimate if partial triumph—what is this but a supreme example of the course of human progress in all generations? As such it has been rehearsed by poet after poet, in dramatic, narrative, and lyric verse.

That so many poets have read into the myths their own stories suggests another possible origin of the myths in the region between myth and history called legend. It is a fairly reasonable view that the myths sprang, not from animism of Nature, but from actual human instances. Hercules, Samson, Beowulf, notable

10

huskies of their time, have become glorified with the heroism that thrives on tradition. Even our "strong boy of Boston" within, or in spite of, two generations of science and enlightenment has already gathered a bit of legendary glamour. This view of ancient myth, or of the origin of certain myths, is called "euhemerism," after the ingenious Greek who first proposed it some 2,200 years ago.

Two other theories of ancient Greek myth may be worth noting. The early Christian fathers, in their struggle with paganism, devised out of Holy Writ, especially the history of Israel, the idea that the pagan deities, including even the glorious gods of Greece, were merely the hosts of the fallen angel Satan, seeking to seduce and pervert mankind by their alluring disguises as Aphrodite, Hermes, Ares, and the rest. Of this theory Milton makes use in *Paradise Lost,* where he lists "the Ionian gods" among the rallied army of Satan:

> Titan, Heav'n's first born
> With his enormous brood, and birthright seized
> By younger Saturn, he from mightier Jove,
> His own and Rhea's son, like measure found;
> So Jove usurping reigned: these first in Crete
> And Ida known, thence on the snowy top
> Of cold Olympus ruled the middle air,
> Their highest heav'n; or on the Delphian cliff,
> Or in Dodona, and through all the bounds
> Of Doric land.

This demotion of the Greek gods has always seemed to me a bit ungrateful of Milton, who owed them so much of his poetic power of expression. He may have thought so, too, for he has mentioned them, though in a brief and inconspicuous manner, at the end of a long and gorgeous catalogue of Semitic deities.

The other explanation of myth finds little room in English

poetry, though it is basic in Dante. By this interpretation the Greek deities were the angelic agencies of God, the divine "Intelligences" through which God works his will on mankind. The ancients recognized these influences of Intelligences in Aphrodite, the agent of human love, in Ares, the agent of human contention, and in others; but they failed to discern the One Divine Will that actuated them. Hence the astrological influence of the planets, Mars to war, Venus to love, Jupiter to rule.

To us the import of all these theories is their insistence on the essential truth at the heart of the myths; only with the poet's sense of this truth can they come alive again.

> O antique fables! beautiful and bright
> And joyous with the joyous youth of yore:
> O antique fables! for a little light
> Of that which shineth in you evermore,
> To cleanse the dimness from our weary eyes,
> And bathe our old world with a new surprise
> Of golden dawn entrancing sea and shore.

CHARLES GROSVENOR OSGOOD

Princeton University
February, 1952

ABSYRTUS (ăb·sîr′tûs) was the brother of Medea. See ARGO·
NAUTS.

ABYDOS (*à*·bī′dŏs) was the home of Leander, lover of HERO

ACETES (*à*·sē′tēz) was a sailor who befriended DIONYSUS.

ACHAEANS (*à*·kē′ănz), one of the chief Greek tribes, migrated
from Thessaly to the Peloponnesus and were the ruling people
there in early times. Because of the importance of this tribe, the
poet Homer often calls all the Greeks Achaeans.

ACHELOUS (ăk′ė·lō′ûs), a suitor of Deianira, was defeated by
HERACLES.

ACHERON (ăk′ĕr·ŏn) is a river of HADES.

ACHILLES (*à*·kĭl′ēz) was the chief Greek hero in the TROJAN
WAR.

ACIS (ā′sĭs) was the lover of GALATEA.

ACRISIUS (*à*·krĭs′ĭ·ûs) was the grandfather of PERSEUS.

ACROPOLIS (*à*·krŏp′ô·lĭs) is the citadel of Athens. See
ATHENE.

ACTAEON (ăk·tē′ŏn), a hunter, by chance saw Artemis naked.
She turned him into a stag, and his own hounds killed him.
See ARTEMIS.

ADMETE (ăd·mē′tē), the daughter of Heracles' master demanded the girdle of Hippolyta, which was obtained for her by
HERACLES.

ADMETUS (ăd·mē′tûs) was the husband of ALCESTIS.

ADONIS (*à*·dō′nĭs), a vegetation god, is beloved by APHRO-
DITE.

ADRASTUS (*à*·drăs′tûs) was one of the Seven against THEBES.

ADRIATIC SEA. See MEDITERRANEAN SEA.

AEACUS (ē′à·kûs), a son of Zeus and the grandfather of Achilles, is a judge in Hades. See HADES, ZEUS.

AEAEA (ē·ē′à) is Circe's island. See ODYSSEUS.

AEETES (ē·ē′tēz) possessed the Golden Fleece sought by the ARGONAUTS.

AEGAEON (ê·jē′ŏn) was a Hecatoncheire. See TITANS.

AEGEAN (ê·jē′àn) **SEA.** See MEDITERRANEAN SEA.

AEGEUS (ē′jūs) was the father of THESEUS.

AEGIALEUS (ē′jĭ·ăl′ōos) was one of the Epigoni. See THEBES.

AEGINA (ê·jī′nà) was one of the mistresses of ZEUS.

AEGIS (ē′jĭs) is the shield or breastplate of ATHENE.

AEGISTHUS (ê·jĭs′thûs), a son of Thyestes, was the lover of Clytemnestra. See ATREUS.

AEGYPTUS (ê·jĭp′tûs) had fifty sons, forty-nine of whom were murdered by their wives on their wedding night. See HADES.

AENEAS (ê·nē′às) was by mythical tradition the founder of the Roman race and a man whose epic adventures paralleled in Roman mythology the career of Odysseus among the Greeks. As the story of Odysseus' life was given poetic form by Homer in the *Odyssey,* so the account of most of Aeneas' life is embodied in a long poem, the *Aeneid,* by the Roman poet Virgil. In the *Odyssey* Homer collected the myths of his people and made of them a poem that gave not only pride of race but a code of morals to his posterity in classic Greece. Impressed by this accomplishment, Virgil, writing in the reign of Augustus at about the turn of the Christian era, set out to achieve the same sort of legendary origin for the Roman race; his work therefore was consciously imitative of Homer's, and he borrowed many incidents and situations from Homer's poems and invented episodes for his hero that are recognizably similar to those of the *Odyssey.* The *Aeneid,* though an excellent poem, is an imitative and a derivative one; but it was enormously successful in its own day and continuingly popular with later generations.

Aeneas, the epic hero of the poem, was the son of **Anchises** of Troy and the goddess Venus. Of semidivine origin, he was fated to survive the fall of Troy to the Greek armies and to find his destiny in faraway Italy after many adventures. While the city was going up in flames after its capture by the Greeks, Aeneas took his aged father Anchises on his shoulders and his young son **Ascanius,** or **Iulus,** by the hand, and with his wife **Creusa** following him, set out to escape. In the confusions of that woeful night Creusa was lost, but with his father and son Aeneas reached a group of other Trojans who had escaped and who then accepted him as their leader in seeking a new life elsewhere.

After a period of preparation, the band of Trojans embarked in twenty ships and soon came to the land of Thrace, not far away, where they thought to settle down. But they were warned by a remarkable event not to do so. When Aeneas, who was about to make a sacrifice, had broken off several twigs from a young sapling, he was astonished to see the broken parts drip blood. A voice from the ground then informed him that he was standing at the grave of the young Trojan prince **Polydorus,** whom Priam had sent away to be safe from the hazards of war. This young man had been murdered for the wealth he had brought with him, and the saplings were the shafts of the spears or arrows that had killed him, grown into living plants. To the divining mind of Aeneas this circumstance was a bad omen, and he and his companions sailed away. This incident Edmund Spenser adapts to his own use in *The Faerie Queene* (1. 2. 30–43). The Red Cross Knight, making love to a false and deceiving witch named Duessa, breaks off the twigs of a tree to make her a garland; from the broken twigs blood flows, and from the tree itself comes a voice that identifies the tree as the enchanted

15

form of a man named Fradubio, a victim of Duessa's baleful magic.

The Trojans came next to the island of Delos, and there Aeneas consulted the oracle of Apollo, which told him to seek the land of his forefathers. He remembered that **Dardanus**, the founder of the Trojan royal family, was said to have come from Crete; so the Trojans set sail for that island. There, however, they met with crop failures and disease, until Aeneas' family gods advised him in a dream that he should move on to **Hesperia**, the western land, which had been the original home of Dardanus. This land was Italy, and for Italy the refugees now set their course.

Their next stop was the island of the **Harpies**, where they were attacked by these violent and malicious birds of prey, who prophesied that before the end of their travels the Trojans would have occasion to eat their own tables as well as the food on them (see Harpies under SEA GODS). The Trojans then went to Epirus, where they were hospitably received by other Trojans who had escaped, and later they passed the island of the Cyclopes, where they saw the dread Cyclops Polyphemus, who had been blinded by Odysseus; but they escaped injury. By not sailing through the terrible strait they also escaped misfortune at the hands of Scylla and Charybdis, who had wrought such destruction on Odysseus' men.

As they were sailing along the coast of Sicily, Juno, as implacable an enemy to Aeneas as Poseidon had been to Odysseus, persuaded Aeolus, the god of the winds, to stir up a terrible storm, which blew them off course toward Africa. Fortunately, before the ships were destroyed, Neptune, annoyed at Juno's intrusion into his realm, rose above the waves and ordered them to subside. Thus the Trojans were able to land safely at **Carthage.**

In Carthage they found a peaceful welcome from Queen **Dido** and her subjects. Dido herself had had to flee from Tyre, where her husband, **Sychaeus,** had been murdered for his wealth; and she had founded Carthage as a refuge, bargaining with the aborigines of the place for as much land as a hide would enclose, and then having the hide cut into long strips that, tied end to end, enclosed enough ground for a comfortable city. Thus she was disposed to be kindly to other refugees.

And kindly did she receive the Trojans; she gave a splendid banquet in their honor and especially in honor of their handsome prince, whose godlike form greatly attracted her. The rich munificence of Dido's banquet and the luxury of her house appear in ironic echo in *The Waste Land* (91–93), when T. S. Eliot describes the wealthy but neurotic woman who is the central figure of *A Game of Chess;* her synthetic perfumes

> . . . fattening the prolonged candle-flames,
> Flung their smoke into the laquearia,
> Stirring the pattern on the coffered ceiling.[1]

Here Eliot consciously parallels Virgil's description (*Aeneid,* 1. 726).

Since he was a son of the goddess Aphrodite, Aeneas was always deeply moved by beauty and love, and he responded ardently to Dido. The affair became so serious that at length Jupiter thought it wise to send Mercury to remind Aeneas of his destiny and to suggest that the quest for it be resumed. Aeneas accepted this call to duty, bade farewell to Dido in spite of her protests, and set sail for Italy. The rejected queen, in despair at the loss of her lover, committed suicide on a funeral pyre. The departing Trojans saw the flames but did not know their meaning.

[1] From "The Waste Land," by T. S. Eliot, in his *Collected Poems, 1909–1935* Copyright, 1934, 1936, by Harcourt, Brace and Company. Reprinted with their permission.

The fatal love of Dido and her operatic demise have naturally attracted the attention of poets. Borrowing most of his ideas from Virgil and Ovid, Chaucer tells her story in *The Legend of Good Women*. In *The Merchant of Venice* (5. 1. 9–12) Shakespeare has Lorenzo allude to her death:

> In such a night
> Stood Dido with a willow in her hand
> Upon the wild sea-banks, and waft her love
> To come again to Carthage.

Dido and Aeneas by the seventeenth-century composer, Henry Purcell, is an excellent English opera, and Dido's farewell lament, "When I Am Laid in Earth," is one of the most moving of all operatic compositions.

Diana, arguing against Venus in John Gay's light poem *The Fan* (95–104), proves man's unreliability by citing the fate of Dido:

> . . . Dido there amidst her last distress,
> Pale cheeks and blood-shot eyes her grief express:
> Deep in her breast the reeking sword is drown'd,
> And gushing blood streams from the purple wound.
> .   .   .   .   .   .
> View this, ye maids; and then each swain believe;
> They're Trojans all, and vow but to deceive.

To Alexander Pope, in equally frivolous mood, Aeneas becomes a symbol of man's immovable firmness of purpose. The Baron, hero of *The Rape of the Lock* (5. 5–6), refuses all pleas to return the stolen lock:

> Not half so fixed the Trojan could remain,
> While Anna begged and Dido raged in vain.

(Anna was Dido's sister.)

18

After leaving Carthage, the Trojans completed the remainder of their voyage to Italy almost without incident, for Venus obtained Neptune's promise to allow no further misfortune except the loss of one more man. A faithful but unfortunate steersman named **Palinurus** was accordingly washed overboard during the night. His fate so impressed Cyril Connolly, editor of the now defunct English magazine *Horizon,* that for his book, *The Unquiet Grave,* he adopted Palinurus' name as his pseudonym. The ship that Palinurus was steering, guided by Neptune, reached the shore of Italy safely, near a place called **Cumae.**

While the others made camp, Aeneas went to seek the **Cumaean Sibyl,** a priestess of Apollo who possessed the gift of prophecy (see Sibyl of Cumae under APOLLO). His purpose was to make his way down into the underworld of Hades to consult his father Anchises, who had died during their travels, and he needed the help of the Sibyl. The aged mystic lady told him first to find in the forest a tree with a **golden bough** that he must pluck as a present for Proserpina, the queen of Hades. When he brought the bough back as the Sibyl had directed, she conducted him to the terrible cavern of Avernus that led to Hades, and she guided him through many perils and past many terrible scenes. (For Virgil's description of the underworld, which is more detailed than that of any other classical poet, see HADES.) Aeneas met the shade of Dido, who refused to answer his greeting and hurried by without speaking to him. At last he found the shade of old Anchises, safe in Elysium, and received from him a prophetic account of the wars that he must still fight and of the great civilization of which he was to be the founder.

When Aeneas returned to the upper world, he and his followers set sail again and landed farther up the coast in the mouth of the Tiber river. Here the prophecy of the Harpies that the Trojans should one day eat their tables was fulfilled when they had nothing left to eat except the hard bread on which they had placed the rest of their food. Conscious of destiny fulfilling itself, they set about to find themselves a home. The land to which Aeneas had led them was called **Latium,** and its aged king **Latinus,** who was the grandson of Saturn, welcomed the Trojans in peace when they made themselves known to him. In fact, he offered Aeneas the hand of his daughter, **Lavinia,** in marriage, for it had been foretold to him that she should take as a husband a stranger from overseas.

The old king's generosity, however, became the cause of trouble, for the king of the neighboring **Rutulians,** a fierce fighter by the name of **Turnus,** had long been a suitor for Lavinia, and he objected to her marrying Aeneas. Furthermore, Juno resumed her troublemaking at this point: she caused Latinus' wife to become antagonistic to Aeneas, and she arranged for the accidental killing of a pet deer, an event that provoked a conflict between Latinus' herdsmen and a group of Trojans. Incited by Juno, war thereupon broke out, in spite of Latinus' unwillingness to fight. Against Aeneas were ranged the Latians, the Rutulians under King Turnus, a cruel warrior named **Mezentius,** and a swift and skillful feminine warrior named **Camilla** about whom Alexander Pope composed a well-known couplet supposed to illustrate swift movement (*Essay on Criticism,* 372–373):

> . . . when swift Camilla scours the plain,
> Flies o'er th' unbending corn, and skims along the main.

Aeneas, however, also had an ally, for to his side came the Arcadian king, **Evander,** who had long been at war with Turnus for his own reasons. In the conflict that followed, many warlike events took place, but in the end the Trojans were victorious, and Aeneas himself slew Mezentius and Turnus. With the death of Turnus the *Aeneid* ends unfinished. Other Latin poets took up the story to tell how Aeneas married Lavinia and founded a city named **Lavinium** for her. His son Iulus built another city called Alba Longa where in a later day were born Romulus and Remus. Romulus became the founder of Rome (see ROME).

For the tradition that Brutus, a great-grandson of Aeneas, was the first king of Britain see TROJAN WAR.

AEOLIA (ē·ō′lǐ·à) is the island of the WINDS.

AEOLUS (ē′ŏ·lûs), the king of the winds, befriended Odysseus. See WINDS, ODYSSEUS.

AËROPE (ā·ĕr′ŏ·pē) was the wife of ATREUS.

AESCULAPIUS (ĕs′kū·lā′pǐ·ûs) is the Roman name of the god of medicine, Asclepius. See APOLLO.

AESON (ē′sŏn) was the father of Jason, the leader of the ARGONAUTS.

AETHRA (ē′thrà) was the mother of THESEUS.

AGAMEMNON (ăg′à·mĕm′nŏn), who was commander in chief of the Greek forces in the Trojan War, was murdered by his wife Clytemnestra when he returned home. See ATREUS, TROJAN WAR.

AGANIPPE (ăg′à·nǐp′ē), a spring on Mount Helicon, is a home of the MUSES.

AGAVE (à·gā′vē) was a daughter of Cadmus. See THEBES.

AGLAIA (à·glā′yà) is one of the three GRACES.

AIAS (ā′yăs), or Ajax, was (1) the son of King Telamon of Salamis, a great Greek hero in the TROJAN WAR; (2) the son of King Oileus of the Locrians, a lesser Greek hero in the TROJAN WAR.

AIDES (ā′ī·dēz) is another name of the god HADES.

AIDONEUS (ā′ī·dō′nūs) is another name of the god HADES.

AJAX (ā′jăks) is the Roman form of Aias, the name of two Greek heroes in the TROJAN WAR.

ALBA LONGA (ăl′bá lŏng′gá). See ROME.

ALBION (ăl′bĭ·ŏn) is an English sea god invented by Spenser. See SEA GODS.

ALCESTIS (ăl·sĕs′tĭs). The story of Alcestis and **Admetus,** like the later story that Chaucer tells of patient Griselda and her lordly mate, glorifies the self-sacrificing devotion of the wife but leaves the character of the husband in doubt.

When Zeus killed Asclepius with a thunderbolt for the sin of restoring Hippolytus to life, Apollo, Asclepius' father, was intensely angry. He dared not attack Zeus himself, but he killed the Cyclopes who produced the thunderbolt. For this murder he was banished from Olympus for one year and condemned to be the slave of a mortal. Fortunately for him, he became the herdsman of King Admetus of Pherae, who treated him kindly, and Apollo in gratitude caused Admetus' farm to be extremely prosperous. This pleasant pastoral year is described by George Meredith in *Phoebus with Admetus.*

Admetus fell in love with Alcestis, daughter of King **Pelias** of Iolcus, but Pelias declared that the man who won his daughter's hand must arrive at his court in a chariot drawn by wild beasts. Admetus, who was no animal trainer, despaired of success, but Apollo solved the problem for him by hitching a well-behaved lion and a tractable boar to his chariot. Admetus married Alcestis and they lived happily together.

Admetus seemed to be a remarkably fortunate man, but Apollo discovered that, according to the decree of the Fates, his mortal friend must soon die. The god, carrying with him a gift of wine, went to beg the Fates to spare Admetus. After they had drunk the wine, the Fates agreed to let him live if he could find someone else to die for him on the appointed day. Admetus was confident that one of his friends would be glad to take his place, because all of them had often said that Admetus' happiness was their chief pleasure. But when he told them what they might do for him, they were all suddenly reluctant to oblige. He therefore went to his mother and father, who were, after all, not only extremely fond of him but extremely old and close to death anyway. They listened to him with sympathy, but they said that neither of them wanted to die, not even for him. At last Alcestis offered her life. Admetus had not suggested that she save him, but he made no great objection when she volunteered. The appointed moment came, Alcestis died, and Admetus wept at the loss of so dutiful a wife.

On the burial day the great hero **Heracles,** who was on his way to capture the man-eating horses of Diomedes, arrived to spend a few days with his friend Admetus. When he found Admetus and the other members of the household in mourning, he offered to go away; but Admetus, remembering the sacred law of hospitality, told Heracles that the dead person was merely a woman of the household. He took the hero to a remote room in the palace where he would not hear the sounds of the funeral, and he sent a number of servants to wait on him. As was his custom, Heracles ate and drank until he was full of cheer, and then he roared out some bawdy songs. The sad, shocked faces of the servants annoyed him. He demanded to know what was wrong with them, and finally they told him that Alcestis was dead.

Then Heracles called himself a great blundering idiot, marveled at the virtue of his friend Admetus, and wondered what he could do to excuse his bad manners. The plan he hit upon was characteristic: it called for action and it required strength and daring that only Heracles possessed. He knew that Thanatos, who is Death, would come to take Alcestis from her tomb. He lay in wait for Death, wrestled with him, and made him give Alcestis back to life. Leading the veiled woman, he came to the

23

weeping Admetus and said, "Do you know this girl?" Admetus muttered something about a ghost, but Heracles said, "No, she is Alcestis. I wrestled for her with Thanatos, and I won."

In English literature many poets have praised Alcestis. In *The Legend of Good Women* Chaucer makes Alcestis the queen of the god of love because she is the most virtuous woman the world has ever known. Milton, in one of his most moving sonnets, uses the return of Alcestis to Admetus as the central image to describe a dream he had about his dead wife, Katherine Woodcock. He never saw Katherine, because he went blind two or three years before they met, and he lost her in childbirth two years after they married (Sonnet 23).

> Methought I saw my late espoused Saint
> Brought to me like *Alcestis* from the grave,
> Whom *Joves* great Son to her glad Husband gave,
> Rescu'd from death by force though pale and faint.

She came, he says,

> . . . vested all in white, pure as her mind:
> Her face was vail'd, yet to my fancied sight,
> Love, sweetness, goodness, in her person shin'd
> So clear, as in no face with more delight.
> But O as to embrace me she enclin'd
> I wak'd, she fled, and day brought back my night.

To the early Greeks who invented the story of Admetus and Alcestis, Admetus was doubtless an admirable person. They considered a man to be much more valuable than a woman, and Admetus was also a king on whom the welfare of his country depended. It was right for him to accept Alcestis' sacrifice, and his observance of the law of hospitality in spite of his great grief proved him worthy of the redeemed Alcestis. However, in the fifth century before Christ, when Euripides wrote his tragic drama

Alcestis, the Greek view, or at least the Euripidean view, was not so simple and straightforward. Euripides presents an Admetus who must have troubled the Greek audience and who is variously interpreted by modern critics. As Douglas Bush observes, certain scholars maintain that the Euripidean Admetus is an ideal king whose actions are fully justified by ancient standards, while others hold that he is a selfish coward who finally reforms because he is made to realize his own baseness. Most critics are closer to the second opinion than to the first.

In *Balaustion's Adventure* Browning creates a Greek girl in his own image—the result is hardly Greek—who gives a good translation of Euripides' play but adds a running commentary and interpretation that reveal Admetus as Browning's favorite kind of hero, the weak man who through suffering achieves goodness. According to Balaustion's interpretation, Alcestis as she dies sees through Admetus' selfishness, and after her death Admetus is miserable in the knowledge that his weakness has betrayed her. Gradually he realizes how little he has gained and how much he has lost, and in this painful discovery he achieves moral stature. Heracles, returning with the veiled Alcestis, tests Admetus until both he and Alcestis are satisfied that her husband has become worthy of her. In Balaustion's version, also, Heracles is much more than the brave, good-natured, but blundering Greek hero; he is the personification of unselfish service, whose mere presence moves men to a desire for goodness.

Balaustion, however, is not satisfied with this interpretation. "Could we too make a poem?" she demands, and proceeds to do so. In her version Admetus, the perfect king, prepares without fear for death but questions the justice of the gods. Alcestis then reveals that she has made a secret agreement with Apollo that she will die to save her husband's life. Admetus passionately protests, but the bargain has been made and Alcestis dies. Yet when she reaches Hades, Persephone says wryly that a death is not a death which doubles another life:

> "Two souls in one were formidable odds:
> Admetos must not be himself and thou!"

> And so, before the embrace relaxed a whit,
> The lost eyes opened, still beneath the look;
> And lo, Alkestis was alive again,
> And of Admetos' rapture who shall speak?

If the reader is disappointed in Balaustion (and her creator Browning) for simplifying and sentimentalizing an interesting story, he should be reminded that William Morris, who wrote *The Love of Alcestis* in 1868, three years before *Balaustion's Adventure,* and all other writers since Browning who have produced versions of the story have, in one way or another, prevented Admetus from easily accepting his wife's sacrifice.

ALCIDES (ăl·sī'dēz) was another name of HERACLES.

ALCINOUS (ăl·sĭn'ō·ŭs) was the Phaeacian king who befriended ODYSSEUS.

ALCMAEON (ălk·mē'ŏn) was one of the Epigoni. See THEBES.

ALCMENE (ălk·mē'nē) was the wife of Amphitryon and the paramour of ZEUS.

ALCYONE (ăl·sī'ō·nē), or Halcyone, was the wife of CEYX.

ALCYONEUS (ăl·sī'ō·nŭs) was one of the GIANTS.

ALECTO (à·lĕk'tō) is one of the three FURIES.

ALECTRYON (à·lĕk'trĭ·ŏn) was a servant of Ares. See APHRODITE.

ALEXANDER was another name of Paris, a prince of Troy. See TROJAN WAR.

ALOEUS (à·lō'ōs) was one of the GIANTS.

ALPHEUS (ăl·fē'ŭs) is a river god who pursued Arethusa. See NYMPHS.

ALTHAEA (ăl·thē′à) was the mother of Meleager, the hero of the CALYDONIAN BOAR HUNT.

AMALTHEA (ăm′àl·thē′à) was the goat whose milk fed the infant ZEUS.

AMAZONS (ăm′à·zŏnz), or **AMAZONES** (ăm′à·zŏn′ēz), were a tribe of warlike women who made constant forays into the battle scenes of Greek mythology. They are often said to be the children of Ares, god of battle, and they appear to owe their origin to the worship of the feminine characteristics of the moon, for which see ARTEMIS. As a tribal custom, they permitted only female children to survive, either killing their male children or sending them away to an early and permanent exile. For their females they provided the warlike disciplines of the Greek fighter, a course of study that began for the Amazons with the amputation of the right breast in order to permit a greater freedom of movement to the fighting right arm.

The Amazons, both as defenders of their own realm and as invaders, fought heroically but unsuccessfully against the Greeks. Bellerophon was victorious against them. Theseus joined Heracles in his task of obtaining the girdle of **Hippolyta,** the Amazonian queen; from this project Heracles returned with the girdle, and Theseus with a wife (either Hippolyta herself or her sister **Antiope,** according to varying accounts). A retaliatory raid against Attica was repulsed by Theseus.

A band of Amazons led by their later queen, **Penthesilia,** fought against the Greeks at Troy; but Achilles overcame Penthesilia herself, and her army was routed. See HERACLES, THESEUS, TROJAN WAR.

AMBROSIA (ăm·brō′zhà) is the food of the gods.

AMOR (ā′môr) is a Roman name of EROS.

AMPHIARAUS (ăm′fĭ·à·rā′ŭs) was one of the Seven against THEBES.

27

AMPHION (ăm·fī′ŏn) was the husband of Niobe and the brother of Zethus, with whom he ruled Thebes. See ARTEMIS, THEBES.

AMPHITRITE (ăm′fĭ·trī′tē) is the wife of Poseidon, the king of the SEA GODS.

AMPHITRYON (ăm·fĭt′rĭ·ŏn) was the husband of Alcmene. See ZEUS.

AMULIUS (á·mū′lĭ·ŭs), the usurping king of Alba Longa, was killed by Remus and Romulus. See ROME.

AMYCUS (á·mī′kŭs) was a famous boxer defeated by Polydeuces, one of the ARGONAUTS.

ANADYOMENE (ăn′á·dĭ·ŏm′ĕ·nē) is a surname for APHRODITE.

ANCHISES (ăn·kī′sēz) was the father of AENEAS.

ANDROMACHE (ăn·drŏm′á·kē) was the wife of Hector, the chief hero of Troy in the TROJAN WAR.

ANDROMEDA (ăn·drŏm′ĕ·dá) was rescued from a sea monster by PERSEUS.

ANTAEUS (ăn·tē′ŭs), an earth Giant, was killed by HERACLES.

ANTEIA (ăn·tī′á) loved BELLEROPHON.

ANTENOR (ăn·tē′nôr) was a Trojan councilor during the TROJAN WAR.

ANTEROS (ăn′tĕ·rŏs), the god of mutual love, is the brother and attendant of EROS.

ANTICLIA (ăn′tĭ·klī′á) was the mother of ODYSSEUS.

ANTIGONE (ăn·tĭg′ŏ·nē) was a daughter of Oedipus, king of THEBES.

ANTINOUS (ăn·tĭn′ŏ·wŭs) was the most insolent suitor of Penelope, the wife of ODYSSEUS.

ANTIOPE (ăn·tī′ŏ·pē) was (1) the sister of Hippolyta (see AMAZONS, THESEUS); (2) the mother by Zeus of Amphion and Zethus, regents of THEBES.

APHRODITE (ăf'rṓ·dī'tē), or **Venus,** is the goddess of beauty and the patroness of love of all kinds, animal and human, spiritual and sensual. According to Homer, Aphrodite is the daughter of Zeus and **Dione;** but her name is more appropriate to the account given by Hesiod that she rose from the foam of the sea where the bits of Uranus' genitals fell when he was castrated by Cronus, for Aphrodite means "foam born." Those who believed in Hesiod's story of her origin often called her Aphrodite Urania, and under this title she was thought to embody the great universe-moving love of the gods; whereas under the name of Aphrodite Pandemos she represented the love of mortals and of animals. In later times these titles changed meaning until Aphrodite was called Urania when she represented spiritual love between mortals, and Pandemos when she represented carnal or sensual love.

When Aphrodite arose from the foam she was wafted among the islands of the Mediterranean, arriving first at **Cythera** or **Cyprus** (accounts vary), for which reason she was often given the surnames **Cytherea** and **Cypris.** She was also called **Paphia** after a city on Cyprus where she performed a miracle (see PYGMA-LION). One of the most famous Renaissance paintings is Botticelli's Aphrodite new-risen from the foam, and floating in a great scallop shell. Her best-known surname among the Romans was **Erycina** from a famous shrine dedicated to her at Mount **Eryx** on the northwest coast of Sicily. Her other nicknames included **Anadyomene,** which means "she who came out of the sea," and **Pelagia.**

When Aphrodite arrived on Mount Olympus she was warmly received. Her presence was so lovely that insatiable Zeus fell in love with her, but she refused to grant him her favors. In a fit of pique, he compelled her to marry Hephaestus, his lame son. Aphrodite, however, was not content with Hephaestus, and she

29

became involved in a love affair with Ares. The relationship produced five children: Eros; Anteros, a lesser god of love; Deimos and Phobos, or Pavor, lesser gods of fear, who attended Ares; and Harmonia, who became the wife of Cadmus, founder of Thebes. Aphrodite and Ares began their love affair in secrecy, having set Ares' servant **Alectryon** as a sentry, but Alectryon fell asleep, and the lovers were discovered by Helios, the sun god. Ares punished Alectryon by changing him into the rooster, which must always crow at the approach of dawn. In the meantime Helios reported the intrigue to Hephaestus; Hephaestus made a great net of metal and threw it over the unsuspecting lovers, imprisoning them together, and summoned the other gods to laugh at them in their shame. But who was most embarrassed— the unfaithful wife, the trapped lover, or the deceived husband —is still doubtful. Chaucer wrote a poem called *The Complaint of Mars,* which gives the thoughts of the god of war

> . . . atte departynge
> Fro fresshe Venus in a morwenynge,
> Whan Phebus, with his firy torches rede,
> Ransaked every lover in hys drede.

Chaucer, however, has rearranged the entire myth to fit the medieval idea of courtly love, and he omits the boisterous ending described here. In John Peale Bishop's *When the Net Was Unwound Venus Was Found Ravelled with Mars* Aphrodite's affair with Ares becomes a more general symbol for an illicit love experience between a soldier and a prostitute.

Aphrodite also had a less successful love affair with a young huntsman named **Adonis,** a personage who originated in mythologies older than the Greek, in which he occupied the position of a vegetation god, that is, a god connected with the return of life to plants in the spring and with their decay in the fall.

According to Ovid, Eros one day accidentally wounded his mother Aphrodite with one of his love-provoking arrows, and as a consequence Aphrodite fell in love with Adonis, a handsome young man and an ardent huntsman. Unfortunately for her, Adonis did not return her love in spite of her endearing advances but continued to prefer the excitement of the chase. Aphrodite besought him to take care of himself for her sake, but in spite of her warnings Adonis was killed by a wild boar. Aphrodite, in her grief, transformed Adonis' spilled blood into a flower, the anemone. In the meantime Adonis' spirit went down to Hades, where Persephone, the queen of the underworld, also fell in love with him. Aphrodite's pleas to Zeus to restore Adonis to her were therefore firmly countered by the pleas of Persephone to be allowed to keep him. Caught in this feminine crossfire, Zeus decided that Adonis should spend six months in Hades with Persephone and six months in the upper world with Aphrodite. When Adonis is with Persephone, nature languishes and appears to die, and fall and winter are at hand; but when he returns to Aphrodite, her joy brings life back into the world, and spring and summer ensue. (For another myth about the annual death and rebirth of nature see Persephone under EARTH GODDESSES.)

The myth of Aphrodite and Adonis has been used many times in English poetry. One of the most richly ornate poems in the language is Shakespeare's long narrative *Venus and Adonis,* in which he plays up the reluctance of Adonis to gratify Venus, as well as the extreme ardor of Venus balked of her desire. Spenser also uses the myth, though more symbolically, in *The Faerie Queene* (3. 1. 35). He describes

> . . . with what sleights and sweet allurements she
> Entyst the Boy, as well that art she knew,
> And wooed him her Paramoure to be

31

as the subject of a tapestry hung in the Castle Joyous, which is one of his allegories of loose living. In this passage Spenser makes of the affair a symbol of lust in action. Later in the same book (3. 6. 29–54) he uses the story as a symbol of the natural order. Here he describes at length a place that he calls the Garden of Adonis, where are accumulated all human spirits waiting to receive the habitation of a body. In the center of this garden is a pleasant arbor of trees grown closely together to form a covert in which Venus is able to delight in

> Her deare *Adonis* ioyous company,
> And reape sweet pleasure of the wanton boy,

no longer troubled by misfortune. Their love here is the symbol of the continuance of life in the world.

Hardly less famous is Aphrodite's love for Anchises, a member of a branch of the royal house of Troy. Aphrodite appeared to him as the daughter of a Phrygian king, and she subsequently bore him a son whom they named Aeneas. He grew up a prince of Troy, and his wanderings after the fall of that city to the Greeks are the subject of Virgil's *Aeneid* (see AENEAS). Aphrodite was in no small degree accountable for the Greeks' war against the Trojans. For her part in provoking that great struggle see the article on the Trojan War.

By Hermes, Aphrodite had a son named after both of them and called Hermaphroditus. For the story of his curious involvement with a river Nymph named Salmacis, see HERMES.

In these myths Aphrodite appears in her many manifestations as the great, complicated love instinct of human nature. In her actions are found the deepest motives and the most complex involvements of love. For the Greeks she was associated with many personal symbols, including the swan, the sparrow, the dove, the apple, the rose, the myrtle, the linden, and the cypress.

She was supposed to have a girdle or cincture of great virtue, which represented her chastity. Spenser makes considerable use of this symbol in *The Faerie Queene* where he relates how Hephaestus wrought it "in *Lemno* with unquenched fire" for Aphrodite and how a beautiful and chaste young lady named Florimell, who had been fostered by the Graces, found it one day in Aphrodite's secret bower where it had been left for the nonce. Florimell took it for her own, and the fifth canto of Book Four relates how, when Florimell had temporarily lost it, the girdle was the subject of an argument among several light ladies, none of whom it would fit because of their lack of chastity. As to how Aphrodite herself, who was certainly not addicted to austere virtue, could comfortably wear so demanding an article, Spenser candidly relates (4. 5. 3):

> That girdle gaue the vertue of chast loue,
> And Wiuehood true, to all that did it beare;
> But whosoeuer contrarie doth proue,
> Might not the same about her middle weare,
> But it would loose, or else a sunder teare.
> Whilome it was (as faeries wont report)
> Dame *Venus* girdle, by her steemed deare,
> What time she vsd to liue in wiuely sort;
> But layd aside, when so she vsd her looser sport.

Aphrodite is the loveliest of the goddesses and the favorite of poets in all languages. Her attributes and her person are referred to in many poems of Spenser's, including the *Epithalamion* and *Prothalamion,* and his poem *An Hymne in Honour of Beautie* is addressed to her. Donne alludes to her in the opening lines of his *Elegie 12.* In *The Rape of the Lock* (5. 135–136) Pope writes of Belinda's lock, transformed after its rape into a shooting star, so that it

> . . . the blest Lover shall for Venus take,
> And send up vows from Rosamonda's lake,

Pope's suggestion being that fond lovers will be unable to distinguish between a shooting star and the planet of Venus. In *Don Juan* (1. 55) Byron describes Donna Julia,

> . . . whom to call
> Pretty were but to give a feeble notion
> Of many charms in her as natural
> As sweetness to the flower, or salt to ocean,
> Her zone to Venus, or his bow to Cupid,
> (But this last simile is trite and stupid).

Here the "zone" is Aphrodite's girdle.

Aphrodite is the subject of a later myth in which she lured a knight named Tannhäuser into a cave and lived with him for seven years, a story that Swinburne made the subject of his poem, *Laus Veneris.* For Dante Rossetti, in *Venus Victrix,* she is still the conquering force in life. In our own times W. H. Auden has called one of his poems *Venus Will Now Say a Few Words,* in which the procreative principle is personified to describe the origin of man.

Astarte, or **Ashtoroth,** is the Phoenician name for Aphrodite, especially in her function as the productive power of nature. Under this name she was particularly well known among the Greek islands, where the trading of the Phoenicians carried her fame. Several English poets have preferred this name. Lord Byron, for example, in *Manfred,* uses Astarte as the name of Manfred's dead lover. Manfred, suffering remorse for a terrible but unnamed crime, lives alone in the Swiss Alps. He calls up a number of spirits of the universe in search of forgetfulness and at last calls up Astarte, who forecasts his death on the next day. In this poem Manfred is clearly Byron himself, and Astarte is

Augusta, his half sister, with whom his reputed incestuous relations led to his exile from England.

Dante Rossetti wrote a sonnet called *Astarte Syriaca*.

APOLLO (*à·pŏl'ō*). The first god of light was **Hyperion,** a Titan. His majesty is recalled by Hamlet when he says that his father, compared to Claudius, was as "Hyperion to a satyr" (*Hamlet,* 1. 2. 140). In English literature Hyperion is occasionally regarded as the reigning sun god, as in Thomas Gray's *The Progress of Poesy* (53); and at times his name is used merely as another name for Apollo: in *Henry V* (4. 1. 289–292), for example, the King speaks of the common laborer who

> . . . from the rise to set,
> Sweats in the eye of Phoebus, and all night
> Sleeps in Elysium; next day after dawn,
> Doth rise and help Hyperion to his horse.

Hyperion, however, lost his powers to younger gods.

His son **Helios** became the god of the sun in its physical aspects. Each morning in his palace in the east, the four horses of the sun are harnessed, the gate is opened by Eos, goddess of the dawn, and Helios drives his flaming chariot across the sky. Because he is one of the few Titans who retained their godhead under Zeus, Helios is simply called "Titan" in Spenser's *Prothalamion* (4) and Robert Herrick's *Corinna's Going A-Maying* (25). For a sun god, however, he lives a rather shadowy existence because the stories connected with him and even his position as heavenly charioteer were eventually attributed to Apollo. Only a few actions of Helios are important: he observed, for example, that Aphrodite was unfaithful to Hephaestus and informed the lame god, he told Demeter who had abducted her daughter Persephone, he required that Odysseus' crew be punished for killing and eating some of the cattle of the sun, and he was the father of Circe. H. D. describes him in her poem *Helios.*

Apollo, the son of Zeus and Leto, replaced Hyperion as god of light and gradually usurped the lesser powers of Helios. He is also called **Phoebus,** which means "shining"; **Pythius,** which refers to his slaying of the Python (see ORACLES); **Lycius,** which is thought to mean "wolf god"; and **Cynthius** and **Delius,** which refer to the mountain and the island on which he was born. **Paean,** which means "healer," is another name sometimes given to Apollo. Originally Paean was an Olympian himself, the physician of the gods, but he was little more than a personified abstraction, and his name was soon attached to Apollo and later to Asclepius. Songs of praise or triumph addressed to Apollo the preserver are called paeans.

The mother of Apollo was **Leto,** or **Latona,** a Titaness. When Zeus's wife Hera learned that Leto was with child by Zeus, she demanded that no people and no place give her refuge. Leto wandered in despair until Poseidon sent a dolphin to carry her to the floating island of **Delos,** which Zeus or Poseidon anchored for her in the Mediterranean. There on Mount **Cynthus** she gave birth to twins, Apollo and Artemis, goddess of the moon. In *The Faerie Queene* (2. 12. 13) Spenser refers to Leto's flight from the anger of Hera and to the anchoring of Delos, and Milton in *I Did But Prompt the Age* recalls the rude Lycian peasants whom Zeus transformed into frogs because they refused to let Leto drink from their lake when she was weary from traveling with her "twin born progeny."

Apollo and Artemis were as devoted to their mother as she was to them. When **Tityus,** a Giant, insulted Leto, her children subdued him with their arrows, and he was then hurled into Tartarus, where his huge bulk covers nine acres. Vultures eternally eat his liver and his liver is constantly renewed; thus his torment never ceases. In English literature he appears, with Tantalus and others, as a great sinner who has received a well-deserved punishment; he is used in this way, for example, in Ben Jonson's *Catiline* (4. 2. 294). Apollo and Artemis also took swift and terrible vengeance on Niobe, who boasted that she was superior to Leto (for details, see ARTEMIS).

Apollo is he god of light, archery, medicine, and poetry and music. Because he is the god of light nothing is hidden from him, and he is therefore a prophet and a speaker of truth. As an archer he is a destroyer; his arrows bring sunstroke and fever. During the Trojan War the daughter of a priest of Apollo was captured by the Greeks and given to the Greek leader, Agamemnon, who refused to release her. The priest prayed to his god, and Apollo sent a pestilence on the Greeks.

The story of **Hyacinthus** symbolizes the destructive power of the summer sun on young people, animals, and plants. Hyacinthus was a handsome youth whom Apollo loved. One day when they were throwing the discus together, Apollo threw, and Hyacinthus, running forward to retrieve the discus, was struck by it and instantly killed. Apollo turned the blood of Hyacinthus into a purple flower on which he put the Greek exclamation of sorrow, "Ai, Ai." The hyacinth thus became a flower of mourning, which Milton refers to in *Lycidas* (106) as "that sanguine flower inscrib'd with woe."

Although the sun sometimes kills, it also causes growth and preserves health. To the Greeks and Romans, Apollo was the ideal of handsome and vigorous youth and the father of medicine. In one of the battles of the Trojan War Diomedes stunned and would have killed Aeneas, but Apollo rescued him and with the aid of Leto and Artemis healed his wounds. Later the god performed a similar service for Hector, who had been wounded by Aias.

Asclepius, or **Aesculapius,** the first physician, was the son of
Apollo by **Coronis,** the daughter of King Phlegyas of Thessaly.
Before Asclepius was born, Apollo was informed by his messenger
the crow (which then had white plumage) that Coronis had a
mortal lover. Apollo killed her at once; but later repented, punished the crow for faithfulness by turning its feathers black, and
saved his unborn son. Asclepius was trained by Chiron, the wise
Centaur, but he far surpassed his tutor in the art of healing.
He became famous throughout Greece, so famous that when
Hippolytus was killed, Artemis, who had been his protector,
offered Asclepius a large fee to restore him to life. Asclepius did
so, and for this impiety he was killed by a thunderbolt of Zeus.
The Greeks and Romans worshiped Asclepius as a god.

In Shakespeare's *Pericles* (3.2) Thaisa appears to die in childbirth and is buried at sea by her husband, Pericles; but her
coffin is cast up on shore and Cerimon, a nobleman who has skill
in medicine, is able to revive her. "Aesculapius guide us!" says
Cerimon. When the Red Cross Knight strikes down Sansjoy in
The Faerie Queene (1. 5. 12–44), Duessa hides Sansjoy in a magic
cloud and later she and Night carry him, almost dead, to hell.
There they persuade Aesculapius to heal his wounds. At his
shrine at **Epidaurus** Asclepius often appeared in the form of a
serpent, and Ben Jonson in *Bartholomew Fair* (2. 1. 5–6) and
Milton in *Paradise Lost* (9. 504–507) refer to this story.

As the god of poetry and music, Apollo is closely associated
with the Muses, who dance and sing to the music of his lyre at
the banquets of the gods. In English literature Apollo is referred
to most frequently as the sun itself and next as the patron of
poetry. Spenser calls him the "god of Poets" (*Faerie Queene,*
7. 7. 12), and in the *Epithalamion* (121–128), his own marriage
song, he describes Apollo as the father of the Muses and
asks his blessing on both the wedding and the poem. When

Milton in *Lycidas* (64–84) questions the value of the poetic discipline:

> Alas! What boots it with uncessant care
> To tend the homely slighted Shepherds trade,
> And strictly meditate the thankles Muse?

Apollo replies and gives what seems to Milton a satisfactory answer. In Keats's sonnet *On First Looking into Chapman's Homer* the "realms of gold"—literature itself—are the demesnes "which bards in fealty to Apollo hold"; and Callicles in the final song of Matthew Arnold's *Empedocles on Etna* sings of the god and the Muses:

> 'Tis Apollo comes leading
> His choir, the Nine.
> —The leader is fairest,
> But all are divine.

The **lyre,** a stringed instrument which the god Hermes invented and gave to Apollo, is a symbol in English literature of beautiful music. In *Love's Labour's Lost* (4. 3. 342–343), for example, Berowne says that love is

> . . . as sweet and musical
> As bright Apollo's lute, strung with his hair.

Terpsichore in Spenser's *Teares of the Muses* (329–330) laments that the spawn of Ignorance have usurped the places of the true singers:

> Mongst simple shepheards they do boast their skill,
> And say their musicke matcheth *Phoebus* quill.

This sort of boast never went unpunished, for Apollo was intensely jealous of his reputation as a musician.

Pan, who was vain of his skill on the pipes he had invented, once challenged Apollo to a contest. **Tmolus,** a mountain god, acted as judge, and King **Midas,** a friend of Pan's, was the audience. The rustic god played well, as Shelley imagines in his *Hymn of Pan* (12–23):

> Liquid Peneus was flowing,
>   And all dark Tempe lay
> In Pelion's shadow, outgrowing
>   The light of the dying day,
>   Speeded ʋy my sweet pipings.
>
> The Sileni, and Sylvans, and Fauns,
>   And the Nymphs of the woods and the waves,
> To the edge of the moist river-lawns
>   And the brink of the dewy caves,
> And all that did then attend and follow,
> Were silent with love, as you know, Apollo,
>   With envy of my sweet pipings.

But Apollo drew music from his lyre that only the Muses could equal, and Tmolus awarded the prize to him. Midas, who didn't know anything about music but knew what he liked, said that the judgment was unfair, and Apollo in contempt gave him a pair of donkey's ears.

Midas concealed his disfigurement under a specially designed cap, but he could not hide it from his barber, whom he swore to secrecy. Barbering has always been a garrulous trade, and this barber almost burst with his secret. Finally he eased his pain by digging a hole in the ground and whispering into it, "King Midas has ass's ears." Reeds grew on the spot, and when the wind blew through them they whispered softly (but loud enough for everyone to hear), "King Midas has ass's ears." Chaucer's Wife of Bath, who got this tale from her fifth husband, a great critic of women, says that it was Midas' wife who revealed his secret

40

(*Canterbury Tales,* III. 950–982). Pope alludes to this version of the story in the *Epistle to Dr. Arbuthnot* (79–82) when he gives his reason for writing *The Dunciad:*

> Out with it, Dunciad! let the secret pass,
> That secret to each fool, that he's an Ass:
> The truth once told (and wherefore should we lie?)
> The Queen of Midas slept, and so may I.

The poor taste of Midas is proverbial. In *Of the Courtier's Life* (48–49), for example, Sir Thomas Wyatt, describing the flattering lies that are expected of a courtier but that he himself is not willing to tell, declares that he cannot

> . . . say that Pan
> Passeth Apollo in music manifold.

And John Lyly in *Euphues: The Anatomy of Wit* describes his knowledgeable young hero as one who "could easily discern Apollo's music from Pan his pipe." (For another story about Midas see DIONYSUS.)

The goddess Athene invented the flute and played it until she discovered that she looked absurd when she puffed out her cheeks. Then she threw it away, and **Marsyas,** a Satyr, found it and learned how to make excellent music on it. Like Pan, he believed his own tunes irresistible, and he finally demanded a trial of skill with Apollo. Apollo agreed on one condition: that the winner should do what he pleased with the loser. When the decision went against the foolish Marsyas, Apollo had him flayed alive. This story, like those of Niobe and Arachne, is intended to show the dreadful punishment that falls on one who defies a god.

From his oracles at Delphi and elsewhere, Apollo foretold the future to his worshipers (see ORACLES), and he granted the gift of prophecy to two women whom he loved. Cassandra, daughter of King Priam of Troy, accepted the gift but refused to yield to Apollo, and he took a terrible revenge: he made all mortals disbelieve her prophecies. The **Sibyl of Cumae** also suffered because she would not become the mistress of Apollo. He gave her prophetic power and promised, if she would love him, to make her immortal. She took a handful of sand and begged him to grant her a year of life for each grain of sand. He agreed, but she forgot to ask for continuing youth, and this he would not give because she refused his love.

The Sibyl lived for a thousand years in her cave at Cumae; she was seven hundred years old when she helped Aeneas, the Roman hero. Usually she wrote her prophecies on the leaves of trees, and the wind blew them about her cave so that many were lost and the rest were in complete disorder. The title of Gerard Manley Hopkins' poem *Spelt from Sibyl's Leaves* alludes to the difficulty of making sense out of her jumbled foretellings of the future. Once, however, she wrote nine prophetic books and offered them to King Tarquin of Rome. He said the price was too high. She burned three of the books and told him that he could have six for the same price. When he still refused to pay, she burned three more and offered him the last three books for the same price. This time he gave her what she asked, and thereafter the **Sibylline Books** were guarded by priests and consulted at moments of crisis. John Donne writes ironically in *Upon Mr. Thomas Coryats Crudities* (71–72), an extravagant book of travels,

> As *Sibyls* was, your book is mysticall,
> For every peece is as much worth as all.

The Sibyl told Aeneas that her body was shrinking as she grew older. According to one story, toward the end of her thousand years she was a tiny shriveled thing that was kept in a cage. In

the *Satyricon* of the Roman writer Petronius one of the characters says, "I myself with my own eyes saw the Sibyl of Cumae
hanging in a cage, and when the boys shouted at her, 'Sibyl,
what do you want?' she used to answer, 'I want to die.' " T. S.
Eliot uses these lines as the epigraph, or motto, of *The Waste
Land.*

It is easy to understand why a mortal maid might be reluctant
to become mistress of a god. He would not be faithful to her,
but he would kill her, as Apollo killed Coronis, if she took
another lover. A jealous wife like Zeus's Hera would persecute
the girl, and if she became pregnant she would be harshly
treated, probably put to death, by her own family. Even the
most religious father was skeptical when his daughter confessed
that she was about to bear the child of a god.

Marpessa was aware of these disadvantages when she was forced
to choose between Apollo and a mortal lover. Apollo tried to
take her away from **Idas,** one of the Argonauts, but Zeus inter-
vened and declared that Marpessa must make the decision. She
chose to marry Idas because he would grow old as she did and
because he promised to remain faithful to her. Stephen Phillips
retold this story at the end of the nineteenth century. In his
Marpessa Apollo offers the girl immortality if she will have him,
but she prefers the humble love of Idas and the opportunity to
live a full mortal life with its sorrows as well as its joys. The
theme unfortunately is too much for Phillips' sweet vagueness.

The most famous of the girls who refused Apollo was **Daphne,**
the daughter of the river god Peneus. She was a huntress who
scorned love, but one day Apollo met her in the woods and
determined to have her at once. She ran, and he ran after her,
shouting that he loved her and telling her who he was, which
frightened her even more. With the god just behind her, she
burst through the trees at the edge of the Peneus and cried,

"Father, help me!" The river god transformed her on the spot, and Apollo found himself embracing not a lady but a laurel. He decreed that the laurel should be sacred to him, and thereafter poets and conquerors were crowned with wreaths of **laurel,** or bay (often called the **bays**), since the tree has both names. The word "laureate," which has had a doubtful value since the British crown established the post of poet laureate, means "crowned with laurel." In *The Rehearsal,* a famous burlesque of the heroic drama of the Restoration, the leading character is an absurd playwright. He is named Bayes because he is intended to represent Dryden, who was made poet laureate shortly before *The Rehearsal* was first acted. Dryden, one of the greatest English satirists, took this satire on himself in good part and often referred to himself as Bayes.

Daphne's story has been used in many ways in English literature. Some writers have been impressed chiefly by the vivid picture of the chase, as was Spenser in *The Faerie Queene* (3. 7. 26 and 4. 7. 22). To others the story has symbolized unattained loveliness. Before Cressida becomes his mistress, Troilus prays, in Shakespeare's *Troilus and Cressida* (1. 1. 101–102),

> Tell me, Apollo, for thy Daphne's love,
> What Cressid is . . . ,

and Lacy in Robert Greene's *Friar Bacon and Friar Bungay* (2. 3. 50–51) compares the girl he thinks he cannot have to

> Daphne, the damsel that caught Phoebus fast
> And locked him in the brightness of her looks.

In Milton's *Comus* (661–662) the enchanter imprisons the Lady in his magic chair, which he says, with unconscious irony, will hold her fast

> . . . as *Daphne* was,
> Root-bound, that fled *Apollo.*

Comus does not realize that although the Lady's body is his prisoner, her virtue protects her from him as securely as Daphne's transformation protected her from Apollo.

The wit of Andrew Marvell in *The Garden* (27–30) turns Apollo's defeat into victory by the suggestion that the deepest desire of men and gods is for the innocent peace of nature:

> The *Gods,* that mortal Beauty chase,
> Still in a Tree did end their race.
> *Apollo* hunted *Daphne* so,
> Only that She might Laurel grow.

In his *Ode upon Dr. Harvey* (5–10) Abraham Cowley tortures the myth into ingenious absurdity. He says that when the scientist Harvey made violent love to Nature, she

> Began to tremble, and to flee,
> Took Sanctuary like *Daphne* in a tree:
> There *Daphnes* lover stop't, and thought it much
>   The very Leaves of her to touch,
> But *Harvey* our *Apollo*, stopt not so,
> Into the Bark, and root he after her did goe . . . .

But James Russell Lowell's puns about Daphne's embarkation in *A Fable for Critics* (1–30) are just as tiresome as Cowley's kind of ingenuity.

Apollo was not always unsuccessful in love. Four of his many mistresses deserve mention here. The Nymph **Cyrene,** who was wrestling with a lion when Apollo first saw her, was the mother of his son Aristaeus, a rustic deity, the inventor of beekeeping. Also, by the Muse Calliope Apollo became the father of Orpheus, the great musician. One of these boys brought tragedy to the other. Aristaeus lusted for Orpheus' wife, Eurydice, and as she fled from him one day she was bitten by a snake and died. The attempt of Orpheus to win her back from Hades is one of the most moving stories in mythology (see ORPHEUS).

Clytie, a water Nymph, was deeply in love with Apollo, but he left her for another girl. She refused to eat or take any care of herself. All day long she watched Apollo as he traveled through the sky, and soon she was turned into a sunflower and became a symbol of faithfulness. William Blake writes of the

> . . . Sun-Flower! weary of time,
> Who countest the steps of the Sun,

and Thomas Moore in *Believe Me, If All Those Endearing Young Charms* uses Clytie to prove that true love never alters:

> . . . the sun-flower turns on her god, when he sets,
> The same look which she turn'd when he rose.

Phaethon's schoolmates laughed at his boast that his father was Apollo. When he asked reassurance of his mother **Clymene,** she sent him to see his father at the palace of the east. There Apollo received him kindly, acknowledged him as his son, and swore by the Styx (the most binding oath of the gods) that he should have whatever he desired. At once the boy asked to drive the chariot of the sun for one day. Apollo tried to dissuade him, telling him of the fierceness of the horses and the perils of the road, but Phaethon would not listen to reason. The Hours harnessed the horses, Eos opened the eastern gate, and out went Phaethon. As soon as they realized that Apollo's hand was not on the reins, the horses ran away. They dashed up and down the heavens, frightening the constellations, making the clouds smoke, and burning the tree-covered hills. Under the terrible heat the **Ethiopians** turned black and Libya became a desert. The suffering earth prayed for relief, and Zeus struck Phaethon with a thunderbolt. Phaethon fell flaming into the great and mysterious river **Eridanus,** and on its shores his sisters the **Heliades** mourned for him until they were turned into poplar trees and their tears into amber.

In English literature Phaethon usually has been a symbol of rash presumption. Spenser calls him *"Phoebus* foolish sonne" (*Teares of the Muses,* 7) and compares his arrogance to that of Lucifera, ruler of the House of Pride in *The Faerie Queene* (1. 4. 9). Valentine in *Two Gentlemen of Verona* (3. 1. 154–155) plans to elope with Silvia, the Duke's daughter. When the Duke discovers the plot, he contemptuously compares Valentine to Phaethon and asks,

> Wilt thou aspire to guide the heavenly car
> And with thy daring folly burn the world?

In *Richard II* (3. 3. 178–179) the King, about to surrender his crown to the rebel Bolingbroke, speaks of himself in bitter irony:

> Down, down I come, like glist'ring Phaeton,
> Wanting the manage of unruly jades.

Spenser in the catalogue of trees in *Virgils Gnat* (198) describes the "Sunnes sad daughters" mourning for Phaethon, and Andrew Marvell recalls them in *The Nymph Complaining for the Death of Her Faun* (99–100):

> The brotherless *Heliades*
> Melt in such Amber Tears as these.

Religious poets of the seventeenth century sometimes represented Apollo as an enemy of Christ and a servant of the Devil, but generally the god of poetry has had an honored place in English literature. Because he is an advanced moralist (in the *Eumenides* of Aeschylus he defends Orestes, who has been purified through suffering, against the Furies, the goddesses of the old law of strict retribution) and because he is the god of light and therefore of truth, Apollo was often used in the nineteenth century as the symbol of intellectual order.

Coleridge, who in his prose writings gave his fellow Romantics a philosophy, contrasts the intellectual Apollo with Dionysus, the symbol of instinctive vigor. Keats makes Apollo the hero of *Hyperion.* The theme of this unfinished poem is the spiritual progress of man, and it is represented through the fall of the Titans and the rise of the new gods. The Titans, though far superior to their predecessors, must yield to the greater excellence of the Olympians; and the qualities essential to progress, greater self-control and greater knowledge, are shown in Apollo. When in his difficult search for godhead he finally arrives at understanding, he says,

> Knowledge enormous makes a god of me.

Shelley's *Hymn of Apollo* (31–36) expresses a similar concept:

> I am the eye with which the Universe
> Beholds itself and knows itself divine;
> All harmony of instrument or verse,
>
> All prophecy, all medicine are mine,
> All light of art or nature;—to my song
> Victory and praise in their own right belong.

Songs of victory and praise—paeans—were always sung to Apollo. In *Empedocles on Etna* Matthew Arnold (perhaps to his embarrassment, for his poetic statement is at variance with his critical belief) shows Empedocles defeated in his attempt to find full satisfaction in the austere Apollonian ideal of intellectual development. While Callicles in the distance sings of the defeat and death of Marsyas (as described earlier), Empedocles commits suicide by leaping into the volcano. Both Marsyas and Empedocles are victims of Apollo.

Swinburne, revolting against Christianity, sees Apollo in *The Last Oracle* (73–76, 83–86) as the one enduring god:

> Thou the word, the light, the life, the breath, the glory,
> Strong to help and heal, to lighten and to slay,
> Thine is all the song of man, the world's whole story;
> Not of morning and of evening is thy day.
>
> . . . . . .
>
> God by god goes out, discrowned and disanointed,
> But the soul stands fast that gave them shape and speech.
> Is the sun yet cast out of heaven?
> Is the song yet cast out of man?

Swinburne's kind of neopaganism, however, would have amazed Apollo.

APPLES OF THE HESPERIDES (hĕs·pĕr'ĭ·dēz) are golden apples guarded by the Hesperides, daughters of Atlas, and the dragon Ladon. Atlas was tricked into giving three of these apples to HERACLES.

AQUARIUS (á·kwār'ĭ·ûs), the Water-Bearer, is a constellation and a sign of the ZODIAC.

AQUILO (ăk'wĭ·lō) is the Roman name for Boreas, the north wind. See WINDS.

ARACHNE (á·răk'nē) was a maiden who challenged Athene to a weaving contest. The goddess defeated her and turned her into a spider. See ATHENE.

ARCADIA (är·kā'dĭ·á), or **ARCADY** (är'ká·dē), is a mountainous region in the Peloponnesus, the central district of the Greek peninsula. Watered by innumerable streams, and protected in many places from the harsher features of a southern climate by its higher altitudes and frequent fogs, it is better suited to the pasturage of flocks than to agriculture. The summer, which burns many parts of Greece brown with its hot sun, leaves Arcadia characteristically green and cool.

The people of Arcadia, therefore, remained for centuries a simple, generally rural folk, even after other areas of Greece had been formed into city-states with more sophisticated civilizations. The Arcadians tended their flocks in the fields and cultivated the arts, music in particular. The god Pan was supposed to have invented the rustic flute in Arcadia (see PAN); and the Arcadian herdsman, whiling away the grazing time of his flocks, traditionally played to himself or his fellows on his flute.

The pastoral quality of Arcadia has left its mark on Greek mythology, and even more decidedly on the literature of classical times and of later days in England. With its glens and coverts of woods, Arcadia was supposed to have been the favorite hunting ground of Artemis, the goddess of the hunt and of chastity. Indeed, it was claimed not only that the human race had originated there but that the Arcadians themselves were Artemis' descendants. Calling themselves "the bear-people," they worshiped her in the form of a bear. According to another story, the Arcadians were descended from Arcas, the son of Zeus and a Nymph named Callisto. Callisto was a follower of Artemis, but when she broke her vow of chastity and yielded to Zeus, Artemis turned her into a bear. For further details see ARTEMIS. Both Zeus and Hermes were born in Arcadia, and the rural areas were the haunts of which Pan was most fond.

As life in ancient times became more complex, the Greeks often turned their minds nostalgically back to the bucolic days of their ancestors, and they naturally found in the life of Arcadia their best symbol of escape. Arcadia became, therefore, the local symbol for poetry that praised the pastoral life, and ultimately it became indissolubly united with the pastoral tradition in both classical and English literature.

The pastoral tradition in literature begins with the work of Theocritus, a Syracusan poet, whose *Idylls* show bucolic life both as it was and as a sort of idealized existence. Following Theocritus' example, the Roman poet, Virgil, in his *Eclogues,* carries the idealization still further. In these poems the shepherds are all exemplary young men, innocent of guile, who compose music and poetry both for their own amusement and to celebrate the pure shepherdesses whom they love. The weather is usually spring or summer, the meadows are green, and the flocks of sheep peaceful and clean. Renaissance writers imitated the classical poets, and in 1504 an Italian poet named Sannazaro wrote *Arcadia,* a collection of poetic eclogues connected by prose passages, which became extremely popular, setting the pattern for a number of Elizabethan writers.

Although the pastoral or Arcadian tradition spread generally over Europe in succeeding years, its greatest exemplar in Elizabethan England was the poet Spenser. To the elements of innocent, sometimes unrequited, love amid the green fields and pretty flocks, Spenser, following Italian models, added the further element of allegory, so that his shepherds and shepherdesses, moving through the usual scenes of pipe playing and love making, became the vehicles for satire and for moral comment. *The Shepheardes Calender* and *Colin Clouts Come Home Againe* remain signal accomplishments in the genre.

Arcadian pastoral life naturally found its way into prose works as well as into poetry. Sir Philip Sidney's prose romance, *Arcadia,* attempts to blend the traditional view of pastoral life with the medieval chivalric tradition. Again, Arcadian life is the subject of both Thomas Lodge's *Rosalind* and *As You Like It,* in which Shakespeare uses Lodge's story, though Arcadia itself is not the scene of either. A more direct dramatic use of the convention, which was extraordinarily popular in Elizabethan and Jacobean times, is John Fletcher's play, *The Faithful Shepherdess* (ca. 1610), which concerns itself altogether with shepherds and shepherdesses of a sort much more likely to be found in fiction than in fact.

The Arcadian tradition did not end with the Jacobeans. Milton, for example, found it a rich field, and the best of his shorter poems draw from it their symbolism. The shortest, though not the best, of these is his *Arcades*, a masque in praise of the Countess of Derby, in which the Genius of the Wood appears to speak the main part:

> Stay gentle Swains, for though in this disguise,
> I see bright honour sparkle through your eyes,
> Of famous *Arcady* ye are, and sprung
> Of that renowned flood, so often sung,
> Divine *Alpheus*, who by secret sluse,
> Stole under Seas to meet his *Arethuse*.

The song that concludes the work says of the Countess herself:

> Such a rural Queen
> All *Arcadia* hath not seen.

Both *Comus* and *Lycidas* are likewise Arcadian pastoral poems. The latter mourns the death of Edward King, whom Milton had known as a fellow student at Cambridge. King is represented as a shepherd whose loss is mourned by the other shepherds still in the pastures, and especially by Milton:

> Together both, ere the high Lawns appear'd
> Under the opening eye-lids of the morn,
> We drove a field, and both together heard
> What time the Gray-fly winds her sultry horn,
> Batt'ning our flocks with the fresh dews of night. . . .

The Arcadian idealization of country life lost none of its literary impetus during the eighteenth century. Nymphs and swains, shepherds and shepherdesses, Strephons and Amaryllises were so widely written about that the terms themselves became unbearable clichés for later writers. The tradition on the one hand retained classic purity in Alexander Pope's *Pastorals;* and on the other hand retained the pastoral spirit but found a local scene in poems such as Oliver Goldsmith's *The Deserted Village,* in which he writes:

> Sweet was the sound, when oft at evening's close
> Up yonder hill the village murmur rose;
> There, as I pass'd with careless steps and slow,
> The mingling notes came soften'd from below;
> The swain responsive as the milk-maid sung,
> The sober herd that low'd to meet their young.

This sort of thing provoked another poet, George Crabbe, to write *The Village,* a poem showing country life in more real colors: his purpose was to

> . . . paint the cot,
> As Truth will paint it and as bards will not.

Cowper in *Hope* also remarks sadly:

> The poor, inured to drudgery and distress,
> Act without aim, think little, and feel less,
> And no where, but in feign'd Arcadian scenes,
> Taste happiness, or know what pleasure means.

Although Wordsworth was not given to classical conventions, in *Michael,* he has, like Goldsmith, found a native scene for an Arcadian mood. Wordsworth, however, avoided the more elaborate falsities that had grown up in literary Arcadias. With his tremendous faith in the purifying and simplifying powers of nature acting on the human mind, and with his close observation of human life in natural surroundings, he created an old shep-

53

herd who has at once the real simplicity of a true rustic and the ideal innocence of Arcadia.

The tradition was still so much alive in the late nineteenth century that W. S. Gilbert made a delightful satire about it in *Iolanthe,* in which a shepherd, born of a brook Nymph, is elected to Parliament. The opening scene is "an Arcadian landscape" with a brook running through it, but by the time Strephon, the shepherd hero, has found his way into Parliament and has succeeded in extricating his loved shepherdess, Phyllis, from the toils of British chancery law, which has made her a ward of the Lord Chancellor, the effect accomplished is something of which Theocritus never dreamed.

In a sonnet that bears the traditional name *Amaryllis* Edwin Arlington Robinson mourns the passing of pastoral life under the modern tide of commercialism:

> It made me lonely and it made me sad
> To think that Amaryllis had grown old.[2]

Yet the pastoral tradition will doubtless survive as long as there are poets who prefer the quiet simplicity of the countryside to the noisy confusions of the city.

ARCAS (är′kȧs), the son of Callisto and Zeus, was sometimes said to be the ancestor of the Arcadians. See ARTEMIS.

AREOPAGUS (ăr′ē·ŏp′ȧ·gûs) is the hill of ARES.

ARES (ā′rēz), or **Mars,** a son of Zeus and Hera, is the god of war. Dressed in magnificent armor and carrying a spear and a flaming torch, Ares swaggers into battle attended by his sons **Deimos and Phobos,** or **Pavor,** gods of tumult and terror; Enyo, the goddess of battle and the destroyer of cities; and Eris, the goddess of discord. Enyo and Eris are variously described as sister, mother, daughter,

[2] From "Amaryllis," by E. A. Robinson, in his *Children of the Night.* Reprinted with the permission of the publisher, Charles Scribner's Sons.

and wife of Ares. As scavengers of the battlefield, the vulture and the dog are Ares' favorite bird and animal.

Ares and Mars hold the same position in Greek and Roman mythology, but their differences in character and achievement point to a significant difference between the two cultures. Although the Greeks were skillful warriors, they thought of Ares as "the blood-stained bane of mortals" (*Iliad*, 5). He was hated and feared by most men and disliked by nearly all the gods, including his parents Hera and Zeus. In one of the battles before Troy the Greek hero Diomedes, with Athene guiding his spear, wounded Ares in the belly. The god roared with pain and ran home to Olympus to complain to Zeus, but Zeus received him with cold contempt. Ares often opposed Athene, who was the goddess of victory, but she always defeated him because she was just and wise as well as warlike.

In contrast to the brutal, cowardly, sometimes unsuccessful Grecian Ares, the Roman Mars is brave, invincible, and glorious. Rome was founded by Romulus, the son of Mars and a Vestal Virgin (after his death Romulus was deified as the lesser god of war, **Quirinus**); and the god's temple within the city was on the **Campus Martius,** or Field of Mars, a favorite place for sports and military exercises. The warriors in the *Aeneid* often seek a glorious death in battle, and Roman generals prayed to Mars for victory and offered him a portion of their plunder. In *The Knight's Tale* by Chaucer, Palamon and Arcite fight for the hand of Emily, and Arcite prays to Mars for victory. Ironically, Arcite gets the victory, but Palamon, who has prayed to Venus, gets the girl.

Like most of the other gods, Ares had several casual love affairs and fathered extraordinary children, including the race of warlike women called the Amazons. His only enduring affection, however, was for Aphrodite, and the most remarkable offspring of this union of delight and terror was Eros, the god of love. (For further details of the affair see APHRODITE.)

When a son of Poseidon raped one of Ares' daughters by a mortal mistress, Ares killed the boy. Poseidon accused Ares of murder, and he was tried and acquitted by the gods, who held court on a hill in Athens. Thereafter this hill was called the **Areopagus,** the hill of Ares. It was the scene of other murder trials presided over by the gods, notably that of Orestes (see ATREUS), and it became the seat of the highest human tribunal in Athens. In Elizabethan times the name was applied by Gabriel Harvey to an informal group of critics who were attempting to reform the meters of English poetry, and John Milton in the seventeenth century called his written address to the English Parliament the *Areopagitica* in recollection of the *Areopagitic Oration* of the Greek Isocrates, who also composed his speeches to be read.

Although the war god is frequently mentioned in Greek and Roman literature, there are few stories about him. When he is not described as the lover of Aphrodite, he almost always appears as a mere personification of war, and that is the way he is used in English literature. Piers, for example, in Spenser's *Shepheardes Calender* (*October,* 39) urges the poet Cuddie to "sing of bloody Mars, of wars, of giusts." In *Richard II* (2. 1. 41) the rhapsodizing John of Gaunt calls England "this seat of Mars," and Thersites in *Troilus and Cressida* (2. 1. 58) describes the boastful, strong, stupid warrior Ajax as "Mars his idiot." The favorite animal of Ares is recalled by Antony in *Julius Caesar* (3. 1. 273) when he says that Caesar's ghost shall "Cry 'havoc!' and let slip the dogs of war."

Enyo, or **Bellona,** receives similar treatment. Spenser (*Faerie Queene,* 7. 6. 3) speaks of her as

> . . . drad *Bellona,* that doth sound on hie
> **Warres** and allarums vnto Nations wide.

One of Macbeth's admirers calls him "Bellona's bridegroom" (*Macbeth,* 1. 2. 54), and this conceit is wittily developed by Richard Lovelace in his apology to his mistress Lucasta for going to the wars:

> True, a new Mistresse now I chase,
>   The first Foe in the Field;
> And with a stronger Faith imbrace
>   A Sword, a Horse, a Shield.

When **Eris,** or **Discordia,** was not invited to the wedding of Peleus and Thetis, she threw among the guests a golden apple inscribed "For the fairest," and this shrewd and spiteful gesture was a main cause of the Trojan War. Eris, however, is only an abstraction. There are no other important stories about her, and she seldom appears in English literature, although in *Paradise Lost* (2. 967; 10. 707–709) she is one of the attendants of.Chaos and, after the fall, she introduces death among the beasts.

In English literature, however, another personification from classical mythology sometimes takes Eris' place. This is **Ate,** the goddess of infatuation, the cause of all rash actions and the originator of mischief. Shakespeare, for example, makes Ate the companion of the ghost of Caesar raging for revenge (*Julius Caesar,* 3. 1. 271). Early in *The Faerie Queene* (2. 7. 55) Ate is mentioned as the false spirit whose golden apple caused the quarrel among the goddesses, and later, in the first canto of Book Four, she takes part in the action. She and her dwelling are described in detail. Born "of hellish brood" and nourished by the Furies, this foul misshapen hag lives on human blood shed in "mischieuous debate, and deadly feood." Her dwelling place, close to the gates of hell, is hung with countless trophies of her victories over men.

ARETHUSA (ăr′ĕ·thū′zȧ) is one of the NYMPHS.

ARGIPHONTES (är′jĭ·fŏn′tēz) is another name for HERMES.
ARGO (är′gō) was the ship of the ARGONAUTS.
ARGONAUTS (är′gȯ·nôts). The story of the expedition of the Argonauts, in spite of its many supernatural elements, possibly had its origin in the real events of some prehistoric quest that set out from Greece to the eastward. Whatever its beginnings in fact, however, the mythological story as we know it has the essence of the Greek heroic spirit, with its mixture of superhuman achievements and human passions, especially as they appeared in the person of **Jason,** the chief and first mover of the expedition.

Jason, like other Greek heroes, came of a distinguished lineage, for he was a great-great-grandson of Deucalion, who with his wife Pyrrha repeopled the earth after the great flood by throwing stones over their shoulders, a method not listed in the Kinsey Report. The line passed from Deucalion through Hellen, the eponymous father of all the Greeks, or Hellenes, through Aeolus (not the wind god, for whose character see WINDS), to Jason's father, **Aeson.** Aeson, possibly because he was forced to do so, gave up the throne of Iolcus, a city in Thessaly, to his brother **Pelias,** but on condition that Pelias return it to Jason when the boy came of age.

Jason was reared by Chiron the Centaur until he was twenty years old. Then an oracle directed him to face Pelias and demand his father's throne. An oracle meantime had informed Pelias that a descendant of Aeolus, who would appear before him wearing only one sandal, would deprive him of the throne. When Jason traveled to Iolcus, he found that he had to cross the river Enipeus, which was flooded at the time. On the bank there was a poor old woman lamenting her inability to reach the other side. He carried her across with difficulty, for the current was swift, and he lost one sandal in the river. The old woman was Hera in mortal disguise, and thereafter she favored Jason for his courtesy. When he arrived at court wearing only one sandal, Pelias recognized him and was prepared with a stratagem. He told Jason that his coming to the throne should be preceded by an heroic achievement, and he suggested that Jason undertake to bring back the **Golden Fleece** from faraway **Colchis.**

The Golden Fleece itself was the center of a colorful myth. Aeson's other brother, **Athamas,** had two children, **Phrixus** and **Helle,** by his wife **Nephele.** Then Athamas tired of her, put her aside, and married Ino, Cadmus' daughter, who developed a traditionally stepmotherly attitude toward the two children and began to mistreat them. In revenge, Nephele brought down a drought on the land, and Ino retaliated by demanding the sacrifice of Phrixus and Helle to relieve it. The children were about to be sacrificed when their mother appeared on the scene with a golden-fleeced ram that had been given to her by Hermes. She placed the children on its back, whereupon the ram sprang into the air and set course for Colchis. Helle, the daughter, fell off into the sea at a place that was therefore given her name and called the **Hellespont;** but Phrixus reached Colchis, sacrificed the ram to Ares, and hung its golden fleece in a sacred grove, where it came to be guarded by a dragon. Thus to Pelias the fleece seemed both remote and secure, the recovery of it impossible. It seemed so to Shakespeare, too, and he borrows its qualities for Portia, the heroine of *The Merchant of Venice* (1. 1. 161–172), whom Bassanio describes thus:

> In Belmont is a lady richly left;
> And she is fair, and, fairer than that word,
> Of wondrous virtues . . . .
>
> . . . . . .
>
> Nor is the wide world ignorant of her worth;
> For the four winds blow in from every coast
> Renowned suitors, and her sunny locks

Hang on her temples like a golden fleece,
Which makes her seat of Belmont Colchos' strond,
And many Jasons come in quest of her.

Jason was pleased with Pelias' suggestion. He first employed **Argus,** the son of Phrixus (not the hundred-eyed person slain by Hermes, for whom see ZEUS), to build a huge ship. Because Jason's contemporaries were accustomed to boats that were scarcely more than oversized canoes, the ship that Argus built to accommodate fifty men seemed in itself of heroic size, and it was named the **Argo** for its builder. Athene aided in the construction of it and even placed in it a piece of oak from the tree of the oracle at Dodona.

Then Jason invited all the heroes of Greece to join him in the expedition, and those who accepted included Theseus, Orpheus, Heracles, Pirithous, Castor and Polydeuces (or Pollux), Meleager, Admetus, Peleus, Nestor, Neleus, and two sons of the north wind Boreas, named **Calais** and **Zetes.**

When the expedition was ready to sail, Jason made a sacrifice to Zeus and asked for an omen. Zeus responded by thundering and flashing his lightning, a favorable sign which satisfied the heroes. They therefore set sail. Their first port of call was **Lemnos,** the Aegean isle, where they found a situation calculated to delight the hearts of heroes. The women of Lemnos, provoked to the act by Aphrodite, had slain their husbands and all the other men on the island (though unknown to them their queen, **Hypsipyle,** had saved her father from destruction). The heroes thus found pleasure enough available, and the use to which they turned it produced another race of heroes. Jason himself had twin sons by Hypsipyle, though later, when the other Lemnian women learned that she had saved her father's life, they killed her sons and sold her into slavery to King Lycurgus of Nemea (for her life in Nemea, see THEBES). Chaucer made a touching love story of this affair between "duc Jason" and "Ysiphile" for his collection called *The Legend of Good Women*. The deserted Ysiphile writes a letter to Jason to tell him that his two children

> . . . ben lyk of alle thyng, ywis,
> To Jason, save they coude nat begile. . . .

Furthermore, says Chaucer,

> . . . trewe to Jason was she al hire lyf,
> And evere kepte hire chast, as for his wif;
> Ne nevere hadde she joye at hire herte,
> But deyede, for his love, of sorwes smerte.
>   (1569–1570, 1576–1579)

Not forgetting their quest, however, in spite of so delectable a life, the heroes at last set sail again and landed next at **Cyzicus.** As they were leaving this island, Heracles pulled too hard on his oar and broke it. He therefore went ashore in the company of a youth named **Hylas** to find another oar, and while they searched, amorous Nymphs fell in love with Hylas and kidnaped him. Because Heracles would not go without him, the Argo had to leave them both behind.

The heroes stopped next in Bithynia, where they were at once challenged to box with King **Amycus,** who ruled the country and took an insolent pride in his ability with his fists. His challenge was accepted by Polydeuces, who quickly vanquished him. The Argo then proceeded to the entrance to the Euxine (now the Black) Sea, where a real peril faced the heroes. This entrance was commanded by two floating cliffs called the **Symplegades,** which crashed together on any vessel that sought to pass through to the inner sea. However, the problem of passage was solved for the Argonauts by old King **Phineus,** whose kingdom of Salmydessus

61

in Thrace lay close by and whom they aided in a problem of his own.

Phineus had got himself into considerable trouble with the gods. He had first married **Cleopatra,** the daughter of Boreas, the north wind (not to be confused with the later famous queen of Egypt) and had two sons by her. After she died, or according to a later story, after Phineus had for some reason imprisoned her, he married **Idaea,** a daughter of Dardanus of Troy. Idaea falsely accused Cleopatra's sons of improper conduct and caused Phineus to blind them. This injustice led Zeus to force on Phineus the choice of being himself blinded or killed. In this dilemma Phineus chose blindness, but in so doing he offended Helios, the god of the sun, because he had chosen not to see the sun again. Consequently, Helios sent the terrible **Harpies** to prey on Phineus. These creatures were the monstrous daughters of the sea deities Thaumas and Electra, and they had the bodies, wings, and claws of birds, but the heads of maidens. From their home, the Strophades islands in the Ionian Sea, they flew into Phineus' kingdom and each day stole his food or defiled it with their excrement (see SEA GODS). Two of the Argonauts, Calais and Zetes, who had been his brothers-in-law when he was married to Cleopatra, drove off the Harpies.

As to the Argonauts' problem, Phineus advised them to release a dove to fly between the cliffs; the cliffs would then crash together on the dove, and while they were moving back into their separate positions, the Argonauts could sail through. This advice the heroes followed and it worked almost perfectly. The Symplegades, in crashing together on the dove, missed all the bird except a few of her tail feathers. The Argo was then rowed swiftly through the reopening passage, and though the cliffs came quickly together again, they missed all the boat except its rudder. Ever after, the two cliffs were united into one rock. The incident supplied Milton with a parallel by which to describe Satan's passage through the realm of Chaos in *Paradise Lost* (2. 1013–1018). Satan sprang upward

> . . . like a Pyramid of fire
> Into the wilde expanse, and through the shock
> Of fighting Elements, on all sides round
> Environ'd wins his way; harder beset
> And more endanger'd, then when *Argo* pass'd
> Through *Bosporus* betwixt the justling Rocks. . . .

The rest of the Argonauts' passage to Colchis was without serious incident except for their experience with the **Stymphalian Birds,** creatures similar to the Harpies, whose feathers were as sharp as arrows and whose talons were of iron. These birds, which attacked the Argonauts by showering down iron feathers that pierced the heroes' skin, were driven off only by a great clamor that the Argonauts set up.

The expedition now reached Colchis in safety, and there Jason found the land ruled by **Aeetes,** a son of Helios. Aeetes consented to give Jason the Golden Fleece only on condition that Jason first perform a task for him, and the task was designed to get rid of Jason. It consisted of yoking Aeetes' brazen-hooved bulls, that breathed fire, of plowing the field of Ares, and of sowing it with dragon's teeth like those sown by Cadmus, teeth that would spring up into armed soldiers who would attack whoever had planted them.

Jason, in the manner characteristic of heroes, accepted the task and set the date on which he would perform it. He then put to use the experience that he had gained on the island of Lemnos, and made love to Aeetes' daughter, **Medea,** whose name means "the counseling woman," and who was actually a powerful sorceress. Medea accepted his love and used her magic powers to provide him with a mixture to make him fire- and sword-proof.

63

Athene also came to his aid. Consequently Jason had no trouble in yoking the fire-breathing bulls to the plow, much to the astonishment of all who watched. Moreover, he made short work of sowing the dragon's teeth. When the armed warriors sprang up from the soil and attacked him, he first displayed an heroic *sprezzatura* and fought them off singlehanded. Then he resorted to what Medea had taught him and threw a stone among them; this ruse caused them to fight among themselves until they finally killed one another off.

Now all that Jason had to do was to best the dragon that guarded the fleece in the sacred wood. Again a woman's wiles were successful where a man's strength would have failed. Medea gave him a liquid that, when sprinkled on the old dragon, put him to sleep for the first time in his life. The fleece itself was then an easy plunder.

To make sure that Aeetes did not change his mind, Jason and the other Argonauts, taking Medea and her brother, Absyrtus, with them, left Colchis secretly. Aeetes, however, soon missed his guests and his children and set out in hot pursuit. He might have overtaken them had not Medea thought of another ruse. She dismembered her brother and threw the pieces out into the sea as the ship moved along. Not only was Aeetes deeply shocked by this device, but he felt bound to collect his disjunct son and give him a decent burial as required by the gods. By the time he had accomplished this sad task, his daughter and her friends were safely beyond pursuit.

The Argonauts reached Iolcus again without mishap, and Jason dedicated the Argo to Poseidon, who had given it such fair passage over his waters. Then Jason demanded the throne of Iolcus from Pelias. According to one story, Pelias refused and Jason slew him. Another myth is more complicated. Jason, it seems, asked Medea to restore his aged father, Aeson, to youth-

fulness by her charms. Medea made elaborate preparations for
the task. She first prayed to numerous deities, including Hecate
and Tellus, the earth. Then she called up her magic chariot
powered by twin-winged serpents and flew off to a place where
she could find the mysterious herbs she needed. Nine nights
were taken up in her search, though Jessica, in Shakespeare's
Merchant of Venice, seems to think that Medea took only one,
and consequently says of the enchanted night that she is spending
with her lover Lorenzo (5. 1. 12–14),

> In such a night
> Medea gathered the enchanted herbs
> That did renew old Æson.

After gathering a collection of items that would put even a
modern drugstore to shame, Medea built altars to Hebe, the
goddess of youth, and to Hecate, the goddess of witchcraft, and
began the final ritual. Into a caldron she put herbs, seeds, sand,
the head and wings of a screech owl, the liver of a stag, the
entrails of a wolf, the beak of a crow, and other exotic things.
She had Aeson brought in, put him into a trance with one of
her spells, and laid him out as if dead, on a bed of herbs.
Then, shutting all others from her magic, she marched three
times around her altars, dipping a burning twig into the blood of
a sacrificed black sheep, and performing other rites. When the
caldron had bubbled sufficiently, she cut Aeson's throat and let
his blood drain forth, after which she poured her potpourri into
his mouth and into the wound in his throat. The effect was as
planned, and Aeson rose up a young man again, his hair
and beard youthful in color although they had been white
with age.

Naturally, Medea's success was received as a sensation. Pelias
too was growing old, and his daughters besought Medea to work

the same rejuvenation on him. Medea pretended to consent, and actually went through the same motions, but this time she put only a few odds and ends, together with some plain water, into the caldron. She then persuaded the daughters to kill their father and put his body in the caldron. Too late they learned that they had killed him to no purpose, and Medea had meantime escaped.

But Medea's magic, powerful as it was, could not keep for her the love of Jason. Although she had two children by him, he fell in love with **Creusa**, or **Glauce**, the daughter of Creon of Corinth, made her his wife, and deserted Medea. Medea's revenge was ruthless and terrible. She prepared a cursed dress by steeping it in a deadly poison. This she sent to Creusa as a reconciliation present. When Creusa put it on, it burned her to death, and her father, too, who tried to save her. Medea also burned down Jason's house. As Jason came to her in great anger, she murdered their two sons and flew away in her serpent chariot to Athens where Aegeus, the father of Theseus, who hoped that she could cure his impotence, gave her protection. The story of Medea's terrible revenge on Jason is the subject of a tragedy by Euripides, which has recently been freely translated by Robinson Jeffers. A crime that she attempted in Athens is told in this book under THESEUS. In *The Legend of Good Women* (1676–1677), Chaucer, intent on the feminine faithfulness that is the subject of the work, omits the violence that Medea did and tells only of her reproaches to Jason, concluding:

> O haddest thow in thy conquest ded ybe,
> Ful mikel untrouthe hadde ther deyd with the!

Jason himself came to a sorry end. Despondent over his misfortunes, which he certainly had brought on himself, he set out for the sacred grove where the Argo had been placed in dedication to Poseidon. There he killed himself, or according to another account, the stern of the Argo fell on him and killed him.

The entire story of Jason is related by the indefatigable William Morris in a long poem called *The Life and Death of Jason,* and Robert Graves has recently retold the voyage of the Argonauts in a novel, *Hercules, My Shipmate.*

ARGUS (är′gŭs) was (1) the hundred-eyed giant who guarded Io on Hera's orders (see ZEUS): (2) the builder of the Argo, the ship of the ARGONAUTS; (3) the dog of ODYSSEUS.

ARIADNE (ăr′ĭ·ăd′nė) aided Theseus in slaying the Minotaur. Theseus deserted her on the island of Naxos, but the god Dionysus fell in love with her and married her. See DIONYSUS, THESEUS.

ARIES (ā′rĭ·ēz), the Ram, is a constellation and a sign of the ZODIAC.

ARION (á·rī′ŏn) was (1) a musician (see SEA GODS); (2) a winged horse (see THEBES).

ARISTAEUS (ăr′ĭs·tē′ŭs) is- the minor god of beekeeping. See ORPHEUS, SEA GODS.

ARSINOE (är·sĭn′ŏ·ē) was the first wife of Alcmaeon, one of the Epigoni. See THEBES.

ARTEMIS (är′tė·mĭs), or **Diana,** the twin sister of Apollo, is the virgin goddess of the moon and the hunt, and the protector of young persons and wild animals. As goddess of the moon, she is also called Phoebe, Selene, Luna, and Hecate. The Titaness **Phoebe,** whose name means "the bright one," seems to have been the first moon goddess; she was the mother of Leto and therefore the grandmother of Artemis. She was replaced as moon goddess by **Selene,** a daughter of the Titans Hyperion and **Thea,** who were also the parents of Helios, the sun god, and Eos, the goddess of the dawn. Selene was gradually overshadowed by Artemis, as Helios was by Apollo, and Artemis finally assumed all the powers of the goddess of the moon and all the stories attributed to her. **Luna,**

which simply means "moon," is, like Diana, a Roman name for Artemis.

The mixture of good and evil that the Greeks and Romans found in their gods is seen most clearly in the moon goddess, who is at once the chaste and lovely Artemis and the mysterious and terrible **Hecate**, the goddess of the dark of the moon. The Roman writers sometimes represent Diana as having three natures as the moon has three phases: she is Luna in the sky, Diana on earth, and Hecate in Hades. This notion appears in English literature also. In *Paradise Lost* (3. 730), for example, Uriel refers to the moon's "countenance triform"; Robin Goodfellow in *A Midsummer-Night's Dream* (5. 1. 391) speaks of "triple Hecate's team"; and Herrick in *A Conjuration: To Electra* adds solemnity to his pleading

> By silent nights, and the
> Three Formes of *Heccate.*

Dogs howl at the approach of Hecate, as they do in the *Aeneid* when the Sibyl of Cumae in the middle of the night sacrifices four black bullocks to the dark goddess. Hecate is the mistress of witchcraft, and she is powerful at graveyards and crossroads. As an attendant of the queen of Hades, she has power over dreams and fantasies and is able to raise the spirits of the dead. In *Macbeth* (3. 5 and 4. 1) Hecate is the mistress of the three witches who offer riddling prophecies and raise apparitions to trick Macbeth. The enchanter in Milton's *Comus* (534) does "abhorred rites to *Hecate*"; and in Spenser's *Faerie Queene* (1. 1. 43) an evil spirit who has been sent to get a false dream from Morpheus frightens the sleepy god into wakefulness with Hecate's "dreaded name." The most recent use of this name is in Edmund Wilson's *Memoirs of Hecate County,* a book of stories that deal with a noticeably sulphurous suburban area of our country.

Artemis is also called **Cynthia** and **Delia** because she was born on Mount Cynthus on the island of Delos (for stories of her birth see APOLLO). Under the names of **Ilithyia**, or **Eileithyia**, and **Lucina** (which are sometimes applied to Hera and sometimes are the names of a separate goddess), Artemis is the goddess of childbirth. She is invoked in this capacity by Spenser in his *Epithalamion* (374–387). That a virgin goddess is often the goddess of childbirth is one of the divine paradoxes that the human authors of this book must leave unexplained. The cypress is the tree of Artemis, and all wild animals are sacred to her, but especially the deer. To the Greeks and Romans she was the ideal of beautiful and vigorous girlhood as Apollo was of robust and handsome young manhood.

Artemis not only gloried in her own virginity but required a vow of chastity from the many Nymphs who were her attendants and her hunting companions. In Pope's *The Rape of the Lock* (2. 105–106) the heroine Belinda, who is a follower of Artemis only in the sense that she is a virgin, is doomed to disaster, but no one knows

> Whether the nymph shall break Diana's law,
> Or some frail China jar receive a flaw.

Artemis protected her attendants, as she did Arethusa when the river god Alpheus attempted to force his love on her (see NYMPHS); and she punished them if they broke their vows. When Callisto, an Arcadian follower of Artemis, yielded to Zeus and bore him a son, Artemis turned her into a bear. (Some writers say that this punishment was imposed by Hera, Zeus's jealous wife.) Years later the transformed Callisto met her son Arcas hunting in the forest. As he raised his spear to kill her,

Zeus translated them both to the sky, making her the Great Bear, Arctus, or Ursa Major, more familiarly known as the Big Dipper, and her son the Little Bear, Arcturus, or Arctophylax, a giant star that has the North Star or Cynosure at the tip of its tail. In Milton's *Comus* (340–341) the Elder Brother, lost in a black night, recalls this story when he says that a candle flame would seem like a

> . . . star of *Arcady,*
> Or *Tyrian* Cynosure.

Arcas was often said to be the father of the inhabitants of Arcadia, a rural district in the heart of Peloponnesus (see ARCADIA).

The goddess of fair and harmless light was quick to resent slights and insults and terrible in her vengeance. When King Oeneus of Calydon at the festival of harvest forgot to sacrifice to Artemis, she sent a great boar to ravage his kingdom (see CALYDONIAN BOAR HUNT); and when Agamemnon, waiting in Aulis to lead the Greeks against Troy, killed a stag sacred to Artemis, she refused to allow the Greek fleet to sail until Agamemnon had atoned for his sin by sacrificing his daughter Iphigenia (see TROJAN WAR).

Artemis and Apollo were exceedingly fond of their mother Leto and fierce defenders of her honor. They killed a Giant named Tityus because he had insulted Leto (see APOLLO), and they wiped out the entire family of a woman who boasted that she was superior to their mother. **Niobe,** the daughter of Tantalus, married **Amphion,** regent of Thebes, and bore him fourteen sons and daughters. Her pride in these children stirred in her the terrible arrogance of her father, and she declared that the Thebans should worship her rather than Leto. "She has only two children," Niobe said, "but I have seven times as many."

Urged to vengeance by their mother, Artemis and Apollo with

their arrows shot down Niobe's seven sons and then her seven daughters as they wept over their brothers' bodies. Amphion, mad with grief, killed himself. Niobe was changed into a stone from which flows continually the stream of her tears. In English literature she is usually a symbol of sorrow rather than foolish pride. Hamlet, for example, bitterly recalls that his mother, now remarried, two months before had followed his father's body "like Niobe, all tears" (*Hamlet*, 1. 2. 149), and in *Childe Harold* (4. 79) Byron describes Rome as

> The Niobe of nations! there she stands,
> Childless and crownless, in her voiceless woe.

Actaeon, a mighty hunter who under other circumstances might have been a favorite of Artemis, was punished by the goddess because through ill luck he offended her modesty. One day when he was hot and tired from hunting, he went to a tree-fringed pool on a little stream. He did not know that this was a favorite bathing place of Artemis, but he surprised the goddess, naked, on the bank of the pool. She threw a handful of water in his face and he was transformed into a stag. When he tried to run away, his own hunting dogs tracked him down and killed him.

The significance of this story for the English Renaissance is clearly represented in a speech by the lovesick Orsino in *Twelfth Night* (1. 1. 19–23):

> O, when mine eyes did see Olivia first,
> Methought she purg'd the air of pestilence!
> That instant was I turn'd into a hart,
> And my desires, like fell and cruel hounds,
> E'er since pursue me.

The hart (by a familiar pun that the Elizabethans always enjoyed) became the human heart awakened by a glimpse of divine beauty, and the passions that could not be satisfied became the

71

hounds that destroyed the heart. Samuel Daniel makes similar use of the story in Sonnet 5 of *Delia*. In the nineteenth century Shelley compares himself to Actaeon in *Adonais* (274–279):

> . . . he, as I guess,
> Had gazed on Nature's naked loveliness,
> Actaeon-like, and now he fled astray
> With feeble steps o'er the world's wilderness,
> And his own thoughts, along that rugged way,
> Pursued, like raging hounds, their father and their prey.

Here the myth represents the fate of man when he bursts in on inner meanings of life and is destroyed by what he has discovered. Writing in our own time, Robinson Jeffers in a poem called *Science* also uses the myth gloomily to predict man's self-annihilation through his increasing knowledge and his misuse of it:

> His mind forebodes his own destruction;
> Actaeon who saw the goddess naked among leaves
>   and his hounds tore him.
> A little knowledge, a pebble from the shingle,
> A drop from the oceans: who would have dreamed
>   this infinitely little too much?[3]

John Peale Bishop expresses man's ignorance of the nature of his guilt and the nature of his quest in *Another Actaeon*.

John Day, a seventeenth-century poet, writes of

> A noise of horns and hunting, which shall bring
> Actaeon to Diana in the spring.

As T. S. Eliot reworks these lines in *The Waste Land* (197–201), the noise of industrialism, which has replaced the hunting horns, heralds a union of vulgarities; and although Diana does not

---

[3] From "Science;" by Robinson Jeffers, in his *Roan Stallion; Tamar, and Other Poems.* Copyright, 1925, by Boni & Liveright; copyright, 1935, by Modern Library. Reprinted with the permission of Random House, Inc.

bathe, she illuminates some rather extraordinary ablutions. One hears

> The sound of horns and motors, which shall bring
> Sweeney to Mrs. Porter in the spring.
> O the moon shone bright on Mrs. Porter
> And on her daughter
> They wash their feet in soda water.[4]

Though she was the virgin huntress who swore her Nymphs to chastity and who protected such scorners of love as Atalanta of Boeotia and Hippolytus, Artemis herself once fell in love. One night she looked down and saw the shepherd **Endymion** sleeping on Mount **Latmos** in **Caria.** He was so handsome that even Artemis' heart was touched. She descended from the sky and kissed Endymion and lay beside him while he slept. Through her power or that of Zeus, Endymion was given eternal youth to be spent in eternal sleep, and night after night Artemis returns to Mount Latmos to lie with her sleeping lover.

This myth is referred to incidentally by many English poets. In *The Merchant of Venice* (5. 1. 109–110), for example, Portia explains a moonless night by saying,

> . . . the moon sleeps with Endymion,
> And would not be awak'd.

Two Elizabethans, John Lyly and Michael Drayton, and one Romantic, John Keats, have developed the theme in detail. Lyly's *Endymion, the Man in the Moon* is an allegorical play in which Endymion forsakes Tellus, the earth, because of his apparently hopeless love for Cynthia. In revenge Tellus has Endymion put into an enchanted sleep from which he is released by a kiss from

---

[4] From "The Waste Land," by T. S. Eliot, in his *Collected Poems, 1909–1935.* Copyright, 1934, 1936, by Harcourt, Brace and Company. Reprinted with their permission.

73

Cynthia, who accepts him as her admirer but does not grant him her love.

Drayton in *Endimion and Phoebe* works out in a more interesting way the relationship between physical and spiritual love. Phoebe, who is devoted to her worshiper Endymion, makes love to him in the guise of a Nymph. He refuses to listen to her because he is "Phoebes servant sworne," but after she leaves him he is consumed with desire. When she wakens him at dawn, he pleads his love, still thinking her a Nymph, but she reveals herself as Phoebe and confesses her love for him. Then she shows him the divine secrets of the sky, causes him to be deified, and takes him back to Mount Latmos, where she will often visit him in his immortal sleep.

In Drayton's poem the myth is made Platonic; Phoebe represents the divine beauty that (according to Plato) all men love in their souls, and her gifts to Endymion are the rewards of the spirit. Although the symbolism of Keats's *Endymion* is somewhat cloudy, it is clear that in this poem, also, Diana represents the ideal beauty that inspires ideal love. Like Drayton's Phoebe, Keats's goddess disguises herself, but she leads Endymion through adventures which cause him to realize that divine love is to be gained only by vigorous participation in human life and by attainment of human sympathy and human love.

Another love story about Artemis—one that was rejected by certain early scholiasts, perhaps because they felt that one love story was enough for a virgin goddess—is alluded to by Virgil in the *Georgics*. In three lines he tells how Pan won Luna's love by offering her a beautiful white fleece of wool. Spenser in his *Epithalamion* (378–381) soothes the commentators by attributing this bribe to Endymion, but Browning in *Pan and Luna* moralizes the tale. In Browning's poem the goddess, realizing that everyone can see her naked beauty, hides herself in a fleecy cloud, but the cloud is a trap of wool devised by Pan; thus her modesty betrays her to his lust.

Artemis has always been a symbol of spiritual beauty, but she appeared most frequently in English poetry during the Renaissance, when she was one of the poetic disguises of Queen Elizabeth. The likeness between the two ladies is remarkable: Elizabeth in her day was as famous a virgin as Artemis; she demanded chastity of her maids of honor, as Artemis did of her Nymphs, and punished them if they transgressed; and she, like Artemis, was suspected of having at least one mortal lover. In Elizabethan poems most references to the moon goddess are addressed as much to Elizabeth as to Artemis.

Spenser often alludes to Diana in his poetry, and she appears in two of the stories in his *Faerie Queene*. In the first of these (3. 6. 1–28) Diana takes Belphoebe, one of the twin daughters of Chrysogonee, to train "in perfect Maydenhed," and Belphoebe's actions in the poem show how well Diana succeeds. Belphoebe (whose name means "beautiful Phoebe") is a type of Diana and Elizabeth; as is Britomart, the warlike virgin who is the heroine of Book Three. Britomart is named for **Britomartis,** a Cretan goddess sometimes identified with Artemis.

Two of the many lyrics that praise the virgin goddess and the virgin queen are Sir Walter Ralegh's *Praised Be Diana's Fair and Harmless Light* and Ben Jonson's song, which begins:

> Queene and huntress, chaste and fair,
> Now the sun is laid to sleep,
> Seated in thy silver chair,
> State in wonted manner keep.
> Hesperus entreats thy light,
> Goddess excellently bright.

Oberon's story in *A Midsummer-Night's Dream* (2. 1. 163–164) also illustrates the technique of double reference. He says that he once saw Cupid shoot his arrow of love at Artemis, but the arrow's fire was quenched in her chaste beams,

> And the imperial vot'ress passed on,
> In maiden meditation, fancy-free.

For the other virgin goddesses see ATHENE and HESTIA.

ASCANIUS (ăs·kā′nĭ·ûs), who was also called Iulus, was the son of AENEAS.

ASCLEPIUS (ăs·klē′pĭ·ûs) is the god of medicine. See APOLLO.

ASHTOROTH (ăsh′tò·rŏth), or Astarte, was the Phoenician name for APHRODITE.

ASOPUS (*à*·sō′pûs) was the father of Aegina, one of the mistresses of ZEUS.

ASPHODEL (ăs′fò·dĕl) is the flower that grows in HADES.

ASTARTE (ăs·tär′tē), or Ashtoroth, was the Phoenician name for APHRODITE.

ASTRAEA (ăs·trē′à) is the goddess of human justice, a symbol of innocence and purity. The daughter of Zeus and Themis, the goddess of divine justice, Astraea lived on earth with mortal beings during the peaceful Golden Age, the Silver Age, and the decaying Bronze Age, as did others of the immortals. But, when the Iron Age came, and with it almost universal wickedness and depravity among mortals, the gods one by one left the earth in disgust, until only Astraea remained. At last, she, too, left and was fixed in heaven by Zeus, where she became the constellation of Virgo, or the virgin. Beside her are her scales of justice, the constellation Libra. Zeus afterward destroyed all human beings except Deucalion and Pyrrha by a great flood, for which see DEUCALION. In *The Faerie Queene* (5. 1. 5–12) Artegall, the knight of justice, is brought up by Astraea. She trains him in her discipline, and before she leaves the earth she gives him the sword with which Jove fought the Titans and leaves to him her servant, the iron man Talus, to carry out his commands. Then she retires to the heavens.

There was a myth among the Greeks that Astraea would some day return, as would other of the Olympians, and bring with her a return of the primal virtues that she represents, an event to which Virgil refers in *Eclogue 4* (6):

> Jam redit et Virgo, redeunt Saturnia Regna
> [Now returns the Virgin, too, the Golden Age returns]

a line that Dryden took as the epigraph of his poem, *Astraea Redux* (1660), which celebrates the return to the English throne of King Charles II after Cromwell's rule. Dryden could hardly have expected as much of Charles' reign as would have been required to recall Astraea, and Charles must have known it; but with kings, flattery is no vice. Alexander Pope somewhat more appropriately applies the myth to the advent of the Christ in his eclogue, *Messiah* (17–20), which is made up of prophecies about Christ's coming:

> All crimes shall cease, and ancient fraud shall fail,
> Returning Justice lift aloft her scale;
> Peace o'er the world her olive wand extend,
> And white-rob'd Innocence from heav'n descend.

One of Pope's contemporaries, a playwright by the name of Mrs. Aphra Behn, gave herself the *nom de plume* Astraea but was fond of providing rather unmaidenly action in her plays. Pope refers to this incongruity in a well-known passage of *Imitations of Horace*, First Epistle, Second Book (290–291):

> The stage how loosely does Astraea tread,
> Who fairly puts all characters to bed!

Wordsworth, reflecting on the past glories of the Swiss people

77

(*Memorials of a Tour on the Continent, 1820,* 24. 2. 2), in a moment of classical reminiscence seldom repeated in his better-known poems, writes,

> But Truth inspired the Bards of old
> When of an iron age they told,
> Which to unequal laws gave birth,
> And drove Astraea from the earth.

After this allusion he reverts sharply to a subject of which he was fonder, a small country boy tending his goats.

ASTYANAX (ăs·tĭ′á·năks) was the infant son of Hector, the chief hero of Troy in the TROJAN WAR.

ATALANTA OF ARCADIA (ăt′á·lăn′tá är·kā′dĭ·á) was the heroine of the CALYDONIAN BOAR HUNT.

ATALANTA OF BOEOTIA (ăt′á·lăn′tá bē·ō′shá) was the daughter of **Schoeneus.** Informed by an oracle that if she married she would bring calamity on herself, she avoided amorous society and gave her time and heart instead to the chase of non-human quarries. In this activity she became extremely fleet of foot and so found a way to deal with the suitors who, in spite of her aversion to them, sought her hand. She informed them that whoever wanted to marry her must first beat her in a foot race, and that whoever lost to her in the race must lose his life.

Atalanta was so lovely that many men tried to outrun her, but Atalanta ran faster than they did, and they were put to death. For one of these extraordinary races a youth named **Hippomenes** was a judge. He immediately fell in love with her and offered to race her as the others had done. First, however, he prayed to Aphrodite, the goddess of love, urging her that she protect him because she was responsible for his ardor. Aphrodite heard his prayer; and moving unseen, she brought three golden apples from her garden on the island of Cyprus and gave them to Hippomenes with directions for their use.

When the race was under way, Hippomenes, finding himself about to be passed by Atalanta, dropped one of the golden apples. It pleased the girl's eye and she slowed down to pick it up. When she caught up with him again, Hippomenes dropped the second apple with the same effect, and in like manner the third. His stratagem worked only narrowly, but it worked; he reached the finish mark just ahead of Atalanta, and she was his by contract.

Atalanta was at first reluctant to keep her word and marry Hippomenes, but she had no alternative. Later the two discovered such bliss in marriage that they forgot the proper gratitude due to Aphrodite, and so the word of the oracle came to pass. Aphrodite, angry at their neglect, caused them to offend Cybele, and that powerful goddess turned them into animals, Atalanta into a lioness and Hippomenes into a lion, after which she yoked them to her chariot for the rest of time (see EARTH GODDESSES).

Although this racing Atalanta is probably better known than her Arcadian namesake, the huntress, she is less famous for what the poets in our language have made of her. Swinburne gives fame to the huntress, but William Morris has little to add to the luster of the racer in his retelling of her feats in *Atalanta's Race,* one of the poems in *The Earthly Paradise.* Morris prefers to conclude his verse with the happy marriage, omitting the later misfortune; but in spite of his subject matter, his poem is pedestrian.

ATE (ā′tē) is the goddess of infatuation. See ARES.

ATHAMAS (ăth′a·măs) was the husband of Nephele and of Ino. See ARGONAUTS, THEBES.

ATHENAEA (ăth′ė·nē′a) is another name of ATHENE.

ATHENE (*à·thḗne*), or **Athena,** or **Minerva,** or **Pallas Athene,** as she is often called, came into the world in an extraordinary manner. Most accounts agree that Zeus swallowed his first wife Metis when she became pregnant because it had been decreed that she would give birth to a child mightier than he. Sometime later Zeus developed a terrible headache and requested Hephaestus to split open his head with an ax. When Hephaestus had

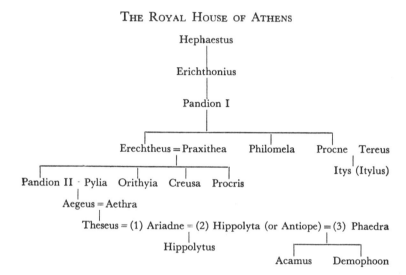

THE ROYAL HOUSE OF ATHENS

done so, out of the cleft sprang Athene in full war dress and with a loud war cry. Thus came into being the virgin goddess of war and of wisdom. This myth seemed to Milton an appropriate way in which to describe the birth of Sin from the head of Satan in *Paradise Lost* (2. 752–758). In these lines, Sin, unrecognized by her father who is attempting to find his way out of Hell, reminds him that in the assembly of revolting angels in Heaven Satan was struck with a headache:

All on a sudden miserable pain
Surpris'd thee, dim thine eyes, and dizzie swumm
In darkness, while thy head flames thick and fast
Threw forth, till on the left side op'ning wide,
Likest to thee in shape and count'nance bright,
Then shining heav'nly fair, a Goddess arm'd
Out of thy head I sprung.

Thus Satan produced sin out of himself, as Zeus was the sole author of wisdom.

As the goddess of war, Athene seems to represent the cunning side of conflict that leads to victory, and for this reason she is usually pictured as holding a small symbolic statue of victory in one hand. Because of her superior wisdom, she always had the better of Ares, the god of rough, crude war, when the two clashed. It was Athene who brought victory to the Greeks at Troy when she had Odysseus arrange the stratagem of the wooden horse (see TROJAN WAR), and thus she was instrumental in defeating the side taken by Ares. Athene is used symbolically on the United States' victory medal that commemorates our victory in World War II. On this medal she appears with her no-longer-needed sword broken and held in her hands, and her foot triumphantly placed on her helmet.

As the goddess of wisdom, Athene has an even more distinguished reputation. She was the mother of contemplation, the practice of wisdom. Furthermore, she was associated with such useful household arts as spinning and weaving; and she was generally credited with having invented the plow, the ship, and the wagon, as well as the craft of shoemaking. The myth of **Arachne** shows Athene's skill in weaving and also serves as an example of the swift and terrible ways in which the gods punish impiety. Arachne was a maiden who was so skillful a weaver that she boasted her prowess was equal to Athene's. Athene thereupon challenged her to a contest. Arachne impudently wove a tapestry showing the love affairs of Zeus, and Athene was forced to admire her skill; but then the goddess put her own hand to the loom and wove a tapestry showing the dignity of the gods and the punishments that they inflict on impious mortals. Thereupon she turned the impious Arachne into a spider that must always stay at the center of its web. This myth is recounted by Spenser in *Muiopotmos* (257–352) where he invents a son of Arachne, named Aragnoll, the villain of the poem.

In a civilization in which wisdom and skill in war were held in high regard, as they were in Greece, Athene was bound to be a popular figure. She suggested to Zeus the means by which he overcame the Giants and thus gained control of the world, and she seems to have been the undoing of most of the violent monsters that were left after Zeus's main battle against them, for she aided Cadmus in overcoming the dragon, Perseus in killing Medusa, Theseus in slaying the Minotaur, and Heracles in all his gigantic achievements. She furthermore aided Bellerophon in securing Pegasus, the winged horse; Jason in obtaining the Golden Fleece; and Odysseus in all his exploits in returning to Ithaca. A hero with Athene on his side was a hero indeed, a symbolism by which the Greeks expressed their opinion that intelligence is an essential in the heroic character. The myths of her aid to heroes are told elsewhere in this book.

If Athene was popular with the Greeks in general, she was especially so with the people of **Athens,** which was named for her. According to myth, the city originally belonged to the Cecropians. The gods, however, decided that the city should belong to either Poseidon or Athene, whichever produced the thing more useful to man. Poseidon, striking the rock with his trident, brought forth the horse; but Athene produced the olive tree, and **Erichthonius** or **Erechtheus,** the king of the Cecropians, awarded the victory to her. According to some versions, Cecrops was the king who judged the contest.

In the hazy genealogy of the royal house of Athens, Erichthonius is given as the grandfather of Erechtheus, but the same stories are told of both kings. Like Cecrops, Erichthonius was a child of earth. Hephaestus, repulsed by Athene, dropped his seed on the ground and the earth bore Erichthonius. The boy was protected by Athene, who put him in a covered chest and gave it to the three daughters of Cecrops with a strict order that it should not be opened. When two of the girls yielded to their curiosity and opened the chest, what they saw drove them mad and caused them to leap to their death from the **Acropolis,** the high tablelike rock on which the city was built. They saw either a child guarded by snakes or a child with snakes for legs, a sight which should hardly have had such a devastating effect on girls whose own father was snake-footed. But after this excitement Athene took care of the boy herself, and when he reached manhood he showed his gratitude by building on the Acropolis a temple in Athene's honor called the **Erechtheum.** Later a much larger and more famous temple called the **Parthenon** was built on the Acropolis, and in this was placed the statue of Athene by the sculptor Phidias. This statue seems to have shown Athene in her most typical pose, standing with a spear in one hand and a small figure of victory in the other, and with her shield leaning against her; on her head a warrior's helmet, and on her breastplate the head of Medusa (see Gorgons under SEA GODS, and PERSEUS). Another statue of Athene by Phidias stood outside the Parthenon on the Acropolis and was of such colossal size that it could be seen from miles away at sea.

The oldest statue said to be of Athene was the **Palladium,** an image so old, in fact, that it was thought to have fallen from heaven. A priestly family in Athens kept charge of this sacred object, and the belief was common that so long as the statue remained safe within the city, the city was safe from capture or destruction. In their day, the Trojans had the Palladium, and their city fell only after the statue had been taken from them, either because it was stolen by Odysseus and Diomedes, or because Aeneas removed it when he departed. Because of these different versions of the story, the possession of the statue was variously claimed by Athens and Argos, and later by Rome, where the Romans held that it had been brought by Aeneas. Matthew Arnold, in *Palladium,* makes the statue, still held by the Trojans safe in their uncaptured city, a symbol of the soul that sends on human life a "ruling effluence." He concludes, remembering the powers of the Palladium,

> And when it fails, fight as we will, we die;
> And while it lasts, we cannot wholly end.

The symbols of Athene include the shield, the spear, the figure of victory, and the **aegis** (which means "shield"), the head of Medusa mounted on a breastplate or a shield. The olive, the cock, the owl, the crow, and the serpent were all sacred to her. Her other names were numerous. The best known was Pallas, a name derived from a word meaning "to brandish." Others were: **Soteira,** or savior; **Parthenos,** the virgin; **Nike,** the victorious one; **Mechanitis,** the ingenious one; **Promachos,** the forefront of battle; and **Tritogeneia, Tritonia,** and **Athenaea.** The **Panathenaea** was a festival in Athene's honor celebrated yearly at Athens.

Well-known appearances of the goddess in English poetry include Byron's witty attack on Lord Elgin for removing the famous marbles from the Parthenon to the British Museum, a poem called *The Curse of Minerva* in which he envisions the goddess, despoiled of her fineness, appearing to him:

Gone were the terrors of her awful brow,
Her idle aegis bore no Gorgon now;
Her helm was dinted, and the broken lance
Seem'd weak and shaftless e'en to mortal glance;
The olive branch, which still she deign'd to clasp,
Shrunk from her touch and wither'd in her grasp.

Athene's curse on Lord Elgin is typical both of her powers and Byron's wit:

Be all the sons as senseless as the sire:
If one with wit the parent brood disgrace,
Believe him bastard of a brighter race.

In Poe's poem *The Raven* this bird of ill omen perches symbolically on a bust of Pallas over his chamber door; and Tennyson, in *Oenone*, gives a description of the goddess that conveys all her chaste and intellectual aloofness from human folly:

. . . Pallas . . . stood
Somewhat apart, her clear and bared limbs
O'erthwarted with the brazen-headed spear
Upon her pearly shoulder leaning cold,
The while, above, her full and earnest eye
Over her snow-cold breast and angry cheek
Kept watch . . . .

Small wonder then that Paris, to whom she appeared thus with Aphrodite and Hera, was more affected by the softer charms of Aphrodite.

For the other virgin goddesses see ARTEMIS and HESTIA.

ATHENS (ăth′ĕnz), the city of Athene, is on the plain of Attica about three miles from the sea. The first settlement was on the Acropolis, a large rock that rises nearly two hundred feet above the plain; later the Acropolis remained the citadel and the town spread out around it. Athens was the center of ancient Greek culture. See ATHENE.

ATLAS (ăt′lăs), a Titan, holds up the heavens on his shoulders. He was tricked into giving three of the golden apples of the Hesperides to HERACLES.

ATREUS (ā′trōōs). The sufferings of the house of Atreus mirror the Greek belief that punishment for sin is visited not only on the sinner himself but also on his children and his children's children until the sin is somehow expiated. The founder of this

THE HOUSE OF ATREUS

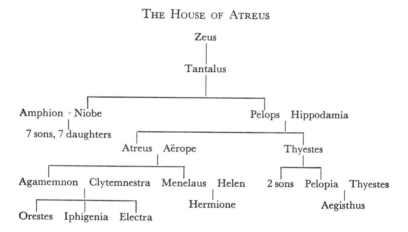

tragic family was **Tantalus,** a son of Zeus. He had great wealth and power; his marriage was blest with a son and a daughter, Pelops and Niobe; and the gods were so fond of him that they often invited him to attend their banquets and councils. His good fortune, however, seems to have unbalanced him, and he became the victim of pride and skepticism: although he doubted the superhuman power of the gods, he aspired to be a god himself.

86

In his insolence Tantalus killed his son **Pelops,** cooked the body, and invited the gods to a banquet, hoping to prove that they could not tell human flesh from animal. At this time Demeter was distracted with the loss of her daughter Persephone, and she absent-mindedly ate a part of Pelops' shoulder, but all the other gods recognized the impiety of Tantalus. They resolved to punish him in a way that would always be an example to erring men, and they therefore confined him in a special place in Hades: he always stands up to his neck in water, but the water recedes whenever he tries to drink; branches loaded with ripe pomegranates and peaches and figs always dangle in front of his eyes, but the fruit is snatched away whenever he tries to pluck it. Sir Guyon, Spenser's knight of temperance, finds Tantalus thus tormented (*Faerie Queene,* 2. 7. 59):

> The knight him seeing labour so in vaine,
> Askt who he was, and what he ment thereby:
> Who groning deepe, thus answerd him againe;
> Most cursed of all creatures vnder skye,
> Lo *Tantalus,* I here tormented lye:
> Of whom high *Ioue* wont whylome feasted bee,
> Lo here I now for want of food doe dye. . . .

From Tantalus' punishment comes our verb "to tantalize."

Pelops was restored to life by the gods and given an ivory shoulder in place of the one that Demeter had eaten. This first instance of bone surgery is recalled lightheartedly by Robert Herrick when he says in *To Electra* that the skin of his mistress is whiter than "Pelops arme of yvorie." In spite of his unfortunate start in life, Pelops won the girl of his choice and ruled the southern part of Greece, which was named for him the **Peloponnesus.**

He fell in love with **Hippodamia,** the daughter of King **Oenomaus** of Pisa, who demanded that her suitors risk their lives for her. Oenomaus had a pair of miraculously swift horses, a gift to him from the war god Ares, and he staged a chariot race with each of his prospective sons-in-law. If he won, he killed the boy; and if the boy won, he got Hippodamia. Twelve suitors had tried and failed when Pelops made his challenge, but he had two special advantages: first, he owned a pair of winged horses that had been given to him by Poseidon; and second, he or Hippodamia bribed **Myrtilus,** Oenomaus' servant, to tamper with one of the wheels of the king's chariot. Pelops won the race, and Oenomaus was killed in the wreck of his chariot. But when Myrtilus claimed his reward, Pelops was moved by his father's violent temper, and he threw Myrtilus in the ocean, where he drowned, cursing Pelops.

Niobe, Pelops' sister, married Amphion, regent of Thebes, and bore him seven sons and seven daughters. As she considered her queenly state and her many children, she was touched by her father's terrible pride, and she demanded that the Thebans worship her instead of Leto, the goddess who was the mother of Apollo and Artemis. Urged on by their mother, Artemis and Apollo killed Niobe's fourteen children, and she was transformed into a stone from which flows continually the stream of her tears. For further details see Niobe under ARTEMIS.

Niobe's end was tragic, but Pelops, although he had tempted the gods to vengeance by killing Myrtilus, lived a long and happy life. Yet the family curse fell heavily on his sons, **Atreus** and **Thyestes.** Atreus married **Aërope** and became king of Mycenae, and Thyestes was honored in the country as the brother of the king; but Thyestes lusted for his brother's wife and finally managed to seduce her. When Atreus learned of this crime, he first acted temperately and merely banished Thyestes from the country, but he continued to brood over his brother's treachery.

Two of Thyestes' children were still at the court, and Atreus decided to use them in his revenge. He pretended to pardon Thyestes and ordered a magnificent banquet to celebrate his return, but the children of Thyestes were the meat for this celebration, and Thyestes, lacking the insight of the gods, ate his own offspring. When Atreus boasted of his trick, Thyestes cursed his brother and departed. Later he learned that he might breed an avenger by mating with his surviving daughter **Pelopia;** the son of this incestuous union was Aegisthus.

The gods were so shocked by Atreus' crime that Apollo for one day turned the course of his sun chariot from west to east. Milton refers to this action in *Paradise Lost* (10. 687–691) when, after telling of Eve and Adam's eating the forbidden fruit, he describes the rearrangements made in the universe to replace the perfect climate of Eden with a climate that included the extremes of heat and cold:

> . . . At that tasted Fruit
> The Sun, as from *Thyestean* Banquet, turn'd
> His course intended; else how had the World
> Inhabited, though sinless, more then now,
> Avoided pinching cold and scorching heate?

In the final scene of *Titus Andronicus,* Shakespeare's most bloody play, Titus—taking his cue from Atreus—revenges himself on the men who have raped and mutilated his daughter; he kills them and serves them in a pie to their mother. Louis MacNeice in *Thyestes,* pondering the question of the complicity in evil of those who have not willed it, asks:

> Did his blood tell him what his mind concealed?
> Didn't he know—or did he—what he was eating?[5]

[5] From "Thyestes," by Louis MacNeice, in his *Springboard, Poems 1941–1944*. Copyright, 1945, by Random House, Inc., and reprinted with their permission.

In *Il Penseroso* (97–100) Milton says,

> Som time let Gorgeous Tragedy
> In Scepter'd Pall com sweeping by,
> Presenting *Thebs,* or *Pelops* line,
> Or the tale of *Troy* divine.

It is not surprising that he mentions Pelops' line, for eight of the surviving tragedies by the three great Greek tragedians concern members of this doomed family: Sophocles' *Electra,* Euripides' *Iphigenia at Aulis, Iphigenia among the Tauri, Electra,* and *Orestes,* and Aeschylus' *Agamemnon, Choephoroe,* and *Eumenides.* Aeschylus' three plays are the most important source of the myth, for they give a connected account of the culmination of the curse in terrible violence within the family of one of Atreus' sons.

Atreus had two sons, **Agamemnon** and **Menelaus,** and both made an excellent start in life. Agamemnon as king of Mycenae was the most powerful man in Greece. He married **Clytemnestra,** a princess of Sparta; and Menelaus won for his wife Helen, the half sister of Clytemnestra and the most beautiful woman in the world. She was later called Helen of Troy. The king of Sparta was so pleased to have Agamemnon and Menelaus as sons-in-law that he resigned his throne to Menelaus, and all went well with the young king until three goddesses disputed over who was the most beautiful and Aphrodite bribed the mortal judge, Prince Paris of Troy, to choose her. The bribe she offered him was the most beautiful woman in the world, and she therefore arranged to have Paris steal Helen from Menelaus. The result was the Trojan War and, for Menelaus, the painful notoriety of becoming the world's most famous cuckold. After Troy was burned, Helen was restored to Menelaus and they lived happily together. (For the birth of Helen and Clytemnestra, the exploits of Agamemnon and Menelaus against the Trojans, and the reuniting of Menelaus and Helen, see TROJAN WAR.)

Agamemnon and his children bore the burden of the family curse. He was the commander in chief of the Greek forces in the Trojan War, but only three of his actions in that campaign contributed directly to his violent death. When the Greek army had assembled at Aulis, on the coast of Boeotia, a contrary north wind blew constantly and prevented the expedition from sailing toward Troy. The soothsayer Calchas declared that Agamemnon had killed a stag sacred to Artemis and that the angry goddess would not permit the fleet to sail until Agamemnon had sacrificed to her his daughter **Iphigenia**. The choice was a terrible one. Agamemnon loved his daughter, but he thought of his brother's desire for vengeance, the army's eagerness to attack Troy, and particularly his own prestige as supreme commander. Finally he sent word to Clytemnestra that he wished to marry Iphigenia to the hero Achilles; and when the lovely girl arrived in happy anticipation of her marriage, he allowed her to be sacrificed to Artemis (for further details see TROJAN WAR).

Clytemnestra never forgave him for this deed. She heard also that in Troy he had taken a girl named Chryseis as his mistress, and that when he had been forced to give her up he had demanded and received another Trojan girl who had been awarded to Achilles (for further details see TROJAN WAR). Finally, when the war was over and Agamemnon returned in triumph to Argos, he brought with him the Trojan princess **Cassandra**. Clytemnestra bitterly resented this flaunting of his mistresses, although she herself had long since taken a lover.

Agamemnon had a quick and easy voyage home, and he was welcomed with all the pomp that befitted a conqueror. He did not sense the tension that underlay his wife's gracious welcome and his subjects' songs of triumph. All the people knew that

Clytemnestra had been living for years with **Aegisthus,** the surviving son of Agamemnon's uncle and enemy Thyestes, and they knew that she had not sent him away. But the prophetic Cassandra, as soon as she approached the palace, felt all its pent-up evil. Apollo had granted her the power to foretell the future but, because she would not yield to him, had cursed her with the terrible sentence that no man should believe her prophecies. When Agamemnon entered the palace, she lingered outside overcome by visions. She saw the multiplying sins of the family from Tantalus to Atreus, and she knew the ugly deed that was even then being done inside the palace. Finally she, too, went inside, saying that she was going to her death.

Soon Clytemnestra threw open the palace door. She had a bloody ax in her hand, and she shouted in wild triumph that she had killed Agamemnon in his bath because he had murdered her child Iphigenia, and that she had also killed his paramour, Cassandra, one of the many paramours with whom he had destroyed his marriage. Her lover Aegisthus then appeared at her side and exulted in this vengeance for Atreus' sin against his father. Thereafter this bloody pair ruled in Argos.

In *Sweeney among the Nightingales* T. S. Eliot introduces us to an evening party in a low dive where some tough characters are plotting against Sweeney. The animality of Sweeney and the others is constantly emphasized. Then Eliot writes,

> The nightingales are singing near
> The Convent of the Sacred Heart,
>
> And sang within the bloody wood
> When Agamemnon cried aloud,
> And let their liquid siftings fall
> To stain the stiff dishonoured shroud.[6]

[6] From "Sweeney among the Nightingales," by T. S. Eliot, in his *Collected Poems, 1909–1935.* Copyright, 1934, 1936, by Harcourt, Brace and Company. Reprinted with their permission.

The two images remind us of the two great western civilizations, the Christian and the classical. In spite of nineteen centuries of Christianity, the low intrigue in the bar is still a typical human scene, and the song of the nightingale (whose unhappy story of love and death is described in Aeschylus' *Agamemnon* by the Chorus and Cassandra shortly before Cassandra enters the palace to die) links the sordid crime about to be committed with the tragic murder of Troy's conqueror. In this sudden vision of man's history of pain and passion, some critics see the grandeur of the past contrasted with the squalor of the present, and others see the sensual Agamemnon equated with the sensual Sweeney. Eliot has transferred the scene of Agamemnon's death from his palace in Argos to the sacred grove in Colonus where Oedipus died (see Oedipus under THEBES).

Two children of Agamemnon and Clytemnestra still lived, **Orestes** and **Electra.** Doubtless Aegisthus would have killed Orestes had the boy been in Argos, but his sister had taken him to the court of **Strophius,** the king of Phocis. For seven years Electra was abused and neglected by her mother and Aegisthus; she hated them and existed only in the hope that Orestes would come back. In the seventh year the oracle at Delphi ordered Orestes to avenge his father's murder. He arrived in Argos in the company of his good friend **Pylades,** the son of his protector King Strophius, and he met Electra at Agamemnon's grave, where she had gone to pray for Orestes' return.

Starved for tenderness, Electra poured out her love to Orestes. "Four places in my heart are yours," she said. "I see my father in your face. You have the love that should belong to my mother, whom I must hate, and to my sister, who is pitifully dead. And you are my faithful brother, who alone has cared for me." Their plan was quickly made. Orestes and Pylades would go to the palace as messengers come to announce the death of Orestes.

Aegisthus and Clytemnestra would be eager to hear this news and to question those who brought it.

Orestes killed Aegisthus and then met his mother. The oracle of Apollo had ordered him to commit a terrible crime in order to avenge a terrible crime: he must murder his mother because she had murdered his father. Clytemnestra held out her arms and said, "My child, can you kill me?" Deeply moved, Orestes asked his friend, "May I let my mother live?" But Pylades reminded him of the words of the oracle, and Orestes killed her.

As he explained to the people of Argos that he had done this deed at the command of Apollo, Orestes suddenly saw in his mind's eye the Furies, the grisly goddesses who represent the agonies of remorse. "They are here," he shouted, "like Gorgons, dressed in darkness, twined with snakes. I am hunted. I shall never rest again." The Furies were agents of a narrow justice completely lacking in mercy; they pursued anyone who offended against the old law, without any regard for his motive. For years Orestes was tormented by these terrible creatures, but finally Athene presided at a court in Athens where the Furies accused, and Apollo defended, Orestes. According to the new dispensation of Zeus, Orestes was judged to have done a necessary evil and to have been purified through suffering. In the last play of Aeschylus' trilogy even the Furies accept the new law of mercy and thereafter are known as the Eumenides, "the kind ones." Orestes by the purity of his intention and by the agonies of his remorse had atoned not only for his own sin but for all the sins of the house of Atreus. He had lifted the curse.

The passionate and lonely Electra found happiness as the wife of Pylades, Orestes' friend; and in a later version of the myth even Iphigenia was recalled to life. As Euripides tells the story in *Iphigenia at Aulis* and *Iphigenia among the Tauri,* Artemis took pity on Iphigenia just as she was about to be sacrificed at

Aulis, snatched her away from the priest's knife, and left a deer in her place. Iphigenia was transported to the land of a barbarian people called the Taurians, and there became the priestess of Artemis; it was her duty to preside over the sacrificial murder of all strangers whom the Taurians captured.

According to Euripides, even after the judgment of Athene some of the Furies were not placated, and Orestes, still suffering, asked the oracle at Delphi what more he must do to free himself from guilt. The oracle replied that he must go to the land of the Taurians, steal a statue of Artemis from the Taurian temple, and bring it back to Athens. His friend Pylades went with him, and they were both immediately captured by the Taurians and sent to Iphigenia to be prepared for death. Orestes and Iphigenia rapturously discovered that they were brother and sister and, through a ruse of Iphigenia's, the three managed to steal the image of Artemis and embark on their ship. Unfortunately at the mouth of the harbor a contrary wind blew them back toward the bloodthirsty barbarians.

At this point Athene came down from Olympus and told the king of the Taurians that he must let the two Greeks and the priestess go free. He agreed; Poseidon altered the wind; and Iphigenia—like Pearl White in the last sequence of an old serial movie—was rescued by the hero and his faithful friend. Although Euripides pleased the crowd by bringing Iphigenia back to life again and by absolving Artemis of cruelty, he did it at the expense of the tragic dignity of the original story.

Cassandra, the prophetess whom nobody believes, appears most frequently in English literature as the sad foreseer of the fall of Troy. She plays this role in Chaucer's *Troilus and Criseyde* and in Shakespeare's *Troilus and Cressida*. The Nymph Oenone, in Tennyson's poem of that name, has been forsaken by Prince Paris of Troy, who has been promised the love of Helen in return for awarding the golden apple to Aphrodite. Oenone believes that she must die of sorrow, but she feels that she will not die alone.

> . . . I will rise and go
> Down into Troy, and ere the stars come forth
> Talk with the wild Cassandra, for she says
> A fire dances before her, and a sound
> Rings ever in her ears of armed men.
> What may be I know not, but I know
> That, wheresoe'er I am by night and day,
> All earth and air seem only burning fire.

Dante Gabriel Rossetti's two sonnets for a drawing of Cassandra show her (as does the drawing) predicting the death of Hector as he sets out to fight Achilles.

In *Cassandra* (46–60, 91–95) George Meredith writes of her last prophecy as she stands before the palace of Agamemnon:

> Still upon her sunless soul
> Gleams the narrow hidden space
> Forward, where her fiery race
> Falters on its ashen goal:
> Still the Future strikes her face.
>
> See toward the conqueror's car
> Step the purple Queen whose hate
> Wraps red-armed her royal mate
> With his Asian tempest-star:
> Now Cassandra views her Fate.
>
> King of men! the blinded host
> Shout:—she lifts her brooding chin:
> Glad along the joyous din
> Smiles the grand majestic ghost:
> Clytemnestra leads him in.
>
> . . . . . .

> Captive on a foreign shore,
> Far from Ilion's hoary wave,
> Agamemnon's bridal slave
> Speaks Futurity no more:
> Death is busy with her grave.[7]

When his hero, Don Juan, loses the lovely Haidée, Byron remembers (*Don Juan*, 4. 52) that the future which Cassandra foresaw was invariably miserable:

> Here I must leave him, for I grow pathetic,
> Moved by the Chinese nymph of tears, green tea!
> Than whom Cassandra was not more prophetic;
>
> .   .   .   .   .   .
>
> 'Tis pity wine should be so deleterious,
> For tea and coffee leave us much more serious.

But Robinson Jeffers in his poem called *Cassandra* delights in the bitterness of her prophecies and at the same time claims her gift and her curse for himself. Men hate the truth, he says; of the poet, the preacher, and the politician they ask only lies. Therefore he advises the prophetess:

> . . . Poor bitch be wise.
> No: you'll still mumble in a corner a crust of truth, to men
> And gods disgusting.   —you and I, Cassandra.[8]

When the Spartans conquered Athens in 404 B.C., they would have destroyed the city if one of their officers had not sung the first chorus of Euripides' *Electra* and reminded them that Euripides was an Athenian. Milton recalls this story in his sonnet

---

[7] From "Cassandra," by George Meredith, in *The Poetical Works of George Meredith*. Copyright, 1912, by Charles Scribner's Sons. Reprinted with their permission.

[8] From "Cassandra," by Robinson Jeffers, in his *The Double Axe and Other Poems*. Copyright, 1948, by Random House, Inc. Reprinted with the permission of the publisher.

When the Assault Was Intended on the City. Most English writers have felt the same high regard for the tragic story of the house of Atreus as told by Aeschylus, Sophocles, and Euripides, but few of them have tried to use the material themselves. Three contemporary writers, however, have made the attempt: T. S. Eliot, Robinson Jeffers, and Eugene O'Neill.

In his inadequate verse play *The Family Reunion*, Eliot tries to create an Orestes-like character of our own time in the person of Harry, Lord Monchensey. Harry feels himself responsible for the death of his wife: he has murdered her or at least has willed her death. Pursued by the Furies, he returns to his mother Amy and a houseful of aunts and uncles. To relieve his mind, his sympathetic Aunt Agatha explains that his father, now long dead, had loved her rather than Amy and had wished to kill Amy. Harry seems to have inherited his father's frustrated desire, and his sense of guilt is for his father as well as himself. Harry does not kill his mother, as Orestes did, but he causes her death by leaving home abruptly even though he has been told that any shock will kill her. He goes off in rather vague pursuit of atonement.

Robinson Jeffers in *The Tower beyond Tragedy*, a long extravagant dramatic poem, retells the action of the first two plays of Aeschylus' trilogy, *Agamemnon* and *Choephoroe*, which deal with the murder of Agamemnon by Clytemnestra and Orestes' ritual slaying of his mother. The violence and passion of the story appeal to Jeffers, and his poem deals chiefly with the characters' feelings and the action, one high point of which is a remarkable strip tease put on by Clytemnestra. In the conclusion, however, the poem becomes didactic. Electra offers herself to Orestes. (Her incestuous passion, which is symbolically important to Jeffers, is recognized by psychologists, who have named the unsatisfied sexual desire of a daughter for her father the Electra complex; here Electra has transferred her passion for her dead father to her brother.) Orestes, however, refuses her, saying that he has "fallen in love outward." The attitudes of Cassandra, Clytemnestra, and Electra are contrasted with that of Orestes. Cassandra only waits for death, and Clytemnestra and Electra have become too deeply involved in human relationships (the commonest symbol of this involvement in Jeffers' poems is incest); but Orestes has

> . . . climbed the tower beyond time, consciously,
>   and cast humanity, entered the earlier fountain.[9]

In his poetry Jeffers has never made his central belief more explicit: that the proper study of mankind is not man but nature.

The best contemporary use of this Greek myth has been made by Eugene O'Neill. In his formidable dramatic trilogy, *Mourning Becomes Electra,* he has worked out the entire tragic story in terms of the New England family of Mannon at the close of the Civil War. Depending equally on Aeschylus and Freud, O'Neill succeeds admirably in recreating the fear and horror and the sense of implacable fate that belong to the original story. But like many of his contemporaries, he is unable to imagine Orestes' purification through suffering as Aeschylus represented it in the *Eumenides.* Orin Mannon, the Orestes of O'Neill's play, shoots himself to escape from the horrors of remorse.

ATROPOS (ăt′rŏ·pŏs) is one of the three Fates. See FATE.

ATTICA (ăt′ĭ·kà) is a region of the Greek peninsula that includes in its bounds the cities of Athens and Eleusis, as well as a great many miles of mostly infertile soil. The Athenians were, naturally, the most prominent inhabitants of Attica, and like

[9] From "The Tower beyond Tragedy," by Robinson Jeffers, in his *Roan Stallion, Tamar, and Other Poems.* Copyright, 1925, by Boni & Liveright; copyright, 1935, by Modern Library. Reprinted with the permission of Random House, Inc.

their fellows, traced their lineage back to **Cecrops.** Cecrops was a child of the earth. He had a man's body, but his legs were snakes. He began the process of civilizing his people, who called themselves **Cecropians,** and some say that he mediated in the famous dispute between Athene and Poseidon as to which of these Olympians was to become the patron of the city. Because Cecrops decided in favor of Athene, the city took her name and bears it to this day. According to other stories, Erichthonius or Erechtheus was the king who meditated this dispute (see ATHENE).

Since Athens became the center of the classical world, particularly in literature and philosophy, Attica has survived as a name for classical purity in the arts. Milton alludes to this significance in his sonnet to Lawrence (20) when he asks,

> What neat repast shall feast us, light and choice,
> Of Attick tast, with Wine, whence we may rise
> To hear the Lute well toucht. . . ,

and Keats also, when he exclaims of the Grecian urn,

> O Attic shape! Fair attitude! with brede
> Of marble men and maidens overwrought. . . .

AUGEAN (ŏ·jē′án) **STABLES** were cleaned in a single day by HERACLES.

AUGEAS (ŏ·jē′ás) owned the filthy stables that were cleaned by HERACLES.

AULIS (ŏ′lĭs) was the port in Boeotia from which the Greeks sailed for the TROJAN WAR.

AURORA (á·rô′rá) is the Roman name of the goddess of the dawn, EOS.

AUSTER (ŏs′tĕr) is the Roman name for Notus, the south wind. See WINDS.

AUTOLYCUS (ŏ·tŏl′ĭ·kŭs), a famous thief, was a son of Hermes. See HERMES, SISYPHUS.

AUTONOE (ŏ·tŏn′ŏ·ē) was the daughter of Cadmus. See THEBES.

AVENTINE (ăv′ĕn·tīn) is one of the seven hills of later ROME.

AVERNUS (à·vẽr′nŭs) is the cave through which Aeneas entered HADES.

B

BACCHANALIA (băk′à·nā′lĭ·à) was a celebration of the rites of Bacchus, or DIONYSUS.

BACCHANTES (bà·kăn′tēz) were followers of Bacchus, or DIONYSUS.

BACCHUS (băk′ŭs) is a name of DIONYSUS.

BASSARIDS (băs′àr·ĭdz) were followers of DIONYSUS.

BAUCIS (bō′sĭs) and Philemon were an aged couple whose charity and piety were signally honored by ZEUS.

BAYS is a name for the laurel. See Daphne under APOLLO.

BELLEROPHON (bĕ·lĕr′ŏ·fŏn), or **BELLEROPHONTES** (bĕ·lĕr′ŏ·fŏn′tēz), the rider of Pegasus and the slayer of the Chimaera, was a prince of Corinth. His father, King **Glaucus,** a skillful horseman, fed his horses human flesh to make them fierce. One day they upset his chariot and ate him. Bellerophon was also a horse fancier, but his great ambition was to ride the winged horse **Pegasus.** This magnificent animal, a son of Poseidon and the Gorgon Medusa, was born of Medusa's blood when she was killed by Perseus. Pegasus flew at once to Olympus, where he was caught and tamed by Athene. He was also the horse of the Muses, and on Mount Helicon the sacred fountain Hippocrene, which means "horse's fountain," sprang up where he stamped his hoof.

Bellerophon had little hope that he could master this animal, but he consulted a wise man who advised him to spend a night in Athene's temple. There he dreamed that the goddess gave him a golden bridle, and when he awoke the bridle was beside him. He rushed out of the temple and found Pegasus grazing tamely beside the spring **Pirene,** ready to be bridled. Soon Bellerophon, astride the marvelous horse, was racing across the sky. He did not forget to give thanks to Athene, and the winged horse never failed him until pride led him into impiety.

Bellerophon killed a man in Corinth, the stories do not say why, and went to Argos to be purified by King **Proetus. Anteia,** the wife of Proetus, fell in love with Bellerophon and, when he refused her advances, told her husband that he had tried to attack her. Because Bellerophon was his guest, Proetus concealed his jealous anger, and sent the young man with a sealed letter to Anteia's father, King **Iobates** of Lycia. The letter asked that Bellerophon be put to death, but Iobates had entertained Bellerophon for several days before he read the letter, and therefore he was in the same dilemma as his son-in-law: the rule of hospitality forbade him to do violence to a guest.

But finally he thought of an honorable way to get rid of Bellerophon. He requested him to free Lycia from the **Chimaera.** This fire-breathing monster, a daughter of Typhon and Echidna, was a lion in front, a dragon behind, and a goat in the middle. In *Paradise Lost* (2. 624–628) Milton puts Chimaeras among the monstrous shapes of hell, and Spenser in *The Faerie Queene* (6. 1. 8) makes the Chimaera and Cerberus the parents of the foulest monster that he can imagine, the Blatant Beast. No man on foot was a match for the Chimaera; but Bellerophon, mounted on Pegasus, kept out of range of her flames and claws and was thus able to shoot her with his arrows.

When Bellerophon returned unharmed to the Lycian court, Iobates sent him to fight first against the **Solymi**, a nation of mighty warriors, and then against the Amazons. Bellerophon was successful in both undertakings, and as he returned from the second campaign he killed a large company of Lycians whom Iobates had sent to ambush him. At this point Iobates decided that Bellerophon was not an ordinary mortal, and he gave him one of his daughters in marriage and half his kingdom. Yet as time passed Bellerophon found himself unsatisfied with his wife and his children and his kingship. Filled with a terrible pride, he declared himself a god, and tried to force Pegasus to carry him to the top of Mount Olympus; but Pegasus, wiser than his temporary master, threw him off in midair. Bellerophon was blinded by the fall but not killed. Thereafter he wandered, bitter and alone, on the Aleïan plain in Asia Minor.

Spenser (*Faerie Queene*, 3. 11. 42) recalls that Poseidon took the shape of a winged horse

> To snaky-locke *Medusa* to repayre,
> On whom he got faire *Pegasus,* that flitteth in the ayre.

Sometimes Pegasus is compared with other wonderful horses, magical or real. In *The Squire's Tale* (V. 207–208) by Chaucer, for example, the people marveled at the horse of brass, and

> . . . seyden it was lyk the Pegasee,
> The hors that hadde wynges for to flee,

and Vernon in *1 Henry IV* (4. 1. 108–110) says that Prince Hal sits his horse with such ease

> As if an angel dropp'd down from the clouds
> To turn and wind a fiery Pegasus
> And witch the world with noble horsemanship.

Usually, however, Pegasus is a symbol of poetic inspiration. Spenser, for example, completely disregards the disastrous conclusion of Bellerophon's ride toward Olympus in an image in which Pegasus represents poetry and his rider any noble person whose fame may be made permanent by a poet (*Ruines of Time,* 425–427):

> Then who so will with vertuous deeds assay
> To mount to heuen, on *Pegasus* must ride,
> And with sweete Poets verse bc glorifide.

In *An Essay on Criticism* (150–153) Pegasus dwindles from horse to abstraction when Pope declares:

> Thus Pegasus, a nearer way to take,
> May boldly deviate from the common track;
> From vulgar bounds with brave disorder part,
> And snatch a grace beyond the reach of art.

Only Milton, remembering (like the others) that Pegasus symbolizes poetic inspiration, also remembers that Pegasus bucked off Bellerophon. In *Paradise Lost* (7. 4–20) Milton asks his Muse Urania, who has helped him to soar "Above the flight of *Pegasean* wing," to help him to descend again:

> . . . Up led by thee
> Into the Heav'n of Heav'ns I have presum'd,
> An Earthlie Guest, and drawn Empyreal Aire,
> Thy tempring; with like safetie guided down
> Return me to my Native Element:
> Least from this flying Steed unrein'd, (as once
> *Bellerophon,* though from a lower Clime)

> Dismounted, on th' *Aleian* Field I fall
> Erroneous, there to wander and forlorne.

BELLONA (bĕ·lō′nȧ) is the Roman name of Enyo, the goddess of battle. See ARES.

BIFRONS (bī′frŏnz) is another name for JANUS.

BLESSED ISLANDS are the equivalent of the Elysian Fields, which are paradise. See HADES, SEA GODS.

BONA DEA (bō′nȧ dē′ȧ), or Fauna, a Roman fertility goddess, is the daughter or wife of Faunus, the Roman PAN.

BOREAS (bō′rē·ȧs) is the north wind. See WINDS.

BOSPHORUS (bŏs′fŏ·rŭs), which means "the ford of the cow," is the strait where the transformed Io crossed to the east. See ZEUS.

BRAZEN AGE preceded the great flood that drowned all mankind except Pyrrha and DEUCALION.

BRIAREUS (brī·ār′ē·ûs), or Aegaeon, was a Hecatoncheire. See TITANS.

BRISEIS (brī·sē′ĭs), a Trojan girl, was captured by the Greeks and given to Achilles. When Agamemnon demanded the girl, Achilles refused to take any further part in the TROJAN WAR.

BRITOMARTIS (brĭt′ŏ·mär′tĭs) is a Cretan goddess often identified with ARTEMIS.

BRUTUS (brōō′tŭs), or **BRUT**, according to medieval but not classical legend, was a great-grandson of Aeneas and the first king of Britain. See TROJAN WAR.

BUSKIN (bŭs′kĭn), or cothurnus, is a high, thick-soled boot, once worn by actors in tragic drama and often used as the symbol of tragedy. Milton says in *Il Penseroso* (97–102):

> Som time let Gorgeous Tragedy
> In Scepter'd Pall com sweeping by,
> Presenting *Thebs,* or *Pelops* line,
> Or the tale of *Troy* divine.

105

Or what (though rare) of later age,
Ennobled hath the Buskind stage.

See Melpomene under MUSES.

CABIRI (kă·bī′rī) are secret deities whose mysteries were celebrated at SAMOTHRACE.

CACUS (kā′kŭs) was killed for stealing cattle from HERACLES.

CADMUS (kăd′mŭs) was the founder of THEBES.

CADUCEUS (kà·dū′shŭs), a golden staff with wings at the top
and intertwined with serpents, is the badge of office of HERMES.

CAELIAN (sē′lĭ·ản) is one of the seven hills of later ROME.

CALAIS (kăl′ā·ĭs) was one of the ARGONAUTS.

CALCHAS (kăl′kảs) was a Greek Prophet prominent in the
TROJAN WAR.

CALLIOPE (kà·lī′ŏ·pē) is the Muse of heroic or epic poetry.
See MUSES.

CALLIRHOE (kà·līr′ŏ·ē) was the second wife of Alcmaeon,
one of the Epigoni. See THEBES.

CALLISTO (kà·lĭs′tō) was a Nymph of ARTEMIS.

CALYDONIAN (kăl′ĭ·dō′nĭ·ản) **BOAR HUNT.** Like the expedition of the Argonauts, the Calydonian Boar Hunt was an
adventure in which many of the great heroes took part; and also
as in many another happening of Greek mythology, the final
result of the hero's actions had been predicted as well as determined by the Fates. The story exemplifies the favorite Greek
concept not only that fate is inescapable but that its decrees

actually come about through the willful acts of man, even when he has been forewarned and has tried to escape his destiny.

The leader of the Calydonian hunt was **Meleager**, prince of Calydon, and son of King **Oeneus** and Queen **Althaea**. Soon after his birth the three Fates, spinning their fatal thread, appeared to his mother, and one of them, Atropos, foretold that the life of Meleager would last only as long as a brand then burning in the fire. Althaea, who appears to have been a woman of action, quickly seized the vital brand from the fire and put out its flames. Then she hid it away, thinking that it and her son's life would be safe. This experience of Althaea's is used as a conceit by Shakespeare in *2 Henry IV* (2. 2. 94, 96–98). Falstaff's page, bandying words with red-nosed Bardolph, exclaims at last:

> Away, you rascally Althaea's dream, away!

When Prince Hal asks him to explain the allusion, he replies:

> Marry, my lord, Althaea dreamt she was delivered
> of a firebrand, and therefore I call him her dream.

Althaea's name is preserved to us, too, in the name of a flower and in the title of Richard Lovelace's well-known lyric, *To Althaea from Prison,* but both usages are fortuitous. The word "althaea" meant originally a marsh plant. Lovelace merely borrowed a classical name as a pseudonym for his mistress, as Cavalier poets were fond of doing.

As Meleager grew to manhood, his father Oeneus one day sacrificed to the gods and, through oversight or neglect, failed to include Artemis in his offerings. The goddess was naturally quick to resent this slight, and she sent a tremendous and terrible boar to ravage the land of Calydon. His bristles were spearlike, and his eyes were red and fiery. He trampled out the crops, wrecked the vineyards and olive groves, and terrorized the herds of cattle. Obviously there was a hero's job to be done, and Meleager decided that he was the man to do it.

Meleager therefore issued an invitation, as Jason had done, to the other heroes of Greece to join with him in hunting the boar. A number of great heroes answered, including Jason, Pirithous, Peleus, Theseus, Telamon, Nestor, Castor and Polydeuces (Pollux), Idas, Lynceus, Admetus, and Anceus. Most important to Meleager, there came **Atalanta of Arcadia** (not to be confused with Atalanta of Boeotia, whose foot race with Hippomenes is told under her name), the beautiful and athletic heroine who had been reared in her early youth by a bear and who consequently had grown up to be a fierce huntress as well as a lovely woman. She came dressed in an off-the-shoulder tunic clasped by a buckle of gold, and with a quiver of ivory over her shoulder, a costume designed to combine the practical needs of a huntress with the usual feminine advantages.

First, as was customary, Meleager offered nine days of hospitable entertainment. On the tenth day the hunt began. The heroes set up a game run by stretching nets between trees, and they brought their best hounds into the field. Soon the boar was attracted by the noise of the hunt and rushed to attack the huntsmen. The first spear cast against him was that of Jason, who accompanied it with a prayer to Artemis. Artemis acknowledged the prayer by allowing the spear to strike the boar lightly, but only after she had removed its tip while it was in flight. In the excitement caused by the attack of the boar, Nestor was forced to climb a tree to escape; and Telamon, rushing forward to cast his spear, tripped over the roots of a tree and fell. At this point Atalanta, with feminine calm in the midst of male confusion, loosed an arrow at the boar and drew first blood, an event which Meleager, already in love with her, proclaimed with more than sportsmanly enthusiasm.

Atalanta's success, slight though it was, excited her masculine rivals to greater efforts. Anceus rushed the boar, defying in one breath the beast and the beauty who had sent it, with the result that he received a mortal wound from the boar's tusk. Both Theseus and Jason were likewise unsuccessful, the former's lance being turned aside in flight by a branch and the latter's going astray to kill one of the dogs. Then Meleager drove his spear into the animal and killed it. Meleager awarded the boar's head and hide to Atalanta because she had drawn the first blood, but this act excited the other huntsmen to unsportsmanlike envy, and especially Plexippus and Toxeus, the brothers of Meleager's mother, who even seized the trophies from Atalanta's hands. This rude act enraged Meleager, and he slew his own uncles.

The news of her brothers' death reached Althaea as she was offering victory sacrifices in the temples. At first she was grief stricken; but later she felt a murderous and revengeful anger toward her son. She took from its hiding place the fated brand and, after many indecisions in which the love of a mother fought against sisterly love, she cast it into the fire and it burned.

As the brand caught fire, it gave a moan; at the same moment Meleager, who was some distance away, was struck with pain. Then, as the brand was consumed by the fire, his life ran out its time in agony, and he died, regretful that his death was not a hero's death and calling the while on his parents and his sisters. When the act was done, Althaea killed herself; and Meleager's sisters gave way to such unremitting grief that Artemis, repenting the misfortune that she had caused, turned them into birds to give them solace. Thus again fate found its long way to fulfillment.

The best-known poetic use of this myth is in Swinburne's

drama, *Atalanta in Calydon,* in which a famous song to Artemis begins:

> When the hounds of spring are on winter's traces,
> The mother of months in meadow or plain
> Fills the shadows and windy places
> With lisp of leaves and ripple of rain. . . .

CALYPSO (ká·lĭp′sō) for eight years held Odysseus captive. See ODYSSEUS.

CAMILLA (ká·mĭl′á) was a feminine warrior who fought against AENEAS.

CAMPUS MARTIUS (kăm′pŭs mär′shŭs) was the field of Mars in Rome. See ARES, ROME.

CANCER, the Crab, is a constellation and a sign of the ZODIAC.

CAPANEUS (kăp′á·nūs) was one of the Seven against THEBES.

CAPITOLINE (kăp′ĭ·tô·līn) is one of the seven hills of later ROME.

CAPRICORNUS (kăp′rĭ·kôr′nŭs), the Goat, is a constellation and a sign of the ZODIAC.

CARIA (kā′rĭ·á) was a section of Asia Minor that contained the cities of Miletus, Halicarnassus, and Cnidus, the river Maeander, and Mount Latmos, where Endymion sleeps immortally. See ARTEMIS.

CARTHAGE (kär′thĭj), one of the most famous cities of ancient times, was situated on a large bay on the northern coast of Africa. For a time the Carthaginians were the most formidable rivals of the Romans, with whom they fought the three Punic Wars. The first war began in 265 B.C., and the last, in which Carthage was captured and destroyed, began and ended in 146 B.C. A myth relates that Carthage was established by Queen Dido, who welcomed and fell in love with Aeneas, the homeless wanderer who was to found the Roman race. Dido committed suicide when she was deserted by AENEAS.

CASSANDRA (kȧ·săn′drȧ), the Trojan prophetess whom nobody believed, became a slave of Agamemnon when Troy fell. See ATREUS, TROJAN WAR.

CASSIOPEA (kăs′ĭ·ȯ·pē′ȧ) was the mother of Andromeda. See PERSEUS.

CASTALIA (kăs·tā′lĭ·ȧ), pursued by Apollo, jumped into a spring on Mount Parnassus. The spring thereafter was named for her and was sacred to Apollo and the Muses. See ORACLES.

CASTOR (kȧs′tȯr) and **Polydeuces,** or **Pollux,** were twins but only half brothers. Their mother Leda, the wife of King Tyndareus of Sparta, was seduced by the god Zeus in the guise of a swan, and she produced two eggs: from one came her immortal son and daughter by Zeus, Polydeuces and Helen; and from the other her mortal son and daughter by Tyndareus, Castor and Clytemnestra. All four children were destined for fame.

The twin brothers became inseparable companions and great heroes. Because there were conflicting stories about their parentage, they were often called the **Dioscuri,** the sons of Zeus, and sometimes the Tyndaridae, the sons of Tyndareus. In Roman times they were frequently called the **Castores.** Polydeuces was a fine boxer and Castor a skillful horseman. They joined the Argonauts in quest of the Golden Fleece; and in Bithynia, where King Amycus insisted on boxing with strangers, Polydeuces represented the Argonauts and knocked out the pugnacious king. The twins also took part in the Calydonian Boar Hunt. Their sister Helen, who was later known as Helen of Troy, was so beautiful even as a child that the hero Theseus, with the aid of his friend Pirithous, carried her off to marry her. But he left her before the marriage in order to help Pirithous, who also wished to steal a bride; and while he was gone Castor and Polydeuces rescued Helen and took her back to Sparta.

Finally the twins quarreled with Idas and Lynceus, who were

111

also brothers. Either they disagreed over the division of spoils in a cattle raid, or the Dioscuri stole the girls to whom the other brothers were betrothed. Whatever the cause of the fight, Castor, the mortal twin, was killed, as were Lynceus and Idas. Polydeuces felt that he could not live without his brother, and he asked Zeus to let him share his immortality with Castor. Zeus agreed, and the twins are always together: they spend one day in Hades and the next day in Olympus. They are patrons of athletes and soldiers, and also of mariners, to whom they appear in the form of what is now called St. Elmo's fire. They are identified with the constellation Gemini, the Twins; and it is usually as the constellation that they appear in English literature. Spenser's reference in the *Prothalamion* is typical; he concludes his praise of two young men by saying,

> . . . like the twins of *Ioue* they seem'd in sight,
> Which decke the Bauldricke of the Heauens bright.

For the adventures of Helen and Clytemnestra, the sisters of these heroes, see TROJAN WAR, ATREUS.

CASTORES (kás·tôr′ēz) was a Roman name for Pollux and CASTOR.

CATTLE OF GERYON (jē′rĭ·ȯn) were captured by HERACLES.

CATTLE OF THE SUN lived on the island of Thrinacia. In spite of Odysseus' warning, his shipmates killed and ate some of these sacred cattle. Soon after the mariners put to sea again, a storm destroyed the ship and all the men were drowned except ODYSSEUS.

CECROPIANS (sē·krō′pĭ·ȧnz) were the original inhabitants of the city that became Athens. See ATTICA.

CECROPS (sē′krŏps) was the first king of ATTICA.

CELAENO (sē·lē′nō) is one of the Harpies. See SEA GODS.

CELEUS (sĕl′ē·ŭs) was the father of a family that befriended Demeter at Eleusis. See EARTH GODDESSES.

CENTAURS (sĕn′tôrz). The offspring of Ixion and a cloud (see IXION), the Centaurs were a race of savage monsters, half-man and half-horse. In classical mythology and English literature they usually appear as fighters, drinkers, and rapists. Their most celebrated brawl occurred at the marriage of Hippodamia and Pirithous, king of the Lapiths. The Centaurs came to the wedding as invited guests, but they soon got drunk; one tried to violate the bride, and the others went after the remaining women. The Lapiths, led by Pirithous and his friend Theseus, killed many Centaurs and drove the rest out of Thessaly.

Heracles, a quarrelsome type himself, had a great deal of trouble with Centaurs. When he and Deianira were first married they wished to cross a river at which the Centaur Nessus acted as ferryman. Nessus insulted Deianira as he was carrying her over the river, and Heracles shot him with a poisoned arrow. Before he died, however, Nessus gave the bride a fatal charm against unfaithfulness (see HERACLES). On another occasion Heracles, who was being entertained by the Centaur **Pholus,** demanded some of the wine that was stored in Pholus' cave but that belonged to the whole community of Centaurs. According to one version of the story, this wine had been given to the Centaurs by Dionysus on the understanding that they share it with Heracles; in another version Heracles has no claim on the wine except his great thirst. But when Pholus reluctantly gave the hero a drink, the other Centaurs attacked, and Heracles killed a great many of them. Spenser describes both this fight and the Lapith-Centaur battle among the tapestries in the house of Ate (*Faerie Queene,* 4. 1. 23):

> And there the relicks of the drunken fray,
> The which amongst the *Lapithees* befell,

> And of the bloodie feast, which sent away
> So many *Centaures* drunken soules to hell,
> That vndèr great *Alcides* furie fell.

In the fight over the wine Heracles not only lost his host Pholus, who while examining one of the hero's poisoned arrows dropped it on his foot and died of the scratch, but inadvertently caused the death of his good friend **Chiron,** who had nothing in common with his fellow Centaurs except his appearance. The son of Cronus and a sea Nymph, Chiron was renowned for his kindness and his wisdom. Apollo and Artemis taught him the arts of hunting, music, medicine, and prophecy, and he became the tutor of such famous men as Asclepius, Jason, and Achilles. In Matthew Arnold's *Empedocles on Etna* Callicles sings:

> In such a glen, on such a day,
> On Pelion, on the grassy ground,
> Chiron, the aged Centaur, lay,
> The young Achilles standing by.
> The Centaur taught him to explore
> The mountains; where the glens are dry
> And the tired Centaurs come to rest,
> And where the soaking springs abound
> And the straight ashes grow for spears,
> And where the hill-goats come to feed,
> And the sea-eagles build their nest.
>
> . . . . . .
>
> He told him of the Gods, the stars,
> The tides;—and then of mortal wars,
> And of the life which heroes lead
> Before they reach the Elysian place
> And rest in the immortal mead;
> And all the wisdom of his race.

When he was wounded by one of Heracles' poisoned arrows, Chiron found the pain unbearable and achieved death by presenting his immortality to Prometheus. Zeus placed Chiron among the stars as the constellation Sagittarius, the Archer.

Not the gentleness of Chiron but the violence of the other Centaurs gave the unhappily married Byron a metaphor for marriage: "that moral Centaur, man and wife" (*Don Juan*, 5. 158).

CEPHALUS (sĕf′ȧ·lŭs), the husband of Procris, was carried off by the goddess Eos, but he remained true to his wife. Eos at last allowed him to return to Procris but contrived to ruin their marriage. See EOS.

CEPHEUS (sē′fūs) was the father of Andromeda. See PERSEUS.

CEPHISUS (sė·fī′sŭs) was the father of NARCISSUS.

CERBERUS (sĕr′bĕr·ŭs) is the three-headed dog who guards the entrance to HADES.

CERCYON (sĕr′sĭ·ŏn), who killed all whom he overcame in wrestling, was defeated and slain by THESEUS.

CERES (sē′rēz) is the Roman name of the Olympian earth goddess, Demeter. See EARTH GODDESSES.

CERMALUS (sĕr′mȧ·lŭs) was one of the seven hills of earliest ROME.

CERYNEIAN (sĕr′ĭ·nē′yȧn) **STAG** was captured by HERACLES.

CETO (sē′tō) is the wife of Phorcys, one of the SEA GODS.

CEYX (sē′ĭks), the son of Hesperus, the evening star, was king of Thessaly. His wife, **Alcyone,** or **Halcyone,** was the daughter of Aeolus, the god of the winds. Two different myths that agree only in their conclusions grew up about Ceyx and his wife. According to the first myth, the two were so happily married that they called themselves Zeus and Hera and thus offended the gods, who changed them into birds as punishment. The better-known myth, however, is of a gentler sort. Ceyx, because of omens attendant on the death of his brother, decided to consult an oracle of Apollo in Ionia, and he set out on a voyage to this place in spite of his wife's direful feminine intuitions. On the way a storm destroyed his boat, and he was drowned with all his men. Alcyone made constant sacrifices to the gods for her husband's safety, and especially she implored Hera for his safe return, until that goddess decided to reveal to the luckless woman that Ceyx had drowned. So Hera sent Iris to the underworld to arrange for a vision to inform Alcyone of her husband's death. Accordingly, Morpheus, the chief god of dreams, appeared to Alcyone as Ceyx and told her that he had drowned.

Alcyone awoke and went down to the seashore, where she soon discovered her husband's body floating in on the tide. In her grief, as she cast herself over the cliff to her death or, according to another version, as she ran down the sea wall to meet her husband's body, she was changed into a bird, the halcyon, and Ceyx likewise. All versions of the myth agree that the two were mated as birds as they had been as human beings and that Aeolus quiets his winds during the season when his daughter sits on her nest, which floats on the waves. These quiet windless days are still called halcyon days.

Chaucer borrowed this story from Ovid as part of the introduction to *The Book of the Duchess,* and although he calls it (60–61)

> . . . a tale
> That me thoughte a wonder thing,

after telling it, he observes that reading it put him to sleep. But since Chaucer was writing a "dream vision," a conventional poem in which the poet is required to fall asleep, we may suppose that poetic necessity, rather than the story itself, got the better of him. Milton turns the myth to a more symbolic use in *On the Morning of Christ's Nativity* (61–68):

But peacefull was the night
Wherein the Prince of light
  His raign of peace upon the earth began:
The Windes with wonder whist,
Smoothly the waters kist,
  Whispering new joyes to the milde Ocean,
Who now hath quite forgot to rave,
While Birds of Calm sit brooding on the charmed wave.

Also, in that compendium of mythological references, *Endymion* (1. 453–455), Keats apostrophizes sleep:

      . . . O comfortable bird,
That broodest o'er the troubled sea of the mind
Till it is hush'd and smooth!

an image that misconstrues the cause of the calmness associated with the halycons but loses nothing of its effect.

CHARICLO (kăr′ĭ·klō) was the mother of TIRESIAS.

CHARITES (kăr′ĭ·tēz) are the GRACES.

CHARON (kā′rŏn) is the boatman who ferries the souls of the dead across the Styx or the Acheron to HADES.

CHARYBDIS (ká·rĭb′dĭs) was condemned by Zeus to live under a rock on the Sicilian straits, where she became a whirlpool. See SEA GODS, ODYSSEUS.

CHIMAERA (kī·mē′rá) was a terrible monster that was killed by BELLEROPHON.

CHIRON (kī′rŏn), a gentle and learned Centaur, was a tutor of heroes. See CENTAURS.

CHLORIS (klō′rĭs), or **Flora,** is the goddess of spring and flowers and the wife of Zephyrus, the west wind. Her use in English literature is typified by Herrick's words to his mistress in *Corinna's Going A-Maying* (15–17):

Rise, and put on your Foliage, and be seene
To come forth, like the Spring-time, fresh and greene,
And sweet as *Flora.*

CHRYSEIS (krī·sē′ĭs), the daughter of Chryses, priest of Apollo, was captured by the Greeks and given to Agamemnon. When Agamemnon refused to release her, her father persuaded Apollo to send a pestilence among the Greeks. See TROJAN WAR.

CHRYSES (krī′sēz) was a Trojan priest of Apollo. See TROJAN WAR.

CICONES (sĭ′kŏ·nēz) fought against ODYSSEUS.

CILIX (sĭl′ĭks), searching for his sister Europa, gave his name to Cilicia. See THEBES.

CIMMERIANS (sĭ·mē′rĭ·ánz) lived in perpetual darkness beyond the great river of Oceanus. See SEA GODS.

CIRCE (sîr′sē) is an enchantress. See ODYSSEUS.

CISPIUS (sĭs′pĭ·ŭs) was one of the seven hills of earliest ROME.

CLEOPATRA (klē′ŏ·pā′trả) was the first wife of Phineus, who aided the ARGONAUTS.

CLIO (klī′ō) is the Muse of history. See MUSES.

CLOTHO (klō′thō) is one of the three Fates. See FATE.

CLYMENE (klĭm′ẻ·nē) was the mother of Phaethon by APOLLO.

CLYTEMNESTRA (klī′tĕm·nĕs′trả), the half sister of Helen of Troy, murdered her husband Agamemnon. See ATREUS, TROJAN WAR.

CLYTIE (klī′tē), a Nymph whose heart was broken when Apollo deserted her, was transformed into a symbol of faithfulness, the sunflower. See APOLLO.

CLYTIUS (clī′tĭ·ŭs) was one of the GIANTS.

CNOSSUS (nŏs′sŭs) was the capital city of Crete and of the Cretan civilization. At Cnossus lived King Minos and Queen Pasiphae, and there Daedalus built the Labyrinth to imprison the Minotaur that Theseus slew. Ancient ruins of great archeological interest have been excavated there. See DAEDALUS, THESEUS.

COCALUS (kŏk′á·lûs) was a protector of DAEDALUS.

COCYTUS (kȯ·sī′tûs) is a river of HADES.

COEUS (sē′ûs) is one of the TITANS.

COLCHIS (kŏl′kĭs) was the place where the Golden Fleece was located. See ARGONAUTS.

CORA (kô′rȧ) is another name of Persephone, the daughter of Demeter and the wife of Hades. See EARTH GODDESSES, HADES.

CORONIS (kȯ·rō′nĭs) was the mother of Asclepius by APOLLO.

CORYBANTES (kŏr′ĭ·băn′tēz) were the half-divine priests of Cybele. See EARTH GODDESSES.

COTHURNUS (kȯ·thûr′nûs) is another name for the BUSKIN.

COTTUS (kŏt′ûs) was a Hecatoncheire. See TITANS.

CREON (krē′ŏn) became regent when Oedipus left the throne of THEBES.

CRETAN BULL, the father by Pasiphae of the Minotaur, was captured by Heracles. See DAEDALUS, HERACLES.

CREUS (krē′ûs) is one of the TITANS.

CREUSA (krê·ū′sȧ) was (1) a Trojan princess, the wife of AENEAS; (2) the second wife of Jason, leader of the ARGO-NAUTS.

CRONIA (krō′nĭ·ȧ) was a harvest celebration in honor of CRONUS.

CRONUS (krō′nûs), or **Saturn,** or **Saturnus. Uranus,** the sky, hated nearly all his children by Gaea, the earth. When he confined a large number of them in Tartarus, which is as far beneath Hades as earth is beneath heaven, Gaea was so angry that she urged her Titan sons to rebel against their father. All except Cronus, the youngest, were afraid to attack him. Armed with a sickle provided by Gaea, Cronus ambushed Uranus and castrated him. The Furies and the Giants sprang up from the blood of the mutilated god, and (according to one

119

story) Aphrodite rose from the sea where the bits of his genitals fell.

Cronus married his sister Rhea and ruled the universe for many centuries. Yet a prophecy troubled him. It had been predicted that one of his children would overthrow him, as he had overthrown his father, and to prevent this eventuality he swallowed each of his children as they were born. One after the other, he gulped down Hestia, Demeter, Hera, Poseidon, and Hades. Rhea, like her mother, preferred her children to her husband, and she watched the regular disappearance of her offspring with growing dismay. When Zeus was born, she hid him away and offered Cronus a stone wrapped in swaddling clothes.

If the stone lay heavy on Cronus' stomach, it did not do so for long. Zeus grew up rapidly and soon challenged his father's power. With the aid of his grandmother, Gaea, he compelled Cronus to disgorge the stone and the five children, and then he and his brothers and sisters fought a great war with Cronus and the other Titans, for a detailed account of which see ZEUS. The Titans were defeated, and most of them were hurled into Tartarus. Comus in Milton's masque of that name (803–804) recalls that Jove proclaimed

> . . . the chains of *Erebus*
> To som of *Saturns* crew.

Certain Greek writers said that Zeus and Cronus were finally reconciled, and that Cronus became the ruler of the Blessed Islands (see HADES, SEA GODS). According to the Roman writers, when Cronus, or Saturn, was defeated in Greece, he fled to Italy, where Janus ruled. In *Paradise Lost* (1. 519–520) Milton refers to this migration to Italy. There Saturn civilized the people, taught them the art of agriculture, and made them prosperous. Janus, impressed by Saturn's wisdom, shared the throne with him, and they ruled amicably together. Sometimes Janus was confused with Saturn (see JANUS).

Few stories are told of Cronus. As supreme ruler he is a remote, crafty, terrible figure who seized the throne by violence and attempted to hold it by the same means. The Greek Hesiod calls him Cronus of the crooked counsel. The only sympathetic portrait of him in English literature is offered by John Keats, who describes him in defeat (*Hyperion*, 1. 1–7, 106–112):

> Deep in the shady sadness of a vale
> Far sunken from the healthy breath of morn,
> Far from the fiery moon, and eve's one star,
> Sat gray-hair'd Saturn, quiet as a stone,
> Still as the silence round about his lair;
> Forest on forest hung about his head
> Like cloud on cloud.

When he speaks to the Titaness Thea, who tries to comfort him, Saturn regrets chiefly the loss of his power to do good:

> . . . I am smother'd up,
> And buried from all godlike exercise
> Of influence benign on planets pale,
> Of admonitions to the winds and seas,
> Of peaceful sway above man's harvesting,
> And all those acts which Deity supreme
> Doth ease its heart of love in.

In English literature Cronus is usually a dark and malignant god. This interpretation depends partly on classical story but chiefly on astrological notions concerning the influence of the planet Saturn. In Spenser's allegorical House of Alma (*Faerie Queene*, 2. 9. 52), for example, Phantastes, the inhabitant of the first room of the human brain, seems young yet full of melancholy:

> . . . one by his vew
> Mote deeme him borne with ill disposed skyes,
> When oblique *Saturne* sate in the house of agonyes.

(The house of agonies is the twelfth heavenly house, but for further explanations the authors refer the reader to any standard work on astrology). In Shakespeare's *Titus Andronicus* (2. 3. 32–39) Aaron, the villainous Moor, tells Tamora that Saturn governs his desires:

> What signifies my deadly-standing eye,
> My silence, and my cloudy melancholy,
>
> . . . . . .
>
> Vengeance is in my heart, death in my hand,
> Blood and revenge are hammering in my head.

And in *The Knight's Tale* by Chaucer (I. 2456–2469) Saturn himself gives a full account of his evil proclivities:

> Myn is the drenchyng in the see so wan;
> Myn is the prison in the derke cote;
> Myn is the stranglyng and hangyng by the throte,
> The murmure and the cherles rebellyng,
> The groynynge, and the pryvee empoysonyng;
> I do vengeance and pleyn correccioun,
> Whil I dwelle in the signe of the leoun.
>
> . . . . . .
>
> And myne be the maladyes colde,
> The derke tresons, and the castes olde;
> My lookyng is the fader of pestilence.

Yet Chaucer, Shakespeare, Spenser, and many others also wrote of the **Golden Age** over which a benignant Saturn reigned. Spenser describes this period of lost innocence in *The Faerie Queene* (5. Prologue. 9):

For during *Saturnes* ancient raigne it's sayd,
That all the world with goodnesse did abound:
All loued vertue, no man was affrayd
Of force, ne fraud in wight was to be found:
No warre was knowne, no dreadfull trompets sound,
Peace vniuersall rayn'd mongst men and beasts,
And all things freely grew out of the ground:
Justice sate high ador'd with solemne feasts,
And to all people did diuide her dred beheasts.

Chaucer, without mentioning Saturn, tells of the delights of this time in *The Former Age,* and Shakespeare several times speaks of the Age of Gold.

This dichotomy in the character of Cronus seems to be the result of his two functions: the first as the dark supreme ruler and the second as the gentle harvest god. In Greece, because his worship coincided with the development of agriculture, he was recognized as a harvest god; and in Athens, Rhodes, and Thebes a festival called the **Cronia** was celebrated in his honor, a happy harvest celebration in which social distinctions were eliminated.

In Roman mythology Saturn was at first a rather humble god of harvest, and his wife Ops was the harvest helper. Later he was identified with Cronus, and Ops with Rhea, and the Golden Age whose departure was lamented by the Greeks was thought by the Romans to have occurred at a later time when Saturn fled from defeat in Greece to peaceful reign in Italy. For many years Saturn shared the rule of Italy with Janus, but one day he suddenly disappeared. In his honor Janus established the **Saturnalia,** which was celebrated in December. As long as the festival lasted, everyone pretended that the Golden Age had returned. Declarations of war were forbidden, executions were postponed, master and man ate at the same table, and people exchanged presents. The season of this festival was later chosen by Christians for the Christmas celebration.

See also TITANS.

CUMAE (kū′mē) is the place where Aeneas first landed in Italy. See AENEAS.

CUMAEAN SIBYL (kū·mē′*a*n sĭb′ĭl), or Sibyl of Cumae, who was given the power of prophecy and a thousand years of life by Apollo, guided Aeneas to Hades. See APOLLO, AENEAS.

CUPID (kū′pĭd) is a Roman name for EROS.

CURETES (kū·rē′tēz), the half-divine priests of Rhea, protected Zeus when he was a child. See EARTH GODDESSES.

CYBELE (sĭb′ė·lē), or **CYBEBE** (sĭ·bē′bē), was the Phrygian name of the Titan earth goddess, Rhea. See EARTH GODDESSES.

CYCLOPES (sī·klō′pēz; singular, **CYCLOPS,** sī′klŏps) are huge one-eyed giants. The first Cyclopes were sons of Uranus and Gaea. They were confined in Tartarus by Uranus and liberated by Zeus when the Olympians were overthrowing the Titans. In gratitude the Cyclopes created for Zeus the thunderbolt, which became his favorite weapon. When Zeus killed Asclepius with a thunderbolt, Apollo, Asclepius' father, was afraid to attack Zeus but took his revenge by killing the Cyclopes. In the *Odyssey,* however, the Cyclopes are giant one-eyed cannibals, the sons of Poseidon, who keep flocks on the volcanic island of Sicily. For them see ODYSSEUS.

CYCNUS (sĭk′nŭs), which means "swan," was the name of three young men who were all turned into swans. The first, a son of Ares, was a thief whom Heracles killed. The second, a son of Poseidon, was abandoned at birth by his mother but was cared for by a swan. He was an ally of the Trojans against the Greeks, and in the first fight the Greek hero Achilles strangled him. The first two Cycnuses became swans after death, but the third was simply translated from youth to swan. He was a friend of Phaethon, the foolish son of Apollo who tried to drive his father's chariot of the sun. Zeus killed Phaethon with a thunderbolt, and Cycnus grieved so bitterly that the gods transformed him into a swan.

These rather vague and unsatisfactory stories are the fore-runners of many later tales of swan transformation found in England and on the continent, both in folk tale and in the literature of conscious art. The best known is the story of the Knight of the Swan, who is called Helias, Lohengrin, and various other names. In 1512, Robert Copland translated from a French version *The History of Helyas, Knight of the Swan* as a compli-ment to the noble English families who claimed descent from the Swan Knight. Edmund Spenser made a swan transformation the central motif of his betrothal poem, the *Prothalamion*.

CYLLENE (sĭ·lē′nē) is the mountain famous as the birthplace of HERMES.

CYLLENIUS (sĭ·lē′nĭ·ûs) is another name for HERMES.

CYNTHIA (sĭn′thĭ·à) is another name for ARTEMIS.

CYNTHIUS (sĭn′thĭ·ûs) is another name for APOLLO.

CYNTHUS (sĭn′thŭs) is the mountain on Delos famous as the birthplace of Artemis and APOLLO.

CYPRIS (sī′prĭs) is another name for APHRODITE.

CYPRUS (sī′prûs) contends with Cythera for the honor of being the island to which Aphrodite floated when she arose from the foam. See APHRODITE.

CYRENE (sī·rē′nē), a Nymph who liked to wrestle with lions, was the mother of Aristaeus by APOLLO.

CYTHERA (sĭth′ẽr·à) contends with Cyprus for the honor of being the island to which Aphrodite floated when she arose from the foam. See APHRODITE.

CYTHEREA (sĭth′ẽr·ē′à) is a name for APHRODITE.

CYZICUS (sĭz′ĭ·kûs) is the island on which Heracles left the expedition of the ARGONAUTS.

DAEDALUS (dĕd′à·lûs), the skillful artificer who anticipated the achievement of the Wright brothers, was a famous inventor and artist, and a descendant of Hephaestus, the god of craftsmen. Athens was his native city, and there he created many marvelous things, including statues that moved of themselves. His nephew, **Perdix**, or **Talus** (not to be confused with the Talus who guarded the shores of Crete, for whom see THESEUS), became Daedalus' apprentice and eventually his rival. Perdix, after brooding over the backbone of a fish, invented the saw; and Daedalus was so filled with jealous rage that he threw Perdix into the sea. The gods transformed the young man into the partridge, which still bears his name.

Daedalus fled to **Cnossus** in Crete, where he was hospitably received by King **Minos**. At this time Minos had incurred the anger of Poseidon. He had prayed to the god for a bull to sacrifice in his honor; but when Poseidon sent him the **Cretan Bull** from the sea, Minos was so delighted with the animal that he kept it and sacrificed an inferior bull in its place. Poseidon, who usually took the simplest means of revenge, this time devised a subtler punishment: he caused **Pasiphae**, Minos' wife, to conceive a violent passion for the bull. When Daedalus appeared, Pasiphae took him into her confidence, and he disguised her as a cow so that she might satisfy her lust. In due time she bore the **Minotaur,** who was half-bull and half-man; and Daedalus, at the command of Minos, built the famous **Labyrinth,** an intricate maze in which the monster was kept. For the story of the human sacrifices offered to the Minotaur and of his death at the hands of Theseus, see the article on that hero.

Daedalus and his son Icarus (who at this point suddenly appears in the story) lived happily in Crete until Minos learned that Daedalus had helped Pasiphae to indulge her unnatural passion for the bull. Then the king confined Daedalus and Icarus in the Labyrinth and thus provided the ultimate proof of its effectiveness, for not even Daedalus, its creator, could find his way out of it. The sky was the only way of escape, and Daedalus therefore made wings of feathers and wax. Before he and Icarus tried to fly, he warned the boy that they must hold to a middle course between sky and sea: if they flew too high the sun would melt the wax and the wings would fall apart. But after they had soared into the air, Icarus was so delighted with his new power that he ranged far up into the heavens. The wax melted, the wings fell from his shoulders, and he plunged down into a sea that thereafter was called the **Icarian Sea.**

Daedalus flew safely to Sicily and sought the protection of King **Cocalus.** When Minos discovered that Daedalus had escaped, he was furiously angry, and he could not rest until he had thought of a way to discover the inventor's hiding place. He sent word through the civilized world that he would give a large reward to anyone who could string a thread through every spiral of a sea shell. Daedalus quickly solved the problem. He tied a thread to an ant, bored a small hole in the closed end of a shell, put the ant in the hole, and then plugged up the hole and secured the end of the thread. The ant worked its way to the open end of the shell and, in doing so, pulled the thread through every spiral. When this shell arrived from Sicily with a request for the reward, Minos was sure that only Daedalus could have accomplished the task, and he set sail at once for Sicily to capture his errant servant. King Cocalus received him with proper ceremony but refused to surrender Daedalus. Doubtless war would have resulted if one of Cocalus' daughters had not ended the dispute by scalding Minos to death in his bath.

In English literature Daedalus and Icarus are sometimes remembered for their boldness. Lord Talbot in Shakespeare's *1 Henry VI* (4. 6. 54–57), for example, urges his son to reckless bravery with these words:

> Then follow thou thy desp'rate sire of Crete,
> Thou Icarus. Thy life to me is sweet.
> If thou wilt fight, fight by thy father's side;
> And, commendable prov'd, let's die in pride.

More frequently, however, Icarus, like Phaethon, symbolizes rash and foolish pride. In *3 Henry VI* (5. 6. 18–25) King Henry in an elaborate image describes himself and his son as Daedalus and Icarus, but his labored comparison is less effective than Gloucester's contemptuous thrust:

> Why, what a peevish fool was that of Crete
> That taught his son the office of a fowl!
> And yet, for all his wings, the fool was drown'd.

Similarly, George Santayana in his sonnet *On the Death of a Metaphysician* represents the failure of the "unhappy dreamer" of his poem in terms of the myth:

> I stood and saw you fall, befooled in death,
> As, in your numbëd spirit's fatal swoon,
> You cried you were a god, or were to be;
> I heard with feeble moan your boastful breath
> Bubble from depths of the Icarian sea.[1]

In *Musée des Beaux Arts* W. H. Auden uses a painter's treatment of the story of Icarus as an example of the irony of human suffering and of human indifference to the suffering of others:

[1] From "On the Death of a Metaphysician," by George Santayana, in *Poems* (New York: Charles Scribner's Sons, 1925). Reprinted with the permission of the publishers.

In Breughel's *Icarus,* for example: how everything turns away
Quite leisurely from the disaster; the ploughman may
Have heard the splash, the forsaken cry,
But for him it was not an important failure; the sun shone
As it had to on the white legs disappearing into the green
Water; and the expensive delicate ship that must have seen
Something amazing, a boy falling out of the sky, .
Had somewhere to get to and sailed calmly on.[2]

Daedalus is often remembered for his inventions: the wings, the statues that moved of themselves, and what Chaucer (*House of Fame,* 1920–1921) calls

> . . . that Domus Dedaly,
> That Laboryntus cleped ys.

Socrates, because he was a sculptor as well as a philosopher, claimed descent from Daedalus (Plato, *Alcibiades* I, 121); and Stephen Dedalus, the aspiring artist who is the hero of James Joyce's *Portrait of the Artist as a Young Man,* prays for help to the first Daedalus: "Old father, old artificer, stand me now and ever in good stead." Spenser borrowed from Greek the adjective "daedal," which means "cunningly wrought," and Shelley and Keats and a number of other poets have also used the word.

DAEMON (dē′mŏn) is usually the guardian spirit of a person, society, or place. See HESTIA.

DANAE (dăn′ā·ē) was a mistress of Zeus whom the god visited as a shower of gold. See PERSEUS, ZEUS.

DANAIDS (dăn′ā·ĭdz) were the fifty daughters of Danaus, who ordered them to murder their husbands on their wedding night. Forty-nine of them obeyed, and they suffer a special torment in HADES.

---

[2] From "Musée des Beaux Arts," by W. H. Auden, in *The Collected Poetry of W. H. Auden.* Copyright, 1945, by W. H. Auden. Reprinted with the permission of the publisher, Random House, Inc.

DANAUS (dăn′ā·ûs) ordered his fifty daughters to murder their husbands on their wedding night. See HADES.

DAPHNE (dăf′nē), pursued by Apollo, was transformed into the laurel, and Apollo adopted the laurel as his tree. See APOLLO.

DAPHNIS (dăf′nĭs) was a shepherd who invented pastoral song and story. He loved Piplea and tried to win her from her master, Lityerses, by defeating him in a reaping contest. Daphnis was losing until Lityerses was killed by HERACLES.

DARDANUS (där′dȧ·nûs) was the founder of the Trojan royal house. See AENEAS.

DEATH. See Thanatos under HADES.

DEIANIRA (dē′yȧ·nī′rȧ) was the second wife of HERACLES.

DEIDAMIA (dē·ĭd′ȧ·mī′ȧ) was the mother by Achilles of Pyrrhus, or Neoptolemus, who fought in the TROJAN WAR.

DEIMOS (dī′mŏs) is an attendant of his father ARES.

DEIPHOBUS (dē·ĭf′ŏ·bûs), a prince of Troy, was a minor hero in the TROJAN WAR.

DELIA (dē′lĭ·ȧ) is another name for ARTEMIS.

DELIUS (dē′lĭ·ûs) is another name for APOLLO.

DELOS (dē′lŏs) is the Aegean island on which Leto gave birth to Artemis and APOLLO.

DELPHI (dĕl′fī), a Greek town at the foot of Mount Parnassus, was the place of the most famous oracle of Apollo. See ORACLES.

DEMETER (dḙ·mē′tḙr) is the Olympian earth goddess. See EARTH GODDESSES.

DEUCALION (dū·kā′lĭ·ȯn). Before the great flood there were three or four ages of man. First was the Golden Age when Cronus ruled. This was a time of innocence, peace, and ease, when the earth provided food without man's labor. For the poets' use of the Golden Age see the article on Cronus. Next came the **Silver Age** in which man suffered from heat and cold and was forced to cultivate the earth to get his food. Men in this time were strong and brave, but their tempers were bad and they often neglected their duties to the gods. In the next period, the **Brazen Age,** mankind was fiercer, crueler, and more impious. One possible survivor of this time was Talus, the brazen giant who is described in the article on Theseus. Byron alludes to the characteristics of this age in his satire, *The Age of Bronze.* There followed the **Iron Age,** a time of pain, sickness, poverty, war, and oppression. One by one the gods departed, and finally Astraea, the goddess of human justice, also abandoned the earth. According to some stories, the great flood followed the Age of Brass and the present age is the Age of Iron, a view for which evidence could be found in ancient Greece and in the world today. But other stories hold that the flood ended the Iron Age, and that the present time might be called the Age of Stone.

In one of the darkest ages, Brass or Iron, mankind became so evil that Zeus determined to destroy the race. With the help of his brother Poseidon, god of the sea and the rivers, he caused such a great flood that all the earth was covered except the tip of the tallest mountain, Mount Parnassus. Prometheus, the benefactor of man, had foreseen the anger of Zeus, and he had instructed his son **Deucalion** to build a chest or ark and to stock it with provisions. When the waters rose Deucalion and his wife **Pyrrha** were safe in their ark, but all other human beings were drowned.

For nine days and nights the two survivors floated on the desert of waters until their ark touched on the tip of Mount Parnassus, and there they landed. Zeus, knowing they were a pious and decent couple, took pity on them and made the flood recede. As they made their way down the mountain, they came to an old, partly ruined temple, where they gave thanks for their deliverance and prayed that the race of man might be restored. This shrine belonged to Themis, goddess of divine justice, and

131

a voice spoke from the temple telling them to throw the bones of their mother behind them. Pyrrha and Deucalion were shocked by this apparently impious command, but it soon occurred to Deucalion that the earth was the mother of all men and that stones might be called her bones. He and Pyrrha took stones and threw them over their shoulders; those thrown by her became women and those thrown by him became men. Thus the race of man was recreated. Pyrrha and Deucalion also had children by the more familiar method, and one of them was **Hellen,** eponymous father of the Greeks or **Hellenes.**

The similarities between classical myth and Biblical story are striking, and Giles Fletcher in *Christs Victorie and Triumph* (3. 7) speaks for many Christians when he says:

> Who doth not see drown'd in Deucalions name,
> (When earth his men, and sea had lost his shore)
> Old Noah . . . ?

In Milton's *Paradise Lost* (11. 9–14), when Adam and Eve have sinned and repented, they pray for forgiveness:

> . . . nor important less
> Seem'd their Petition, then when th' ancient Pair
> In Fables old, less ancient yet then these,
> *Deucalion* and chaste *Pyrrha* to restore
> The Race of Mankind drownd, before the Shrine
> Of *Themis* stood devout.

The most effective use of the myth, however, is made by Spenser in a lament for the decline of civilization in his time (*Faerie Queene,* 5. Prologue. 2):

> For from the golden age, that first was named,
> It's now at earst become a stonie one;
> And men themselves, the which at first were framed
> Of earthly mould, and form'd of flesh and bone,

Are now transformed into hardest stone:
Such as behind their backs (so backward bred)
Were throwne by *Pyrrha* and *Deucalione*.

DIANA (dī·ăn′*à*) is a Roman name of ARTEMIS.

DICTYS (dĭk′tĭs), a fisherman who befriended Perseus and his mother, was later made a king by PERSEUS.

DIDO (dī′dō), queen of Carthage, committed suicide when she was deserted by her lover AENEAS.

DIOMEDES (dī′ō·mē′dēz) was (1) one of the Epigoni who conquered Thebes and a Greek hero in the Trojan War (see THEBES, TROJAN WAR); (2) a son of Ares who owned man-eating horses for which he was killed by HERACLES.

DIONE (dī·ō′nē) was said by Homer to be the mother of APHRODITE.

DIONYSUS (dī′ō·nī′sŭs), or **Bacchus,** or **Liber,** is a god of the general fertility of nature, and as such is related to the earth goddesses, to Poseidon, and to Priapus, but he is doubtless known best for only one of his many attributes, and that is as the god of the vine and the wine that it produces. Dionysus was the son of Zeus by **Semele.** Hera, in her unceasing campaign to discourage Zeus's amours, persuaded Semele to ask her lover for a sight of him in his full splendor. When Zeus accordingly appeared in his panoply of thunder and lightning, Semele was burnt to ashes by the splendor of the sight, but Zeus seized her unborn son, Dionysus, and, as some accounts have it, implanted the child in his own thigh until it was ready for birth. Dionysus' other name **Dithyrambus** is thus thought to have meant "twice-born."

The infant Dionysus was given at first to Ino, his mother's sister, to tend at Mount Nysa; but later he was reared by **Silenus,** a son of Pan. Silenus was a fat old Satyr who loved to drink and usually appeared riding on a donkey. Hera's anger against Dionysus did not cease, and while he was still a young man she drove him mad and sent him wandering about the world. Dionysus was restored to his senses by the earth goddess Rhea, and afterward continued in his travels for the purpose of teaching the cultivation of the vine and the use of wine. He was variously received in different countries. While in the kingdom of **Midas** in Asia Minor, Silenus became lost during a bout of drunkenness and was rescued and kindly treated by Midas. For this courtesy Dionysus granted Midas the choice of his own reward, and Midas asked that everything that he touched be turned to gold. He enjoyed his magic touch immensely until he discovered that the food he wished to eat also turned to the valuable but indigestible metal. Then he prayed for release from the power, and the god directed him to bathe in the river **Pactolus,** an act which freed Midas but changed the sands of the river to gold. (For another story about Midas see APOLLO.)

At another time, Dionysus was seized by sailors who wished to sell him into slavery in Egypt. During the course of the voyage, however, vines grew up out of the sea and entwined the mast of the ship, while Dionysus himself was released from his bonds and appeared in his godly person, attended by his symbolic wild beasts and crowned with ivy. All the sailors were turned into dolphins except one named **Acetes** who had recognized and attempted to befriend the god. Acetes then piloted the ship to the island of Naxos, where the god wished to go. Alfred Noyes uses this myth in *Bacchus and the Pirates*. On Naxos Dionysus found **Ariadne,** who had been deserted by Theseus. The god comforted Ariadne, made her his wife, and persuaded Zeus to grant her immortality. The golden crown that was her wedding gift from Dionysus appears in the constellation of Taurus, and is called the Corona Borealis.

Dionysus sometimes met with opposition to his teachings. Such was the situation when he brought them to his own city of

Thebes. King **Pentheus** opposed the cultivation of the vine and the celebration of the god's rites. He even attempted to put Acetes, whom he captured, to death for celebrating the rites, but Dionysus rescued Acetes and caused Pentheus to be torn to pieces by his own mother when Pentheus interrupted the Dionysian rites that the women were celebrating on Mount Cithaeron. A similar fate the god provided for King **Lycurgus** of Thrace who opposed him. He drove Lycurgus mad and caused him to slay his own son under the impression, some accounts say, that his son was a vine in the need of pruning.

By whatever means they were spread, Dionysus' rites and the worship of the god became general in Greece and later in the western Mediterranean. Because nature flourishes in the spring and summer, Dionysus was associated with Demeter as a seasonal divinity. Consequently he was thought to suffer during the winter months, and festivals were held to comfort and honor him. These festivals usually took the form of orgiastic celebrations by women. One such was held in Athens in December; another in January was featured chiefly by a nocturnal procession of women; a third in February celebrated the opening of the wine and the pouring of it; and the last of the series in March ran for six days and was called the Great Dionysia. These festivals, when they spread to Rome, were called **Bacchanalia,** a name that survives today.

Dionysus, or Bacchus, is well known in our time as the figure of a man crowned with ivy leaves and holding aloft a bunch of grapes in one hand and a cup in the other. In ancient times, however, Dionysus was sometimes represented as old and sometimes as young and delicate, nearly always crowned with the traditional ivy and wearing a stag's skin on his shoulders. He was usually attended by lynxes, tigers, and panthers, and he carried a staff, called a **Thyrsus,** tipped with a pine cone. Besides

Silenus, his inveterate companions were the **Satyrs** and the older Satyrs, or **Sileni,** of whom Silenus was the prototype. The Satyrs were human in form except that they had the ears, legs, and tails of horses or goats. They were always inflamed with wine and sexual passion, so that there are many stories of their pursuit of the woodland Nymphs (for further details see PAN). Centaurs, who had the trunks of men but the full bodies of horses, also attended the god. The female followers of Dionysus were usually called **Maenads, Bacchantes,** or **Bassarids.** In *Ode to the West Wind* (20–23) Shelley uses the disordered hair of a Maenad as an image of gathering storm clouds:

> Like the bright hair uplifted from the head
>
> Of some fierce Maenad, even from the dim verge
> Of the horizon to the zenith's height,
> The locks of the approaching storm,

and Swinburne in the first chorus (41–44, 49–52) of *Atalanta in Calydon* recalls the female followers of the god:

> And Pan by noon and Bacchus by night,
> Fleeter of foot than the fleet-foot kid,
> Follows with dancing and fills with delight
> The Maenad and the Bassarid;
>
> . . . . . .
>
> The ivy falls with the Bacchanal's hair
> Over her eyebrows hiding her eyes;
> The wild vine slipping down leaves bare
> Her bright breast shortening into sighs. . . .

Dionysus' connection with poetry was a close one. The choral songs sung in his honor, as Aristotle observes in *The Poetics,* led ultimately to the development of the drama, of which Dionysus was the patron god, in association with Apollo and the **Muses.** At the Theatre of Dionysus in Athens, against the foot of the Acropolis, were played the great comedies and tragedies of classical times. The **dithyramb,** a wild and vehement song improvised and sung by the Bacchanals, has given its name to a kind of poetry that appears to be written under strong inspiration and consequently makes up in fervor what it often lacks in significance. To Plato all good poetry seemed to be of this sort. In a famous passage in the *Ion,* Socrates tells Ion that "all good poets, epic as well as lyric, compose their beautiful poems not by art, but because they are inspired and possessed." He compares the poets thus to Dionysian maidens "who draw milk and honey from the rivers when they are under the influence of Dionysus, but not when they are in their right mind," a dictum which has been the subject of much subsequent debate. Spenser allows one of his shepherds to express this idea in *The Shepheardes Calender* (*October,* 103–114).

In English poetry Dionysus appears most frequently as the god of revelry. Allusions to Bacchanalian festivals are numberless. Herrick wrote several poems about Bacchus. Milton rejects the Bacchanalia as a form of pagan idolatry in *Paradise Lost* (7. 31–33) in the famous lines where he calls on the Muse to govern his song and

> . . . fit audience find, though few.
> But drive farr off the barbarous dissonance
> of *Bacchus* and his Revellers.

In his poem *Upon Drinking in a Bowl,* on the contrary, John Wilmot, Earl of Rochester, declares:

> *Cupid* and *Bacchus* my Saints are;
> May Drink and Love still reign.

Another well-known allusion to Bacchus is in Keats's *Ode to a Nightingale:*

> Away! Away! for I will fly to thee,
> Not charioted by Bacchus and his pards,
> But on the viewless wings of Poesy,

lines in which Keats rejects the intoxicating power of wine for that of poetry, and in which many an American school boy has found a mistaken reference to the world of cowboys ("pards" means "leopards"). Yet in *Endymion* (4. 193–267) Keats gives a colorful description of a Bacchanalian procession; and Matthew Arnold, in a poem called *Bacchanalia: or, The New Age,* makes of the Bacchanalia a symbol of the triumph of the future over the past. Ralph Waldo Emerson, also, wrote a poem called *Bacchus,* in which he calls on the god to restore the past in memory through the power of his wine. Frederick Faust wrote *Dionysus in Hades.*

DIOSCURI (dī'ŏs·kū'rī) were Polydeuces and CASTOR.

DIRAE (dī'rē) is a Roman name of the FURIES.

DIRCE (dîr'sē) was the wife of Lycus, regent of THEBES.

DIS (dĭs) is a Roman name of the god HADES.

DISCORDIA (dĭs·kôr'dĭ·à) is the Roman name for Eris, goddess of discord. See ARES.

DITHYRAMB (dĭth'ĭ·răm) was a wild song sung by the Bacchanals, followers of DIONYSUS.

DITHYRAMBUS (dĭth'ĭ·răm'būs) is another name for DIONYSUS.

DODONA (dò·dō'nà), a city in Epirus, was the place of the most famous oracle of Zeus. See ORACLES.

DOLPHINS are sacred to Poseidon, the Olympian ruler of the SEA GODS.

DORIS is the wife of Nereus, one of the SEA GODS.

DRYADS (drī'ădz) are tree NYMPHS.

DRYOPE (drī'ò·pē), a mortal girl, was transformed into a Dryad. See NYMPHS.

E

EARTH GODDESSES. The first divinity of the Greeks was **Gaea,** or **Ge,** the goddess of the earth, whom the Romans called **Tellus,** or **Terra Mater.** Her son and husband **Uranus,** the sky, was not worshiped, apparently because he was so vaguely imagined. Gaea's chief characteristic was fecundity. Not only was she the mother by Uranus of the creatures of the earth, but she also mated with her son Pontus and her grandson Poseidon to produce various creatures of the sea.

She always sided with a son against his father, but when son or grandson opposed son or grandson her allegiance wavered. Because Uranus confined most of his children in Tartarus, Gaea persuaded her son Cronus to attack and castrate his father. Cronus then became the supreme ruler and took Rhea for his queen. Knowing that one of his offspring was fated to overthrow him, Cronus swallowed his first five children; but after Zeus was born, when Cronus asked for what he had bred, Rhea gave him a stone.

As soon as Zeus reached maturity, Gaea helped him to compel Cronus to disgorge the other children, and then the Olympians and the Titans fought a great war. At first Gaea assisted her grandchildren against her children, and her excellent advice was chiefly responsible for the defeat of the Titans; but when some of the Titans were confined in Tartarus, she mourned for them and created a monster named Typhon and incited her children the Giants to fight against Zeus. The Olympians needed the help of Heracles to subdue the last of Gaea's children.

Rhea, the wife of Cronus and the daughter of Gaea, assumed all the attributes of her mother. She was called **Cybele,** or **Cybebe,** in Phrygia, and the Romans named her **Ops.** Like Gaea, Rhea was inexhaustibly fertile, and she helped her children against their father. A part of her plot against Cronus has already been described. After saving Zeus's life, she sent him to Crete to be raised by her half-divine priests the **Curetes,** who drowned out his cries by beating their spears against their shields.

In Phrygia, where she was worshiped as Cybele, her half-divine followers were called **Corybantes.** Like the Curetes, they honored their goddess with wild and warlike dances; Spenser (*Faerie Queene,* 1. 6. 15) speaks of "*Cybeles* franticke rites." In art Cybele is usually veiled, and she sits on a throne with lions by her side or in a chariot drawn by lions. Her crown is shaped in the form of towers and battlements. Other priests of Rhea or Cybele were the **Idaean Dactyls,** fabulous discoverers of iron and copper and workers of magic. Their home was on Mount Ida in Crete or Phrygia, and their number was variously said to be five, nine, ten, twenty, or a hundred. According to one writer, there were thirty-two Dactyls who worked evil charms and twenty Dactyls who prevented the charms from taking effect. All of these numbers or combinations of numbers were significant in the Pythagorean system, and for explanations the authors of this book refer the reader to the works of Pythagoras.

When Dionysus was driven mad by Hera, Rhea cured him and taught him her religious rites. This instruction was to be expected, since Dionysus and the earth goddess, whatever her name, were both deities of fertility. Because Atalanta of Boeotia and Hippomenes, in their happiness after their marriage, forgot to offer sacrifices to Aphrodite, she caused them to offend Cybele, and Cybele turned them into a lioness and a lion and yoked them to her chariot.

Spenser and Milton both remember this goddess as **Cybele** rather than Rhea, and call her the great mother and the goddess of cities. Spenser (*Faerie Queene,* 4. 11. 28) sees her as

> Old *Cybele,* arayd with pompous pride.
> Wearing a Diademe embattild wide
> With hundred turrets,

and also (*Ruines of Rome,* 6) as

> . . . that great *Phrygian* mother
> Renowm'd for fruite of famous progenie.

In *Arcades* (21–22) Milton echoes Spenser when he describes

> . . . the towred *Cybele,*
> Mother of a hunderd gods,

and Byron (*Childe Harold,* 4. 2) says of Venice:

> She looks a sea Cybele, fresh from ocean,
> Rising with her tiara of proud towers. . . .

Demeter, or **Ceres,** a daughter of Rhea and Cronus, is the Olympian goddess of the earth and especially of agriculture. Corn and poppies are sacred to her and her daughter Persephone, and cows, sheep, and pigs are sacrificed to the two goddesses. In art Demeter is represented as carrying a cornucopia of plenty filled with ears of corn. Ceres means "corn," and in English poetry corn is often related to or personified as the goddess of agriculture. Pope, for example, in his *Moral Essays* (4. 176) sees "laughing Ceres re-assume the land," and in *The Progress of Poesy* (9) Gray speaks of "Ceres' golden reign." Demeter was associated with Dionysus and Poseidon and other deities of fertility; and because agriculture was the basis of civilization, she was also a goddess of law and marriage. In the betrothal masque of *The Tempest* (4. 1) Ceres and Juno together bless the troth-plight of Miranda and Ferdinand.

Persephone, or **Cora**, or **Proserpina**, or **Libera**, was the daughter of Demeter by Zeus. Once when Hades, the god of the underworld, made one of his infrequent visits to earth, he saw the lovely Persephone gathering flowers with her attendants in the vale of **Enna** in Sicily. The dark god immediately fell in love with her, caught her up into his chariot, and disappeared beneath the earth. Demeter heard her daughter's cries but arrived too late to save her. After she had wandered nine days in sorrow looking for Persephone, Helios, the sun, who sees everything, told Demeter what had happened.

In terrible anger she cursed the earth for allowing Hades passage to the underworld. Thereafter drought and flood and all sorts of disasters plagued the earth, and mankind came close to death through famine. The fountain Nymph Arethusa, who in her journey under the ocean had seen Persephone in the underworld, told Demeter that her daughter looked sad but queenlike, and begged Demeter to be merciful. The goddess demanded that Zeus restore Persephone. Although he was reluctant to assert his authority over his powerful brother Hades, Zeus agreed to require that Persephone be returned to earth on condition that she had eaten nothing while in the underworld. Before Hades let her go, he persuaded Persephone to eat four pomegranate seeds, and thereafter, according to the decree of the Fates, she spent four months of each year with Hades and the rest of the time with her mother. (For Persephone as the queen of the underworld see HADES, and for another myth about the annual death and rebirth of nature see Adonis under APHRODITE).

This myth symbolizes the yearly death and rebirth of nature and especially of what the English call corn and we call wheat.

In the winter the seed belongs to Hades, but in the spring it is restored to Demeter. In the course of her sorrowful search for her daughter, Demeter was kindly entertained at **Eleusis** in Attica by **Celeus** and **Metanira** and their children. Later one of these children, **Triptolemus,** became a priest of Demeter. She gave him a chariot drawn by dragons, and he traveled around the world teaching men the art of planting. Spenser (*Virgils Gnat,* 208) speaks of the time before men knew the seed of Ceres, "which first *Triptoleme* taught how to be sowne," and in Swinburne's *At Eleusis* Demeter tells of her stay with Celeus and Metanira. At Eleusis were established the **Eleusinian Festivals** and **Mysteries,** both of which were celebrated in February and September. The festivals were open to all, but the mysteries were restricted to initiates and little is known of them except that they probably interpreted the annual death and rebirth of Persephone as a symbol of the immortality of the human spirit.

The myth of Demeter and Persephone is the only tragic story about the gods. Olympians are often involved in dark and violent happenings and sometimes they feel intense sorrow, but their hurts are rather quickly healed. One sentence frequently repeated by Homer seems to symbolize their lives on Olympus: "Laughter unquenchable arose among the blessed gods." In English literature many poets have recalled the rape of Persephone. Milton (*Paradise Lost,* 4. 268–272) describes

> . . . that faire field
> Of *Enna,* where *Proserpin* gathring flours
> Her self a fairer Floure by gloomie *Dis*
> Was gatherd, which cost *Ceres* all that pain
> To seek her through the world.

(Dis is a Roman name for Hades.) In *The Winter's Tale* (4. 4. 116–118) Perdita, as the hostess of the sheepshearing feast, wishes for spring flowers:

> . . . O Proserpina,
> For the flowers now that, frighted, thou let'st fall
> From Dis's wagon!

Shelley wrote a *Song of Proserpine, While Gathering Flowers on the Plain of Enna:*

> Sacred Goddess, Mother Earth,
>   Thou from whose immortal bosom
> Gods, and men, and beasts have birth,
>   Leaf and blade, and bud and blossom,
> Breathe thine influence most divine
> On thine own child, Proserpine.
>
> If with mists of evening dew
>   Thou dost nourish these young flowers
> Till they grow, in scent and hue,
>   Fairest children of the Hours,
> Breathe thine influence most divine
> On thine own child, Proserpine.

Tennyson in *Demeter and Persephone* tells with warm sympathy the story of the rape of the daughter, the mother's search and sorrow, and their final reunion. In *The Appeasement of Demeter* George Meredith alters the myth. In his version, the curse is lifted from the dying earth, not by the return of Persephone, but by a pitiful attempt at play between a thin stallion and a thin mare. Instinct stirs faintly in them, Demeter sees and laughs kindly at their parody of pleasure, and the earth then revives. Meredith also makes an addition to mythology in *The Day of the Daughter of Hades.* In springtime in the vale of Enna a mortal boy sees Demeter and Persephone reunited. As their chariot starts toward Olympus, a girl, Skiageneia, the daughter of Persephone and Hades, leaves the chariot and joins the boy. They wander about together with the girl delighting in the life of the earth. Finally her lovely song of growing things tells her father where she is, and the daughter of Hades and springtime is taken back to the house of death.

Many poets in English literature, drawing on classical and other pagan traditions as well as the Christian tradition, have written of the majesty and fruitfulness of nature. Probably the most impressive results are Spenser's description of Dame Nature in *The Faerie Queene* (7. 7. 5–13) and Milton's account of the creation of the earth and of the creatures of the earth in *Paradise Lost* (7).

ECHIDNA (ĕ·kĭd′nȧ) was the wife of TYPHON.

ECHO (ĕk′ō) was a Nymph. See NARCISSUS, NYMPHS.

EILEITHYIA (ī′lĭ·thī′yȧ), or Ilithyia, is the goddess of childbirth. See ARTEMIS, HERA.

ELECTRA (ĕ·lĕk′trȧ) (1) was the daughter of Agamemnon and Clytemnestra, who aided her brother Orestes in the ritual killing of their mother as retribution for the murder of their father (see ATREUS); (2) is a Pleiad who had a love affair with Zeus that resulted in the birth of Dardanus, the founder of the royal house of Troy (see ZEUS); (3) is an Oceanid who married Thaumas and became the mother of Iris, goddess of the rainbow, and of the Harpies (see SEA GODS).

ELEUSINIAN (ĕl′oo·sĭn′ĭ·ȧn) **FESTIVALS** and **MYSTERIES** were celebrated at Eleusis in February and September in honor of Demeter and Persephone. See EARTH GODDESSES.

ELEUSIS (ĕ·loo′sĭs) is a town in Attica where Demeter, searching for her daughter Persephone, was kindly entertained, and where the Eleusinian Festivals and Mysteries were established in honor of Demeter and Persephone. See EARTH GODDESSES.

ELPENOR (ĕl·pē′nôr) was a follower of ODYSSEUS.

ELYSIAN (ĕ·lĭzh′ȧn) **FIELDS** are the paradise in HADES.

ELYSIUM (ĕ·lĭzh′ûm) is the paradise in HADES.

ENCELADUS (ĕn·sĕi′ȧ·dŭs) was one of the GIANTS.

ENDYMION (ĕn·dĭm′ĭ·ŏn) is the shepherd who is visited each night in his immortal sleep by ARTEMIS.

ENNA (ĕn′à) is the vale in Sicily where Persephone was gathering flowers when she was kidnaped by Hades. See EARTH GODDESSES.

ENYO (ê·nī′ō) is the goddess of battle. See ARES.

EOS (ē′ŏs), or **Aurora**, or **Mater Matuta**, each morning opens the eastern gate of heaven for the chariot of the sun. "Morn," says Milton *(Paradise Lost, 6. 2–4)*,

> Wak't by the circling Hours, with rosie hand
> Unbarr'd the gates of Light.

Countless English poets have echoed Homer in describing the goddess of the dawn as rosy fingered and saffron robed. Many of these references are mere formal *periphrases,* but sometimes they express the deep joy men feel at the coming of day, as when Herrick happily says *(Corinna's Going A-Maying, 3–4),*

> See how *Aurora* throwes her faire
> Fresh-quilted colours through the air!

The Greek Eos is a daughter of Hyperion, and the sister of Helios and Selene, Titan deities of the sun and the moon. The Romans usually recognized Aurora as the dawn goddess, but sometimes they gave her office to Mater Matuta, who was also a goddess of sea travel. Matuta was identified with Leucothea, a minor Greek sea goddess, and Milton therefore once speaks of Leucothea as the goddess of the dawn *(Paradise Lost, 11. 135).*

According to classical myth, the dawn likes men as much as men like her. Her most famous love affair was with **Tithonus,** a son of King Laomedon of Troy. Eos persuaded Zeus to make Tithonus immortal, but she forgot to ask that he be given eternal youth. Tithonus, like the Sibyl of Cumae, grew old, then shriveled with age; finally there was nothing left of him but a voice. According to one version of the story, Eos transformed him into a grasshopper. This love affair is mentioned by many poets, as, for example, Spenser in *The Faerie Queen* (3. 3. 20):

> . . . faire *Aurora,* rising hastily,
> Doth by her blushing tell, that she did lye
> All night in old *Tithonus* frosen bed. . . .

But Tennyson provides the most extended and effective treatment of this myth in *Tithonus,* a dramatic monologue in which the aged mortal addresses the goddess:

> The woods decay, the woods decay and fall,
> The vapours weep their burthen to the ground,
> Man comes and tills the field and lies beneath,
> And after many a summer dies the swan.
> Me only cruel immortality
> Consumes: I wither slowly in thine arms. . . .

In the gentle elegiac mood established by these lines, Tithonus recalls his love for Eos and begs for death:

> Release me, and restore me to the ground;
> Thou seëst all things, thou wilt see my grave:
> Thou wilt renew thy beauty morn by morn;
> I earth in earth forget these empty courts,
> And thee returning on thy silver wheels.

Among others whom Eos loved and carried off to her palace in the east were **Cephalus** and Orion. Cephalus was married to **Procris,** a daughter of Erechtheus, and he remained true to her in spite of Eos' beauty. The goddess finally released him, but not before she had cast doubt on his wife's fidelity. With the help of Eos, he disguised himself and made love to Procris. She did not yield to him, but once she was so tempted that she did not object to his wooing. At once he revealed his identity and

147

accused her of unfaithfulness. Procris, to show her scorn of such jealousy, became a servant of Artemis and received from her a hound that never lost his quarry and a spear that never missed its mark. Cephalus begged her to take him back, and finally she did so and gave the unerring spear to him as a proof of her forgiveness. Soon, however, she became as jealous as he had been and followed him wherever he went. One day when he was hunting he saw in the underbrush what he thought was an animal, hurled his spear, and killed his wife. For Eos' affair with Orion see the article under his name.

Having many lovers, Eos also has many children. By Tithonus she was the mother of **Memnon** and Emathion. Memnon, king of Ethiopia, fought against the Greeks at Troy and was killed by Achilles. Eos in great sorrow carried his body back to Ethiopia, and the tears that she still weeps for him appear to men as dewdrops. Her grief is recalled perpetually at Thebes, in Egypt, where a statue of Memnon was erected: when dawn came and the sun's rays first touched the statue, it made a sound like the twanging of a harp string. In our day the statue stands but the sound of grief is no longer heard.

Eos was also the mistress either of the wind god Aeolus, or of the Titan Astraeus, by one of whom she became the mother of the winds and the stars. Her favorite son is **Phosphor**, the morning star, whom Shakespeare calls "Aurora's harbinger" (*Midsummer-Night's Dream*, 3. 2. 380). Milton in *Paradise Lost* (5. 6–7) alludes to the winds as the sons of Eos when he speaks of the sound

> Of leaves and fuming rills, *Aurora's* fan,
> Lightly dispers'd. . . .

EPAPHOS (ĕp′á·fŏs) was a son of Io and ZEUS.
EPHIALTES (ĕf′i·ăl′tēz) was one of the GIANTS.

EPIDAURUS (ĕp'ĭ·dô'rŭs) was a city-state of Greece famous for its temple of Asclepius. See APOLLO.

EPIGONI (ê·pĭg'ô·nī) were the sons of the Seven against THEBES.

EPIMETHEUS (ĕp'ĭ·mē'thŭs) was the brother of PROME-THEUS.

EPIRUS (ê·pī'rŭs) was a Grecian kingdom in which was located the city of Dodona, famous for its oracle of Zeus. See ORACLES.

ERATO (ĕr'å·tō) is the Muse of love poetry and marriage songs. See MUSES.

EREBUS (ĕr'ê·bŭs) is a name of HADES.

ERECHTHEUM (ĕr'ĕk·thē'ûm) was a temple in Athens sacred to ATHENE.

ERECHTHEUS (ê·rĕk'thŭs), who is usually identified with Erichthonius, was an early king of Athens. See ATHENE.

ERICHTHONIUS (ĕr'ĭk·thō'nĭ·ûs), who is usually identified with Erechtheus, was an early king of Athens. See ATHENE.

ERIDANUS (ê·rĭd'å·nûs) is the mysterious river into which Phaethon fell. See APOLLO.

ERINYES (ê·rĭn'ĭ·ēz) are the FURIES.

ERIPHYLE (ĕr'ĭ·fī'lē) was the wife of Amphiaraus, one of the Seven against THEBES.

ERIS (ē'rĭs) is the goddess of discord. See ARES.

EROS (īr'ŏs), or **Cupid**, or **Amor**, is the god and personification of love. According to one myth, he is one of the oldest of the gods, arising out of Chaos and helping to shape the world from that formless mass. In this origin he is thought of, as in Spenser's *Hymne in Honour of Love,* as the organizing and unifying power of love. According to another and widely accepted myth, however, he is the son of Aphrodite, the goddess of love and beauty, and Ares, the god of war. In either case, the relationship of Eros to the other gods and goddesses is a symbolic one in that he has the power to make any of them fall in love as he chooses. This power is well illustrated in the stories of Apollo and Daphne, of Aphrodite and Adonis, and of all the love affairs of Zeus.

Eros was commonly figured as a handsome young man. In Alexandrian times he degenerated into a fat little boy, although his power was undiminished. Equipped with a pair of golden wings, he could fly about at will, and with his bow and quiver of arrows he caused mortals and gods alike to fall uncontrollably in love. Sometimes he was pictured as blindfolded, to signalize the unexplainably random quality of some of the affairs that he caused. In one of his songs Sir Charles Sedley gives a reason for the troubles of lovers:

> Love still has something of the sea,
>> From whence his mother rose;
> No time his slaves from doubt can free,
>> Nor give their thoughts repose.
>
> They are becalmed in clearest days,
>> And in rough weather tossed;
> They wither under cold delays,
>> Or are in tempests lost.

Eros' close associates are usually his brother, **Anteros,** the god of mutual love; **Peitho,** the goddess of persuasion; **Himeros,** the god of desire; **Pothos,** the god of longing; and the Muses and Graces.

The best-known myth concerning Eros is his love affair with **Psyche,** the personification of the human soul. Psyche was a young woman of such great beauty that Aphrodite became jealous of her and sent Eros to make her fall in love with some base mortal. Eros, gazing on her beauty, accidentally wounded himself with his dart and fell in love with her himself. He carried her off to a hideaway to live with her, but he came to her only in the darkness of night. All would have been well had not Psyche's sisters, the traditional interfering relatives, stirred up her curiosity about her husband on the pretext that he might be some ugly beast. In the night Psyche arose and lit a lamp. While she was leaning over Eros, she spilled a drop of hot oil on him and woke him. He flew away and left her inconsolable, though he still loved her.

To regain Eros, Psyche wandered about until she came to the temple of Demeter, whose aid she sought. Demeter advised her to seek Aphrodite's forgiveness, but Aphrodite agreed to forgive her only if she would perform a series of difficult tasks. The first of these consisted in trying to separate a large heap of mixed grains into types, an assignment that Psyche accomplished with the help of ants sent by Eros. The second task required her to obtain a bit of fleece from each member of a large flock of sheep; but a river god aided her by suggesting that she gather the samples from the thorns along the river after the sheep had watered. Finally she was sent to Hades for a box of the ointment with which Persephone maintained her beauty. The queen of Hades gave her the desired box, but warned her not to look inside it. On the way back, Psyche was overcome by curiosity and opened the box, for which act she would inevitably have had to return to Hades had not Eros persuaded Zeus to rescue her. Zeus also made her immortal and permitted Eros to marry her. The daughter of this marriage was **Voluptas**, the goddess of pleasure. Spenser (*Faerie Queene*, 3. 6. 50) calls this child Pleasure and makes her a symbol of ideal love.

According to some mythologists, the story of Psyche represents the human soul as passing through three conditions: a prenatal state of blessedness, followed by life on earth in its difficulties and struggles, and afterwards by the return of the soul to beatitude. Psyche was so often portrayed as a butterfly, which shows a similar transition as it passes from the caterpillar stage to the beauty of the winged insect, that the word "psyche" came ultimately to mean "butterfly." The butterfly therefore is still a symbol of the soul.

The myths of Eros naturally appeal to poets, both for their romantic associations and for their symbolic value. Allusions to Eros and his power are without number in English poetry. The story of his love for Psyche has frequently been retold. In *The Faerie Queene* (3. 11. 29–30, 35) Spenser holds Eros responsible for all the love affairs of the gods described in the tapestries of the House of Busyrane the enchanter. John Lyly in *Cupid and My Campaspe Played at Cards for Kisses* gives a pleasant account of how Cupid came to be blind. The song explains that Campaspe, in what appears to have been an early instance of strip poker, won all of Cupid's accouterments and his eyes as well. Milton ends *Comus* (1004–1007) with an allusion to Eros, who

> Holds his dear *Psyche* sweet intranc't
> After her wandring labours long,
> Till free consent the gods among
> Make her his eternal Bride,

and Milton attributes to this marriage not one child but two, Youth and Joy. In *Endymion* (2. 535–544), that texture of so many classic myths, Keats gives a colorful description of Cupid:

> . . . Love's self, who stands superb to share
> The general gladness: awfully he stands;
> A sovereign quell is in his waving hands;
> No sight can bear the lightning of his bow;
> His quiver is mysterious, none can know
> What themselves think of it; from forth his eyes
> There darts strange light of varied hues and dies:

A scowl is sometimes on his brow, but who
Look upon it feel anon the blue
Of his fair eyes run liquid through their souls.

In his *Ode to Psyche* he describes Eros and Psyche in one
another's arms, and pledges to make for them and their love a
shrine in his imagination.

A famous statue of Eros stands in the center of Piccadilly
Circus, London.

ERYCINA (ĕr′ĭ·sī′nȧ) is a Roman surname for APHRODITE.

ERYMANTHIAN (ĕr′ĭ·măn′thĭ·ȧn) **BOAR** was captured by
HERACLES.

ERYX (ē′rĭks) is a mountain on the northwest coast of Sicily
where there was a famous shrine to APHRODITE.

ESQUILINE (ĕs′kwĭ·līn) is one of the seven hills of later ROME.

ETEOCLES (ê·tē′ȯ·klēz) and Polynices, sons of Oedipus, vied
for the kingdom of THEBES.

ETHIOPIANS (ē′thĭ·ō′pĭ·ȧnz) lived in the south beyond the
great river of Oceanus. They were burned black on the day that
Phaethon tried to drive the chariot of the sun. See APOLLO,
SEA GODS.

EUMAEUS (ū·mē′ûs) was the faithful swineherd of ODYSSEUS.

EUMENIDES (ū·měn′ĭ·dēz) is a name of the FURIES.

EUPHROSYNE (ū·frŏs′ĭ·nē) is one of the three GRACES.

EUROPA (ū·rō′pȧ) was one of the mistresses of ZEUS.

EURUS (ū′rûs) is the east wind. See WINDS.

EURYCLEIA (ū′rĭ·klē′yȧ) was the aged nurse of ODYSSEUS.

EURYDICE (ū·rĭd′ĭ·sē) was (1) the wife of ORPHEUS; (2) the
wife of Creon, king of THEBES.

EURYLOCHUS (ū·rĭl′ȯ·kûs) was a follower of ODYSSEUS.

EURYNOME (ū·rĭn′ȯ·mē), a great ruler, is one of the TITANS.

EURYSTHEUS (ū·rĭs′thūs) commanded the labors of HERA-
CLES.

EURYTION (ū·rĭ′tĭ·ŏn), the herdsman of Geryon's cattle, was killed by HERACLES.

EURYTUS (ū′rĭ·tûs), a renowned archer, was killed by Heracles for refusing to permit his daughter Iole to marry that hero. Iphitus, the son of Eurytus, gave his father's famous bow to Odysseus. See HERACLES, ODYSSEUS.

EUTERPE (ū·tẽr′pē) is the Muse of music. See MUSES.

EVADNE (ê·văd′nē) was the wife of Capaneus, one of the Seven against THEBES.

EVANDER (ê·văn′dẽr) was an ally of AENEAS.

F

FAGUTAL (fă′gū·tả̇l) was one of the seven hills of earliest ROME.

FATAE (fä′tē) are the three Fates. See FATE.

FATE. According to the Greeks and Romans, there is a fate that is stronger than the gods, and there are also three **Fates,** or **Moerae,** or **Parcae,** or **Fatae,** who are goddesses. Fate itself is not personified, but its power is manifest. It has dethroned two kings of the gods, Uranus and Cronus, and in time it may also dethrone Zeus. Shelley makes skillful use of the idea of the fall of Zeus in *Prometheus Unbound.*

The Moerae are the daughters of Zeus and Themis, the goddess of divine justice, and thus the Hours are their sisters. If it is possible to relate the Fates clearly to the universal fate, they are the part of fate that is known to the gods. They are thought of as presiding especially over birth and death, but every moment of human life is subject to their decree. Sometimes they appear to be old and sometimes young, but they are always grave faced and are dressed in long garments. **Clotho** carries the spindle, **Lachesis** a scroll or globe, and **Atropos** the shears. The first spins the thread of life, the second decides how long it shall be, and the third cuts it.

No mortal can escape the life allotted to him by the Fates, nor can any god compel them to alter their decrees. At the urging of Apollo, they agreed to let Admetus live beyond the day fixed for his death, but only on condition that someone else die for him (see ALCESTIS). The mother of Meleager was informed of her son's doom. When he was a week old, the Fates appeared to her and said that he would die as soon as a log then burning in the fire was consumed. She snatched the log from the hearth, quenched its flame, and hid it away, but this knowledge, which made her believe that her son was safe from death, later forced upon her a tragic choice that involved her death as well as her son's (see CALYDONIAN BOAR HUNT).

In addition to fate and the three Moerae, there is also **Tyche**, or **Fortuna**, the goddess of chance, whose symbol is a wheel that shows her fickleness. As long as belief in the gods was strong, Tyche was no more than a servant of the Fates; their eternal decrees were sometimes hidden behind her giddiness. When men lost their faith, however, Fortune became the ironic substitute for divine order, ruling by her whims all the mutable world beneath the moon.

The Furies and Nemesis, the goddesses of vengeance, are also associated with the Fates (see FURIES). The relation between the power of fate and these powers of vengeance depends on the notion that the gods punish sin and that this punishment is part of a sinner's destiny. The concept involves a profound irony, for if a man is fated to do evil, how can he be considered responsible for his sin? The Greeks and Romans found no satisfactory solution for this problem of predestination and free will, and for Christians it is still a major paradox.

English literature has made much use of what Launcelot Gobbo in *The Merchant of Venice* (2. 2. 65–67) calls the "Fates and Destinies and such odd sayings, the Sisters Three and such branches of learning." One of the commonest images is that of the thread of human life. In Elizabethan times Thomas Sackville in his *Induction* (300–301) writes of Old Age who feared the time when the Fates would have untwined

> His vital thread and ended with their knife
> The fleeting course of fast declining life,

and Pistol pleads in *Henry V* (3. 6. 49–50):

> . . . let not Bardolph's vital thread be cut
> With edge of penny cord and vile reproach.

In the seventeenth century George Herbert, in a letter to his mother, changes the pagan symbol into a thoroughly Christian one. "I have alwaies observ'd the thred of Life to be like other threds . . . , full of snarles and incumbrances: Happy is he, whose bottom [skein] is wound up and laid ready for work in the New *Jerusalem*." And John Donne, using the thread and the shore of the Styx in *A Hymne to God the Father*, characteristically alters the image to rob fate of its power and to make him responsible for his actions:

> I have a sinne of feare, that when I have spunne
> My last thred, I shall perish on the shore.

In our own time Henry C. Calhoun, a character created by Edgar Lee Masters, ruminates bitterly on his father, who demanded that his son avenge him on Spoon River:

. . . what did he do but send me along
The path that leads to the grove of the Furies?
I followed the path and I tell you this:
On the way to the grove you'll pass the Fates,
Shadow-eyed, bent over their weaving.
Stop for a moment, and if you see
The thread of revenge leap out of the shuttle
Then quickly snatch from Atropos
The shears and cut it, lest your sons,
And the children of them and their children
Wear the envenomed robe.[1]

(For the envenomed robe see HERACLES).

The three witches in *Macbeth* owe something to the Moerae but more to the notions of witchcraft in Shakespeare's time. Like the Fates, the witches have power to foretell the future, and Macbeth calls them "the weird sisters" ("weird" is the Anglo-Saxon word for "fate"). There is no suggestion, however, that the witches control the future, as the Fates do. The Fates, moreover, are instruments of divine order, whereas the witches, with their charms and apparitions, are doers of evil and servants of evil. They offer Macbeth incomplete and riddling prophecies that are designed to lead him on to further crimes and eventually to his downfall.

In contrast to these "secret, black, and midnight hags," the Parcae of Ben Jonson's *Epitaph on Solomon Pavy* are absent-minded but tenderhearted creatures. Solomon, a thirteen-year-old actor in one of the children's companies, had played the parts of old men so well

As, sooth, the Parcae thought him one,
He played so truly.

[1] From "Henry C. Calhoun," by Edgar Lee Masters, in his *Spoon River Anthology*. Copyright, 1915, by The Macmillan Company. Reprinted with the permission of the estate of Edgar Lee Masters.

They therefore cut his thread. As soon as they discovered their mistake, they tried to restore him to life, but heaven resolved to keep him because he was too good for earth.

In the nineteenth century neither Byron nor Browning found much kindness in the Fates. The three Destinies in *Manfred* are servants of Arimanes, the devil. Byron modeled them on the witches in *Macbeth* but tried to give them more dignity, with the unfortunate result that they are much less terrifying than he intended them to be. In *Apollo and the Fates* Browning makes the three goddesses express the idea that life is blank and evil except when touched by the illusion of Apollo's sunshine. Browning, disguised as Apollo, argues that life is good. Not with his argument but with a gift of wine, he persuades the Fates to agree with him that man's struggle is "no defeat but a triumph!" An explosion from the earth's center ends the discussion, but the goddesses admit that they have spoken a truth that Apollo can interpret.

Since western culture has fostered a belief in free will, it is not surprising that in English literature the Moerae usually are regarded either as servants of evil or as powers at best unsympathetic to man and at worst inimical to him. As Atropos says in Browning's poem:

> My shears cut asunder: each snap shrieks "One more
> Mortal makes sport for us Moirai who dangled
> The puppet grotesquely till earth's solid floor
> Proved film he fell through, lost in Nought as before."

Fate makes free will impossible and reduces man to an ignorant but obedient actor doing the deeds and saying the words prepared for him by necessity. This view of human life is expressed, for example, in *Lear* (4. 1. 36–37) by Gloucester:

> As flies to wanton boys are we to th' gods.
> They kill us for their sport.

The same attitude is found in every one of Thomas Hardy's novels and in John O'Hara's *Appointment in Samarra*. Most western writers, however, have refused to accept this idea.

A related notion, but one that does not necessarily destroy the possibility of free will, is that the punishment for the sin of a father is visited not only on him but on his children and his children's children until the sin is expiated. (See Masters' poem quoted earlier.) This belief is a powerful force in both classical and Christian cultures. It is the cause of the terrible sufferings of the Greek house of Atreus, and its simplest Christian statement is

> In Adam's fall
> We sinned all.

Shakespeare in *Romeo and Juliet* uses this notion in an extreme form. The Prologue explains that the tragedy is the result of the feud between the Montagues and the Capulets and also the means of bringing the two families together. Romeo and Juliet have no opportunity to exercise free will. They are "star-cross'd lovers," the Prologue says, and throughout the play there are references to the "yoke of inauspicious stars" that dooms them to unhappiness and violent death.

The stars are Shakespeare's symbol for fate because the Elizabethans inherited from the late classical era and the Middle Ages a belief that the stars strongly influenced human life. This notion was systematized into the pseudo science of astrology, which still has its devotees today. In Christian times the powers of the goddess Fortune and the stars were reconciled with the power of God. God's providence was above all. However, when Adam and Eve sinned, the universe was wrenched from its perfect order, and thereafter the planets had evil influences on human life. Beneath the lowest heavenly body, the mutable moon, the evil and inexplicable earth was ruled by Fortune. Because of his sins, man must suffer on earth the cruel whimsicalities of Fortune and the malignancy of the stars. Theologians encouraged this view. They urged men to withdraw as much as possible from worldly life and to fix their minds on heaven.

This kind of thinking strongly colored the minds even of men like Chaucer who found joy and beauty in life on earth. Chaucer's Monk, for example, tells a series of medieval tragedies, each designed to show that Fortune capriciously raises men to great prosperity and then hurls them down again; and the influence of the stars on the rival lovers is carefully worked out in *The Knight's Tale.*

The stars and **Fortune's Wheel** are common images in medieval and Renaissance literature, even though in Elizabethan times men were rejecting the notion that these influences ruled their lives on earth, and asserting that they themselves were responsible for what happened to them. Cassius, for example, says in *Julius Caesar* (1. 2. 140–141):

> The fault, dear Brutus, is not in our stars,
> But in ourselves, that we are underlings,

and Edgar in *Lear* (1. 2. 128–137) sneers at Gloucester's belief in fate:

> This is the excellent foppery of the world, that, when we
> are sick in fortune, often the surfeit of our own behaviour,
> we make guilty of our disasters the sun, the moon, and
> the stars; as if we were villains on necessity; fools by
> heavenly compulsion; knaves, thieves, and treachers by
> spherical predominance; drunkards, liars, and adulterers
> by an enforc'd obedience of planetary influence; and
> all that we are evil in, by a divine thrusting on.

Yet Fortune and the stars continued to be important not only because they were traditional but also because most men were keenly aware of a stream of circumstance that sometimes brought them good luck or bad luck without reference to their intentions or their efforts.

The mournful Alcyon in Spenser's *Daphnaida* (498–502) offers the customary warning:

> And ye fond men, or fortunes wheele that ride,
> Or in ought vnder heauen repose assurance,
> Be it riches, beautie, or honours pride:
> Be sure that they shall haue no long endurance,
> But ere ye be aware will flit away.

Nearly all the great ones that ebbed and flowed by the moon spoke their complaint to Fortune at the moment of their downfall. Mortimer in Marlowe's *Edward II* (5. 6. 58–60) uses the common image:

> Base Fortune, now I see that in thy wheel
> There is a point, to which when men aspire,
> They tumble headlong down,

but Richard II in Shakespeare's play of that name (4. 1. 184–189) invents a new image to convey the old idea. As he is forced to offer the usurping Bolingbroke the crown, he says:

> Now is this golden crown like a deep well
> That owes two buckets, filling one another,
> The emptier ever dancing in the air,
> The other down, unseen, and full of water.
> That bucket down and full of tears am I,
> Drinking my griefs whilst you mount up on high.

Only Marlowe's Tamburlaine continues to triumph in spite of his boast (1. 2. 174–175):

> I hold the Fates bound fast in iron chains,
> And with my hand turn Fortune's wheel about.

Yet there is irony in this arrogance, although Tamburlaine is not aware of it. As Marlowe seems to conceive of the situation, Tamburlaine's successes have been decreed by the fate that is stronger than the gods.

Since the Renaissance, Fortune has been represented in various ways. Tennyson, for example, produces in *Enid* a typically Victorian song about the goddess:

> Turn, Fortune, turn thy wheel with smile or frown;
> With that wild wheel we go not up or down;
> Our hoard is little, but our hearts are great.
> Smile and we smile, the lords of many lands;
> Frown and we smile, the lords of our own hands;
> For man is man and master of his fate.

In our own time Phelps Putnam has written a *Hymn to Chance,* whom he celebrates as the masculine creative force of the universe ("We have insulted you as Lady Luck"[2]), and W. H. Auden in his poem *In War Time* has given a witty turn to the traditional image:

> Abruptly mounting her ramshackle wheel,
> Fortune has pedalled furiously away. . . .[3]

FAUNA (fõ′na), or Bona Dea, a Roman fertility goddess, is the daughter or wife of Faunus, the Roman PAN.

FAUNS (fõnz), or **FAUNI** (fõ′nī), are wood gods, followers of PAN.

FAUNUS (fõ′nûs) is a Roman name for PAN.

FAUSTULUS (fõs′tyû·lûs), a shepherd, adopted Remus and Romulus, founder of ROME.

[2] From "Hymn to Chance," by Phelps Putnam, in his *The Five Seasons.* Copyright, 1927, 1931, by Charles Scribner's Sons. Reprinted with the permission of the publisher.

[3] From "In War Time," by W. H. Auden, in *The Collected Poetry of W. H. Auden.* Copyright, 1945, by W. H. Auden. Reprinted with the permission of the publisher, Random House, Inc.

FAVONIUS (fȧ·vō′nĭ·ûs) is the Roman name of Zephyrus, the west wind. See WINDS.

FLORA (flô′rȧ) is the Roman name of the goddess of spring, CHLORIS.

FORTUNA (fôr·tū′nȧ) is the Roman name of Tyche, the goddess of fortune. See FATE.

FORTUNE'S WHEEL. See FATE.

FURIAE (fū′rĭ·ē) are the Roman FURIES.

FURIES. From the blood of Uranus, castrated by his son Cronus, sprang the three **Erinyes,** the goddesses of vengeance, whom the Romans called the **Furiae** and the **Dirae.** Their names are **Alecto, Tisiphone,** and **Megaera,** and (as Orestes sees them) they are dressed in black, with snakes for hair, and their eyes weep blood. Cleopatra (*Antony and Cleopatra,* 2. 5. 40) says to a messenger who she fears is bringing her bad news of Antony, "Thou shouldst come like a Fury crown'd with snakes." On earth the Furies implacably pursue anyone guilty of a crime against the old law, and in Hades they continue the sinner's punishment. They are the agents of a narrow justice completely lacking in mercy, and they represent the agonies of remorse. Yet after they had tormented Orestes for many years, he was judged by Athene and her court to be purified through suffering, and Athene even succeeded in persuading the Furies to accept the new law of mercy. Thereafter they were known as the **Eumenides,** the kind ones (see ATREUS). This is one story. It is also said that the Furies are called the Eumenides in the vain hope of placating them.

In English literature they are usually seen where Virgil put them, in hell tormenting the guilty. In *Richard III* (1. 4. 55–63) they seize the Duke of Clarence in his dream of damnation, and in *Paradise Lost* (2. 596) they are the jailors of the damned. In *Lycidas* (75) Milton calls Atropos, the Fate who cuts the threads of men's lives, "the blind *Fury*." The Fates and the Furies are often linked in classical mythology, and here Milton probably wanted to join the images of terrible violence and doom. W. B. Yeats in *To Dorothy Wellesley* represents the Furies in their greatest dignity:

> What climbs the stair?
> Nothing that common women ponder on
> If you are worth my hope! Neither Content
> Nor satisfied Conscience, but that great family
> Some ancient famous authors misrepresent,
> The Proud Furies each with her torch on high.[4]

A figure closely associated with the Furies is **Nemesis,** the personification of the righteous anger of the gods. This terrible creature punishes mortals who are arrogant because they have been lucky, especially holders of great place and scorners of love. Thus Nemesis pursues Agamemnon for his pride in victory and Narcissus for his contemptuous rejection of the love of Echo. In the mock-heroic introduction to *Muiopotmos* (2), Spenser says that the deadly quarrel he celebrates was stirred up by wrathful Nemesis. An untraditional Nemesis appears in Byron's *Manfred* (2. 3), where she describes her day's work as a servant of Arimanes, the devil:

> I was detain'd repairing shatter'd thrones,
> Marrying fools, restoring dynasties,
> Avenging men upon their enemies,
> And making them repent their own revenge;
> Goading the wise to madness; from the dull
> Shaping out oracles to rule the world
> Afresh, for they were waxing out of date,
> And mortals dared to ponder for themselves.

[4] From "To Dorothy Wellesley," by W. B. Yeats, in his *Last Poems and Plays.* Copyright, 1940, by Georgie Yeats. Reprinted with the permission of The Macmillan Company.

G

GAEA (jē′à), or Ge, is the first of the EARTH GODDESSES.
GALATEA (găl′à·tē′à), the Nereid sister of Thetis and Amphitrite, fell in love with a youth named **Acis**. For this reason,
and doubtless for others, she refused the advances of **Polyphemus**
the Cyclops, the terrible and crude one-eyed son of Poseidon (for
his other adventures, see ODYSSEUS). Polyphemus nevertheless
continued to yearn for her. He even tried to make himself more
presentable by combing his hair and trimming his beard, and
he sang long laments to her by the seashore; but Galatea continued to prefer Acis.

One day Polyphemus, in the melancholy of unrequited love,
came suddenly on Galatea and Acis enjoying each other's attentions in the covert of a rock. He was overcome with jealous rage.
Galatea fled into the sea, where she was safe; but Acis could not
escape Polyphemus' violence. Running along the shore and
calling for refuge in the sea, he was crushed by a huge rock
which Polyphemus hurled at him. According to Ovid, his blood
gushed purple at first from under the rock, but gradually it
turned into water that flowed down into the sea. Thus was Acis
finally granted the safety of the sea with Galatea, and the
fountain on the slopes of Mount Aetna in Sicily that originated in
this event still bears Acis' name.

Theocritus, the Sicilian poet, in his *Idylls* (11) and Ovid in his
Metamorphoses (13) give good accounts of this myth, and both
dwell on the love laments of Polyphemus. English poets have
generally followed their conception of the story. Thomas Lodge

in *Rosalind* provides for his character Montanus a lyric that
describes

> The lovesick Polypheme that could not see,
> Who on the barren shore,
> His fortunes doth deplore,
> And melteth all in moan
> For Galatea gone.

Montanus, a shepherd in love with a maid, wonders whether she
will reject him as Galatea rejected Polyphemus. John Gay made
of the myth a light opera, *Acis and Galatea,* in which Acis'
unfortunate demise is surrounded with many songs and the whole
matter is carried off in the gayest possible fashion. And the
nineteenth-century poet Austin Dobson found for the myth a
sentimental parallel in *A Tale of Polypheme,* in which he recounts the vain love of a one-eyed blacksmith hermit for a young
girl who came to his neighborhood as a tourist. The parallel
ends in a much less intense fashion than its original and is in
fact not much of a parallel nor much of a poem.

GANYMEDES (găn'ĭ·mēd'ēz) was the paramour and cupbearer of
ZEUS.

GATE OF HORN is the gate through which true dreams come
to men from the cave of Hypnos, god of sleep. See HADES.

GATE OF IVORY is the gate through which deceitful dreams
come to men from the cave of Hypnos, god of sleep. See HADES.

GATES, or Pillars, **OF HERACLES** are two mountains which
face each other across the strait where the Mediterranean Sea
meets the great river of Oceanus, now called the Atlantic Ocean.
These mountains, one of which is now called the Rock of
Gibraltar, were raised by HERACLES.

GE (jē), or Gaea, is the first of the EARTH GODDESSES.

GEMINI (jĕm'ĭ·nī), the Twins, is a constellation and a sign
of the ZODIAC.

GENIUS (jēn′yûs) is the Roman name of the guardian spirit of a person, society, or place. See HESTIA.

GERYON (jē′rĭ·ŏn), a triple man of great strength, owned a herd of cattle for which he was killed by HERACLES.

GIANTS were huge creatures, usually the sons of Titans or Olympian gods. The best-known group of Giants sprang up from the blood of the mutilated Uranus as it mingled with Gaea, the earth, who thus became their mother. These Giants had snakes for legs. Gaea, by means of a miraculous herb, made them invulnerable against the weapons of the gods, but she neglected to protect them similarly against the weapons of mortals. Led by **Porphyrion,** they established themselves on the peninsula of Pallene, near Mount Olympus, and declared war on the gods. Others in the group included **Alcyoneus,** the greatest fighter of them all, and **Pallas** (not Athene), **Enceladus, Polybotes, Ephialtes, Rhoetus,** and **Clytius.**

In the war that followed, the gods seemed likely to be defeated until Athene, remembering that the Giants were not proof against wounds caused by human weapons, brought Heracles into the fray. The gods took the precaution of destroying the magic herb that had given invulnerability to the Giants, and Zeus extinguished the lights of heaven, the sun and moon. Then Heracles slew Alcyoneus with his arrows, an event that seems to have broken the charm, for Athene was then able to slay Pallas and Enceladus, and Poseidon to kill Polybotes. The rest were forced to surrender.

A similar myth concerns Ephialtes and **Otus,** another Giant, who made a kind of private attack on the gods. These two were the sons of the god Poseidon or of his son **Aloeus,** whose name means "the planter," and their career illustrates the power of agriculture to produce strength. Ephialtes and Otus were born small and weak; but, nourished by the grain of the fields, they

167

grew rapidly to gigantic size and strength. As farmers, they soon saw that war and agriculture are enemies; so they captured Ares, the god of war, and imprisoned him in a large brass jar, where he might still be had Hermes not released him after thirteen months.

The brothers now were so confident of their strength that they decided to attack the gods en masse. In order to reach the abode of the immortals, they first put Mount **Ossa** on top of Mount Olympus, and then Mount **Pelion** on top of Mount Ossa, but as they worked, Apollo killed them with his arrows. In his translation of the *Odyssey* (9. 387–388) Pope writes:

> Heav'd on Olympus tott'ring Ossa stood;
> On Ossa Pelion nods with all his wood.

"Piling Pelion on Ossa" still survives as a description of extraordinary activity, and this idea was in Shakespeare's mind when he caused Hamlet to say (*Hamlet,* 5. 1. 302–306), as he seeks to rival Laertes in a demonstration of his love for Ophelia,

> Be buried quick with her, and so will I.
> And if thou prate of mountains, let them throw
> Millions of acres on us, till our ground,
> Singeing his pate against the burning zone,
> Make Ossa like a wart!

Other well-known Giants were Antaeus, the son of Poseidon and Gaea, whose story is told under HERACLES; and Tityus, whose story is told under APOLLO.

GLAUCE (glō′kē) was another name for Creusa, the second wife of Jason. See ARGONAUTS.

GLAUCUS (glō′kŭs) (1) is one of the SEA GODS; (2) was the father of BELLEROPHON; (3) was a Trojan ally in the TROJAN WAR.

GOLDEN AGE was an age of innocence. See CRONUS.

GOLDEN BOUGH was the passport to Hades obtained by AENEAS.

GOLDEN FLEECE was sought by the ARGONAUTS.

GORDIAN (gôr′dĭ·ȧn) **KNOT** was tied by **Gordius,** the father of King Midas of Phrygia. Gordius was a plain man who came riding into Phrygia in a wagon with his wife and son at the very moment when the people of that land were puzzling over a message from an oracle which said that their king would come to them in a wagon. He thus became king. In gratitude he dedicated his wagon to the god of the oracle and tied it in its dedicated place with an intricate and subtle knot that provided John Milton with a metaphor in *Paradise Lost* (4. 347–350). Describing the blissful condition of Adam and Eve in Eden before the Fall of Man, Milton writes of the guileful serpent:

> . . . close the Serpent sly
> Insinuating, wove with Gordian twine
> His breaded train, and of his fateful guile
> Gave proof unheeded.

After Gordius had tied his knot, the legend grew up that whoever could untie it would rule over all of Asia. For a long time no one succeeded, though many tried. Then Alexander the Great, passing by on his road of conquest, tried his hand at the project. When he also was unsuccessful, with imperial impatience he drew his sword and cut the knot in two. Since he later became ruler of a great deal of Asia, he appeared to have fulfilled the legend, and his act has become proverbial. "Cutting the Gordian knot" is still today the figure for solving a problem by direct action.

GORDIUS (gôr′dĭ·ûs) tied the GORDIAN KNOT.

GORGONS (gôr′gŏnz) are monsters whose glance turns men to stone. See SEA GODS.

GRACES. The three **Charites,** or Graces, give inward happiness and outward charm to those whom they favor. Although they almost always appear together, they are thought of as representing different qualities of grace: **Euphrosyne** mirth (Milton invokes her in *L'Allegro*), **Aglaia** splendor, and **Thalia** bloom. They are the handmaidens of Aphrodite; the companions of the Muses, with whom they often dance to the music of Apollo's lyre; and the close associates of all the other powers who make life delightful.

In English literature the Graces frequently appear dancing with the Hours in fields of eternal beauty. Milton's description in *Comus* (984–991) is typical. To the Elizabethans the Graces symbolized the ideal of courtesy, which demanded the perfect fusion of good intentions and good manners. As Spenser says in *The Faerie Queene* (6. 10. 23):

> These three on men all gracious gifts bestow,
> Which decke the body or adorne the mynde,
> To make them louely or well fauoured show,
> As comely carriage, entertainment kynde,
> Sweete semblaunt, friendly offices that bynde,
> And all the complements of curtesie:
> They teach vs, how to each degree and kynde
> We should our selues demeane, to low, to hie;
> To friends, to foes; which skill men call ciuility.

The hopeless struggle of the dull for the patronage of these ladies is described by John Donne in *The True Character of a Dunce:* ". . . the Muses and the Graces are his hard Mistresses, though he daily invocate them, though he sacrifice *Hecatombs,* they still look asquint."

GRAEAE (grē′ē) are three hags of the ocean. See PERSEUS, SEA GODS.

GRIFFINS (grĭf′ĭnz) were monsters half-eagle and half-lion.

GYGES (jī′jēz) was a Hecatoncheire. See TITANS.

HADES (hā′dēz) is the name both of the underworld and of its ruler. The Greeks also called the god **Aides, Aidoneus,** and **Pluton,** or **Pluto,** which means "giver of wealth" and refers to the god's ownership of the precious metals under the earth; and the Romans usually called him Pluto, **Dis** (which means "rich"), and **Orcus,** which is also a name of his kingdom. Frequently confused with Pluto was **Plutus,** a figure that in ancient times symbolized agricultural wealth but later came to represent the wealth of money. In English literature this god of wealth has been replaced by Mammon, whose name comes from a Syriac word for riches and who appears in the New Testament as the personification of wealth and worldliness. The shrewd and avaricious Mammon has pled his case many times in English poetry, most brilliantly in Spenser's *Faerie Queene* (2. 7) and Milton's *Paradise Lost* (1. 678–692; 2. 228–298).

After the Titans were defeated, the three male Olympians, Hades, Poseidon, and Zeus, divided the universe by lot, and the underworld where men's souls go after death became the kingdom of Hades. The attributes of this dark god are the scepter, the horn of plenty, and the helmet that makes its wearer invisible (the name Hades means "unseen"). Since Hades rules the land of death, men seldom tell stories about him and even fear to speak his name. He is not, however, the god of death (who is Thanatos), and he is not evil. Hades has none of the qualities of the Christian Satan. He is a stern but just god who, according to the ancients who believed in judgment after death, acts through his chosen judges to reward the good and punish the wicked. This terrible but kingly figure looks like Jove, says the Roman Seneca, but like Jove when he thunders.

Except for his deeds in the war against the Titans, Hades' only notable action above ground was to acquire a queen. **Persephone,** or **Cora,** or **Proserpina,** or **Libera,** is the daughter of the earth goddess Demeter. One day Hades saw this lovely girl gathering flowers with her attendants in the vale of Enna. He at once fell in love with her, pulled her into his chariot, and disappeared with her beneath the ground. When Demeter demanded that her daughter be returned, Zeus agreed to order Hades to release her on condition that she had eaten nothing while in the under-world. Before he let her go, however, Hades persuaded her to eat four pomegranate seeds, and thereafter she was destined to spend the four winter months in the underworld and the months of spring, summer, and autumn on earth. (For further details of this fertility myth see Persephone under EARTH GODDESSES.)

Persephone, ruling in Hades, looks forward to the release of springtime. To many English poets she is, as Spenser describes her (*Ruines of Time,* 373), "sad *Proserpina.*" From a hint in the Roman poet Claudian, Spenser develops the beautiful but baleful "*Gardin* of *Proserpina*" (*Faerie Queene,* 2. 7. 51–56), garnished with herbs and fruits

> . . . direfull deadly blacke, both leafe and bloom,
> Fit to adorne the dead, and decke the drery toombe,

containing the tree of the golden apples of the Hesperides but surrounded by the black waters of Cocytus, one of the rivers of Hades, in which damned souls were tormented for their crimes on earth. The list of deadly herbs in Spenser may have suggested to Keats the reference in *Ode on Melancholy* to "nightshade, ruby grape of Proserpine."

Swinburne's version of *The Garden of Proserpine* (49–52) lacks the deceptive glamour of Spenser's garden. Here are the plants of death, but here is no mocking contrast between the glittering apples of the Hesperides and the damned souls in the black river. Swinburne in his neopaganism represents Proserpina simply as the giver of endless sleep:

> Pale, beyond porch and portal,
>   Crowned with calm leaves, she stands
> Who gathers all things mortal
>   With cold immortal hands. . . .

His *Hymn to Proserpine* (103–104, 109–110) reaffirms the theme:

> Thou art more than the Gods who number the days of
>   our temporal breath;
> For these give labor and slumber; but thou, Proserpina,
>   death.
>
>   .   .   .   .   .   .
>
> So long I endure, no longer; and laugh not again,
>   neither weep.
> For there is no God found stronger than death; and
>   death is a sleep.

Ernest Dowson, also, in *Villanelle of Acheron,* looks forward to "the sleep of immortality":

> Life, of thy gifts I will have none,
>   My queen is that Persephone,
> By the pale marge of Acheron,
>   Beyond the scope of any sun.[1]

In English poetry, however, these pale romantic echoes of one

---

[1] From "Villanelle of Acheron," by Ernest Dowson, in *Poems* (New York: Dodd, Mead & Company, 1929). Reprinted with the permission of the publisher.

pagan view of Persephone are much less frequent than references to her as the terrible queen of the hell of damned souls. Yet in Thomas Campion's song, *Hark, All You Ladies,* she is imagined as the charming ruler of fairyland:

> Hark, all you ladies that do sleep!
>   The fairy queen Proserpina
> Bids you awake, and pity them that weep.
>   You may do in the dark
>   What day doth forbid.
>   Fear not the dogs that bark;
>   Night will have all hid.
>
> But if you let your lovers moan,
>   The fairy queen Proserpina
> Will send abroad her fairies everyone,
>   That shall pinch black and blue
>   Your white hands and fair arms,
>   That did not kindly rue
>   Your paramours' harms.

No one escapes after death from the vast shadowy region ruled by Hades and Persephone, but six living people—one girl and five heroes—went to the underworld on various errands and returned to earth. These were Psyche, Odysseus, Orpheus, Theseus, Heracles, and Aeneas (for their stories see Psyche under EROS and the articles under the heroes' names). From their adventures come descriptions, sometimes incomplete and contradictory, of the geography of Hades, which is also called **Erebus,** Tartarus, and Orcus.

There are various entrances to Hades, one far in the unknown west and several in Greece and Italy. When Odysseus visited the underworld, he sailed across the great river of Ocean and past the dark land of the Cimmerians until he found the entrance; but Aeneas, guided by the Sybil of Cumae, descended to

Hades in the volcanic region of Vesuvius, through the cave of **Avernus** beside the foul-smelling lake of that name. This cave has become so well known as an entrance to the underworld that its name is sometimes given to Hades itself. Ezra Pound, for example, in *Prayer for His Lady's Life,* a poem based on the Roman poet Propertius, pleads with Pluto and Persephone:

> So many thousand beauties are gone down to Avernus,
> Ye might let one remain above with us.[2]

When a man died, his spirit was claimed by Thanatos, the god of death (who is discussed later on); and Hermes, the messenger of Zeus, escorted the spirit to the underworld. According to Virgil in the *Aeneid,* the dark neutral region between earth and Hades is filled with terrible monsters that once preyed on man: Hydras and Chimaeras, and also grim figures representing human troubles: disease, fear, grief, hunger, poverty, and old age. Hades itself is bounded by four rivers and contains at least one other stream. These are **Styx,** the abhorrent river; **Acheron,** the river of woe; **Cocytus,** the river of lamentation; **Phlegethon,** or **Pyriphlegethon,** the river of fire; and Lethe, the river of forgetfulness. Milton describes them in *Paradise Lost* (2. 577–584):

> Abhorred *Styx* the flood of deadly hate,
> Sad *Acheron* of sorrow, black and deep;
> *Cocytus,* nam'd of lamentation loud
> Heard on the ruful stream; fierce *Phlegeton*
> Whose waves of torrent fire inflame with rage.
> Farr off from these a slow and silent stream,
> *Lethe* the River of Oblivion roules
> Her watrie Labyrinth. . . .

The Styx—from which comes our adjective "stygian"—was the

---

[2] From "Prayer for His Lady's Life," by Ezra Pound, in his *Personae.* Reprinted with the permission of the publishers, New Directions.

name by which the gods swore their most binding oaths. Zeus granted the river this honor because, when the Olympians fought the Titans, the Styx sent her children to support the Olympians. The Nymph Thetis dipped her infant son Achilles in the Styx to make him invulnerable to weapons, but she held him by one heel and he finally received his death wound there (see **TROJAN WAR**). Thinking of the remorse from which all human beings suffer, Byron comments ironically in *Don Juan* (4. 4):

> Thetis baptized her mortal son in Styx;
> A mortal mother would on Lethe fix.

The Lethe is discussed later in this article.

A spirit of the dead gained entrance to Hades by being ferried across the river Styx or Acheron by an ill-tempered old creature named **Charon.** If the spirit's body had not been given proper burial, or if he had not been provided with an obolus, or penny, to pay his fare, Charon refused to take him, and he must wait a hundred years before he was permitted to enter. The second epigraph of T. S. Eliot's *The Hollow Men*—"A penny for the Old Guy"—refers to Guy Fawkes, whose straw-stuffed effigy is hung each year in England in celebration of Guy Fawkes Day, but it also refers to Hades' crusty boatman and his fare. By Acheron, says Spenser (*Faerie Queene*, 1. 5. 33), "many soules sit wailing woefully"; these have not come properly prepared for admission to the underworld. Walter Savage Landor writes of the death of the beautiful but cruel Dirce (for whose life see **THEBES**):

> Stand close around, ye Stygian set,
> With Dirce in one boat conveyed,
> Or Charon, seeing, may forget
> That he is old, and she a shade.

On the other side of the river the spirit of the dead encountered Cerberus, a three-headed dog with a mane and tail of snakes. Spenser describes the beast in *The Faerie Queen* (1. 5. 34):

> Before the threshold dreadfull *Cerberus*
> His three deformed heads did lay along,
> Curled with a thousand adders venemous,
> And lilled forth his bloudie flaming tong.

In Sheridan's comedy *The Rivals* (4. 2. 296–297) Mrs. Malaprop demands of Captain Absolute, who she knows has been masquerading as Ensign Beverley, "You are not like Cerberus, *three* gentleman at once, are you?" This watchdog, a son of Typhon and Echidna, is supposed to allow only the spirits of the dead to enter and none to leave. There have been some notable exceptions, however: Psyche and the Sybil of Cumae, Aeneas' guide, appeased Cerberus with cakes; Orpheus charmed him with music; and Heracles, having received permission from Hades to capture the dog if he did so without using weapons, seized Cerberus in his hands and carried him up to earth but later returned him to his place.

Beyond the river stretch the shadowy plains of **asphodel,** the pale flower of Hades. Sometimes this middle region is called Erebus, but the name is also applied to the entire underworld. In this dreary place, according to the belief of many Greeks and Romans, the spirits of the dead exist as vague shadows of their former selves. When Odysseus on his visit to Hades encountered the shade of the great hero Achilles, Achilles said, "I would rather be the basest slave on earth than a prince among the dead."

Not all the dead, however, suffer this dull eternity. Some who are highly favored by the gods are taken to the **Elysian Fields,** or **Elysium,** where they live in endless happiness. This paradise is sometimes imagined as the **Blessed Islands,** located outside of Hades and far to the west of the great river of Ocean. On the other hand, those who have greatly offended the gods are thrown into the abyss of **Tartarus,** which is as far below the rest of Hades as Hades is below the earth. Originally this great pit seems to have been merely a prison for troublesome creatures. When Uranus ruled the universe, he hurled a number of his children into Tartarus simply because they annoyed and frightened him; and when the Olympians finally defeated the Titans, they confined a number of these dangerous older gods in the abyss.

Although many ancients believed that all except the special favorites and special enemies of the gods must endure the vague miserable afterlife that Achilles' shade despises and that A. E. Housman imagines in *To an Athlete Dying Young* as the life of "the strengthless dead," many others—influenced probably by the Mysteries, especially those of Eleusis, and by the Orphic faith (see ORPHEUS, and Eleusinian Mysteries under EARTH GODDESSES)—believed in an afterlife of rewards and punishments. They conceived of the Elysian Fields, not as a place of privilege for those whom the gods happened to like, but as a paradise reserved for the virtuous; and of Tartarus, not as a convenient prison for those who annoyed the gods, but as a place of torment reserved for the wicked.

Since Hades himself rarely sits in judgment on the souls of the newly dead, this office is usually performed by the shades of three celebrated men: **Rhadamanthus, Minos,** and **Aeacus.** Rhadamanthus and Minos were both sons of Zeus and Europa. On earth Rhadamanthus had a rather shadowy career as a law giver, but in Hades he is well established as a judge. He is perhaps the only Greek whose real career began after death. Sometimes he or Cronus is represented as the ruler of the Elysian Fields. Minos was king of Crete. Because he was the mightiest ruler of his time, his name is associated with law and order even though his actions as related under DAEDALUS and THESEUS hardly offer a pattern for the just man to follow. Aeacus was the son of Zeus and Aegina and the grandfather of Achilles. He was made a judge in Hades because of his great piety.

In Tartarus the wicked suffer all the punishments that the Furies can devise (see FURIES), but the most ingenious torments are reserved for the most celebrated sinners. Spenser describes them in *The Faerie Queene* (1. 5. 35):

> There was *Ixion* turned on a wheele,
> For daring tempt the Queene of heauen to sin;
> And *Sisyphus* an huge round stone did reele
> Against an hill, ne might from labour lin;
> There thristie *Tantalus* hong by the chin;
> And *Tityus* fed a vulture on his maw;
> *Typhoeus* ioynts were stretched on a gin,
> *Theseus* condemned to endlesse slouth by law,
> And fifty sisters water in leake vessels draw.

Typhoeus, or Typhon, a monster who terrified the gods until Zeus thrust him into Tartarus, is not usually represented as enduring a special punishment—Spenser seems to have invented this detail—and Theseus, though for a long time bound to a rock for helping his friend Pirithous in an attempt to abduct Persephone, was finally released by the hero Heracles. But the others named in this stanza of Spenser's are the most famous sinners suffering their special tortures.

Ixion, who tried to make love to Zeus's wife Hera, is bound to a fiery wheel that turns forever; for further details see the article under his name. **Sisyphus,** a king of Corinth, saw Zeus in the form of an eagle carrying off Aegina; this affair, as was noted earlier, produced Aeacus, the third judge in Hades. When Aegina's father asked help in finding his daughter, Sisyphus revealed what he had seen. Thereafter Zeus was his enemy, and in Tartarus Sisyphus is compelled to try to roll a huge rock up a hill. John Dyer (*Epistle to a Famous Painter,* 58–61) describes his eternal frustration:

> Sisyphus, with toil and sweat,
> And muscles strain'd, striving to get
> Up a steep hill a ponderous stone,
> Which near the top recoils, and rolls impetuous down.

For the life of the wily Sisyphus see the article under his name. Tantalus is "hong by the chin" in the sense that he stands always in water up to his neck, but the water recedes whenever he tries to drink. Both his thirst and his hunger are unceasing. Close to his hands hang branches covered with ripe fruit, but whenever he tries to pick the fruit, the branches move out of his reach. Tantalus suffers this punishment because he killed his son Pelops and served his cooked flesh to the gods at a banquet. This terrible crime bred further crimes and caused his descendants for four generations to be cursed; for the details see **ATREUS.**

Tityus was a Giant who insulted the goddess Leto. Her children, Apollo and Artemis, killed him with their arrows, and in Tartarus he lies chained to the ground while two vultures eternally eat his liver and his liver is constantly renewed. The "fifty sisters" whom Spenser mentions are the **Danaids,** forty-nine of whom sinned at the command of their father. **Danaus and Aegyptus** were brothers; the first had fifty daughters and the second fifty sons. The brothers quarreled, and Danaus left Egypt for Argos, but his nephews followed to claim their cousins in marriage. This was according to Greek law and custom, which held that a girl who had no brothers was an encumbrance to the estate and should marry her next of kin. Danaus pretended to accept his nephews as sons-in-law, but secretly he ordered his daughters to kill their husbands on the wedding night. All but one, **Hypermnestra,** who married **Lynceus,** carried out their father's command. The forty-nine Danaids who murdered their husbands (Spenser was wrong to include Hypermnestra in the punishment) are condemned in Tartarus always to draw water in leaky vessels or to fetch water to fill a large jar that is so leaky that it always remains empty. Chaucer tells the story of Hypermnestra in *The Legend of Good Women* (2562–2723), but he leaves out her sisters and Lynceus' brothers, and makes her the daughter of Aegyptus and Lynceus the son of Danaus.

Far from the abyss of Tartarus the virtuous souls enjoy the eternal felicity of the Elysian Fields. Here, as Robert Herrick says (*The Apparition of His Mistresse Calling Him to Elizium,* 13), "in green meddowes sits eternall May," and all that may comfort and please the inhabitants has been provided. When Aeneas visited his father Anchises in Elysium, he saw nearby a large valley through which flowed the river **Lethe,** and many spirits of the dead wandered along its banks. Anchises explained that these were souls who were to live again on earth and that while they waited to be reborn they drank of the river and forgot their former existence. The river of forgetfulness is a symbol frequently used by English poets. "May this be wash'd in Lethe and forgotten?" asks the new King Henry in Shakespeare's *2 Henry IV* (5. 2. 72); and in *Julius Caesar* (3. 1. 205–206) the gushing of the murdered Caesar's blood is described as his own river of oblivion:

> . . . here thy hunters stand,
> Sign'd in thy spoil, and crimson'd in thy lethe.

John Keats twice uses Lethe to mean death of the senses in forgetfulness, once in the well-known opening lines of the *Ode to a Nightingale:*

> My heart aches and a drowsy numbness pains
> My sense, as though of hemlock I had drunk
> Or emptied some dull opiate to the drains
> One minute past, and Lethe-wards had sunk,

and once in the first line of the *Ode on Melancholy:*

> No, No! go not to Lethe. . . .

In our time, John Crowe Ransom in *Parting at Dawn* ironically advises two parting lovers

> . . . if no Lethe flows beneath your casement,
> And when ten years have not brought full effacement,
> Philosophy was wrong, and you may meet.[3]

At a remote place on the bank of the Lethe is the cave of the twin sons of Night, **Thanatos,** or **Mors,** the god of death, and **Hypnos,** or **Somnus,** the god of sleep. The Elizabethans were particularly fond of this symbolic relationship, and Samuel Daniel in Sonnet 51 of *Delia* is one of the many poets who put it into verse:

> Care-charmer Sleep, son of the sable Night,
> Brother to Death, in silent darkness born. . . .

As was mentioned earlier, it is the duty of Thanatos to claim the spirits of the newly dead. Once he was defeated by the hero Heracles, who fought with him for the spirit of Alcestis and restored her to life (see ALCESTIS), and once he was outwitted by Sisyphus (see SISYPHUS). When. Sarpedon, a son of Zeus,

[3] From "Parting at Dawn," by John Crowe Ransom, in his *Selected Poems.* Reprinted with the permission of the publisher, Alfred A. Knopf, Inc.

fell in the defense of Troy, Thanatos and Hypnos carried his body
back to his native Lycia for burial.

Hypnos is usually deep in sleep. "Flat on the ground and still
as any stone," he appears in Thomas Sackville's *Induction to the
Complaint of the Duke of Buckingham* (282, 288–294):

> The body's rest, the quiet of the heart,
> The travail's ease, the still night's fere was he,
> And of our life in earth the better part;
> Reaver of sight, and yet in whom we see
> Things oft that tide, and oft that never be;
> Without respect, esteeming equally
> King Croesus' pomp, and Irus' poverty.

Hypnos' gifts to men are rest and dreams. The gods of dreams
are his sons: **Morpheus,** who creates dreams of human beings;
Icelus, who creates dreams of birds and beasts; and **Phantastus,**
who creates dreams of inanimate objects. Morpheus is so well
known that he often takes his father's place. He is "the god of
slep" to Chaucer (*Book of the Duchess*, 137), as he is to many
other poets and to many less gifted mortals today who say that
when they sleep they are "in the arms of Murphy."

The cave of Hypnos and Thanatos has two gates, one of ivory
and one of horn; the dreams that come through the **Gate of
Ivory** are deceitful, but those that come through the **Gate of
Horn** are true. In Chaucer's *Book of the Duchess* (136–213)
Morpheus shows Alcyone in a true dream that her husband is
dead (for the rest of the story see CEYX), and in Spenser's
Faerie Queene (1. 1. 39–44) Morpheus sends a false dream to
delude the Red Cross Knight. The notion that true dreams issue
from the gate of horn and false dreams from the gate of ivory,
which is found first in Homer (*Odyssey*, 19), is used somewhat
cryptically by T. S. Eliot in *Sweeney among the Nightingales,*
where "Sweeney guards the hornèd gate." The image suggests not

only that Sweeney is an instinctive enemy of true dreams, but also that he has shrugged off any foreboding that he may have had of the violent death that awaits him.

HAEMON (hē′mŏn) killed himself for grief at the death of Antigone. See THEBES.

HALCYONE (hăl·sī′ŏ·nē), or Alcyone, was the wife of CEYX.

HAMADRYADS (hăm′a·drī′ădz) are tree NYMPHS.

HARMONIA (här·mō′nĭ·a) was the wife of Cadmus, founder of THEBES.

HARPIES are monsters, half-woman and half-bird. See SEA GODS, AENEAS, ARGONAUTS.

HEBE (hē′bē), a daughter of Zeus and Hera, is the goddess of youth, and Milton salutes her in this capacity in *L'Allegro* (26–29) when he asks for

> Jest and youthful Jollity,
> Quips and Cranks, and wanton Wiles,
> Nods, and Becks, and Wreathed Smiles,
> Such as hang on *Hebe's* cheek . . . .

She was also the cupbearer of the gods until that job was given to Ganymedes. When Endymion in Keats's poem of that name (4. 415–419) dreams of Olympus,

> . . . arch Hebe brings
> A full-brimmed goblet, dances lightly, sings
> And tantalizes long; at last he drinks
> And lost in pleasure at her feet he sinks,
> Touching with dazzled lips her starlight hand.

After the hero Heracles finished his life on earth, he was taken to Olympus and made the husband of Hebe. As a reward for his great deeds, Spenser says (*Ruines of Time*, 384–385), the hero enjoys

> All happinesse in *Hebes* siluer bowre,
> Chosen to be her dearest Paramoure.

HECATE (hĕk′à·tē) is Artemis in her evil aspect as goddess of the dark of the moon. See ARTEMIS.

HECATONCHEIRES (hĕk′à·tŏn·kī′rēz) were hundred-handed monsters. See TITANS.

HECTOR, a royal prince, was the chief hero of Troy in the TROJAN WAR.

HECUBA (hĕk′ū·bà) was queen of Troy at the time of the TROJAN WAR.

HELEN OF TROY was the daughter of Zeus and Leda. Her eloping with Paris was the immediate cause of the TROJAN WAR.

HELENUS (hĕl′ê·nûs) was a Trojan prince who had the gift of prophecy. The Greeks captured him and forced him to assist them in the TROJAN WAR.

HELIADES (hê·lī′à·dēz) were the sisters of Phaethon. See APOLLO.

HELICON (hĕl′ī·kŏn) is a mountain sacred to the MUSES.

HELIOPOLIS (hē′lĭ·ŏp′ò·lĭs) was an Egyptian city; the temple of the sun to which the Phoenix made its regular pilgrimage was located here. See PHOENIX.

HELIOS (hē′lĭ·ŏs) is a Titan sun god. See APOLLO.

HELLE (hĕl′ē) fell off the golden-fleeced ram into the Hellespont. See ARGONAUTS.

HELLEN (hĕl′ĕn), the mythical ancestor of the Greeks, or Hellenes, was the son of Pyrrha and DEUCALION.

HELLENES (hĕl′ēnz) are the Greeks. Their mythical ancestor, Hellen, was the son of Pyrrha and DEUCALION.

HELLESPONT (hĕl′ĕs·pŏnt) is a narrow strait between Europe and Asia where the sea of Marmora flows into the Aegean. It was named for Helle, who fell into it from the golden-fleeced ram (see ARGONAUTS). Leander swam the Hellespont to see his lady HERO.

HEPHAESTUS (hĕ·fĕs′tŭs), or **Vulcan**, or **Mulciber**, is the god of fire. The son of Zeus and Hera, he is most famous as the blacksmith of the gods and their chief artificer and builder. He is supposed to have forges on Olympus; under Moschylus, the now extinct volcano on the island of Lemnos; and under Mount Aetna, the Sicilian volcano. Hephaestus' association with fire and the forge led to his becoming the god of pottery, metalwork, and the other artifices that make use of fire. He is famed in Homer and other classical poets for his skill as a metalsmith and builder, and in these capacities he is supposed to have built the dwelling places of the gods, to have forged Zeus's scepter and aegis (shield), and to have made the breastplate of Heracles and the shield and armor of Achilles. On Zeus's orders, he created the girl Pandora for the purpose of penalizing man for his acquisition of fire from Prometheus.

Hephaestus is lame. Some stories attribute this characteristic to the flickering of fire, his native element. Other stories say that he was born lame, and that Hera his mother was ashamed of him and threw him out of Olympus, whereupon he was rescued by the Nymphs Thetis and Eurynome, who kept him under the sea and reared him. As Hephaestus grew in strength and skill, he took his revenge by constructing a throne of metal for Hera. When she sat on it, she found herself held so firmly that only Hephaestus could release her, and this he refused to do until Dionysus, his trusted friend, tricked him into returning to Olympus and releasing her. There is another myth, however, that Hephaestus' lameness resulted from a fall. He interceded one day between Zeus and Hera while they were quarreling, and Zeus, in anger seized him by the heel and hurled him from Olympus. Milton tells the end of this story in *Paradise Lost* (1. 738–746), where he pictures Hephaestus as the architect of Pandemonium, the council hall of Hell,

Nor was his name unheard or unador'd
In ancient *Greece;* and in *Ausonian* land
Men call'd him *Mulciber;* and how he fell
From Heav'n, they fabl'd, thrown by angry *Jove*
Sheer o're the Chrystal Battlements: from Morn
To Noon he fell, from Noon to dewy Eve,
A Summers day; and with the setting Sun
Dropt from the Zenith like a falling Star,
On *Lemnos* th' *Aegaean* Ile.

On **Lemnos** Hephaestus was rescued by the Sintians, and the island remained one of his principal places of worship.

Accounts vary as to whom Hephaestus married. Some say he was the husband of Aglaia, one of the Graces, but according to most accounts he married Aphrodite, whom he afterward trapped in a metal net when she was being unfaithful to him with Ares (see APHRODITE). Hephaestus seldom appears in English poetry. In addition to Milton's reference to his fall there is Hamlet's speech to Horatio, which concerns his own sick imaginings as well as his plot to discover King Claudius' guilt by the play-within-the-play (*Hamlet,* 3. 2. 85–89):

> . . . if his occulted guilt
> Do not itself unkennel in one speech,
> It is a damned ghost that we have seen,
> And my imaginations are as foul
> As Vulcan's stithy.

The stithy in this image is the forge blackened by smoke and soot.

Volcanoes are named for Vulcan, who is also the source of our verb "to vulcanize," which refers to a chemical process for treating crude rubber.

HERA (hē'rȧ), or **Juno,** like Zeus, her brother and husband, is the child of Cronus and Rhea. Less fortunate than Zeus, however, she was swallowed by Cronus along with her other brothers and sisters, and was subsequently rescued by Zeus when he made Cronus disgorge them all. Zeus had a particular fondness for Hera, and after two other marriages that did not satisfy him, he married her. Hera thus became the queen of all the gods, and in this capacity she came to represent for the Greeks and the Romans the great feminine element of motherhood in the natural order of things.

Like Zeus, however, Hera developed two rather different sets of characteristics. As the suspicious wife of Zeus, she was imagined as jealous and demanding, even willing to overthrow her husband if she could. Zeus gave her many justifications for her jealousy, and she vented her anger sometimes in reproaches against him and sometimes in persecutions directed against his lovers and their children. She plotted so much against Heracles, Zeus's son by Alcmene, that Zeus in exasperation hung her out of Olympus with golden chains on her wrists and anvils on her ankles. On another occasion, Homer tells us, Hera, in conspiracy with Athene and Poseidon, attempted to overcome Zeus and nearly succeeded.

Hera's benignant characteristics, however, are those of the faithful wife and mother, and she is therefore the patroness of those who endure the labor pains of motherhood. In this character, Hera was known as a woman of supreme dignity and virtue. Her name was variously interpreted to mean "splendor of heaven" or "the lady," and she was complimented by Homer with the epithet, "ox-eyed." She was especially fond of Argos, Mycenae, and Sparta, and every fifth year a festival was held in her honor at Olympia. The Romans, calling her Juno and emphasizing her connection with childbirth, gave her a festival called the **Matronalia** on the first day of March. The most famous statue of her was that by Polyclitus at Argos, so splendid that it rivaled Phidias' statue of Zeus at Olympia. Hera's favorite companions are the Graces and the Hours, and her favorite bird is the peacock, whose tail she made brilliant with the eyes of Argus, the watchman whom she placed on guard over Io, and whom Hermes slew. The Greeks gave Hera many nicknames, the best known of which, **Parthenia,** refers to her as a bride. She bore Zeus four children, Hephaestus, Hebe, Ares, and **Ilithyia, or Eileithyia,** who became the goddess of childbirth and who had, according to Homer, a cave dedicated to her in Crete. The function and the name of Ilithyia, who was called **Lucina** by the Romans, were given sometimes to Hera and sometimes to Artemis.

Hera's faithfulness to her marriage vows and her disapproval of all who lived loosely outside of wedlock became proverbial. In the higher sense she became the symbol of married virtue, and in the lower order of things she became the prototype of the shrewish and suspicious wife who checks the roving eye of her husband from following the passing blonde. She was the forceful personification of monogamy.

References to Hera's severe virtues are common in English poetry. In his *Epithalamion* (390–397), the song for his own marriage, Spenser asks for her blessing as the patron of faithful and happy wedlock. Richard Cleveland strikes a keynote for her personality when he writes in his poem, *Mark Antony,* that she graces Zeus "with embraces more stately than warm." Milton follows the same vein in *Paradise Lost* (4. 497–502) when he lends chasteness to the love of Adam and Eve before the fall by comparing their innocent embraces to those of Zeus and Hera. Adam

> . . . in delight
> Both of her Beauty and submissive Charms
> Smil'd with superior Love, as *Jupiter*
> On *Juno* smiles, when he impregns the Clouds

189

That shed *May* Flowers; and press'd her Matron lip
With kisses pure.

Tennyson gives a vivid description of her dignity and grandeur in *Oenone,* using her advent as a golden cloud that encircles her sacred bird, the peacock:

On the tree-tops a crested peacock lit,
And o'er him flow'd a golden cloud, and lean'd
Upon him, slowly dropping fragrant dew.
Then first I heard the voice of her, to whom
Coming thro' Heaven, like a light that grows
Larger and clearer, with one mind the Gods
Rise up for reverence.

Robert Bridges is more detailed in *Eros and Psyche* (*October,* 25):

Her curling hair with plaited braid and brail,
Pendant or loop'd about her head divine,
Lay hidden half beneath a golden veil,
Bright as the rippling ocean in sunshine:
And on the ground, flashing whene'er she stept,
Beneath her feet the dazzling lightnings lept
From the gold network of her sandals fine.[4]

HERACLES (hĕr′á·klēz), or **Hercules,** the Greek hero and prototype of great physical strength, at the end of his mortal life gained immortality not alone among the Olympian deities but among all succeeding generations in Western Europe. His fame has remained secure, and though shorn of an attribute here and there by the forgetfulness of time, it has continued remarkably true to its original character as conceived by the Greek mythmakers.

The Greeks were apparently unable wholeheartedly to admire

[4] From "Eros and Psyche," by Robert Bridges, in his *Poetical Works.* Reprinted with the permission of the publisher, Clarendon Press, Oxford.

any man for his physical strength alone, and originally the strength of Heracles was matched by the sturdiness of his moral fiber. He was an early symbol of patience, determination, and dutifulness; and he used his great strength primarily to fulfill the moral obligations that were placed squarely before him by his destiny. Though he erred occasionally, being half-mortal, he remained dutiful even in the preparation of his own funeral rites at the end of his life, and symbolically his immortal half, when his mortal half had been burned away by the funeral fire, was carried up to Olympus and immortality.

Heracles was the son of Zeus and of a mortal girl named Alcmene (the details of this ungodly affair can be found under ZEUS), though many supposed him to be the son of Alcmene's husband Amphitryon, and Heracles was therefore sometimes called **Alcides,** as a descendant of Alcaeus, Amphitryon's father. Since Hera, the wife of Zeus and the goddess of matrimony, habitually and energetically opposed her husband's affairs with mortals, she resolved to make life difficult for Heracles. First, having determined the day on which the hero was to be born, she extracted from Zeus the promise that whatever boy should be born on that day should have command over all his neighbors. Then she arranged to delay the birth of Heracles and at once hurried down to Argos, where she caused the wife of **Sthenelus** to give premature birth to a weakly son named **Eurystheus** on the day on which Heracles' birth had originally been scheduled. By this arrangement, she managed to give Eurystheus command over Heracles, and thus she hoped to deny fame and importance to Heracles.

Zeus, however, was not without stratagem, too; he had Hermes bring the infant Heracles to Hera to suckle without telling her the child's identity. Hera, with a motherly generosity rare in our times, gave the child her breast, and from it he drew the great strength that became his chief virtue. His first use of this strength was to protect himself and Iphicles, his twin and half brother, from Hera's wrath. While the boys were still in their cradles, Hera discovered the identity of Heracles and sent two huge snakes to kill him and his brother; but he strangled the snakes. In *On the Morning of Christ's Nativity* (227–228) Milton by a kind of parallelism attributes this precocious act to the newborn Christ, in that Christ's birth put an end to all the pagan mythologies of false gods:

> Our Babe to shew his Godhead true,
> Can in his swadling bands controul the damned crew.

Heracles spent the rest of his youth in a manner no less heroic than its beginning. He was first given to be educated to Rhadamanthus, the learned and just son of Zeus and Europa, and to Linus, a famous singer who was a son of Apollo. From the former he acquired much of his moral character; the latter, from whom he was learning music, he slew in a fit of anger at being disciplined. Because of his slaying of Linus, the hero was taken away from more formal training and given over to the herdsmen of the kingdom to rear. The effect of his life among these rugged fellows was to develop Heracles' great physical strength.

The freedom of his youth and the first phase of his life were brought to an end when he was eighteen, by two remarkable demonstrations of his strength. First he slew a tremendous lion that had been ravaging flocks in the vicinity of Mount Cithaeron. Then, on his way to Thebes to display the skin of the lion as evidence of his feat, he offended and rejected the ambassadors of the king of the Minyae who were coming to claim annual tribute from Thebes. This offense naturally led to war between Thebes and the Minyae, and in this war Heracles by his great deeds gave proof that he was undeniably a hero.

His prowess and growing reputation were noticed by none more than Hera, who was annoyed to see her maneuvers coming to nothing. She therefore prompted Eurystheus, her protégé, to claim the service that was due him because of his fateful birth. Heracles was reluctant to serve Eurystheus. He asked the oracle at Delphi whether he could refuse and received the reply that he could not. The oracle informed him, however, that in Eurystheus' service he would perform twelve labors that would gain his immortality; he therefore yielded to his duty and presented himself to Eurystheus at Mycenae.

Eurystheus' motives in demanding the services of Heracles may have been partly humanitarian, but they appear also to have been colored with envy and the hope of killing the hero. Many of the labors that he required Heracles to perform represented great accomplishments for public welfare, but each also might well have been fatal.

Heracles' first task was to kill the **Nemean Lion**. This child of Typhon and Echidna was a terribly destructive beast that was invulnerable against mortal weapons. It had been sent by Hera to terrorize the plain of Nemea and it accomplished its mission with a success so conspicuous that it was to become proverbial for violent strength. Prince Hamlet, about to accost his father's ghost, protests against the restraining hands of his friends (*Hamlet,* 1. 4. 81–83) with the exclamation:

> My fate cries out
> And makes each petty artire in this body
> As hardy as the Nemean lion's nerve.

Heracles, however, bearded the lion in its den and strangled it with his bare hands. Its invulnerable hide he tore off and made into a garment for himself.

His second task was to destroy the **Lernean Hydra**, a child of the same parentage as the lion. This monster had nine heads, one of which was immortal, and it infested a swamp near the spring of Amymone where it gave off a foul smell scarcely less fatal than its heads. Assisted by his nephew and close friend, **Iolaus,** Heracles first drove the hydra into the open by shooting arrows at it, and then he began cutting off its heads. To his chagrin he found that each head that he lopped off was replaced by two new heads. With his hands occupied by an arithmetical progression of monstrous heads, the hero now found his handicap increased by the arrival of a huge crab that took hold of his foot. He therefore wisely retired to a prepared position to replan his tactics. First he had Iolaus set fire to the woods nearby; then with a brand from the fire he renewed his attack on the hydra by cauterizing each stump as he cut off the head. This process brought him at last to the immortal head, which he cut off and buried. The hydra being now dead, he dipped his arrows into the poison and returned to report his success to Eurystheus.

Eurystheus was not pleased; he claimed that Heracles, because he used the aid of Iolaus, had not lived up fully to the terms of his contract. But he sent him off next to capture, as his third labor, the **Erymanthian Boar.** As the hydra symbolized the unhealthy qualities of a swamp, the boar seems to have figured forth the wild dangers of the mountains, especially of Mount Erymanthus where it lived. Yet Heracles was native to this rugged life, and his fulfillment of the task was correspondingly easy and was even characterized by an element of low comedy. Indeed, Heracles' chief exertions on this task had little to do with the boar itself. In searching out the boar he came across the Centaur Pholus living in a cave on Mount Pholoe and maintaining guard over the wine supply of the Centaur race. According to one version of the story, the wine had been given to the Centaurs by

Dionysus on the express understanding that Heracles have some of it when he passed by; in another version this detail is omitted. However, whether or not Pholus was justified in doing so, he poured Heracles a drink. The bouquet of the wine was extremely powerful, and it soon reached the sensitive noses of the other Centaurs, who gathered intent on mayhem. There was a wild fight on which the clouds, whose children the Centaurs were (see IXION), poured down torrents of rain. Heracles, however, was equal to the odds against him, and with the aid of his poisoned arrows succeeded in driving off the enraged Centaurs, though he killed by mistake his old friend Chiron and lost Pholus when this inquisitive soul, examining one of the hero's arrows, dropped it on his foot and died of the scratch (see CENTAURS). Capturing the wild boar alive, as Heracles had been ordered to do, was something of an anticlimax after this fight; but as he approached Mycenae with it, the sight so frightened Eurystheus that he hid himself in a great bronze pot. Heracles, looking about for a safe place in which to confine the boar, put it into the same pot, and the comic consequences are easily imagined.

Heracles' fourth labor was to capture alive the **Ceryneian Stag**, which was sacred to Artemis. Of this labor little need be said except that Heracles had to pursue the stag for a full year, following it over the open countryside wherever it fled. At one time it took refuge in a temple of Artemis and had to be routed. At another time Heracles was on the point of killing it, but both Artemis and Apollo appeared to prevent him. In the end he caught it.

His fifth labor was to drive the fierce, destructive birds out of the vale of Stymphalus. These **Stymphalian Birds** were similar to the Harpies (see Harpies under SEA GODS). They had iron talons, and their feathers, which they cast downward, were as sharp as arrows; they killed human beings and ate them. Heracles' method of attack was typically direct. He first rang a bell to arouse the birds and then fired his arrows at them as they flew about. Frightened, the birds flew away forever to an island in the Black Sea from which they flew into mythology at least once more when they attacked the Argonauts (see AR-GONAUTS).

For a sixth labor, Eurystheus provided a somewhat less exciting project. Prince **Augeas** of Elis, a son of Helios, the sun god, was the owner of a tremendous herd of cattle that he stabled in buildings on the banks of the river Alpheus. The **Augean Stables,** partly because they held a large number of cattle and partly because they had not been cleaned for a long time, gained a permanent reputation for overwhelming filth, which William Wordsworth echoed in *The Prelude* (10. 583–585) when he described Robespierre's followers in the French Revolution as a group

> . . . who with clumsy desperation brought
> A river of Blood, and preached that nothing else
> Could cleanse the Augean stable

of French politics. What was a familiar figure to Wordsworth is even today a continuing figure of speech, for "cleaning out the Augean Stables" still means cleaning up an awful mess.

Eurystheus made the task doubly hard for Heracles by requiring that he clean out the stables not only by himself but in a single day's time. When Heracles appeared at Elis, Augeas himself was so pleased with the idea that he offered the hero a tenth of his herds as a reward for completing the job. Heracles then cleverly diverted the river Alpheus into the stables and the waters washed them clean within a single day, as required. Augeas, however, when he discovered that Heracles had been compelled by Eurystheus to perform the task, refused to pay the reward he had offered; Heracles in retaliation killed him and his sons.

Eurystheus now sent Heracles to capture the **Cretan Bull,** a magnificent animal that Poseidon, the sea god, had presented to King Minos of Crete. Minos' wife, Pasiphae, fell in love with this bull and bore it a child, the Minotaur, after which the bull roamed at will over the island of Crete. Heracles captured it without unusual difficulty and caused it to swim back to Mycenae bearing him on its back. He presented it to Eurystheus, who either sacrificed it to Hera or turned it loose again, according to varying accounts.

For an eighth labor Heracles was sent to fetch the carnivorous **Horses of Diomedes.** Diomedes, a fierce warrior who was said to be a son of Ares, the god of war, customarily fed these horses on the flesh of men who were shipwrecked on his coast. This diet imbued the horses with such violence that they had to be confined with iron chains. Their fierce wildness, however, was no protection against the might of Heracles, who first overcame their keepers and then led the horses away. When Diomedes and his men sought to prevent him, Heracles not only routed their forces but retributively fed Diomedes himself to his horses. The horses did not long belong to Eurystheus, however, for they escaped into the Arcadian hills where they were thought to have been eaten by wolves.

Eurystheus' daughter, **Admete,** provided the ninth labor by desiring the girdle of Hippolyta, the queen of the Amazons. This girdle, an outer garment, Heracles dutifully procured, even though according to some accounts he had to kill its owner in the process. He was accompanied on this raid by the hero Theseus, who brought back Hippolyta or her sister Antiope as his wife (for further details see THESEUS).

The tenth labor is the story of an anticlimax. Eurystheus demanded that Heracles bring him the **Cattle of Geryon.** Geryon, the son of Callirhoe the Oceanid, was a triple man of great strength and gigantic size. He possessed three bodies, three heads, and six arms, not to mention a pair of wings. Furthermore, he dwelt far beyond the known world in the distant west on an island called Erytheia, where he kept his cattle in a dark cave, and where he was aided in protecting them by a two-headed dog and a fierce herdsman named **Eurytion.**

Heracles made his way westward in a vessel that may have been the cup in which Helios, the sun, nightly returns to the east, until he found himself at the point where Europe and Africa give way to the great stream of Oceanus. Here he set up two mountains as markers of his progress. These mountains are still called the **Pillars** or **Gates of Heracles,** though one of them is better known as the Rock of Gibraltar. Spenser in the *Protha-lamion* (147–149), praising the Earl of Essex for a successful raid against the Spanish, declares that his

> . . . dreadfull name, late through all *Spaine* did thunder,
> And *Hercules* two pillars standing neere,
> Did make to quake and feare.

Sailing westward, Heracles ran into a terrible storm and had to threaten Oceanus himself with his arrows in order to still it. When he reached Erytheia he was attacked first by the two-headed dog, which he killed, and then by Eurytion, whom he also slew. Even Geryon himself quickly fell before the hero's arrows when he sought to prevent the theft of his cattle. With this part of his mission accomplished, Heracles drove Geryon's cattle into his vessel and set sail again for Mycenae.

For some reason he chose to land in Spain and to make a rather circuitous way back to Greece by crossing the Alps and making a round trip down the west coast of Italy and up the east coast. On the spot that was later to become Rome he had a curious adventure. While he was sleeping, a son of Hephaestus named **Cacus** stole some of his cattle. He led them off backward by their tails, so that when Heracles awoke and missed them, he found their footprints leading toward him and was deceived. However, as he was about to abandon the search, he heard the stolen cattle lowing and found them hidden in Cacus' cave. Naturally he slew Cacus and retrieved his cattle. The event was memorialized with an altar by the Romans, who had their cattle market on this place in later years. Cacus' method of disguising his theft was the same as that of the infant Hermes when he rustled some of the cattle of Apollo.

Further south in Italy Heracles had some minor adventures. At Cumae he fought a set of Giants. Past Rhegium he found that the grasshoppers interfered with his sleep, and his prayer that something be done about the nuisance led to grasshoppers being forever banned from the area by the gods. Later one of his oxen escaped and swam across the strait into Sicily, so that to recover it Heracles had to make his way across the strait on the back of another ox and travel all the way around Sicily. But in spite of these delays, he succeeded at last in driving most of the cattle up the east coast of Italy and down the Greek peninsula to Mycenae, whereupon Eurystheus promptly sacrificed the entire lot to Hera. What Heracles must have said about this event has not been recorded.

His eleventh labor, which consisted in obtaining the **Apples of the Hesperides** for Eurystheus, involved him in no less varied adventures. These apples were golden, and they were guarded by Atlas' daughters, the Hesperides. **Atlas,** who was a son of the Titan Iapetus, had fought with the Titans against the gods, and as punishment he was made to hold up the heavens on his shoulders. The golden apples had been the wedding gift of Gaea to Hera; they were tended in an orchard by the Hesperides, with the assistance of a dragon named **Ladon**.

Heracles' first problem was to find Atlas, whose habitat was a matter of much argument at the time, because some averred that the garden of the Hesperides was in the country of the northern Hyperboreans, and others held that it lay far to the west. According to one myth, he set out to the north until he reached the Rhone river, whose Nymphs informed him that Nereus, the old man of the sea (see SEA GODS), could tell him where to find Atlas. Nereus had the power to change his form at will, but Heracles caught and held him in spite of his changes and forced him at last to reveal the location of Atlas, which proved to be in Libya.

Journeying through Libya, Heracles encountered almost at one time two extremes of size and strength. The first of these was **Antaeus**, the Giant son of Poseidon and Gaea, the Titan earth goddess; his strength remained unconquerable as long as he was in actual contact with his mother the earth. Wrestling with him, Heracles was unable to overcome him, for the Giant's strength was constantly renewed. At last he conceived the idea of holding the Giant in the air and strangling him as his power waned away. In Spenser's *Faerie Queen* (2. 11. 23–46) the leader of the evil forces who attack the castle of Temperance is Maleger, a son of earth, whom Sir Guyon finally kills in much the same way that Heracles killed Antaeus. As Heracles was resting from this struggle, he was attacked by a band of **Pygmies**, an unpleasant little folk 13½ inches in height. Heracles was amused by their attack and met it by simply wrapping them up in his lion's skin; some accounts say that he killed them, and others that he brought them back to Eurystheus.

In Egypt Heracles was seized by King Busiris, who had the habit of sacrificing all strangers on his altar. In Heracles, however, he found more of a stranger than he could handle, and the hero turned the tables by bursting free and sacrificing Busiris himself. He now made his way to India and thence to the Caucasus mountains, where he freed Prometheus, an act related somewhat perfunctorily by Shelley in his long poetic drama *Prometheus Unbound* (3. 3). In myth, though not in Shelley's account, Prometheus gave Heracles final instructions as to how to find Atlas (see PROMETHEUS).

When Heracles at last found Atlas, he conceived a stratagem to obtain the apples without a struggle. He offered to hold up the heavens in Atlas' place if the giant would obtain for him three of the golden apples from the garden. To this the tired old giant agreed and did so without delay, saving Heracles what might well have been an impossible task. Berowne, in *Love's Labour's Lost* (4. 3. 340–341), seems not to have heard of this arrangement nor to have regarded the difficulties of the project with much seriousness, because he asks:

> For valour, is not Love a Hercules,
> Still climbing trees in the Hesperides?

When Atlas had brought the apples back to Heracles, he proposed that he himself should deliver them to Eurystheus. For a moment the hero's fate hung in the balance, but his shrewdness saved him. He agreed to Atlas' proposal on the condition that Atlas relieve him of the weight of the heavens long enough for him to find a pad for his shoulders. Atlas was taken in by this ruse, and once he had the heavens firmly back on his shoulders, Heracles took the apples and returned with them to Eurystheus.

The last labor that Eurystheus provided seemed impossible even for Heracles. He directed Heracles to bring back from Hades' kingdom in the underworld the three-headed dog Cerberus, the guardian of the entrance to this awful place. Fortunately,

Athene and Hermes came to the assistance of Heracles and guided him down to Hades' presence. Hades granted Heracles permission to seize Cerberus and carry him to the upper world if he could do so without using weapons. Having first freed his friend Theseus, who was imprisoned there for having tried to kidnap Hades' wife, Persephone, Heracles seized Cerberus with his bare hands and carried him off to Eurystheus, who ordered that the monster be returned to the lower regions. Holofernes the Pedant, in Shakespeare's *Love's Labour's Lost* (5. 2. 539), in the manner of pedants seems to have had the wrong information on this point, for he says that Heracles killed Cerberus with his club.

Thus Heracles completed his long term of servitude, but his heroic life did not end with his obligations to Eurystheus. Indeed, he appears to have got so habituated to heroic deeds that he continued to indulge in them as a kind of reflex action up to the moment of his death, whose circumstances he arranged to fit the heroism of his inner nature. His rescue of Alcestis from death, for example, remarkable as it was (see ALCESTIS), was only a minor action in the course of his obtaining the man-eating horses of Diomedes.

When he was free of Eurystheus' yoke, Heracles put aside his wife **Megara** because in his first fit of madness he had killed their children, and he considered that his wedlock must have been counter to the will of the gods. As if to contradict his reasoning, however, the gods put on him another fit of mad violence, during which he committed a murder and even profaned the oracle of Apollo at Delphi by trying to make off with the sacred tripod of the temple. When he regained his senses, the oracle informed him that he must expiate his insane misdeeds by becoming the slave of Queen **Omphale** of Lydia for three years. A curiously mixed affair resulted from his acceptance of this second period of servitude. In the first place, Omphale seems to have made Heracles become extremely effeminate, so that he gave over to her his lion's skin and took up weaving and spinning with the ladies of her court; but when Omphale fell in love with him, he caused her to produce a son whom they named **Ladus.**

As if to counterbalance his effeminacy during this period, Heracles took an early part in the expedition of the Argonauts (see ARGONAUTS) and he made war on Troy. Laomedon, the king of old Troy, had promised Heracles the hand of **Hesione,** his daughter, in return for Heracles' having rescued her from a sea monster; but he later changed his mind and would not live up to his promise. Heracles therefore gathered around him Telamon, the father of Aias, Peleus, the father of Achilles, and others, with whom he laid siege to Troy. They captured the city and slew Laomedon and all his family except Hesione, whom Heracles gave as wife to Telamon, and her brother Priam, who fathered the royal family that was to defend the city in the major Trojan War of later times (see TROJAN WAR).

Heracles also found time to rescue the shepherd youth **Daphnis** from the cruelty of King **Lityerses** of Phrygia. This youth was the son of Hermes and a Sicilian Nymph who brought him to the favorable attention of Apollo by placing him as a babe in a grove of laurel, a tree sacred to the god. In return for this thoughtful compliment, Apollo gave Daphnis a talent for idyllic song and caused him to invent pastoral song and story. He grew up an innocent and pure shepherd among the Nymphs and shepherds who kept flocks near Mount Aetna in Sicily. As even innocent shepherds will, he fell in love with a maiden. Her name was **Piplea,** and she was soon after abducted by robbers who carried her to Phrygia. Daphnis naturally followed, and found Piplea in the possession of King Lityerses. Lityerses, it seems, was proud of his ability to reap grain, so proud that he habitually challenged strangers to a reaping contest and killed them if he won. Daphnis accepted his challenge, and they both fell to reaping and singing appropriate songs. Daphnis was losing when Heracles arrived and put an end to the match by cutting off Lityerses' head and throwing it into the river Maeander. Matthew Arnold, mourning the loss of his friend A. H. Clough in his elegiac poem *Thyrsis* (182–185), recalls the reaping contest:

> Putting his sickle to the perilous grain
> In the hot cornfield of the Phrygian king,
> For thee the Lityerses-song again
> Young Daphnis with his silver voice doth sing.

Daphnis, according to the version of the myth that Arnold mentions in a note to his poem, later fell in love with a princess and was struck blind by jealous Piplea.

Lesser exploits of Heracles are without number. The manner of his death, however, was in many ways the greatest of his deeds. Still in search of a wife, he tried to win **Iole,** the daughter of King **Eurytus** of Oechalia, but the king refused to permit the marriage although Heracles fulfilled all the conditions that had been imposed. He therefore asked the hand of **Deianira,** the daughter of King Oeneus of Calydon. To win her, Heracles had to outwrestle the river god **Achelous,** who was also her suitor, but this he was able to do without unusual difficulty. For three years he lived happily with Deianira. But in the first days of their marriage, they came to a river across which the Centaur **Nessus** offered to ferry them. Heracles swam the river but entrusted Deianira to Nessus, who, in a manner native to the lusty and bestial Centaurs, tried to carry her off for his own pleasure. Heracles at once killed him with an arrow, but as he died he confided in Deianira that she should save some of his blood and put it on Heracles' garments as a love potion if he should ever appear to be unfaithful to her.

Later Heracles decided on revenge against King Eurytus. He besieged Oechalia and with his customary success killed the king and almost all his family except Iole, whom he proposed to sacrifice to the gods. As he was proceeding to this sacrifice, Deianira, misunderstanding and fearing that she was losing his love to Iole, soaked his sacrificial robe in Nessus' blood and sent it to him by his friend **Lichas.** When Heracles put on the robe, it immediately seized him with its poison and began to kill him. All his efforts to remove it were in vain, for his flesh itself came away with the robe. In his agony he threw Lichas into the sea. The terrible effects of this robe, or shirt as it is more commonly called, have become proverbial for unbearable and inescapable pain. The use to which Shakespeare puts it in *Antony and Cleopatra* (4. 12. 43–47) is typical; Antony, who considers himself to be the descendant of Heracles and who finds his fortune running out in defeat, calls out in despair:

> The shirt of Nessus is upon me. Teach me,
> Alcides, thou mine ancestor, thy rage.
> Let me lodge Lichas on the horns o' th' moon
> And with those hands that grasp'd the heaviest club
> Subdue my worthiest self.

The event served Milton as an image for violent upheaval when in *Paradise Lost* (2. 543–547) he described the tumultuous activities of the reviving fallen angels:

> As when *Alcides* from *Oechalia* Crown'd
> With conquest, felt th' envenom'd robe, and tore
> Through pain up by the roots *Thessalian* Pines,
> And *Lichas* from the top of *Oeta* threw
> Into th' *Euboic* Sea.

The incident seems to have been in T. S. Eliot's mind when he

wrote the fourth movement of *Little Gidding,* the final poem of
Four Quartets:

> Love is the unfamiliar Name
> Behind the hands that wove
> The intolerable shirt of flame
> Which human power cannot remove.[5]

Knowing now that death was near, Heracles returned home to
die. Deianira hanged herself when she learned what she had
brought on him, but Heracles prepared to die atop Mount **Oeta.**
There he had a funeral pyre built, and when it was ready he
gave his bow and arrows to his friend Philoctetes or Philoctetes'
father Poeas and then lay down on the pyre with his lion skin
and his club. At Heracles' signal, Philoctetes or Poeas lighted
the pyre, and the hero was enveloped in its flames (see PHIL-
OCTETES).

The gods, however, had not forgotten the promise they made
to Heracles through the Delphic oracle. Zeus permitted only his
body to be burned; he sent down Iris to conduct his spirit to
Olympus where promised immortality awaited him. There he
was at last reconciled to Hera, who became his mother-in-law in
fact, as she had been in practice, by marrying him to her daughter Hebe.

Heracles, like Samson, continues to be a symbol of great
strength. Shakespeare, for example, mentions him thirty-six times;
and his figure, clothed in a lion skin and carrying a club, is
today the trade-mark of a manufacturer of explosives. Herculean
labors are still what they have always been: tasks of overwhelming difficulty required by duty. The gods kept their word when
they promised Heracles immortality.

[5] From "Little Gidding," by T. S. Eliot, in his *Four Quartets.* Copyright,
1943, by T. S. Eliot. Reprinted with the permission of the publisher,
Harcourt, Brace and Company.

HERCULES (hĕr′kū·lēz) is the Roman name of HERACLES.
HERMAPHRODITUS (hĕr·măf′rŏ·dī′tûs), a son of Hermes and
Aphrodite, was united with the Nymph Salmacis and became a
hermaphrodite. See HERMES.
HERMES (hĕr′mēz), or **Mercury,** is the son of Zeus and Maia.
The exact meaning of his name is not known, but it is thought
to be "the hastener." His attributes are the most varied and
complex of all the major gods. He is best known as the herald
and messenger of Zeus, but he is also generally thought of as
the god responsible for breeding and increase in the animal
world, especially for the increase of cattle. This latter responsibility led to a whole chain of associated duties. Since wealth
in agrarian Greece consisted mostly of cattle, he became a deity
of wealth; since wealth was derived from trade, he became the
god of trade and, by association, of travelers who carry on trade;
since trade in its general form is commerce, he became the god
of commerce. From these major fields of responsibility several
other responsibilities were derived. Smoothness of tongue and
shrewdness of mind make for successful trade, and Hermes thus
became the god of oratory. It is but a step from high-pressure
salesmanship to cheating and thievery, of which Hermes also
became the patron. Because he was a god of luck, he became the
protector of gamblers. Somewhere along the line, he became
also the patron of athletes and a god of the wind, with whose
speed he was able to move about.

Hermes' precociousness was as great as his versatility of inter-
ests. He was born on **Mount Cyllene,** and therefore is often called
Cyllenius. Within a few hours of his birth he had stolen some
of Apollo's cattle by tying brush to their hooves and driving
them backward into a cave at Pylos, so that their tracks made it
appear that they had gone in the opposite direction. Apollo
quickly discovered the thief, however, and haled him before
Zeus for justice. Hermes, meanwhile, had taken a tortoise from

its shell, stretched strings across the empty shell, and thus invented the lyre. He so amused Zeus with this instrument and with his feigned naïveté that Zeus forgave him on condition that the cattle be returned to Apollo. Hermes also made Apollo a present of the lyre, in return for which Apollo forgivingly gave Hermes the **Caduceus,** a golden staff with wings at the top and intertwined with serpents, the symbol of his authority as messenger of the gods, and today the symbol of the medical profession. Apollo also gave him the power to prophesy to human beings, though in actions instead of words.

Hermes appears not to have married, but he was the father of Pan by a Nymph, and he had a son by Aphrodite, whom they named **Hermaphroditus.** A river Nymph named **Salmacis** fell in love with Hermaphroditus, but he ignored her. One day when he was bathing in her river, however, Salmacis seized him and prayed the gods to unite her with him. Taking her prayer perhaps more literally than she had intended, the gods fused the two into a single person having the characteristics both of Hermaphroditus and of Salmacis, and therefore both a male and a female. The word "hermaphrodite" survives today to mean any organism which is able to reproduce by fertilizing its own eggs, or which has both male and female sex organs.

Hermes had another son named **Autolycus** who became the champion thief of the world, an achievement less surprising in view of his ability to cast invisibility on himself and what he stole. He was the grandfather of Odysseus, and he has a namesake in Shakespeare's play *The Winter's Tale* (4. 3. 24–28), who describes himself thus:

> My father nam'd me Autolycus, who being, as I am,
> litter'd under Mercury, was likewise a snapper-up
> of unconsidered trifles. With die and drab I pur-
> chas'd this caparison, and my revenue is the silly
> cheat.

For an adventure in which Autolycus was outwitted see SISY-PHUS.

The inventiveness of Hermes was not limited to thievery, for he was credited with instituting the sacrifice of animals to the gods and with inventing the alphabet and numbers. His position as messenger of Zeus gave him many important duties. He conducted the souls of the dead down to Hades, for which task he had the name **Psychopompos;** he brought Hera, Athene, and Aphrodite to Mount Ida for the judgment of Paris (see TROJAN WAR); and he was the companion of Zeus in his visit to Philemon and Baucis. As a constant traveler himself, he was thought to be the friend of travelers, much as St. Christopher is in our time, and for this reason many highway posts were made with his head on the top and called Hermae. His best-known nickname, however, was **Argiphontes,** which he earned for killing the hundred-eyed Argus, whom Hera had set to watch over Io (see ZEUS). Hermes played to Argus on his pipes and told him the story of Pan and Syrinx and many other stories. Gradually Argus closed all his hundred eyes, whereupon Hermes quickly killed him.

Hermes is pictured typically as a young god. His special symbols are his Caduceus, already described; his low-crowned hat with wings, called a **Petasus;** and his winged sandals, which are called **Talaria.** Hermes in his hat and sandals, and carrying his Caduceus, is a favorite symbol for transportation agencies and telegraph companies today. In English poetry he has usually served as a symbol of the messenger, or of speed and majesty in flight. Milton uses him to add a note of gaiety in *Comus* (963–964), where he pictures him somewhat out of character dancing

> With the mincing *Dryades*
> On the Lawns, and on the Leas;

and he uses him again in *Paradise Lost* (5. 285–287) to give vividness to the flight of Raphael, the sociable spirit, sent down to warn Adam and Eve against the guile of Satan:

> Like *Maia's* son he stood,
> And shook his Plumes, that Heav'nly fragrance filld
> The circuit wide.

John Keats describes him more fully in *Lamia,* the story of a serpent whom Hermes changed into a woman and who nearly succeeded in entrapping a Corinthian youth named Lycias. The poem opens with Hermes, "ever-smitten" with love, departing from Olympus in search of a favorite Nymph. He cannot find her until Lamia charms his eyes against the Nymph's invisibility. The poem contains a famous image of Hermes as "the star of Lethe" (81), a reference to Hermes' duties in conducting the souls of the dead to Hades, where the river of Lethe flows. Shelley translated the fourth Homeric hymn, which tells the amusing story of the infant Hermes, under the title *Hymn to Mercury.* In our own times, in the *New Year Letter* (1. 301–306), W. H. Auden alludes to Hermes' ability to prophesy through actions:

> And often when the searcher stood
> Before the Oracle, it would
> Ignore his grown-up earnestness
> But not the child of his distress,
> For through the Janus of a joke
> The candid psychopompos spoke.[6]

HERMIONE (hĕr·mī'ŏ·nē) was the daughter of Helen and Menelaus. See **TROJAN WAR.**

---

[6] From the "New Year Letter," by W. H. Auden, in his *The Double Man.* Copyright, 1941, by W. H. Auden. Reprinted with the permission of the publisher, Random House, Inc.

HERO (hĭr′ō) and **Leander** were a famous pair of lovers of later classical times who resided one on each side of the **Hellespont,** the narrow strait that separates Europe from Asia where the sea of Marmora flows toward the Aegean. Hero, to the eternal confusion of her name, was a beautiful woman who lived in **Sestos** on the European side of the strait and who served there as a priestess of Aphrodite. Leander lived in **Abydos** on the Asiatic side. One day while he was in Sestos to celebrate a festival in honor of Aphrodite, he saw and fell in love with Hero. Thereafter, guided by a torch that she placed on a tower, he swam the strait each night to be with her. At last, however, he was caught in a storm and drowned, whereupon Hero, discovering his body, cast herself into the sea and was drowned also.

The most famous treatment of this story in English poetry is undoubtedly Christopher Marlowe's long and ornately sensuous poem, *Hero and Leander.* The meeting of the two lovers produced one of Marlowe's best known lines (1. 176):

> Who ever lov'd, that lov'd not at first sight?

a line that is echoed by Shakespeare in *As You Like It* (3. 5. 81–82) where he has Phebe exclaim:

> Dead shepherd, now I find thy saw of might,
> "Who ever lov'd that lov'd not at first sight?"

Since it describes what often happens, "love at first sight" has become a cliché. Marlowe handled the story so brilliantly that no other English poet has been able to touch it without showing his influence.

It is not surprising that the tale had an especial appeal for Romantic and later-nineteenth-century poets. Byron, in *The*

Bride of Abydos (2. 1–5), a poem about a different love affair altogether, was moved by the identity of locale to write:

> The winds are high on Helle's wave,
>   As on that night of stormy water
> When Love, who sent, forgot to save
> The young, the beautiful, the brave,
>   The lonely hope of Sestos' daughter.

Briefly he adds that although Hero's "turret-torch was blazing high" and although the storminess of the weather acted as a warning, Leander set out to swim the strait and was drowned. Byron himself had swum this course and was proud of having done so.

Keats, too, seeing a gem with Leander's form cut into it, states the theme in a sonnet, *On an Engraved Gem of Leander,* in which he describes the unfortunate and imprudent youth

> Sinking bewilder'd 'mid the dreary sea.

In *Hero to Leander,* a poem that is not one of his most successful, Tennyson imagines a plea from Hero to her lover not to leave her:

> No Western odors wander
>   On the black and moaning sea,
> And when thou art dead, Leander,
>   My soul must follow thee!
> Oh go not yet, my love!

Dante Gabriel Rossetti, in Sonnet 88 of *The House of Life,* makes use of a subsidiary myth, that the torch or lamp which Hero had lit each night to guide Leander had, after their deaths, been dedicated in a temple and was not to be relit until some mortal had experienced a life of successful love.

A contemporary poet, Malcolm Cowley, resensing the myth,

says in *Leander* that the drowned lover returned into the natural order of things:

> his hair is wreathed with algae; his eyes gleam
> luminous with jellyfishes; coral
> blooms on his thighs . . . ,[7]

lines that recall Ariel's song in *The Tempest* about the sea change which he told Prince Ferdinand had occurred to his father.

HESIONE (hē·sī′ô·nē) was rescued from a sea monster by HERACLES.

HESPERIA (hĕs·pē′rĭ·à), the western land, was the name by which Italy was known to AENEAS.

HESPERIDES (hĕs·pĕr′ĭ·dēz), the daughters of Atlas, guard the tree on which grow the golden apples. See HERACLES.

HESPERUS (hĕs′pĕr·ûs), or **HESPER** (hĕs′pĕr), or **Vesper,** is the evening star and the king of the west. He is the father of Ceyx and the grandfather of the Hesperides, who guard the golden apples that were Gaea's wedding present to Hera. Sometimes Hesperus is said to be the father rather than the grandfather of the Hesperides; Milton in *Comus* (980–982) describes

> . . . the Gardens fair
> Of *Hesperus,* and his daughters three
> That sing about the golden tree . . . .

Usually, however, Hesperus is seen in English literature as the evening star. He appears thus in Ben Jonson's song to the moon goddess:

> Hesperus entreats thy light,
> Goddess excellently bright,

[7] From "Leander," by Malcolm Cowley, in his *Blue Juniata* (New York: Jonathan Cape and Harrison Smith, 1929). Copyright, 1929, by Malcolm Cowley. Reprinted with the permission of the author.

and in Milton's *Paradise Lost* (9. 50–51) he is the bringer of

> Twilight upon the Earth, short Arbiter
> Twixt Day and Night . . . .

Because in Greek and Roman writers Hesperus is often the morning star also, taking the place of, or becoming, his brother Phosphor, Spenser in *The Faerie Queene* (1. 2. 6) speaks of him as bringing "forth dawning light."

The star Hesperus is the planet Venus and therefore, as Spenser says in the *Epithalamion* (288), the "glorious lampe of loue." In the sixteenth and seventeenth centuries writers of marriage songs frequently praised Hesperus not only because he was the lamp of love but also because his coming showed that the long day of public celebration was past and the married couple might soon be alone together. John Donne, for example, writes in his *Epithalamion Made at Lincolnes Inne,*

> The amorous evening starre is rose,
> Why then should not our amorous starre inclose
> Her selfe in her wish'd bed?

HESTIA (hĕs′tĭ·á). The virgin goddess Hestia, or **Vesta,** the first-born child of Cronus and Rhea, is the oldest and most sacred of the Olympians. The Greeks and Romans swore their most binding oaths in her name. She is the goddess of the hearth and the symbol of home. Each meal began and ended with prayers to Hestia. The hearth of every house was sacred to her, and in each city she had a public hearth on which the fire was never allowed to go out. Colonists carried with them coals from this public hearth and used them to kindle the perpetual flame on the public hearth of the new city that they founded.

In the temple of Vesta at Rome the eternal flame was kept by six priestesses called **Vestal Virgins.** These girls, between the ages of six and ten, were chosen from the best families of Rome, and they promised to remain chaste and to serve the goddess for thirty years. The Vestals were honored by the Romans and given many special privileges, but anyone who broke her vow was cruelly put to death. Although there was no statue of the goddess in the temple, it contained the sacred fire and the Palladium (see ATHENE), the two symbols essential to the welfare of the city.

Because the chaste protectress of the household is not to be gossiped about, the Greeks and Romans told no stories of Hestia. In English literature she is seldom mentioned; yet Milton in *Il Penseroso* (23–30) makes her the mother of Melancholy. It seems curious that he should invent this myth about the virgin goddess, but perhaps he intended to indicate the purity in which Melancholy was conceived. Vesta's priestesses appear much more frequently than she does in English literature, but the word "vestal" loses its relation to the goddess and signifies "dedicated virgin" or simply "virgin." In Pope's *Eloisa to Abelard* (207), for example, "the blameless vestal" is a Christian nun, and Romeo (*Romeo and Juliet*, 3. 3. 38) speaks of the "pure and vestal modesty" of Juliet's lips.

In a Roman household Vesta was worshiped along with the **Penates,** the **Lar,** and the Genius of the father of the family. The Penates were gods of the storeroom; they watched over the food supply and the general welfare of the household. The Lar was a benevolent spirit of the dead, an ancestor who protected the members of the family and shared their secrets. Each household had one Lar, but he and the Penates were often referred to together as **Lares** or Penates or both. There were public as well as family Lares and Penates. Herrick in *Hymn to the Lares* worships his own household gods

> With crowns of greenest Parsley,
> And Garlick chives not scarcely,

and in *A Panegerick to Sir Lewis Pemberton* (3–4) he sends his
salt and sacrifice

> To Thee, thy Lady, younglings, and as farre
> As to thy *Genius,* and thy *Larre.*

In *The Dunciad* (4. 366) Pope writes of a dishonest antique
dealer who hopes to persuade each young collector to pay through
the nose for false antiquities with the ironic result that he will
"keep his Lares though his house be sold." The Romans also
believed in the **Manes,** the good spirits of the dead in Hades,
and the **Lemures,** or **Larvae,** the evil spirits of the dead who
wandered on earth at night and haunted the living. Richard
Aldington in his poem *Lemures* describes man's fear of the spirits
of the dead even in our skeptical age that says, "They are not."
And in James Joyce's *Ulysses* Stephen Dedalus, in the drunken
scene in Bella Cohen's brothel, sees in his mind's eye his mother,
whose death has haunted him all day. "Lemur," he says in horror, "who are you? What bogeyman's trick is this?"

The Roman **Genius** is related to one conception of the Greek
Daemon. The Greeks sometimes applied this term to the gods
and sometimes reserved it for spirits like the Satyrs who were
neither gods nor human beings, but they also conceived of the
Daemon as a protective spirit like the Roman Genius. Human
beings, social groups, and places all had these guardian spirits. A
man's Genius came into being at his birth, accompanied him
through life, and became his living soul after death. His Genius
was the essence of him, his personality. Since every Roman family
worshiped a Lar, the benevolent spirit of an ancestor, it was
natural that they should also worship the Genius of the living
head of the household. A Genius of place was represented as a
serpent, but a personal Genius was usually portrayed as a likeness of the person whom he protected. Sometimes the Genius

had wings and sometimes not. In *The Comedy of Errors* (5. 1. 332–334), when the Duke first sees the twin Antipholi and the twin Dromios together, he says,

> One of these men is genius to the other;
> And so of these. Which is the natural man
> And which the spirit?

In his *Epithalamion* (398–399) and in his description of the Garden of Adonis (*Faerie Queene*, 3. 6. 31–32), Spenser refers to Genius as the god of generation, and three times he uses the notion of the Genius of place (*Ruines of Time*, 19; *Ruines of Rome*, 27; *Faerie Queene*, 2. 12. 46–49). Milton describes the retreat of the pagan gods in *On the Morning of Christ's Nativity* (184–186),

> From haunted spring, and dale
> Edg'd with poplar pale,
> The parting Genius is with sighing sent;

and similar references to the Genius of place occur in *Il Penseroso* (154); in *Arcades,* where the Genius of the Wood is one of the characters in the masque; and in *Lycidas* (182–185), where Milton imagines Edward King as the local god of the Irish Sea, in which he was drowned:

> Now *Lycidas* the Shepherds weep no more;
> Hence forth thou art the Genius of the shore,
> In thy large recompense, and shalt be good
> To all that wander in that perilous flood.

For the other virgin goddesses see ARTEMIS and ATHENE.
HIMEROS (hǐ′mĕr·ŏs), the god of desire, is an attendant of EROS.
HIPPOCRENE (hǐp′ô·krēn) is a spring on Mount Helicon, a home of the MUSES.

HIPPODAMIA (hĭp'ŏ·dȧ·mī'ȧ) was (1) the mother of Thyestes and ATREUS; (2) the wife of Pirithous, a friend of THESEUS.
HIPPOLYTA (hĭ·pŏl'ĭ·tȧ) was a queen of the warlike women called the Amazons. One of the twelve tasks of Heracles was to obtain Hippolyta's girdle. Some accounts say that Theseus, who assisted Heracles in this task, abducted and married Hippolyta. See AMAZONS, THESEUS.
HIPPOLYTUS (hĭ·pŏl'ĭ·tŭs) was the son of Theseus who rejected the love of his stepmother Phaedra and was killed because of her false accusation to THESEUS.
HIPPOMEDON (hĭ·pŏm'ê·dŏn) was one of the Seven against THEBES.
HIPPOMENES (hĭ·pŏm'ê·nēz) was the lover of ATALANTA OF BOEOTIA.
HIPPOTADES (hĭ·pŏt'ȧ·dēz) is another name of Aeolus, king of the WINDS.
HORAE (hô'rē) are the HOURS.
HORSES OF DIOMEDES (dī'ŏ·mē'dēz), which ate men, were captured by HERACLES.
HOURS. The **Horae,** or Hours, are the daughters of Zeus and Themis, the goddess of divine justice. The Hours regulate the days and the seasons, and they stand at the cloud gate of Olympus through which the gods pass when they descend to the earth. The happy conjunction of the Hours and the Graces lends beauty to people and occasions, and therefore these goddesses are attendants of Aphrodite and patrons of every pleasant event and gracious season. In the *Epithalamion* (98–105) Spenser asks them and the Graces to attend on his bride as they do on Aphrodite:

> . . . come ye fayre Houres which were begot
> In *Ioues* sweet paradice, of Day and Night,
> Which doe the seasons of the yeare allot,
> And al that euer in this world is fayre

Doe make and still repayre.
And ye three handmayds of the Cyprian Queene,
The which doe still adorne her beauties pride,
Helpe to addorne my beautifullest bride.

HYACINTHUS (hī′a·sĭn′thûs) was a boy whom Apollo loved but killed by accident. From his blood grew a flower of mourning. See APOLLO.

HYLAS (hī′lăs) was the youth for whom Heracles deserted the expedition of the ARGONAUTS.

HYMEN (hī′mĕn), or **HYMENAEUS** (hī′mĕ·nē′ûs), the god of marriage, appears to have been born of an exclamation. Shouts of "Hymen io Hymen!" were a traditional part of the Greek marriage festival, and when the meaning of the expression became obscure, people assumed that Hymen was the god of marriage. He was imagined as a handsome young man dressed in a saffron-colored robe and carrying the traditional marriage torch. Apollo and the Muse Urania were said to be his parents. A. E. Housman in *Last Poems* XXIV writes,

> He is here, Urania's son,
> Hymen come from Helicon.[8]

He has no existence apart from the marriage feast, and the only story in which he has a dramatic role is that of Orpheus and Eurydice. At the celebration of their marriage, which was fated to be unfortunate, he arrived without a lucky omen, and his torch went out in spite of his attempts to keep it burning. In English literature he appears in marriage songs and masques that imitate the classical epithalamia. A typical reference is

[8] From "Poem XXIV," by A. E. Housman, in his *Last Poems*. Copyright, 1922, by Henry Holt and Company, Inc. Reprinted with the permission of the publisher.

found in Spenser's *Epithalamion* (25–29) when Spenser asks
that his bride be waked from her sleep:

> Bid her awake; for Hymen is awake,
> And long since ready forth his maske to moue,
> With his bright Tead that flames with many a flake,
> And many a bachelor to waite on him,
> In theyr fresh garments trim.

HYPERBIUS (hĭ·pẽr′bĭ·ûs) helped Eteocles defend THEBES.
HYPERBOREANS (hī′pẽr·bō′rĭ·ȧnz) lived in perpetual spring-
time to the north of the great river of Oceanus. See SEA GODS.
HYPERION (hī·pīr′ĭ·ȯn) was the first sun god. See APOLLO.
HYPERMNESTRA (hī′pẽrm·nĕs′trȧ) was the only one of the
fifty Danaids who did not murder her husband on her wedding
night. See HADES.
HYPNOS (hĭp′nŏs) is the god of sleep. See HADES.
HYPSIPYLE (hĭp·sĭp′ĭ·lē) was first queen of Lemnos and then a
slave of the king of Nemea. See ARGONAUTS, THEBES.

I

IAPETUS (ī·ăp′ė·tûs), a Titan, was the father of PROME-
THEUS.
ICARIAN (ī·kār′ĭ·ȧn) SEA is the sea in which Icarus fell when
he tried to fly with wings invented by his father DAEDALUS.
ICARUS (ĭk′ȧ·rûs) was the son of DAEDALUS.
ICELUS (ĭs′ė·lûs) is a god of dreams. See HADES.
IDA (ī′dȧ) is the mountain near Troy that was the home of

Oenone and the scene of the judgment of Paris. See NYMPHS, TROJAN WAR.

IDAEA (ĭ·dē′ȧ) was the second wife of Phineus, a king who aided the ARGONAUTS.

IDAEAN DACTYLS (ĭ·dē′ȧn dăk′tĭlz), who lived on Mount Ida in Crete or Phrygia, were workers of magic and priests of Rhea, or Cybele. See EARTH GODDESSES.

IDAS (ī′dȧs) was chosen by Marpessa as her lover, although she was also wooed by APOLLO.

ILIAD (ĭl′ĭ·ȧd) is the epic poem by Homer about the TROJAN WAR.

ILION (ĭl′ĭ·ŏn), which was also called Troy, was the chief Trojan city. See TROJAN WAR.

ILITHYIA (ĭl′ĭ·thī′yȧ), or Eileithyia, is the goddess of childbirth. See ARTEMIS, HERA.

INO (ī′nō), a Theban princess, became the sea goddess Leucothea. See SEA GODS, THEBES.

IO (ī′ō) was one of the mistresses of ZEUS.

IOBATES (ī·ŏb′ȧ·tēz) was first the enemy and then the patron of BELLEROPHON.

IOLAUS (ī′ȯ·lā′ŭs) was the nephew and companion of HERACLES.

IOLE (ī′ȯ·lē) was wooed unsuccessfully by HERACLES.

IONIAN (ī·ō′nĭ·ȧn) SEA was named for Io, who wandered beside it, along the west coast of the Greek peninsula. See ZEUS.

IPHICLES (ĭf′ĭ·klēz) was a son of Amphitryon, whereas his twin Heracles was a son of ZEUS.

IPHIGENIA (ĭf′ĭ·jĕ·nī′ȧ) was sacrificed to Artemis by her father Agamemnon. See ATREUS, TROJAN WAR.

IPHITUS (ĭf′ĭ·tŭs) gave the bow of his father Eurytus to ODYSSEUS.

IRIS (ī′rĭs), a daughter of the sea deities Thaumas and Electra, is the goddess of the rainbow, and she shows its varied colors on her dress and on her wings. One of her functions is to fill the clouds with water so that they may rain on the earth and fructify the soil, and her rainbow has thus become a symbol of the blessings of rain, promising the early Greeks as much as Noah's rainbow promised his people.

Iris' chief duty, however, is as messenger of Hera, the queen of the gods, and in this capacity she is the feminine counterpart of Hermes, who serves Zeus in the same way. Running errands for Hera, she uses her rainbow as a pathway from heaven to earth or to other parts of the mythological world. Paintings of her show her as a lovely maiden of varicolored clothes and wings, with sometimes a nimbus behind her head. Naturally the peacock is her favorite bird.

For poets, Iris provides an image of airy colorfulness. Milton, for example, uses her for this purpose, once in *Paradise Lost* (11. 244) to describe the vestment of the angel Michael and again in *Comus* (83) where this malicious spirit says that his "skie robes" were "spun out of *Iris* Wooff."

IRON AGE is either the present time or the time just before the great flood that drowned all mankind except Pyrrha and DEUCALION.

ISMENE (ĭz·mē′nē) was a daughter of Oedipus, king of THEBES.

ITYS (ī′tĭs), or **ITYLUS** (ĭt′ĭ·lŭs), was the son of Procne and Tereus. See PHILOMELA.

IULUS (ī·ū′lŭs) was another name for Ascanius, the son of AENEAS.

IXION (ĭks·ī′ŏn), like Tantalus and Sisyphus, was a celebrated sinner for whom a special torment was devised in Hades. When Ixion married, he promised rich bridal gifts that he hated to give. He therefore murdered his father-in-law, who would have received the gifts. No earthly means could purify Ixion of this crime; but Zeus, taking pity on him, carried him to Olympus, purified him, and made him a guest at the banquet of the gods. Ixion at once began to make love to Hera, Zeus's wife. For this ingratitude Zeus found ingenious punishment. He created out of a cloud a phantom that resembled Hera; Ixion made love to the phantom and fathered the monstrous race of Centaurs (see CENTAURS). In Hades Ixion was tied to the side of a fiery wheel that turns endlessly.

Ixion's father and his reputed son Pirithous were also famous for their impiety. His father **Phlegyas** set fire to Apollo's temple at Delphi because Apollo had got Ixion's sister Coronis with child (see APOLLO). Phlegyas was put to death by the god, and in Hades he is forced to stand under a huge rock that is always on the point of falling, while his food is constantly befouled by a Fury. For the sin and punishment of Pirithous, who some say was Ixion's son and some say the son of Zeus, see THESEUS.

In literature Ixion usually appears in Hades on his wheel. He is seen there by Orpheus, Aeneas, and others, including Duessa in Spenser's *Faerie Queene* (1. 5. 35). In Browning's philosophical poem *Ixion* the hero gains spiritual insight through his suffering and becomes conscious of a divine justice higher than that of Zeus. Pope uses Ixion's punishment charmingly in *The Rape of the Lock* (2. 133) and pretentiously in *Ode on St. Cecilia's Day*. In one image of Sonnet 45 in *Delia*, Samuel Daniel recalls Ixion's deluded love-making and uses it as a symbol of hopeless passion. Only Herrick, characteristically avoiding the thought of consequences, takes pleasure in the story of Ixion. He praises the incomparable whiteness of the skin of his mistress Electra, but confesses that she will not fully please him

> Till, like *Ixion's* cloud you be
> White, warme, and soft to lie with me.

223

J

JANUS (jā′nŭs), whose name comes from the Latin word for "going," is the most important of the Latin deities who were not borrowed from the Greeks. Although Janus was unknown to the Greeks, the Romans believed that he had come over from Greece in ancient times and had reigned benevolently as King of Latium, the region of Italy in which Rome was founded. He was thought to have civilized the early Romans, teaching them to farm and to build buildings, especially temples in honor of the gods. Because these achievements were also credited to Saturn (see CRONUS), Janus was sometimes confused with this Titan, whom all agreed he had at least befriended when Saturn, cast out of Greece by Zeus, fled to Italy and spread his useful arts of husbandry there.

The place of Janus in Roman theology seems to have been second only to that of Jupiter. Worship of him began in earliest Roman times not only because of the cultural advantages that he brought but because he was of material assistance in warding off enemies. At a critical moment in a Sabine attack against the early city, a spring of boiling water appeared by means of which the Romans were able to beat off their attackers. On the location of this spring a temple to Janus was built, and thereafter, whenever Rome was at war, the gates of the temple stood open. As history has recorded the matter, the gates were in fact almost never closed. Augustus claimed with pride that during his long reign (27 B.C.–14 A.D.) they were closed three times.

Janus' significance to the Romans begins in the concrete

symbol and ends in the abstract. His name is closely associated with the Latin word "janua," which means a passageway or door. Thus he is the god of openings and therefore of beginnings. Moreover, because the beginning of an undertaking has much to do with its ending (an undertaking well begun has the best chance of ending well), he is also the god of endings. Like a door, Janus faces two ways; and he is usually depicted as having two faces, one that of a youth, to represent the beginning, and the other that of an old man, to represent the ending. Hence his other name, **Bifrons.** His temple also faced two ways, one of its doors toward the east, where the day begins, and the other toward the west, where it ends. Naturally, too, the first month of the calendar, January, was named after him, and the first day of this month, which looks backward on the old year and forward into the new one, was his holiday (though the first day of every month, having the same kind of significance on a smaller scale, was also a day of sacrifice to him). Every enterprise, and especially war, was begun with an invocation of his aid; and even though the final decision as to what must happen was left to Jupiter, after Jupiter had decided, Janus was in charge.

Though not signally popular in English poetry, Janus has provided his share of allusions. To Milton (*Paradise Lost,* 11. 128–129), wishing to describe the Cherubim who were preparing to descend with Michael and evict Adam and Eve from Eden, he suggested a simile:

> Four faces each
> Had, like a double *Janus* . . . .

Also, for Salarino, a Venetian gentleman (*Merchant of Venice,* 1. 1. 50–51), he provided an oath suitable to the context:

> Now, by two-headed Janus,
> Nature hath fram'd strange fellows in her time. . .

Dean Jonathan Swift, seeking a vehicle for wit, found the god adequate to a short poem, *To Janus on New Year's Day* (1729):

> Two-fac'd Janus, God of Time,
> Be my Phoebus while I rhime.
> To oblige your crony S[wif]t,
> Bring our Dame a New-Year's Gift:
> She has got but half a Face;
> Janus, since thou hast a Brace,
> To my lady once be kind;
> Give her half thy Face behind.

Swift apparently wanted the lady to look backward so that she would not see the ruin that, he said, was coming; but she wittily declined:

> Give me Time when coming on:
> Who regards him when he's gone?
> By the D[ea]n though gravely told,
> New Years help to make me old.

But she agreed to accept a gift.

In *The Faerie Queene* (4. 10. 12) Doubt, the gatekeeper of the temple of Venus, has two faces,

> Th'one forward looking, th'other backeward bent,
> Therein resembling *Ianus* auncient . . . .

For Spenser the double face symbolizes uncertainty, and for W. H. Auden, who speaks in the *New Year Letter* (1. 305) of "the Janus of a joke," it suggests a significant ambiguity.

JASON (jā′sŏn) was the chief of the ARGONAUTS.

JOCASTA (jồ·kăs′tȧ) was the mother and later the wife of Oedipus, king of THEBES.

JOVE (jōv) is a Roman name for ZEUS.

JUNO (jōō′nō) is the Roman name of HERA.

JUPITER (jōō′pî·tẽr) is a Roman name for ZEUS.

L

LABDACUS (lăb′dȧ·kŭs) was a king of THEBES.

LABYRINTH (lăb′ĭ·rĭnth), an intricate maze on Crete in which the Minotaur was imprisoned, was built by DAEDALUS.

LACEDAEMON (lăs′ė·dē′mŏn) was the son of Zeus and a Nymph **Taygeta**. He married **Sparta,** and because he succeeded in uniting the various peoples of **Laconia,** he became king of the region and gave both his own and his wife's name to the chief city and to the area. Thus the Laconians, famous for their military prowess, are also known in mythology and history both as the Spartans and the Lacedaemonians.

LACHESIS (lăk′ė·sĭs) is one of the three Fates. See FATE.

LACONIA (lȧ·kō′nĭ·ȧ) was a name of the country first ruled by LACEDAEMON.

LADON (lā′dŏn), a dragon, helps to guard the golden apples of the Hesperides. See HERACLES.

LADUS (lā′dŭs) was the son of Omphale and HERACLES.

LAERTES (lā·ĕr′tēz) was the father of ODYSSEUS.

LAESTRYGONIANS (lĕs′trĭ·gō′nĭ·ȧnz), or Lestrygonians, fought against ODYSSEUS.

LAIUS (lā′yŭs), the father of Oedipus, was a king of THEBES.

LAOCOÖN (lā·ŏk′ō·wŏn) was the Trojan priest of Poseidon who feared the Greeks even when they bore gifts. See TROJAN WAR.

LAODAMIA (lā′ō·dȧ·mī′ȧ) persuaded the gods to bring her husband Protesilaus back to her from Hades for three hours. See TROJAN WAR.

LAPITHS (lăp′ĭths) were a Thessalian people who warred con-tinually against the Centaurs. See THESEUS.

227

LAR (lär; plural, **LARES,** lā′rēz) is a Roman household god. See HESTIA.

LARVAE (lär′vē), or Lemures, according to Roman mythology, are evil spirits of the dead. See HESTIA.

LASTHENES (lăs′thĕ·nēz) helped Eteocles defend THEBES.

LATINUS (là·tī′nŭs) was king of the Latians, who fought against AENEAS.

LATIUM (lā′shŭm) was a region in Italy conquered by AENEAS.

LATMOS (lăt′mŏs) is the mountain in Caria where Endymion sleeps immortally and is visited each night by ARTEMIS.

LATONA (là·tō′nà) is the Roman name of Leto, the mother by Zeus of Artemis and APOLLO.

LAUREL, into which Daphne was transformed, is sacred to APOLLO.

LAVINIA (là·vĭn′ĭ·à) was the second wife of AENEAS.

LAVINIUM (là·vĭn′ĭ·ŭm) was a city founded by AENEAS.

LEANDER (lē·ăn′dĕr) was the lover of HERO.

LEDA (lē′dà) was the mother of Helen of Troy. See TROJAN WAR.

LEMNOS (lĕm′nŏs) is the island on which Hephaestus fell when Zeus hurled him out of heaven, and the first port of call of the Argonauts. See ARGONAUTS, HEPHAESTUS.

LEMURES (lĕm′ū·rēz), or Larvae, according to Roman mythology, are evil spirits of the dead. See HESTIA.

LEO, the Lion, is a constellation and a sign of the ZODIAC.

LERNEAN HYDRA (lĕr·nē′àn hī′drà), a water serpent with nine heads, was killed by HERACLES.

LESTRYGONIANS (lĕs′trĭ·gō′nĭ·ànz), or Laestrygonians, fought against ODYSSEUS.

LETHE (lē′thē) is a river of HADES.

LETO (lē′tō) is the mother by Zeus of Artemis and APOLLO.

LEUCOSIA (lōō·kō′sĭ·à) is one of the three Sirens. See SEA GODS.

LEUCOTHEA (lōō·kŏth′ė·à) was the name given to Ino when she became a sea goddess. See SEA GODS, ODYSSEUS.

LIBER (lī′bĕr) is a Roman name of DIONYSUS.

LIBERA (lī′bĕr·à) is a Roman name of Persephone, the daughter of Demeter and the wife of Hades. See EARTH GODDESSES, HADES.

LIBRA (lī′brà), the Scales, is a constellation and a sign of the ZODIAC.

LICHAS (lī′kàs), a friend of Heracles, was thrown into the sea by the hero in his death agony. See HERACLES.

LIGEIA (lī·jī′à) is one of the three Sirens. See SEA GODS.

LIRIOPE (līr·ĭ′ō·pē) was the mother of NARCISSUS.

LITYERSES (lĭt′ĭ·ĕr′sēz) was killed by HERACLES.

LOTOS EATERS were visited by ODYSSEUS.

LUCINA (lōō·sī′nà) is the Roman name of Ilithyia, the goddess of childbirth. See ARTEMIS, HERA.

LUNA (lōō′nà) is a Roman name of ARTEMIS.

LUPERCALIA (lōō′pĕr·kā′lĭ·à) was a festival in honor of Faunus, the Roman PAN.

LUTINUS (lōō·tī′nûs) is a Roman name for PRIAPUS.

LYCIUS (lĭs′ĭ·ûs) is a name of APOLLO.

LYCOMEDES (lī′kŏ·mē′dēz) was the king of Scyros who was suspected of murdering Theseus. On his island Thetis hid Achilles disguised as a girl. See THESEUS, TROJAN WAR.

LYCURGUS (lī·kûr′gûs) was driven mad for opposing DIONYSUS.

LYCUS (lī′kûs) was the husband of Dirce and a regent of THEBES.

LYNCEUS (lĭn′sōōs) was the only one of fifty brothers who was not murdered by his wife on his wedding night. See HADES.

LYRE is a musical instrument that Hermes invented by taking a tortoise from its shell and stretching strings across the empty shell. He presented the lyre to APOLLO.

MACHAON (mȧ·kā'ŏn), a son of Asclepius, was a Greek leader in the TROJAN WAR.

MAEANDER (mē·ăn'dĕr) is a river (now called Menderes) of central Asia Minor that flows in so circuitous a course that its name has come down to our times as a symbol for aimless and involved movement. It played a small part in many myths. It smoked, for example, with other rivers when Phaethon allowed the chariot of the sun to approach too close to the earth; Heracles, having rescued Daphnis from bloodthirsty Lityerses, threw Lityerses' severed head into its stream; and its involutions were said to have served Daedalus as a model for the complex passages of the Labyrinth.

The most famous attribute of the Maeander, next to its wandering course, was its fine swans. Some myths relate that all swans, when they felt the approach of death, returned to the banks of the Maeander to sing their dying swan song; and it is to this idea that Pope alludes in *The Rape of the Lock* (5. 65–66) when he describes the fall of Sir Fopling under the attack of the enraged virago Thalestris:

> Thus on Maeander's flowery margin lies
> Th' expiring Swan, and as he sings he dies,

lines that echo the Roman poet Ovid.

MAENADS (mē′nădz) were followers of DIONYSUS.

MANES (mā′nēz), according to Roman mythology, are the good spirits of the dead in Hades. See HESTIA.

MARPESSA (mär·pĕs′a) chose for her lover the mortal Idas instead of the god APOLLO.

MARS is the Roman name of the god of war, ARES.

MARSYAS (mär′sĭ·as) was a Satyr who entered a musical contest with APOLLO.

MATER MATUTA (mā′tĕr ma·tōō′ta), or **MATUTA**, is a Roman goddess of dawn and sea travel; in the second aspect she is identified with Leucothea. See EOS, and Leucothea under SEA GODS.

MATRONALIA (măt′rŏ·nā′lĭ·a) was a festival in honor of HERA.

MECHANITIS (mĕk′a·nī′tĭs) is a surname of ATHENE.

MEDEA (mĕ·dē′a) was the wife of Jason and a powerful enchantress. See ARGONAUTS, THESEUS.

MEDITERRANEAN SEA was given its name because it lay in the midst of most of the lands known to the ancients and was therefore in a sense the middle of the world. Located between the Dardanelles and Gibraltar on its east-west axis and between Europe and the continents of Asia and Africa on its north-south axis, it has not entirely lost title to its name even with the discovery of new lands in later days. Into this sea from its European side thrust out the Greek and Italian peninsulas, the two great centers of classic civilization. In early times Greek culture spread out across its waters into Asia Minor, Egypt, and Sicily, even before the military genius of Alexander the Great spread its seeds in the recesses of Asia. Later, from Italy, the Roman civilization reached out to include all the lands that surround the sea.

The Mediterranean includes several lesser seas or subdivisions, of which the best known are the **Aegean Sea,** lying between Greece and Asia Minor; the Ionian Sea, lying off the west coast of the Greek peninsula; the **Adriatic Sea,** lying between the Italian peninsula and the coast of modern Yugoslavia; and the **Tyrrhenian Sea,** lying between the west coast of Italy and the island of Sardinia. In classic times the straits of Gibraltar were known as the Gates of Heracles and were thought to open out on a waste of water, the great river of Oceanus, which extended all the way to the end of the world.

MEDUSA (mĕ·dū'sȧ) was the mortal Gorgon; the other two are immortal. See PERSEUS, SEA GODS.

MEGAERA (mĕ·jē'rȧ) is one of the three FURIES.

MEGARA (mĕg'ȧ·rȧ) was the first wife of HERACLES.

MEGAREUS (mĕg'ȧ·rōōs) helped Eteocles defend THEBES.

MELAMPUS (mĕ·lȧm'pŭs) became a prophet because he was allowed to share some of the wisdom of the serpent. Learning that his servants had killed two snakes, Melampus burned their bodies as if they had been human beings and protected their offspring. When the two young snakes grew up, they came one night where Melampus was sleeping and licked his ears. He woke up in a terrible fright, but he soon discovered that he could understand the speech of all creatures.

Shortly after he acquired this gift Melampus tried to steal some of the cattle of Iphiclus for his brother, who was forbidden to see the girl he loved until he presented these cattle to his prospective father-in-law. The cattle were closely guarded, and Melampus was captured and imprisoned in a room in Iphiclus' house. After nearly a year of captivity he heard two termites chuckling because the beams were almost eaten through and the house was about to fall. Melampus warned Iphiclus, who humored his prisoner by taking him outside. At once the house collapsed, and Iphiclus, with a new respect for Melampus, offered him a herd of cattle in return for a cure for his impotence. From a bird Melampus learned that Iphiclus as a child had been frightened by the bloody knife with which his father had been castrating goats. Melampus prescribed a glass of wine mixed with rust from the knife, and within nine months Iphiclus became a father. The herd of cattle Melampus gave to his brother, who was thus able to marry the girl of his choice. Melampus continued his career as a soothsayer with great success.

MELANIPPUS (měl'*a*·nĭp'ûs) helped Eteocles defend THEBES.

MELANTHIUS (mě·lăn'thĭ·ûs) was the unfaithful goatherd of ODYSSEUS.

MELEAGER (měl'ĭ·ā'jěr) was the hero of the CALYDONIAN BOAR HUNT.

MELICERTES (měl'ĭ·sěr'tēz), a mortal, became the sea god Palaemon. See SEA GODS.

MELPOMENE (měl·pŏm'ě·nē) is the Muse of tragedy. See MUSES.

MEMNON (měm'nŏn), a king of Ethiopia, fought with the Trojans against the Greeks. See EOS, TROJAN WAR.

MENELAUS (měn'ě·lā'ûs) was the husband of Helen of Troy. See ATREUS, TROJAN WAR.

MENOECEUS (mě·nē'sōōs), because of a prophecy, sacrificed his life to save THEBES.

MERCURY is the Roman name for HERMES.

MEROPE (měr'ŏ·pē) (1) was loved by ORION; (2) was the wife of SISYPHUS.

METAMORPHOSES (mět'*a*·môr'fŏ·sēz), a Greek word meaning "transformations," is the title of a large group of poems in Latin hexameters by the Roman poet P. Ovidius Naso or, more familiarly, Ovid. These poems take their title from the fact that each story is at least theoretically based on a miraculous transformation, such as that of Narcissus into a flower, though actually the transformation often plays a rather minor part in the story. Ovid's tales of transformations range all the way from the change of Chaos into the created world down to the change of Julius Caesar into a god, and they include the myths of Aphrodite and Adonis, Pyramus and Thisbe, Perseus and Andromeda, Jason and Medea, and Ceyx and Alcyone, to name but a few (all of these are recounted elsewhere in this book). Indeed, the *Metamorphoses* is one of the great sources of information about myths of this kind, and it has been a quarry for poets and prose writers of all succeeding ages.

METANIRA (mĕt′à·nĭr′à) was the mother of a family that befriended Demeter at Eleusis. See EARTH GODDESSES.

METIS (mē′tĭs) was the goddess of cleverness and the first wife of ZEUS.

MEZENTIUS (mĕ·zĕn′shĭ·ûs) fought against AENEAS.

MIDAS (mī′dàs), king of Phrygia, was given two gifts by two gods. Because Midas did him a favor, Dionysus granted him one wish. Midas chose that everything he touched should turn to gold, but he found this talent so troublesome that he had to ask the god to take it away from him. On another occasion Midas declared that Pan's music was superior to Apollo's, and Apollo gave Midas a pair of donkey's ears. See APOLLO, DIONYSUS.

MINERVA (mî·nĕr′và) is the Roman name for ATHENE.

MINOS (mī′nŏs), once king of Crete, is a judge in Hades. See DAEDALUS, HADES, THESEUS.

M. NOTAUR (mĭn′ô·tôr) was a monster, half-bull and half-human. See DAEDALUS, THESEUS.

MNEMOSYNE (nĕ·mŏz′ĭ·nē) is the goddess of memory and the mother by Zeus of the MUSES.

MOERAE (mē′rē) are the Fates. See FATE.

MOLY (mō′lē) is the magic herb that saved Odysseus from Circe's enchantment. See ODYSSEUS.

MOMUS (mō'mŭs), a son of Night, is the god of faultfinding and mockery. As the licensed grumbler of Olympus, he blamed Zeus for putting the bull's horns on its head rather than on its shoulders, which were stronger; and he found fault even with the beauty of Aphrodite—he criticized her shoes. Finally the gods tired of his mockery and kicked him out of Olympus. In *Ode to the Comic Spirit* George Meredith uses Momus as a symbol of the healthy criticism that is needed to keep both gods and men sane. In this poem, after Momus is thrown out of Olympus, all the other gods degenerate.

MORPHEUS (môr'fūs) is the chief god of dreams. See HADES.

MORS (môrz) is the Roman name of Thanatos, the god of death. See HADES.

MULCIBER (mŭl'sĭ·bẽr) is a Roman name for HEPHAESTUS.

MUSES. The Muses, or the **Pierides,** as they are often called after their birthplace, the spring **Pieria** on the slopes of Mount Olympus, are goddesses whose special nature is to inspire and encourage the arts. They are supposed to be the daughters of Zeus and the Titaness **Mnemosyne,** who is the goddess of memory. The symbolism is obvious: divine inspiration and memory produce the arts.

The Muses are nine in number, and each has a single art or group of related arts as her province. Each also has associated with her name a symbol or symbols drawn from the art that she patronizes. The nine Muses with their associated arts and symbols are:

Clio	history	wreath of laurel and scroll
Melpomene	tragedy	tragic mask and **buskin,** or **cothurnus** (a high, thick-soled boot worn by actors in tragic drama)

Thalia	comedy and pastoral poetry	comic mask, **sock** (a light, thin-soled shoe worn by actors in comedy), and shepherd's staff
Urania	astronomy	globe and pair of compasses
Calliope	heroic or epic poetry	stylus and tablet
Euterpe	music	flute, sometimes a double flute
Erato	love poetry and marriage songs	lyre
Polyhymnia or **Polymnia**	sacred song and oratory	veil
Terpsichore	dancing	wreath, lyre, and cymbals

Traditionally the Muses reside in several springs, Castalia on Mount Parnassus, and **Aganippe** and **Hippocrene** on Mount Helicon. Hippocrene sprang from a place where Pegasus, the winged horse of the Muses, stamped his hoof on dry ground (for this famous horse see BELLEROPHON). The waters of these springs were supposed to give inspiration in the arts to whoever drank of them. Worship of the Muses seems to have been located originally on Mount Olympus where they were thought to have been born, but it later spread to Mount Helicon and also to Mount Parnassus, where Apollo, who is a close associate of the Muses, had his oracle at Delphi on the steep side of the mountain.

Besides inspiring poets and other artists, the Muses themselves engage in the arts, sometimes providing entertainment for the gods on Olympus, and sometimes even appearing at human occasions such as the marriage of Peleus and Thetis. They also engaged in a contest with the nine daughters of a man named Pierus who boastfully had said that his daughters were their equals; when the Muses had won, the daughters were changed into birds.

In English poetry the Muses are referred to probably more often than any other classical figures, for poets have habitually called on them to supply the inspiration with which to make good poetry or have habitually complained about their unreliability when they were needed most. *The Teares of the Muses* (1591) by Edmund Spenser shows them lamenting individually the low state to which letters in England had fallen at that time, a lament that must be considered to have had a good effect in view of the literary works that were produced in the next fifteen or twenty years. William Blake expresses a similar complaint about letters in his own time, in a short poem called *To the Muses,* in which he surmises that they must be absent from the scene. Milton, whose love of things classical was second only to his love of Christian theology, turns the Muse Urania to special use in the first book of *Paradise Lost* where he converts her to Christianity as the inspirer of the Hebrew prophets and calls her to sing of man's first disobedience, an invocation that he varies at the beginning of the seventh book of the same poem. In his *Essay on Criticism* (1. 215–216) Pope warns the critic,

> A *little learning* is a dang'rous thing;
> Drink deep, or taste not the Pierian spring;

here he alludes to the ability of the Muses to inspire through the waters of the spring in which they were born. Nearer to our own times, in 1807, Lord Byron wrote his *Farewell to the Muse,* bidding her an "eternal Adieu"; but in 1812 he was still on familiar terms with her and her sisters and spoke of them in

237

admiring lines in *Childe Harold* (1. 62) where he memorializes Mount Parnassus. It remained for Walt Whitman, beginning his unclassical yawp, *Song of Myself,* to invoke himself as his own Muse, using the poetic formula found in most classical epics and in other poems. Perhaps the best-known allusion to the Muses in our own day is Archibald MacLeish's *Invocation to the Social Muse,* a poem in which he explains the dangers of being inspired to write contemporary political events into one's poetry.

MYRMIDONS (mîr′mĭ·dŏnz) were the ant people given to Aeacus by ZEUS.

MYRTILUS (mîr′tĭ·lûs), the servant of King Oenomaus, was bribed to betray his master by Hippodamia or Pelops, the parents of ATREUS.

NAIADS (nā′ădz) are water NYMPHS.

NARCISSUS (när·sĭs′ûs) was the handsome son of **Liriope** and a river god named **Cephisus.** Many fell in love with him, but he was indifferent to their advances and rejected their love. The Nymph **Echo** was so fond of him that when he refused her attentions, she wasted away until only her voice remained (see NYMPHS), whereupon the other unfortunates prayed to the gods that Narcissus be punished, and their prayer was answered. Some say the goddess Nemesis, who destroys the arrogant, brought about his punishment. One day Narcissus saw his own reflection in the clear water of a fountain and fell in love with it. He became himself the victim of unrequited love, finally wasting away until only the flower that bears his name remained in his place.

Thus did divine irony make the punishment fit the crime, and thus did it provide also an appealing image to poets. Spenser in *The Faerie Queene* (3. 6. 45) refers to

> Foolish *Narcisse,* that likes the watry shore,

and Christopher Marlowe in *Hero and Leander* (1. 74–76), wishing to make a comparison favorable to his hero, writes that Leander's features exceed his

> That leapt into the water for a kiss
> Of his own shadow, and despising many,
> Died ere he could enjoy the love of any.

Marlowe followed a postclassical version of the myth that attributed Narcissus' death to drowning. The original version seems to have been in Milton's mind when in *Paradise Lost* (4. 460–467) he has Eve describe how first she saw her own reflection in limpid water:

> As I bent down to look, just opposite,
> A Shape within the watry gleam appeerd
> Bending to look on me, I started back,
> It started back, but pleas'd I soon returnd,
> Pleas'd it returnd as soon with answering looks
> Of sympathie and love, there I had fixt
> Mine eyes till now, and pin'd with vain desire,
> Had not a voice thus warnd me. . . .

John Keats, who left few myths untouched, in *I Stood Tip-toe upon a Little Hill* (163) summarizes briefly the tale of

> Narcissus pining o'er the untainted spring,

239

and Shelley, describing other flowers in *The Sensitive Plant,*
allows three lines to the narcissi (1. 18–20):

> . . . the fairest among them all
> Who gaze on their eyes in the stream's recess
> Till they die of their own dear loveliness.

Doubtless the best-known contemporary use of the myth is
that of the psychologists, who apply the term "narcissism" to the
condition of abnormal self-love.

NAUSICAA (nō·sĭk′ā·à) was a lovely Phaeacian princess who befriended ODYSSEUS.

NECTAR (nĕk′tĕr) is the drink of the gods.

NEMEAN (nê·mē′àn) **GAMES** originated in a funeral celebrated
by the Seven against THEBES.

NEMEAN (nê·mē′àn) **LION** was killed by HERACLES.

NEMESIS (nĕm′ê·sĭs) is the personification of the righteous anger
of the gods. See FURIES.

NEOPTOLEMUS (nē′ŏp·tŏl′ê·mŭs), who was also called Pyrrhus,
was the son of Achilles. He fought in the TROJAN WAR.

NEPENTHE (nê·pĕn′thē), a magic drink that banished sorrow,
was given by the queen of Egypt to Helen of Troy after the
TROJAN WAR.

NEPHELE (nĕf′ê·lē) was the mother of Phrixus and Helle. See
ARGONAUTS.

NEPTUNE is the Roman name for Poseidon. See SEA GODS.

NEREIDS (nĭr′ĭ·yîdz) are the Nymphs of the Mediterranean Sea.
See NYMPHS, SEA GODS.

NEREUS (nĭr′ōōs) is one of the SEA GODS.

NESSUS (nĕs′ŭs), a Centaur, tried to attack Deianira, Heracles'
wife, and was killed by Heracles. Before he died, he persuaded
Deianira to save some of his blood as a charm against unfaithful-

ness. A sacrificial robe envenomed with his blood caused the death of HERACLES.

NESTOR (nĕs′tôr) was a Grecian councilor in the TROJAN WAR.

NIKE (nī′kē), the goddess of victory, is one of the aspects of ATHENE.

NINUS (nī′nûs) was a king of ancient Babylon; his tomb was the trysting place of Thisbe and PYRAMUS.

NIOBE (nī′ŏ·bē) boasted that she was superior to Leto; therefore Apollo and Artemis, the children of Leto, took a terrible vengeance. See ARTEMIS, ATREUS.

NOTUS (nō′tûs) is the south wind. See WINDS.

NUMITOR (nŭm′ĭ·tôr) was the grandfather of Romulus and Remus. See ROME.

NYCTEUS (nīk′tūs) was the father of Antiope and a regent of THEBES.

NYMPHS are lesser divinities in the Greek hierarchy, a group of beings who have the form of lovely girls and live in the world with human beings but are more closely kin to the gods, whose children or wives they often are. The word "nymph" is derived from the Greek word for "bride," which became generalized to mean "maiden."

Specifically, the Nymphs are nature spirits. Each tree, stream, meadow, and mountain has living in it one such guardian spirit, and consequently there are thousands of them in the world of nature. Nymphs are classified by the part of nature that they inhabit, and of the many such classifications, the most important are:

Oreads	mountain Nymphs
Dryads and **Hamadryads**	tree Nymphs
Naiads	Nymphs of rivers and fountains

Oceanids	Nymphs of the great river of Oceanus
Nereids	fifty daughters of Nereus who are the Nymphs of the Mediterranean Sea

Greek mythology recounts many involvements between the Nymphs and the gods and between the Nymphs and the human race. The Nymphs were frequent attendants at divine weddings, or at the weddings of mortals of whom they were fond. It is with this in mind that Spenser, having called on the Muses to aid him in the celebration of his own wedding in his *Epithalamion* (37–39), asks these divine ladies to bring with them

> all the Nymphes that you can heare
> Both of the riuers and the forrests greene:
> And of the sea that neighbours to her neare,

to deck the bridal bower of his beloved. Also, in the *Prothalamion* (34–36), a poem written to celebrate the betrothal of the two daughters of the Earl of Worcester, he describes the Nymphs of the Thames River gathering flowers along the riverbank as if all were brides who wished

> To decke their Bridegromes posies
> Against the Brydale day, which was not long:
> Sweet *Themmes* runne softly till I end my song.

For Spenser these Nymphs express the spiritual loveliness of nature, and his description made an impression on T. S. Eliot, who echoes it ironically when he wishes to express the debasement of values in our own materialistic times (*The Waste Land*, 179–183):

> The nymphs are departed.
> And their friends, the loitering heirs of city directors;
> Departed, have left no addresses.
>
> .   .   .   .   .   .
>
> Sweet Thames, run softly till I end my song.[1]

There is irony, too, in Pope's use of the word "nymph" as a description of Belinda, the heroine in *The Rape of the Lock* (2. 19–20):

> This Nymph, to the destruction of mankind,
> Nourished two Locks, which graceful hung behind.

Among all the thousands of Nymphs who expressed nature for the Greeks, a good many were the subjects of individual myths. According to one myth, an Oread named **Echo** talked so much that she annoyed Hera, the queen of the gods, who in exasperation at last laid on her the curse of not being able to speak at all except to repeat what others said in her hearing. Subsequently Echo fell in love with Narcissus, and when her love was unrequited, she gradually faded away until only her voice remained, still echoing what she heard among the hills and valleys (see NARCISSUS). Milton has a song about her in his masque *Comus* (229–242), and allusions to Echo are frequent in other English poetry.

Another Nymph, **Arethusa,** was pursued in passion by the river god **Alpheus.** When Arethusa called on Artemis for help, Artemis changed her into a stream and caused her to flow under the ground and under the sea to return to the surface on the island of **Ortygia.** Alpheus, however, was equal to the occasion and flowed after her, ultimately mingling his waters with Arethusa's as he desired. Spenser gives a parallel to this

[1] From "The Waste Land," by T. S. Eliot, in his *Collected Poems, 1909–1935*. Copyright, 1934, 1936, by Harcourt, Brace and Company. Reprinted with their permission.

myth in his story of Molanna and Fanchin, two Irish streams, in *The Faerie Queene* (7. 6. 40–55), his purpose being to add the patina of myth to the countryside of Ireland. He also echoes the Arethusa story in *Colin Clouts Come Home Againe* in the story of Bregog and Mulla. John Keats, in *Endymion* (2. 936–1017), takes up where the myth leaves off and tells a symbolic aftermath in which Arethusa, still treasuring her chastity and still ebulliently pursued by Alpheus, still refuses and still flees him as the two streams rush through Keats's fanciful countryside. Shelley provides a colorful retelling of this myth in his poem *Arethusa.*

Another Nymph who has been the subject of much attention in later poetry is **Oenone,** a Nymph of Mount **Ida,** who lived with Prince Paris of Troy for several years. When Paris left her to marry Helen, she foretold that he would be wounded in the Trojan War and made him promise to return to her to be healed. Paris was wounded just as she had foreseen, and he did have himself carried back to Oenone; but she exercised a feminine privilege and refused to help him, and he consequently died. Oenone then regretted her refusal and, according to some accounts, died on Paris' funeral pyre. Tennyson has retold Oenone's story in two poems. In *Oenone* the Nymph speaks for herself and, in her grief at Paris' desertion, recounts all the events leading up to his departure to seek Helen; she closes with a foreboding of the coming war. In a much later poem, *The Death of Oenone,* Tennyson returns to the theme to tell the rest of the story of Oenone's refusal to see her former lover and of both their deaths.

Several other Nymphs are the subject of notable reference in English poetry. Three of the Nereids are well known: Thetis as the mother of the great Achilles; Amphitrite as the wife of Poseidon, the Olympian sea god; and **Panope** as the Nymph whom Milton describes in *Lycidas* (50–51, 98–102) where he first

blames the Nymphs for allowing his and their beloved friend
Lycidas to drown in the sea:

> Where were ye Nymphs when the remorseless deep
> Clos'd o're the head of your lov'd *Lycidas?*

and then exonerates them of negligence, blaming Lycidas' misfortune on the unlucky ship in which he sailed,

> The Ayr was calm, and on the level brine,
> Sleek *Panope* with all her sisters play'd.
> It was that fatall and perfidious Bark
> Built in th'eclipse, and rigg'd with curses dark,
> That sunk so low that sacred head of thine.

Dryope, a mortal girl, was transformed into a Dryad because
she injured the Dryad of the lotus tree. The story illustrates the
ancients' reverence for the spirits who inhabited and protected
the forms of nature. One day Dryope with her child and her sister
was picnicking by a pool on a tree-fringed stream. When the child
cried for a lotus flower, Dryope picked one, but she saw blood
drip from the stem. She had hurt the Dryad Lotis. In horror
Dryope tried to run, but her feet were rooted in the ground and
soon bark covered her body. As she lost the last of her mortality
she begged her sister to teach the child not to pick flowers or tear
branches off trees. Walter Savage Landor tells this story in a poem
called *Dryope.*
Calypso, the Nymph of the island of Ogygia, kept the home-
seeking Odysseus as her prisoner of love for eight years and
released him only on orders from Zeus himself. A Nymph of
latter-day creation is **Sabrina,** whom Milton in his masque *Comus*
invented to be the resident Nymph of the Severn river. The most
frequent use of Nymphs in English poetry, however, is doubtless
the generalized use of the word to mean merely a beautiful

woman. It is in this sense that Hamlet uses the word in speaking
to Ophelia (*Hamlet*, 3. 1. 88–89):

> . . . Nymph, in thy orisons
> Be all my sins rememb'red.

OCEANIDS (ō·sē′á·nĭdz) are the Nymphs of the great stream
of Oceanus. See NYMPHS, SEA GODS.
OCEANUS (ō·sē′á·nûs) was the first of the SEA GODS.
ODYSSEUS (ō·dĭs′ōŏs), or **Ulysses,** in his heroic character com-
bined greatness of physical strength and skill with greatness of
mind; thus he was the prototype of classical greatness and a
fitting hero for Homer's epic poem, the *Odyssey*. His huge stature
and his great strength caused strangers constantly to mistake him
for a god, and his resourceful wisdom was responsible not only
for the Greeks' winning the war against Troy but for making
possible his own survival against years of hardships on his way
home, hardships that cost the lives of all his men and left him
a solitary survivor. Perhaps the key to all Odysseus' greatness,
in Greek eyes, was his piety, especially for Zeus and Athene, who
were his patrons, for it was this piety, added to his wisdom and
strength, that won him the immortal favors necessary to provide
the happy ending to all his struggles. Odysseus was for the
Greeks the figure of heroic success against all the hardships of
this world, and as such a figure he has survived even to the
twentieth century.

Odysseus was the son of **Anticlia** and **Laertes,** king of Ithaca and the neighboring islands. His young manhood was distinguished by at least two incidents that were important to his later life. The first of these occurred on a visit to his grand-

THE FAMILIES OF ODYSSEUS, PENELOPE, AND HELEN OF TROY

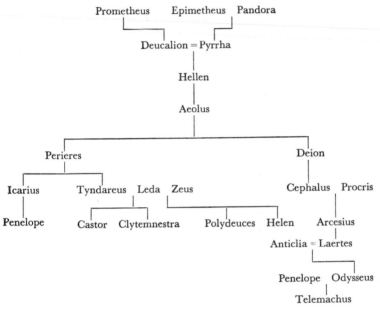

parents, who lived on the slopes of Mount Parnassus. Odysseus killed a great boar, but not before he had been wounded on the knee by the boar's tusks, a wound that left a scar during his entire life and made identification of him always possible to all who knew of it.

The second incident brought him a bow of great strength. Laertes sent Odysseus as an ambassador to Lacedaemon, and there

247

he became friendly with **Iphitus,** who gave him the bow of his father **Eurytus,** a bow that in later times only Odysseus himself had the strength to bend. This fact his wife's insolent suitors found out to their grief.

When Odysseus reached young manhood, his father retired from the throne and gave over the kingdom to him. Shortly thereafter Odysseus became a suitor for Helen, the most beautiful woman of classic times (see TROJAN WAR). Because many other kings of Greece were also suitors for her hand, Odysseus proposed that she be allowed to make her own choice but that first all her suitors take an oath to protect and defend her wedlock. This scheme being agreed on, Helen chose Menelaus. Odysseus prudently found another object for his affections and married **Penelope,** a young lady of virtue as great as her wealth, who in due course bore him a son, **Telemachus.**

Odysseus for some years found himself in the enviable position of being happily married and in control of a peaceful and prosperous kingdom. Such happiness could not last long, and its end came abruptly. Queen Helen, moved by the mortal charm of Prince Paris of Troy and the immortal urgings of Aphrodite, left her husband and eloped to Troy. Menelaus therefore demanded the fulfillment of the contract that all his fellow kings had sworn to at the time of the marriage, and he called on them to make war against the Trojans for the recovery of his wife.

Odysseus, who had invented the contract, could hardly refuse the summons; yet he found the leaving of his wife and infant son too much to face. Moreover, an oracle had told him that if he went he would return only after severe hardship and the loss of friends. He therefore resorted to guile and pretended to be insane; as proof of his insanity, he yoked together a horse and an ox and set about plowing the sands of the seashore. Yet method showed through his madness, for when his friends, to try him, placed the baby Telemachus in the path of the plow, he turned aside to spare the child. They accused him of sanity, and he had to abandon the ruse.

Odysseus' first task was to draw another great hero out of hiding. This hero was Achilles, who was destined to live a long undistinguished life or to win fame and die young in the siege of Troy. His mother Thetis was determined to prevent him from going to Troy, and she disguised him as a woman and hid him in the court of King Lycomedes on the island of Scyros. Odysseus donned a disguise to detect a disguise. Dressed as a trader, he traveled about seeking Achilles. At the court of Lycomedes, while showing his wares to the ladies, he showed also a splendid suit of armor and at the same time had a call to arms sounded. The martial combination was too much for Achilles, who with unladylike eagerness seized on the armor and thus revealed his identity. He readily accepted the invitation to war.

Odysseus' other services to the Greek cause at Troy were numerous. The details are given in the article on the Trojan War; so here it will suffice to name them briefly. Most of them show the ingenuity of Odysseus and his skill with words. He was the chief mediator between the quarreling Greek leaders, Agamemnon and Achilles; and later, when Achilles was killed by the arrow from Paris' bow, Odysseus rescued his body and fought his way back with it to the Greek camp so that it might have fitting burial. Achilles' armor was awarded to Odysseus.

Late in the war, when the Greek cause was making little headway, a son of King Priam of Troy was captured. His name was Helenus, and he had the gift of prophecy. To the Greeks he prophesied that in order to obtain victory they must do three things: obtain the fighting aid of Achilles' son, Neoptolemus; procure the bow and arrows of Heracles; and, finally, secure possession of the Palladium (see ATHENE), a sacred statue of Athene whose presence in Troy guaranteed the security of the city.

Odysseus was able to accomplish all three of these tasks. First he sailed to Scyros again and won the aid of Neoptolemus by presenting to him his father's armor. Neoptolemus promptly joined the Greek forces. The second task was more difficult, for Heracles' bow and arrows belonged to Philoctetes, a wounded hero whom the Greeks had abandoned on Lemnos because his screams and the smell of his wound had been too much for Greek nerves. Philoctetes had naturally resented this treatment and was not kindly disposed to his former friends, but Odysseus and Neoptolemus or Diomedes persuaded him to join the Greek forces again (see PHILOCTETES). The third project also was compassed by Odysseus' wile. Disguised as a beggar, he made his way into the citadel of Troy and found where the Palladium was kept. Later he returned with Diomedes and carried it off to the Greek camp. The preliminary steps had now been taken, and all that remained was to force the issue with the Trojans, no small problem in view of their resolute refusal to come out of the town. Prompted by Athene, his patroness, Odysseus proposed the stratagem of the wooden horse, which carried the day.

When Troy had been captured and sacked and when all the spoils of the city had been divided, the Greek chieftains set out for their homes. For some this was only a short journey, but for Odysseus, who was soon to be cursed by the sea god Poseidon, the journey ended only aften ten long years and brought him home, as Poseidon decreed, late, "in evil case, with the loss of all his company, in the ship of strangers, and [to] find sorrows in his house" (*Odyssey*, 9). The story of his travels forms the subject of Homer's *Odyssey*, an epic poem whose title has survived as the modern word for a long adventuresome journey and whose contents have proved a rich quarry for English poets for the past four centuries. In the following brief account of this journey, a few typical literary references have been included.

When Odysseus and his men set sail for Ithaca, they began at once to suffer the hardships foreseen by the oracle that Odysseus had consulted before he embarked for Troy. Landing at Ismarus, the city of the **Cicones,** the Ithacans captured it and seized a great deal of spoil; but the Cicones gathered together a larger force and counterattacked. In the battle that ensued, Odysseus lost six of his men from each ship and had to flee seaward. On the sea, a tempest beset them for two days and two nights, so that they had to furl their sails and run before the north wind. On the third day, the tempest having subsided somewhat, they tried to sail around Cape Malea, the southernmost point of the Greek mainland, and to turn northward toward Ithaca; but the north wind renewed its fury and drove them off course.

For nine days they were blown across the seas, and on the tenth they landed in the country of the **Lotos Eaters.** Here they were able to get fresh water, and Odysseus sent a scouting party inland to see what the inhabitants were like. There they found men who ate the "honey-sweet" fruit of the lotos, an enchanted fruit. These men gave the fruit to some of the Ithacans, and its magic effect caused them to lose all desire to return home. Instead, they wished to remain forever with the Lotos Eaters in the sweet forgetfulness caused by the fruit. Their feelings are described by Tennyson in *The Lotos Eaters:*

> They sat them down upon the yellow sand,
> Between the sun and moon upon the shore;
> And sweet it was to dream of Fatherland,
> Of child, and wife, and slave; but evermore
> Most weary seem'd the sea, weary the oar,
> Weary the wandering fields of barren foam.
> Then someone said, "We will return no more";
> And all at once they sang, "Our island home
> Is far beyond the wave; we will no longer roam."

Odysseus, however, forced them to return to the ships, where he had them bound so that they could not escape; and the Ithacans set out once more. They came next on the island of the **Cyclopes** (whose name means "round-eyes"). The Cyclopes, sons of Poseidon, were a fierce and unruly race of giants, each of whom had but a single eye placed in the middle of his forehead. They were shepherds who lived on their flocks and on the crops that grew without cultivation on the island.

Fearing danger, Odysseus left eleven of his twelve ships beached on a waste island offshore, and in the twelfth ship went to the main island to explore, taking along a goatskin full of wine for a present. On the main island he and his men found a great cave stored plentifully with cheeses and with young lambs and kids. Ignoring his men's urgings that they content themselves with taking the cheeses and escaping, Odysseus resolved to await the return of the giant Cyclops to whom the cave belonged. Soon their waiting was rewarded, and the Cyclops **Polyphemus** came back, shepherding his flocks. He drove his flocks inside the cave and then blocked its entrance with a stone so great that twenty-two wagons could not hold it.

Polyphemus first milked his ewes and then, discovering his guests, asked who they were. Odysseus replied that they were Greeks and asked hospitality in the name of Zeus. Polyphemus replied that he had no regard for Zeus; and he seized two of the men, dashed out their brains, and ate them raw. The Ithacans watched in horror while he finished his dinner, and then waited until he fell asleep. They took counsel as to whether they should murder him before he awoke again, but Odysseus perceived that if they did so they would perish because of the great stone blocking the entrance of the cave.

In this dilemma, Odysseus was able to devise a stratagem. He and his men waited until the Cyclops had left with his flocks for the next day, and then they took his club, a large pole of olive wood, and sharpened its end. When they had hardened the point in the fire, they put it in hiding until the following night. The Cyclops took two more Ithacans for his supper. Odysseus then gave him the skin of wine for dessert; thus Polyphemus went drunk to sleep. When he was deeply asleep, Odysseus and his men took out the pointed pole, heated it again in the fire, and plunged its point into the giant's eye.

Polyphemus awoke in a rage of pain and called on the other Cyclopes to aid him. Unfortunately for him, the wily Odysseus had assumed the pseudonym of "Noman" in his conversations with Polyphemus, and when the other Cyclopes asked Polyphemus who was injuring him, the giant replied, "Noman," to which his fellows counseled him somewhat dryly to turn for aid to his father, the god Poseidon.

On the following morning the Cyclops rolled away the stone to permit his flock to go out to graze, but he felt the back of each sheep as it passed by him. Odysseus tied the rams together in threes, and his men, one by one, suspended themselves under the middle ram of each group. In this way they all escaped; Odysseus himself came out under the last ram.

They had embarked safely and were making for the open sea when pride overcame Odysseus, and he could not resist calling back to the giant to taunt him. He even told Polyphemus his true identity and thus laid himself open to the wrath of Poseidon, whose curse was quoted earlier in this account. Polyphemus cast a great stone that nearly swamped the ship, but Odysseus and his men safely rejoined the other Ithacans waiting on the small island, and all put out to sea, leaving the frustrated violence of Polyphemus on the receding shore. T. S. Eliot draws from that brutal personality its essence for ironic use in *Sweeney Erect* where he describes Sweeney, the symbol of coarse vulgarity, in bed with an epileptic prostitute:

> Morning stirs the feet and hands
> (Nausicaa and Polypheme),
> Gesture of orang-outang
> Rises from the sheets in steam.[1]

Here he probably intends a contrast between Sweeney, who though physically healthy, is all violence and lust, and the woman, who though epileptic has about her nonetheless some possibility of the sweet innocence of Nausicaa whom Odysseus will meet later in his journeyings. (For another story about Polyphemus see GALATEA.)

Odysseus and his men next encountered **Aeolus,** the god of the winds, on his island. The god was kind to the wanderers from Ithaca, and they stayed to enjoy his hospitality for an entire month, during which time Odysseus told him about the Trojan War. Then as a parting gift, Aeolus gave to Odysseus a bag in which he had enclosed all adverse winds; he also gave him a favorable west wind to blow him on his way. For nine days the expedition sailed securely toward home, and the travelers were actually in sight of their native land when the curiosity of the men as to what the bag contained overcame them and they opened it. At once the stormy winds burst forth and blew them all the way back to Aeolus' island, where the god met them with disfavor because he interpreted their misfortune to mean that they were in bad standing with the Olympians. He asked them to leave his island at once, and they did so, heavy of heart.

After six more days of sailing the seas, they came on the seventh to the island of the **Laestrygonians,** or **Lestrygonians,** a race of giant man-eaters who, like the Cyclopes, were children of the god Poseidon. A reconnaissance party of three whom Odysseus sent to examine the place was attacked and one man eaten. There followed a fierce battle in which the Laestrygonians

[1] From "Sweeney Erect," by T. S. Eliot, in his *Collected Poems, 1909–1935.* Copyright, 1934, 1936, by Harcourt, Brace and Company. Reprinted with their permission.

fought with huge stones as their cousin Polyphemus had done, and the outcome was that only Odysseus and his single ship escaped death and destruction.

This single boatload, escaping in hasty flight, came next to **Aeaea,** an island on which lived the enchantress **Circe,** a daughter of Helios, the sun. Here they spent a day or two in peace, but Odysseus while hunting saw the smoke rising from Circe's house. He divided his men into two groups, and they drew lots to see which would explore the island. The band led by **Eurylochus** drew the lot, and they set off in the direction of Circe's house. There they found an abundance of wild animals who fawned about them instead of attacking them, and they heard Circe singing as she wove her web. After some hesitation they entered and greeted the enchantress, all except Eurylochus, who suspected a trap. Circe gave them magical food, and when they had eaten it, she turned them into swine and drove them off to the pigpen.

All this Eurylochus reported to Odysseus. The hero decided therefore that he himself must face the enchantress, and, girding on his sword, he set off for Circe's house. On the way he was met by Hermes, the messenger of the gods, who not only forewarned him of Circe's power but provided him with a charmed herb called **Moly,** which would counteract her enchantments. When Odysseus reached Circe's house, she prepared a repast for him also, into which she put the customary charms; and when these failed, she struck him with her wand and commanded him to be changed into a hog. At this point, in accordance with Hermes' advice, Odysseus sprang up, drew his sword, and threatened to kill her. Circe then fell at his feet and acknowledged him her superior in occult charms, calling him by his own name and in the same breath inviting him to bed with her. Carrying out Hermes' instructions, Odysseus first extracted a promise that she would try no more mischief and then accepted her invitation. After the lovemaking, Odysseus persuaded Circe to return his companions to their former selves. Then the entire company, overriding the objection of Eurylochus, settled down to a year of feasting and drinking.

The myth of Circe has been a popular theme for English poets, who usually have seen it as a symbol of the power of the sensual life to transform men into beasts. Spenser, modifying it to suit his needs, embedded it in the final canto of the Second Book of *The Faerie Queene,* where it appears as the "Bower of Bliss," a wonderful garden ruled over by an enchantress named Acrasia who has Circe's power. To this bower comes Guyon, the Red Cross Knight of temperance, guided by a holy man, and violently destroys it. By a stroke of the holy man's "vertuous staffe" the victims of Acrasia are returned from beastly to human form, all of them except a hog named Grill, who so much prefers being a hog that he is allowed to remain one. Spenser's point is clearly made by Guyon (2. 12. 87):

> . . . See the mind of beastly man,
> That hath so soone forgot the excellence
> Of his creation, when he life began,
> That now he chooseth, with vile difference,
> To be a beast, and lacke intelligence.

This fragment of the main theme was also taken up in the nineteenth century by Thomas Love Peacock and made into a satirical novel under the title of *Grill Grange.*

Milton provides Circe and Bacchus with a son Comus, whose name is the title of Milton's poem and who was in olden time a minor god of mirth and orgy. The theme of *Comus* is the power of virtue to triumph over vice. The conflict is between a lovely Lady symbolizing chastity and the licentious and sensual Comus (46–58):

Bacchus that first from out the purple Grape,
Crush't the sweet poyson of mis-used Wine

. . . . . .

On *Circes* Iland fell (who knows not *Circe*
The daughter of the Sun? Whose charmed Cup
Whoever tasted, lost his upright shape,
And downward fell into a groveling Swine)
This Nymph that gaz'd upon his clustring locks,
With Ivy berries wreath'd, and his blithe youth,
Had by him, ere he parted thence, a Son
Much like his Father, but his Mother more,
Whom therefore she brought up and *Comus* nam'd.

In the poem we find the tempter up to Circe's tricks. Comus, who (like his mother) has a horde of human beings whom he has changed into beasts, tries to win the Lady to his way of life. He is able to imprison her in a magic chair, but he cannot persuade her to accept him. Her brothers—with the aid of a guardian spirit who gives them the magic herb (here called Haemony), and with the help of the river Nymph Sabrina—finally rescue their sister.

Circe also appears in Matthew Arnold's poem, *The Strayed Reveller,* where she provides a weaker drink whose power does not transform but merely affords a wonderful vision of pleasure; and her magic is the subject of Dante Gabriel Rossetti's poem, *The Wine of Circe:*

Dusk-haired and gold-robed o'er the golden wine
  She stoops, wherein, distilled of death and shame,
  Sink the black drops; while, lit with fragrant flame,
Round her spread board the golden sunflowers shine.
Doth Helios here with Hecatè combine
  (O Circe, thou their votaress?) to proclaim
  For these thy guests all rapture in Love's name,
Till pitiless Night give Day the countersign?
Lords of their hour, they come. And by her knee

> Those cowering beasts, their equals heretofore,
> Wait; who with them in new equality
>   Tonight shall echo back the sea's dull roar
>   With a vain wail from passion's tide-strown shore
> Where the dishevelled seaweed hates the sea.

This description is based on a painting by Burne-Jones.

When the seasons began to repeat themselves, the men reminded Odysseus that they ought to be getting home. The hero thereupon called on Circe to fulfill her promise and give them their freedom. Circe agreed but informed him that first he must seek out **Tiresias,** the blind soothsayer, in the underground realm of Hades. At this news, Odysseus, in a classic manner not fashionable in our times, sat down on her bed and wept; but the goddess was adamant and gave him full instructions as to how to perform the task.

Accordingly, the Ithacans set sail again, and the wind brought them at last to the entrance of Hades, which was close to the land and the city of the Cimmerians, on the western side of Oceanus' stream. Here, taking with him **Perimedes** and Eurylochus, Odysseus made his way into the underworld and, by performing the sacrifices that Circe had specified, caused the strengthless dead to swarm around him. The first to appear was the spirit of **Elpenor,** who had fallen off Circe's roof and broken his neck. Then came Odysseus' mother, Anticlia, whom he had left alive when he sailed for Troy. Finally came Tiresias, who prophesied hardships yet to come on the journey back to Ithaca and who warned Odysseus that when he and his men should land on the island of Thrinacia they must avoid doing harm to the cattle of Helios, the sun. Failure to obey this warning, said Tiresias, would bring destruction to the ship and death to the men, though Odysseus himself would escape. The Theban seer also told Odysseus that his house in Ithaca was filled with unruly suitors seeking the hand of his faithful wife, Penelope, and eating her lord's substance away. These, however, Odysseus was to overcome and slay in revenge.

Odysseus also held conversation with his mother, who told him that Penelope remained alive and faithful to him. When she had done, he talked to Achilles and was struck with grief to hear from Agamemnon the story of Clytemnestra's treachery (see ATREUS), which had sent Agamemnon's spirit to Hades. Looking about him, Odysseus saw many of the famous inmates of Hades' kingdom, such as Sisyphus and Tantalus. Then Odysseus returned to his ship and set sail with his men again on the stream of Oceanus.

When they had returned to Circe's isle, their first act was to carry out a promise made to the spirit of Elpenor: they gave his body a suitable funeral and burial. Then Circe foretold to Odysseus how he might escape destruction by the Sirens, whom he must pass, and how he must deal with the two monsters, Scylla and Charybdis. The **Sirens** were mermaids who lived on a rocky island and sang so enchantingly that passing mariners leaped in the sea or ran their ships against the rocks and were drowned. **Scylla** and **Charybdis** were two monsters who guarded either side of a narrow passage of the sea, Scylla with her body half-sunk into a cliff so that her six dogs' heads reared themselves into the air over the strait, and Charybdis in a deep cave on the other side, into which three times a day she sucked down the waters of the sea and then spewed them up. Both these monsters and the Sirens are discussed in more detail under SEA GODS.

Before passing the Sirens' isle, Odysseus followed the advice of Circe and stopped the ears of his men with wax. He also had them bind him to the mast of the ship, so that he could hear the fatal song but be powerless to yield to it. The Sirens tempted him in every way, but his men, following their instructions, refused to loose him, and the ship consequently passed safely by. They now heard the sea roaring and saw the smoke rising above it; so they knew that they were approaching Scylla and Charybdis. Odysseus ordered the helmsman to steer away from Charybdis, for that monster would have taken the whole ship; but this course naturally caused them to pass close by six-headed Scylla, and she snatched up six of the men and devoured them, to the great distress of their fellows.

In spite of this disaster, the ship itself escaped and came safely to the island of **Thrinacia** where the **cattle of the sun** lived. Odysseus, remembering the words of Tiresias and of Circe, urged his men not to stop there, but they listened to the persuasions of Eurylochus and decided to land. There they were delayed an entire month by the blowing of a southeast wind, which was unfavorable to their course. During this time they kept their oath to Odysseus and did not disturb the cattle of the sun as long as they had corn and wine; but one day, when their provisions were gone, and while Odysseus was asleep, they slew some of the cattle and prepared to eat them. Odysseus expected the worst when he discovered what they had done, and Helios on Olympus demanded revenge from Zeus.

A few days later the unfavorable wind fell off, and the men put their ship to sea again. Zeus kept his promise to Helios. He sent a great storm and then struck the ship suddenly with a thunderbolt. The ship came apart, and the men were drowned; only Odysseus, who had not offended Helios, survived. He kept himself afloat by clinging to the mast and keel of the ship, which he had been able to bind together. Floating along in this manner, he came again to Scylla and Charybdis. Though Charybdis swallowed down the fragments to which he clung, Odysseus was able to save himself by seizing on a fig tree that grew over her mouth and waiting there for her to spew up the wreckage again.

After floating along on the sea for nine days, he came to the island of **Ogygia,** which belonged to the Nymph **Calypso, who** gave him refuge.

Calypso not only gave him refuge; she also gave him her love, though Odysseus, remembering Penelope, accepted her love, as he had that of Circe, only because of necessity. For eight years the Nymph kept him on her island while he yearned for home. At the end of this time, Athene set about having him released. She chose a time when Poseidon was away from Olympus on a visit to the Ethiopians, and she persuaded Zeus that Odysseus had suffered enough to compensate Poseidon for his anger at Odysseus for blinding Polyphemus. Zeus accordingly sent Hermes with orders to Calypso that she not only release Odysseus but help him on his way.

These orders Calypso received with regret, but she obeyed them. With her help, Odysseus fashioned a raft and set off again for home. Unfortunately, Poseidon on his way back from the land of the Ethiopians saw Odysseus and stirred up a storm to destroy him. A great wave turned over the raft and threw the hero into the sea, where he nearly drowned; but the sea goddess **Leucothea** took pity on him. She gave him a veil to wind around his chest and promised that it would bring him safely to shore. Thus Odysseus reached the shore naked except for the veil, and without mortal friend.

The land to which he had come was **Scheria,** the land of the **Phaeacians,** of whom **Alcinous** was king. While Odysseus slept off his weariness in a small grove of trees, Athene went to the house of Alcinous and put into the head of his daughter **Nausicaa** the idea that she should go down to the river to wash clothes. This lovely girl did so, taking along a cart full of clothes and some maidens as attendants. When they had done their washing, they played a game of ball, and their shouts awakened Odysseus.

261

The hero looked forth from the grove, saw the young ladies, and decided to throw himself on their mercy. When he approached, they all fled except Nausicaa, to whom Athene gave courage. Odysseus used all his guile in a winning speech, and as a result Nausicaa gave him clothes and took him back to her father's house.

Alcinous accorded to Odysseus all the hospitality due a stranger. He offered him aid on his homeward journey, although he did not know who Odysseus was, and on the following day he called in his people to celebrate games in Odysseus' honor. During these games Odysseus, though at first unwilling to take part, yielded to provocation, seized a large stone, and threw it far beyond where anyone else had been able to throw it. This feat proved him a hero, and Alcinous persuaded him then to tell his long story to the court.

When Odysseus had completed the account of his wanderings, Alcinous suggested in the manner of the times that all should give gifts to Odysseus that he might not return home empty handed from their hospitality. The next morning the Phaeacians provided a ship and stowed in it all these gifts. For Odysseus they prepared a pallet so that he might sleep. Odysseus was still deep asleep when they reached Ithaca, but the Phaeacians carried him and his possessions safely ashore. Thus he at last escaped the wrath of Poseidon, who, discovering the deed, worked his vengeance on the Phaeacian sailors by turning them to stone just as they were about to reach their home port.

Meanwhile Athene, in the form of a herdsman, woke up the sleepy Odysseus and asked him who he was, a question that the crafty king, who never trusted prying strangers, answered with an elaborate lie worthy in later days of Huckleberry Finn. Then the goddess resumed her own form and received with good temper his mistaken reproach that she had for a long time deserted him. Athene instructed him not to go directly to his palace, where the suitors of his wife were living a violent and debauched life, but to go instead to the cottage of an old and faithful swineherd named **Eumaeus;** she promised to send him further instructions there. For a disguise, she changed him into an old man.

When Odysseus reached the cottage of Eumaeus, the old swineherd did not recognize him but received him hospitably anyway. He told Odysseus how the suitors were wasting his master's goods in their riotous ways, and Odysseus gave him a long fictitious account of his own identity. Soon they were joined by Telemachus, who had been off searching for news of his father and who had escaped the murderous hands of the suitors only by Athene's aid. Telemachus sent the old swineherd off to the palace to tell his mother of his safe return, and in Eumaeus' absence, Odysseus disclosed his identity to his son. Together father and son planned the destruction of the suitors. Then Telemachus went to the palace and gave his mother Penelope an account of his trip. Following Odysseus' orders, he did not tell her that he had seen his father; but he assured her that Odysseus was still alive, and to this encouragement one of his companions on the journey added that the omens showed that Odysseus was actually in Ithaca somewhere.

Soon Odysseus, guided by Eumaeus and in disguise, made his way toward his palace. In the fields he encountered a friend to the suitors, an unfaithful goatherd named **Melanthius,** who kicked Odysseus as he passed; but Odysseus restrained his wrath, and he and Eumaeus at last came to his palace where the suitors were as usual in the midst of a party. Pausing before the gate, Odysseus was recognized even in his disguise by his dog **Argus,** now old and outcast, lying on a heap of dung. This wagging of his tail was his last gesture, for as Odysseus passed on into the palace, old Argus died.

Inside the palace Odysseus received hard words and slight courtesy from the suitors. One of them, **Antinous,** even struck him with a stool; but Odysseus invoked the wrath of the gods against inhospitality to a stranger, and thereafter the suitors treated him more kindly. When Penelope heard of the presence of the stranger, she wished to talk with him in the hope of hearing news of her lord, but Athene put her to sleep and thus postponed the interview. In the night, Odysseus and Telemachus, aided by Athene, stowed in a private room all the weapons that usually hung in the hall.

Afterward, while the suitors slept, Odysseus remained in the hall, and there Penelope came to talk to him by the fire. She did not penetrate his disguise, and he told her an elaborate lie about his identity. He also told her that her lord was not far away and would return, word which he reinforced with such a good description of his real self that Penelope was moved, though in her despair she did not believe the prophecy. As a courtesy, however, she ordered Odysseus' old nurse, **Eurycleia,** to wash his feet. This old woman, while washing him, recognized him by the scar that he had received in his youth from the boar, and Odysseus was barely able to prevent her giving away his secret.

The night was a fateful one, for Penelope, despairing of her lord's return, had agreed to choose from among the suitors a new husband on the next day, her choice to be based on two conditions: the first, that they should rival one another to present lavish gifts to her, her favors to incline to the most generous: and the second, that she would choose whoever could bend and string the great bow of Odysseus and with it shoot an arrow through twelve axheads set in a row. These were the last of the devices of faithful Penelope to stave off an unwelcome marriage. Six years after the victory at Troy, when her husband's return had begun to seem impossible, she tried to keep off the suitors with the pretext that she could not marry until she had completed the weaving of a suitable shroud for old Laertes, Odysseus' father. For three years each day she worked on the web, but at night she secretly unraveled her work. During the fourth year, one of her maidens betrayed her secret, and the suitors forced her to finish the robe. She had scarcely finished it and taken it to Laertes when this fateful night forced decision on her. Thus Penelope became the symbol of the faithful wife, as she appears, for example, in Spenser's *Amoretti* (23), though Thomas Carew in *A Rapture* (125–130) seeks to impugn her virtue in order to persuade his mistress to yield to him:

> The Grecian dame,
> That in her endless web toyl'd for a name
> As fruitless as her work, doth there display
> Herself before the youth of Ithaca,
> And th' amorous sport of gamesome nights prefer
> Before dull dreams of the lost traveller.

When the others had gone to bed, Odysseus made himself a pallet of sheepskins and slept apart. Athene appeared to him, promised him aid, and gave him sleep. The next day Odysseus revealed himself to Eumaeus and another herdsman, asking their help in bolting the doors so that he might come at the suitors without giving them an opportunity to escape. The suitors now gathered for the celebration. Penelope had brought before them the great bow of her lord and set the test. Telemachus placed the twelve axheads in a row. One by one, each of the suitors tried his hand at bending the bow, and all failed. They warmed it by the fire and greased it with lard, but still they could not bend it. Then they decided to make sacrifices to Apollo, the god of archery, and to try the bow again the next day.

At this point, Odysseus, in spite of their protests, seized

the bow. He bent it easily and strung it. Then he fitted an arrow to the string and pierced the axheads; his second arrow killed the insolent Antinous. A violent fight ensued, in which Odysseus soon used up all his arrows; but Telemachus supplied him with other arms and fought by his side. The suitors, too, obtained arms, through the treachery of Melanthius, the wicked goatherd, but Athene gave the victory at last to Odysseus and his son. All the suitors save one or two, for whom Telemachus asked mercy, were slain. Odysseus then sent for the maidens of the house who had lived loosely with the suitors. He had them clean out the mess of battle and stack the dead suitors neatly on the outside. Then he had Telemachus hang these girls in an outer hall.

When Penelope came down into the hall, she found order restored. She refused to believe the old nurse Eurycleia, who told her that Odysseus had returned and won this battle. Only after a long conversation with Odysseus himself was she at last persuaded that the good news was true; he finally convinced her by his knowledge of the nature of his own bed, which he had fashioned out of a growing olive tree.

Now there remained for Odysseus only to make himself known to his father Laertes. With Telemachus, he set off for the old man's house. He found Laertes working in his garden in filthy old clothes and in great grief of mind that his son was lost. Odysseus was moved by the sight, and after lengthy conversation, showed the old man that his grief was now without foundation. Their reunion was interrupted by the news that the kinsmen of several of the dead suitors were approaching, armed and intent on revenge; but these Odysseus and Telemachus, with the aid of Athene, soon routed, and in fact Odysseus would have slain them all had not Athene stayed his hand.

Odysseus' troubles, as they are recorded in the *Odyssey*, were now over, and he was free to return to Penelope and live out his days, awaiting the peaceful death at sea that Tiresias had foreseen for him. It remained for a poet of a later day, Lord Tennyson, to take up the story here. In the poem that bears the Roman equivalent of Odysseus' name, *Ulysses,* Tennyson imagines that the active old hero had been unable to live a quiet and peaceful life after so much activity. He shows Ulysses setting forth to seek death at sea on another quest for knowledge and adventure. Reading this poem, one is more impressed with the Victorian mind of its author than with the classic personality of its subject; for Tennyson, tired of the Victorian effort to reconcile science and religious faith, sees in the figure of Ulysses the person who must go on learning, though what he learns does not comfort him. It is restlessness that drives him on, and the final statement has become famous for its stoic attitude:

> To strive, to seek, to find, and not to yield.

The use that James Joyce made of the Odyssean myths in his novel, *Ulysses,* though conventional in the basic respect that it represents Ulysses as the symbolic wanderer of the world, is strikingly unconventional in other respects. Joyce has created a modern counterpart of Ulysses in the person of Bloom, and for him he provides a series of incidents that are parallel to those of the *Odyssey;* but like the character of the protagonist, the events have all been translated into modern counterparts as they would occur in everyday Dublin, and all the incidents occupy the space of only twenty-four hours. In this way the commonplace and ineffectual Bloom is ironically contrasted with the heroic and successful Odysseus, and at the same time the carefully worked out parallel touches the acts and character of Bloom with pathos and a certain dignity.

ODYSSEY (ŏd′ĭ·sē) is an epic poem by Homer about the wanderings of **ODYSSEUS.**

OEDIPUS (ĕd′ĭ·pŭs) unknowingly killed his father and married his mother. See THEBES.

OENEUS (ē′nūs) was the father of Meleager, hero of the CALYDONIAN BOAR HUNT.

OENOMAUS (ē·nŏ′mā·ŭs) was killed in a chariot race with Pelops, father of ATREUS.

OENONE (ē·nŏ′nē) is one of the NYMPHS.

OENOPION (ē·nŏ′pĭ·ŏn), avenging an insult to his daughter, blinded ORION.

OETA (ē′tà) is the mountain on which Heracles prepared his own funeral pyre. See HERACLES.

OGYGIA (ō·jĭj′ĭ·à) is the island of Calypso. See ODYSSEUS.

OILEUS (ō·wī′lōōs) was the father of the lesser Aias. See TROJAN WAR.

OLYMPIC (ō·lĭm′pĭk) **GAMES** were established in honor of ZEUS.

OLYMPUS (ō·lĭm′pŭs) is the mountain on whose summit the gods live.

OMPHALE (ŏm′fà·lē) was served for three years by HERACLES.

OMPHALUS (ŏm′fà·lŭs) is a sacred stone at Delphi. See ORACLES.

OPHELTES (ō·fĕl′tēz), who was killed by a serpent, was renamed Archemorus and given a splendid funeral by the Seven against THEBES.

OPHION (ō·fī′ŏn) is one of the TITANS.

OPPIUS (ŏp′ĭ·ŭs) was one of the seven hills of earliest ROME.

OPS (ŏps) is the Roman name of the Titan earth goddess Rhea. See EARTH GODDESSES.

ORACLES. The two most famous oracles of the ancient world were the oracle of Zeus at **Dodona** in **Epirus** and the oracle of Apollo at **Delphi** on the slope of Mount **Parnassus.** Zeus's was the oldest oracle in Greece, but Apollo's was the most renowned;

so many pilgrims visited Delphi that it was said to be the center of the earth. When people were perplexed by fears and uncertainties they took their questions to the oracles and, if the gods were willing and the attendants of the oracles skillful, they received the answers of the gods.

At Dodona, in the land of oak trees, Zeus answered questions by causing a wind to rustle the branches of the oaks. The priests who interpreted these answers hung brass vessels on the branches to make the god's voice clearer to them. At Delphi the priestess of Apollo—who was sometimes called **Pythia,** or the **Pythoness,** because a great serpent named **Python** had possessed the place of the oracle until Apollo killed him—sat on a tripod over a cleft in the rocks; the vapor rising from this cleft put her into a trance and caused her to speak with the wisdom of the god.

A. E. Housman writes in *The Oracles:*

'Tis mute, the word they went to hear on high Dodona mountain,
When winds were in the oakenshaws and all the cauldrons tolled,
And mute's the midland navel-stone beside the singing fountain,
And echoes list to silence now where gods told lies of old.[2]

In these lines the cauldrons are the brass vessels that the priests hung in the oak trees at Dodona; "the cauldrons tolled" when they were struck together by the wind blowing through the branches. As the oracular symbol at Delphi Housman uses not the tripod of the Pythoness but the **Omphalus.** This is a large stone pierced with a knifelike piece of iron; the archaic letters carved on the stone seem to spell "Earth's." Housman calls it "the midland navel-stone" because Delphi, as explained earlier, was considered the center of the earth, and Omphalus means "central point." Probably the oracle originally belonged to Gaea, the

[2] From "The Oracles," by A. E. Housman, in his *Last Poems.* Copyright, 1922, by Henry Holt and Company, Inc. Reprinted with the permission of the publisher.

ancient earth goddess and the mother of the Titans and many of the monsters. The Python who guarded the oracle until Apollo killed him was one of Gaea's sons.

The Omphalus was believed to be the stone that Cronus swallowed, thinking it was Zeus. Cronus learned that one of his children by Rhea was fated to dethrone him, so he swallowed the first five as soon as they were born. After the birth of Zeus, however, Rhea wrapped a stone in swaddling clothes and gave it to Cronus. As soon as Zeus was grown he sought the aid of his grandmother Gaea, and together they compelled Cronus to disgorge the five children and also the stone, which was then placed at Delphi.

The "singing fountain" that Housman mentions is the spring near Delphi named **Castalia** for the daughter of a river god who took refuge in it when she was pursued by Apollo. The spring thereafter was sacred to Apollo and the Muses, and those who drank of it or bathed in it were touched by poetic inspiration.

Tennyson in *The Talking Oak* refers to Dodona when he speaks of the Thessalian tree

> In which the swarthy ringdove sat,
> And mystic sentence spoke.

The oracle at Dodona was founded because a black dove alighted there and commanded the people to establish an oracle of Zeus.

Sometimes the oracles spoke plainly to men, as when the oracle at Delphi ordered Orestes to avenge his father's murder by killing his mother and her lover; but often they spoke in riddles, as when Apollo's oracle at Delos told Aeneas, who had asked guidance in his wanderings, to seek the land of his forefathers: it took time and trouble and finally the advice of Aeneas' family gods for him to discover where the land of his forefathers was. Because oracular utterances were so frequently ambiguous, they required the interpretation of wise men; and the wise men's interpretations were sometimes as obscure as the oracles. In *The Winter's Tale* (3. 2. 133–137) the Delphic oracle speaks as clearly as it did to Orestes. In *Cymbeline* (5. 5. 443–458), however, the oracle of Jupiter is so mysterious that it can be explained only by a soothsayer, and then only after the events it predicts have taken place. Similarly, in John Ford's *The Broken Heart* (4. 3. 35–38) the dark prophecy of the oracle at Delphi is only partly explained by the sage Tecnicus. As the king and his courtiers attempt to construe the meaning, one of the councilors declares:

> . . . the pith of oracles
> Is to be then digested when th' events
> Expound their truth, not brought as soon to light
> As utter'd. Truth is child of Time . . . .

An unbeliever would describe the same phenomenon by saying that any guess about the future, if expressed with sufficient ambiguity, can by hindsight be made to apply to the events that it purported to foretell.

In Christian times a belief grew up that Satan and his rebel angels (as Robert Burton says) "gave oracles at Delphos, and elsewhere," and that the birth of Christ silenced the oracles forever. Housman alludes to this silence in the lines quoted earlier, but he does not describe it as a triumph for Christ, as Milton does in *On the Morning of Christ's Nativity* (173–180):

> The Oracles are dum,
> No voice or hideous humm
>   Runs through the arched roof in words deceiving.
> *Apollo* from his shrine
> Can no more divine,
>   With hollow shreik the steep of *Delphos* leaving.
> No nightly trance, or breathed spell,
> Inspires the pale-ey'd Priest from the prophetic cell.

In English literature, however, the oracles and the prophets of classical mythology usually represent divine rather than satanic inspiration. Their utterances, as the illustrations have shown, are often difficult to understand. In *Paradise Lost* (10. 163–191) the words of the Son of God to the serpent are typically oracular not only because they are spoken by a divinity but also because they are ambiguous; what the Son means when he says that the seed of the woman shall bruise the serpent's head is revealed only in the fullness of time. Satan misinterprets the oracle and does not recognize the doom that awaits him.

Describing a considerably less reliable prophet, Byron says of Rousseau in *Childe Harold* (3. 81):

> . . . he was inspired, and from him came,
> As from the Pythian's mystic cave of yore,
> Those oracles which set the world in flame,
> Nor ceased to burn till kingdoms were no more.

W. B. Yeats writes of Plotinus' mystical vision of truth in *The Delphic Oracle upon Plotinus.*

ORCUS (ôr′kûs) is a Roman name of the god and of the place HADES.

OREADS (ô′rî-ădz) are mountain NYMPHS.

ORESTES (ō-rĕs′tēz) was ordered by Apollo to kill his mother Clytemnestra because she had murdered his father Agamemnon. See ATREUS.

ORION (ō-rī′ŏn), a son of the sea god Poseidon, was a huge handsome fellow and a mighty hunter. His first wife was **Side**, whose name means "pomegranate"; she was cast into Hades for boasting that she was more beautiful than Hera, the queen of the gods. (For the connection of the pomegranate with the underworld, see Persephone under HADES.) Orion then fell in love with **Merope,** the daughter of King **Oenopion** of the island of Chios.

While he wooed this girl, Orion hunted so successfully that he practically cleared the island of wild beasts. The king, however, found many reasons to put off the marriage, and one day Orion got drunk and seduced Merope. Oenopion caught him in his drunken sleep and blinded him; but Orion learned that he might regain his sight from the rays of the rising sun, and he therefore went to the island of Lemnos and got one of the attendants of the god Hephaestus to guide him toward the east. The sun restored his sight, and he hurried back to Chios to take his revenge on Oenopion, but the king had been hidden away by Poseidon.

Accounts differ as to Orion's later adventures. Some say that he went to Delos to become a servant of Artemis, the goddess of hunting, and that she grew so fond of him that her brother Apollo disapproved and tricked her into shooting him. According to another version, Orion met Artemis on Chios and tried to rape her. She summoned a huge scorpion which stung him to death, and then both he and the scorpion were turned into constellations. Spenser alludes to this myth in *The Faerie Queene* (7. 7. 39). A third story maintains that while Orion was serving Artemis, he was seen by Eos, the goddess of the dawn, who fell in love with him and carried him off. Then Artemis grew jealous and killed him. The love affair between Orion and the goddess of the dawn caused Keats to produce his wonderful line (*Endymion*, 2. 198), "blind Orion hungry for the morn."

At one time in his crowded life Orion met and desired the **Pleiads,** or **Pleiades,** seven Nymphs who were the daughters of Atlas. The ladies ran and Orion pursued. Some say that the chase lasted for years until Zeus, taking pity on the Nymphs, turned them into stars; but when Orion was killed by Artemis, he became a constellation, and ever since he has continued to pursue the

Pleiades across the heavens. It is not surprising that the king of the gods decided to help these ladies. Before they made a career of escaping from Orion, three of them had been the mistresses of Zeus: by him Maia became the mother of the god Hermes; Electra, of Dardanus, founder of the royal house of Troy; and Taygeta, of Lacedaemon, the first king of Sparta. In the sky Orion appears as he did on earth, the mighty hunter with his sword, club, and lion's skin. According to certain stories, his dog was also translated to the skies and became the dog star Sirius. Spenser (*Faerie Queene,* 1. 3. 31) calls this star "fierce *Orions* hound," and T. S. Eliot, creating an atmosphere of foreboding in *Sweeney among the Nightingales,* writes:

> Gloomy Orion and the Dog
> Are veiled; and hushed the shrunken seas.[3]

In English literature Orion is mentioned most frequently as a constellation, and often in connection with the Pleiades. Since Orion usually rises in a period of storms, Milton (*Paradise Lost,* 1. 305–306) speaks of the roiling of seaweed

> . . . when with fierce Winds *Orion* arm'd
> Hath vext the Red-Sea Coast. . . .

Tennyson recalls in *Locksley Hall* (7–10):

> Many a night from yonder ivied casement, ere I went to rest,
> Did I look on great Orion sloping slowly to the West.
>
> Many a night I saw the Pleiads, rising through the mellow shade,
> Glitter like a swarm of fire-flies tangled in a silver braid.

And in *More Poems* XI A. E. Housman writes:

[3] From "Sweeney among the Nightingales," by T. S. Eliot, in his *Collected Poems, 1909–1935.* Copyright, 1934, 1936, by Harcourt, Brace and Company. Reprinted with their permission.

The rainy Pleiads wester,
    Orion plunges prone,
And midnight strikes and hastens,
    And I lie down alone.

The rainy Pleiads wester
    And seek beyond the sea
The head that I shall dream of
    That will not dream of me.[4]

The most extended and serious use of the myths about Orion was made by the nineteenth-century poet Richard Henry Horne, whose long narrative poem *Orion* is an allegory of spiritual progress. The hero, a giant of the earth, falls in love with Artemis and aspires to intellectual and spiritual understanding; but he is distracted by sensual passion for the lovely Merope, another creature of earth, until he is blinded by her father's soldiers and she is taken away from him. His misery, however, leads him to happiness, for he goes to Eos, and she restores his sight and gives him her love. This love is not all spirit, like that of Artemis, nor all passion, like that of Merope, but a blend of the two. Orion learns that man, to be happy and useful, must achieve this balance between the intellect and the emotions. As Douglas Bush points out, Horne's poem is strongly influenced by Keats's *Endymion* and *Hyperion*.

ORITHYIA (ŏr′ĭ·thī′yȧ) was kidnaped by Boreas. See WINDS.

ORPHEUS (ôr′fĭ·yûs) the Thracian, the son of the Muse Calliope and Apollo, the patron of artists, was the greatest singer and musician of classical myth. When he sang and played on the lyre, his father's instrument, he moved men and gods to do his

---

[4] From "Poem XI," by A. E. Housman, in his *More Poems*. Copyright, 1936, by Barclays Bank, Ltd. Reprinted with the permission of Henry Holt and Company, Inc.

bidding and, when he chose, charmed wild beasts and (as John Fletcher * writes)

> . . . made trees
> And the mountain tops that freeze
>   Bow themselves when he did sing.
> To his music plants and flowers
> Ever sprung as sun and showers
>   There had made a lasting spring.

Lorenzo in *The Merchant of Venice* (5. 1. 79–82), made wise by love, moonlight, and music, moralizes the powers of Orpheus:

> . . . therefore the poet
> Did feign that Orpheus drew trees, stones, and floods,
> Since naught so stockish, hard, and full of rage
> But music for the time doth change his nature.

In ancient Greece, however, all poems were made to be sung, and Orpheus composed his own poems; thus he has come in English literature to symbolize the great poet as well as the great musician.

He sailed with the Argonauts and, as Spenser says in the *Amoretti* (44),

> When those renoumed noble Peres of Greece,
> thrugh stubborn pride amongst themselues did iar
> forgetfull of the famous golden fleece,
> then Orpheus with his harp theyr strife did bar.

He was called on many times to lift their drooping spirits and compose their quarrels, but his most notable deed on this expedition was to outsing the **Sirens.** These lovely but cruel mermaids lived on a rocky island and lured mariners to death by their

---

* This song from Shakespeare and Fletcher's *Henry VIII* (3. 1. 3–8) is usually attributed to Fletcher.

seductive music. On the return voyage the Argonauts passed close to this island, and they would have wrecked their ship and drowned if Orpheus had not sung louder and sweeter than the Sirens and thus persuaded the heroes to hold their course. Some versions of the story say that the Sirens committed suicide after this failure, but there is contrary evidence (see Sirens under SEA GODS). William Morris (*The Life and Death of Jason,* 14) invented antiphonal songs for the Sirens and Orpheus, but the songs seem oddly interchangeable, and are not good enough to make men either wreck a ship or keep on rowing.

Orpheus married a beautiful Dryad named **Eurydice,** but their time of happiness was short. **Aristaeus,** a half brother of Orpheus, lusted for Eurydice, and one day when he found her alone he tried to force his attentions on her. As she ran from him she stepped on a poisonous snake, and its bite killed her. Orpheus found his sorrow unbearable, and finally he resolved to go to the underworld and beg the return of Eurydice. This journey was forbidden to any living man, but Orpheus subdued the guards with his music and presented himself at the palace of Pluto and Persephone. As he sang his grief for Eurydice, the Furies wept and the spirits tormented in Tartarus forgot their own suffering. His song touched the heart of Persephone and, as Milton says (*Il Penseroso,* 107–108),

> Drew Iron tears down *Pluto's* cheek,
> And made Hell grant what Love did seek.

Pluto gave him permission to take Eurydice back to life on condition that she follow behind him and that he refrain from turning to look at her until they reached the upper world. He kept his word. They passed all the perils of Hades, but although he feared for her safety and yearned to see and touch her, he looked straight ahead. At last he stepped out into daylight and turned to embrace her, but he turned too soon. She was still in the darkness; and as his arms went around her, she faded. She could only whisper, "Goodbye." Even Orpheus' great courage and genius had not, in Milton's words (*L'Allegro*, 149–150),

> . . . set free
> His half-regain'd *Eurydice*.

Robert Browning in *Eurydice to Orpheus,* writing about a painting of the couple by Lord Leighton, imagines the thoughts of Eurydice at the parting:

> But give them me, the mouth, the eyes, the brow!
> Let them once more absorb me! One look now
>   Will lap me round forever, not to pass
> Out of its light, though darkness lie beyond:
> Hold me but safe again within the bond
>   Of one immortal look! All woe that was,
> Forgotten, and all terror that may be,
> Defied,—no past is mine, no future: look at me!

When Orpheus found that he could not return to Hades, he abandoned himself to despair. He avoided other people and wandered in the wild places of Thrace, singing his songs. One day he was found near Mount Rhodope by a band of Maenads who were drunk in the celebration of the rites of Dionysus. They drowned out his music with their shouts, killed him, and tore his body to pieces. His lyre and his bloody head were thrown in the river Hebrus, and they floated to the island of Lesbos. Milton, lamenting in *Lycidas* (58–63) the untimely death of a fellow poet, first asks the Nymphs (in the traditional fashion of the pastoral elegy) why they could not save Lycidas, and then he realizes the emptiness of his question:

> What could the Muse her self that *Orpheus* bore,
> The Muse her self, for her inchanting son

Whom Universal nature did lament,
When by the rout that made the hideous roar,
His gory visage down the stream was sent,
Down the swift *Hebrus* to the *Lesbian* shore?

Musing on duty and fame and the uncertainty of human life,
Milton relates the myth of Orpheus not only to Edward King, the
Lycidas of his poem, but also to himself.

Later, when he writes *Paradise Lost* (7. 26–27, 32–39),

On evil days though fall'n, and evil tongues;
In darkness, and with dangers compast round,

he returns to the death of Orpheus. He asks his own Protestant
Muse Urania to guide his song,

But drive farr off the barbarous dissonance
Of *Bacchus* and his Revellers, the Race
Of that wilde Rout that tore the *Thracian* Bard
In *Rhodope*, where Woods and Rocks had Eares
To rapture, till the savage clamor dround
Both Harp and Voice; nor could the Muse defend
Her Son. So fail not thou, who thee implores:
For thou art Heav'nlie, shee an empty dreame.

Even when classical myth moved Milton most deeply, he never
forgot to point out that to a Christian mind it was false. Yet
in this particular myth he found a partial parallel between the
circumstances of Orpheus' death and his own immediate circumstances—he was also a successful artist but a deeply disappointed man to whom many of his countrymen were hostile;
and he found a poetic truth more important than the parallel.
Orpheus, with his supreme accomplishment, his terrible failure,
and his violent death at the hands of his own people, was a
symbol of the tragic fate of human greatness.

Though Orpheus' life was sad and his death shocking, he and

Eurydice were reunited for eternal happiness in the Elysian Fields, and his lyre, according to certain versions of the myth, was translated to the heavens to become the constellation Lyra. Lamenting the death of Sir Philip Sidney in *The Ruines of Time* (607–615), Spenser tells this story of the lyre but transfers its ownership to Sidney, whom he calls Philisides, "the lover of the star," a name that Sidney invented for himself because his love poems were addressed to Stella. Spenser sees floating down a river a harp made of gold and ivory,

> The harpe, on which *Dan Orpheus* was seene
> Wylde beasts and forrests after him to leade,
> But was th' Harpe of *Philisides* now dead.

> At length out of the Riuer it was reard
> And borne aboue the cloudes to be diuin'd,
> Whilst all the way most heauenly noyse was heard
> Of the strings, stirred with the warbling wind,
> That wrought both ioy and sorrow in my mind:
> So now in heauen a signe it doth appeare.

In later times an oracle of Orpheus was established on Lesbos, the island to which his bloody head had floated, and Orpheus was endowed with magical and prophetic powers and made the center of the **Orphic** religion, which flourished from about the sixth century before Christ until the coming of Christianity. The Orphic worshipers believed in the divine origin of man, original sin, reincarnation, and the ultimate translation of the virtuous soul to paradise. The Renaissance poet Giles Fletcher in *Christs Victorie and Triumph* (3. 7) has in mind the religious figure of Orpheus when he writes:

> But he that conquer'd hell, to fetch againe
> His virgin widowe, by a serpent slaine,
> Another Orpheus was then dreaming poets feigne.

ORPHIC (ôr'fĭk) religion was centered on the figure of ORPHEUS.

ORTYGIA (ôr·tĭj'ĭ·ă) is the island on which the waters of Arethusa and Alpheus were finally joined. See NYMPHS.

OSSA (ŏs'ă) is a mountain which two Giants placed on Mount Olympus; then they piled Mount Pelion on top in their attempt to reach and attack the gods. See GIANTS.

OTHRYS (ŏth'rĭs) was the mountain stronghold of the Titans. See ZEUS.

OTUS (ō'tŭs) was one of the GIANTS.

PACTOLUS (păk·tō'lŭs) is the river whose sands turned to gold when Midas bathed in it. See DIONYSUS.

PAEAN (pē'ăn) is a name given to Apollo and also Asclepius. Paeans were songs of praise cr triumph addressed to APOLLO.

PALAEMON (pà·lē'mŏn) was the name given to Melicertes when he became one of the SEA GODS.

PALATINE (păl'à·tīn) is the hill on which Romulus founded ROME.

PALATIUM (pà·lā'shŭm) was one of the seven hills of earliest ROME.

PALINURUS (păl'ĭ·nū'rŭs), a steersman, was washed overboard from one of the ships of AENEAS.

PALLADIUM (pà·lā·dĭ·ûm), which was reputed to guarantee the security of any city that held it safely, was an ancient image of ATHENE.

281

PALLANTIDES (păl′ăn·tī′dēz) were the fifty sons of Pallas whose attempt to put their father on the throne of Athens was defeated by THESEUS.

PALLAS (păl′ăs) (1) is another name for ATHENE; (2) was one of the GIANTS; (3) was a brother of Aegeus who tried to usurp the throne of Athens but was defeated by THESEUS.

PAN (păn), or **Faunus**, or **Sylvanus**, the son of Hermes and a Nymph, is the Arcadian god of the fields and woods and the patron of hunters and shepherds. He protects flocks and herds, and he inspires travelers in wild and lonely country with panic. He has the legs and hooves of a goat but the trunk and arms of a man. Goat horns sprout from his head, his ears are pointed, and his bearded face is jovial and ugly. Because he has the gift of prophecy, the Romans established a shrine to the prophet Faunus at Lupercal, at the foot of the Palatine Hill, where the festival of **Lupercalia** was held in his honor. Usually, however, Pan has no temples; offerings of milk, honey, and lambs are made to him anywhere in the woods and fields. As Swinburne explains, rather feverishly, in *The Palace of Pan* (36–40), this god has

> A temple whose transepts are measured by miles,
>   Whose chancel has morning for priest,
> Whose floor-work the foot of no spoiler defiles,
> Whose musical silence no music beguiles,
>   No festivals limit its feast.

As a symbol of the vital powers of nature, Pan is associated with Dionysus, the earth goddesses, and Aphrodite. He is a simple god, lustful and playful, short tempered only if disturbed in his midday nap. He appears in scenes of rustic beauty surrounded by a happy crew of Satyrs, Fauns, Sileni, Sylvans, and Nymphs. In *Virgils Gnat* (178) Spenser imagines the vale of Tempe where "Woodgods, and Satyres, and swift Dryades" play together on the grassy green; and Milton says in *Paradise Lost* (4. 705–708), describing the nuptial place of Adam and Eve,

> . . . In shady Bower
> More sacred and sequesterd, though but feignd,
> *Pan* or *Silvanus* never slept, nor Nymph,
> Nor *Faunus* haunted.

Pan is always lecherous. The lecherous old churchman in Browning's *The Bishop Orders His Tomb at St. Praxed's Church* understands this side of Pan's nature well enough when he asks that the bas relief on his tomb show the god "Ready to twitch the Nymph's last garment off." But Pan is usually an unfortunate lover, probably because he is ugly. His rumored affair with Artemis is described in the article on that goddess. When he fell in love with a Nymph named **Pitys,** she fled from him, prayed for protection, and was transformed into the pine tree, which thereafter was sacred to Pan. Another metamorphosis thwarted his passion for **Syrinx,** a Hamadryad. When Pan ran after her, she jumped in the river Ladon and asked the river god to save her. He turned her into a bunch of reeds, and Pan took a melancholy satisfaction in cutting reeds of various lengths, tying them together, and creating his musical instrument, the syrinx, or pipes of Pan. As he says in Phelps Putnam's *Ballad of a Strange Thing,*

> Sometimes there's music in these girls,
> Sometimes.[1]

Keats retells this myth in the first poem (157–158) of his 1817 volume,

> . . . how fair, trembling Syrinx fled
> Arcadian Pan, with such a fearful dread.

[1] From "Ballad of a Strange Thing," by Phelps Putnam, in his *Trinc.* Copyright, 1927, by Charles Scribner's Sons. Reprinted with their permission.

Andrew Marvell gives the myth fresh meaning in *The Garden* (31–32) when he implies that Pan intended the change:

> . . . *Pan* did after *Syrinx* speed,
> Not as a Nymph, but for a Reed.

Pan was proud of his skill on the pipes, and the tale of his unsuccessful musical contest with Apollo is told in the article on that god. On one occasion he turned warrior and fought for the Athenians at Marathon. His exploits are described by Browning in *Echetlos:*

Nor helmed nor shielded, he! but, a goat-skin all his wear,
Like a tiller of the soil, with a clown's limbs broad and bare,
Went he ploughing on and on: he pushed with a ploughman's share.

. . . .

Did the steady phalanx falter? To the rescue, at the need,
The clown was ploughing Persia, clearing Greek earth of weed,
As he routed through the Sakian and rooted up the Mede.

After their victory, the grateful Athenians built a shrine to **Pan** under the Acropolis. Ordinarily, however, Pan is no warrior but the simple god of nature whom shepherds worship. He has this familiar aspect in, for example, John Fletcher's *The Faithful Shepherdess* and the last eclogue of Spenser's *Shepheardes Calender* (7–18), in the prayer of Colin Clout:

> O soueraigne *Pan* thou God of shepheards all,
> Which of our tender *lambkins* takest keepe:
> And when our flocks into mischaunce mought fall,
> Doest saue from mischiefe the vnwary sheepe:
> Als of their maisters hast no lesse regarde,
> Then of the flocks, which thou doest watch and ward:
>
> I thee beseche (so be thou deigne to heare,
> Rude ditties tund to shepheards Oaten reede,

Or if I euer sonet song so cleare,
As it with pleasaunce mought thy fancie feede)
Hearken awhile from thy greene cabinet,
The rurall song of carefull Colinet.

Along with this idea of the god, however, there grew up another more exalted conception in which Pan is the symbol of the universe. The notion depends largely on a mistaken etymology; the name "Pan" means "the feeder," that is, the feeder of flocks, but it was taken to mean "all." This conception lies behind Milton's image (*Paradise Lost*, 4. 266–267) of the eternal spring led on by

> . . . Universal *Pan*
> Knit with the *Graces* and the *Hours* in dance.

The exalted notion of the god was given force in English literature by the elaborate allegory of pastoral poetry. In *The Shepheardes Calender,* as we have already seen, Pan sometimes appears as the mere rustic god of shepherds; but more frequently he represents Christ (*May,* 54; *July,* 49) or the Christian God (*May,* 111; *September,* 96). Since Christian poets wrote of their contemporaries as shepherds, the pastoral disguise necessarily turned Christ or God into Pan. In *On the Morning of Christ's Nativity* (89–90) Milton speaks of the simple shepherds who were still unaware

> That the mighty *Pan*
> Was kindly com to live with them below.

In the same poem, however, Milton describes the retreat of the pagan gods at the birth of Christ, and in *Paradise Lost* he represents Greek gods and other pagan deities as deceiving shapes taken by the fallen angels. On the one hand, then, Pan became a symbol of the Christian God; and on the other hand, he or Apollo or Dionysus became the symbol of all false religions defeated by the spread of Christianity. Plutarch tells a story of the days when Tiberius ruled the Roman empire. A ship piloted by a man named Thamuz sailed from Greece toward Italy but was becalmed near the island of Paxi. A voice from the shore three times shouted, "Thamuz!" and when the pilot finally replied, the voice said, "When you reach Palodes, tell them that great Pan is dead." Thamuz did as he was told, and was answered at Palodes by a great wail of surprise and sorrow.

This story was often repeated by the poets of triumphant Christianity. In the seventeenth century Abraham Cowley in *On the Death of Mr. Crashaw* (19–22) used it in his reproof to his fellow poets:

> Nor have we yet quite purg'd the *Christian land;*
> Still *idols* here, like *calves* at *Bethel,* stand.
> And though *Pans Death* long since all *oracles* broke,
> Yet still in Rhyme the *Fiend Apollo* spoke.

In the nineteenth century the contest between Christ and Pan was revived; and while sturdy Christians like Elizabeth Barrett Browning declared with delight that Pan was dead, neopagans like Swinburne lamented the triumph of Christ ("Thou hast conquered, O pale Galilean; the world has grown grey from thy breath").

Much more important to literature was the fresh imaginative use of Pan in the works of such poets as Wordsworth and Keats. In *The Excursion* (4. 883–887) Wordsworth writes of the presence that the shepherd of pagan Greece felt, heard, and saw in nature:

> And, sometimes, intermixed with stirring horns
> Of the live deer, or goat's depending beard,—
> These were the lurking Satyrs, a wild brood
> Of gamesome Deities; or Pan himself,
> The simple shepherd's awe-inspiring God!

Keats in his hymn to Pan (*Endymion,* 1. 232–306) invokes the god as the lover and protector of woods, meadows, and cultivated fields, the hunter, the tender of flocks, the king of Fauns and Satyrs, and, finally, the universal Pan:

> Be still a symbol of immensity;
> A firmament reflected in a sea;
> An element filling the space between;
> An unknown—but no more: we humbly screen
> With uplift hands our foreheads, lowly bending,
> And giving out a shout most heaven rending,
> Conjure thee to receive our humble Paean,
> Upon thy Mount Lycean!

Although Ezra Pound titled one of his poems *Pan Is Dead,* he seems to have been mistaken. Pan is active enough, for example, in the novels and tales of E. M. Forster (for a brilliant evocation of Pan-inspired fear see *The Story of a Panic*). In the first of E. E. Cummings' *Chansons Innocentes*

> it's
> spring
> and
>   the
>   goat-footed
> baloonMan   whistles
> far
> and
> wee.[2]

And Harpo Marx always plays the role of Pan.

Silenus, the son or brother of Pan, is an old fat Satyr who loves to drink and who usually has to ride on a donkey because

---

[2] From "Chansons Innocentes, I," by E. E. Cummings, in his *Collected Poems* (New York: Harcourt, Brace & Company, 1938). Copyright, 1923, by E. E. Cummings. Reprinted with the permission of Brandt & Brandt.

he is too fat and too drunk to walk. He was the tutor and later the follower of Dionysus, and his adventures are related in the article on that god. The **Sileni,** of whom Silenus is the prototype, are old Satyrs. The **Satyrs,** or **Satyri,** are first represented as human in form but with the tails of horses; later they have the goatlike ears, horns, legs, and hooves of Pan. The **Fauns,** or **Fauni,** the sons of Faunus, are Roman Satyrs. **Fauna,** or **Bona Dea,** the daughter or wife of Faunus, is a Roman fertility goddess. The **Sylvans,** or **Sylvani,** who are named for Sylvanus, are Roman spirits of the woods.

Although the Sileni are usually drunk, they are skillful musicians and they have a certain amount of homely wisdom. In Ben Jonson's *Oberon,* a masque for Prince Henry, there is a Silenus who explains the action to a chorus of Satyrs; these were the stock characters of the Satyr-drama of classical Greece. In English literature the Satyrs usually represent two different but related qualities. Sometimes they symbolize brutish disregard for art and ethics, and brutish lust. In Spenser's *Teares of the Muses* (265–282) Ignorance leads a rout of Fauns and Satyrs to tear down the bowers of the Muses, and Sir Satyrane in *The Faerie Queene* (1. 6. 22) is the son of a modest matron and a Satyr who found her wandering in the woods,

> And kindling coles of lust in brutish eye,
> The loyall linkes of wedlocke did vnbinde,
> And made her person thrall vnto his beastly kind.

This interpretation of the Satyr is reflected in the modern English term for uncontrollable sexual desire in men, satyriasis. Yet sometimes the Satyr symbolizes the morally unconscious child of nature. In Hawthorne's *The Marble Faun* Count Donatello is such a man until tragedy awakens his moral sense.

288

PANATHENAEA (păn'ăth·ê·nē'á) was a festival celebrated yearly at Athens in honor of ATHENE.

PANDARUS (păn'dá·rûs) was a foolish Trojan who fought in the TROJAN WAR.

PANDION (păn·dī'ŏn) was the father of Procne and PHILO-MELA.

PANDORA (păn·dō'rá), the first woman, was the wife of Epimetheus. See PROMETHEUS.

PANIC is a sudden fear inspired by PAN.

PANOPE (păn'ŏp·ē) is one of the Nereids. See NYMPHS.

PAPHIA (pā'fĭ·á) is a name for APHRODITE.

PAPHOS (pā'fŏs) was the son of Pygmalion whose name the Cyprians gave to their city because of Aphrodite's miraculous gift to PYGMALION.

PARCAE (pär'sē) is a Roman name of the Fates. See FATE.

PARIS (păr'ĭs), a prince of Troy, eloped with Helen and thus provided the immediate cause of the TROJAN WAR.

PARNASSUS (pär·năs'ûs) is a mountain sacred to the Muses and to Apollo. See MUSES, ORACLES.

PARTHENIA (pär·thē'nĭ·á) is another name for HERA.

PARTHENON (pär'thê·nŏn), on the Acropolis at Athens, was the chief temple of ATHENE.

PARTHENOPAEUS (pär·thê'nŏ·pē'ûs) was one of the Seven against THEBES.

PARTHENOPE (pär·thĕn'ŏ·pē) is one of the three Sirens. See SEA GODS.

PARTHENOS (pär'thê·nŏs) is a surname of ATHENE.

PASIPHAE (pá·sĭf'ā·ē) was queen of Crete and mother of the Minotaur. See DAEDALUS.

PATROCLUS (pá·trō'klûs) was the retainer and close friend of Achilles in the TROJAN WAR.

PAVOR (pā'vôr) is the Roman name for Phobos, an attendant of ARES.

PEGASUS (pĕg′à·sŭs), the winged horse, is a symbol of poetic inspiration. He was the horse of the hero BELLEROPHON.

PEITHO (pī′thō), the goddess of persuasion, is an attendant of EROS.

PELAGIA (pė·lā′jĭ·à) is a name for APHRODITE.

PELEUS (pē′lōos) is usually remembered as the husband of **Thetis** and the father of Achilles, but not all his accomplishments were connubial. He was the king of Phthia in Thessaly; and he sailed with the Argonauts, took part in the Calydonian Boar Hunt, and helped Heracles conquer Troy in the days when it was ruled by Priam's father Laomedon.

At one time Peleus unintentionally killed a man and went to be purified of his blood guilt at the court of King Acastus of Iolcus. The wife of Acastus took a fancy to the handsome hero, but he paid no attention to her. When she spitefully told her husband that Peleus had tried to seduce her, Acastus plotted revenge. He took Peleus hunting on the wild slopes of Mount Pelion, and soon established the custom of resting for an hour or two at noontime, with only two or three hunters keeping guard against Centaurs and wild beasts. One day, in the middle of the siesta, Acastus hid Peleus' sword and then he and the other hunters stole away, leaving Peleus asleep and weaponless. Doubtless the hero would have perished there if Chiron, the wise and gentle Centaur, had not waked him and returned his sword. With this much aid, Peleus acquitted himself well against wild beasts and fierce Centaurs. Zeus, when he heard the whole story, praised Peleus for his chastity, a virtue which the king of the gods frequently admired in others.

This adventure recommended the hero to Zeus as a husband for the Nereid Thetis, a fateful lady whose charms almost lost Zeus his godhead. Thetis was destined to have a son greater than his father; and if Zeus had made love to her as he intended, his universal rule would soon have ended. Thetis' destiny was known only to Prometheus and his mother Themis. According to some stories, Prometheus refused to reveal the secret in spite of his constant torment; other stories say that he told Zeus and thus regained the god's favor. Whoever his informer was, Prometheus or his mother, Zeus learned the decree of fate, gave up his courtship of Thetis, and decided that she should marry the mortal Peleus.

Although the heavens favored Peleus' suit, Thetis was a sea Nymph, and before he could marry her he had to catch and tame her. This was no easy task because she, like her father Nereus and Poseidon's son Proteus, could change her shape at will; but Peleus persisted and at last Thetis yielded. Their magnificent wedding, which was attended by the gods, is frequently mentioned in English literature. Edmund Spenser, for example, says in *The Faerie Queene* (7. 7. 12),

> Was neuer so great ioyance since the day,
> That all the gods whylome assembled were,
> On *Haemus* hill in their diuine array,
> To celebrate the solemne bridall cheare,
> Twixt *Peleus* and Dame *Thetis* pointed there;
> Where *Phoebus* self, that god of Poets hight,
> They say did sing the spousall hymne full cleere,
> That all the gods were rauisht with delight
> Of his celestiall song, and Musicks wondrous might.

The only goddess not invited was Eris, the goddess of discord, and she threw into the assembly a golden apple inscribed "For the fairest." This spiteful gesture began the contest among the goddesses that caused the Trojan War. The rich wedding presents included a pair of immortal horses, the gift of Poseidon; these horses drew Achilles' chariot at Troy.

Because Thetis was immortal, she wished to have an immortal child; and as her first seven children were born she threw each

291

one into fire or boiling water to burn away its mortal part. This was the usual way in which goddesses conferred immortality, but Thetis somehow failed to wind up the charm because when the mortal part of her babies was burned away, nothing was left. The eighth child was Achilles. Peleus refused to have him treated as the others had been, and Thetis, in the fashion of supernatural brides, departed in great anger. But she was always very fond of Achilles who, in spite of her efforts to protect him, became, as fate had decreed, much greater than his father. For what happened to the golden apple, Thetis' efforts on behalf of Achilles, and Achilles' brief glory see TROJAN WAR.

PELIAS (pē'lĭ·as) was the father of Alcestis and the uncle of Jason, the leader of the Argonauts. See ALCESTIS, ARGONAUTS.

PELION (pē'lĭ·ŏn) is a mountain that two Giants piled on top of Mount Ossa and Mount Olympus in their attempt to reach and attack the gods. See GIANTS.

PELOPIA (pĕ'lŏ·pī'a), the daughter of Thyestes, bore him a son, Aegisthus. See ATREUS.

PELOPONNESUS (pĕl'ŏ·pŏ·nē'sŭs), the southern peninsula of Greece, was named for its first ruler Pelops, the father of ATREUS.

PELOPS (pē'lŏps) was the father of Thyestes and ATREUS.

PENATES (pĕ·nā'tēz) are Roman household gods. See HESTIA.

PENELOPE (pĕ·nĕl'ŏ·pē) was the faithful wife of ODYSSEUS.

PENEUS (pĕ·nē'ûs), the principal river of Thessaly in Greece, flows through the lovely vale of **Tempe**. The most famous lines about the vale and the river occur in Spenser's *Prothalamion* (78–80), where Nymphs had thrown flowers on the waves of the Thames River

That like old *Peneus* Waters they did seeme,
When downe along by pleasant *Tempes* shore
Scattred with Flowres, through *Thessaly* they streeme.

Peneus is also the name of the god of the river. For the story of his daughter Daphne see APOLLO.

PENTHESILIA (pĕn'thḗ·sî·lē'ạ), a queen of the Amazons, was an ally of Troy in the Trojan War. See TROJAN WAR, AMAZONS.

PENTHEUS (pĕn'thūs), a king of Thebes, was killed by his mother Agave in a Dionysian frenzy. See DIONYSUS, THEBES.

PERDIX (pĕr'dĭks), or Talus, who invented the saw, was a nephew and apprentice of DAEDALUS.

PERIBOEA (pĕr'ĭ·bē'ạ) was foster mother of Oedipus, king of THEBES.

PERIMEDES (pĕr'ĭ·mē'dēz) was a follower of ODYSSEUS.

PERIPHETES (pĕr'ĭ·fē'tēz), a brigand of Epidaurus who killed travelers with his iron club, was slain by THESEUS.

PERSEPHONE (pĕr·sĕf'ȯ·nē) is the daughter of Demeter and the wife of Hades. See EARTH GODDESSES, HADES.

PERSES (pĕr'sēz), from whom the Persian kings claimed descent, was a son of PERSEUS.

PERSEUS (pĕr'sōōs). The story of Perseus, which culminates in his winning of Andromeda and the rescue of his mother from the fell intent of an island king, is one of the best known and pleasantest of the Greek myths. It is a story that begins in miracle and ends in domestic commonplace. To King **Acrisius** of Argos, who had no children, the Delphic oracle sent word that he would have a daughter whose son would cause the death of Acrisius. Therefore, when his daughter **Danae** was born, he imprisoned her underground, or, according to some accounts, in a brazen tower, so that she might never have a son; but Zeus fell in love with her beauty and manifested himself to her in a shower of

293

gold. As a result of this visit, Danae bore a son who was named Perseus. (For the poets' use of this myth see ZEUS.)

THE FAMILY OF PERSEUS AND HERACLES

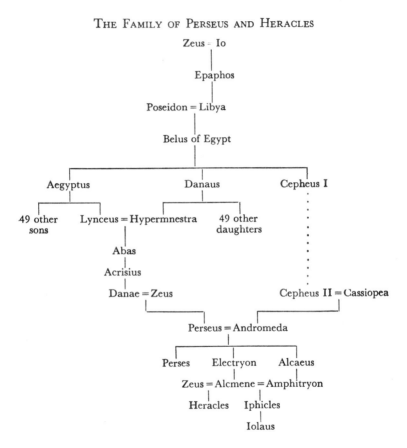

When Acrisius heard of the birth of his grandson, he was greatly worried. Not believing Danae's story of the cause of the event, he put both mother and child into a wooden chest that he set adrift on the sea. The chest floated to the island of Seriphos where

294

Danae and Perseus were rescued by a fisherman named **Dictys,** who cared for them and later introduced them to his brother, King **Polydectes.** Polydectes fell in love with Danae, and when he found that Perseus was likely to hamper his intentions, he persuaded Perseus to seek the head of **Medusa,** the Gorgon, whose glance turned men to stone (see SEA GODS).

In his project Perseus was aided by both Hermes and Athene. Hermes led him first to the **Graeae,** sisters of the Gorgons, three old women who had only one eye and one tooth, which they passed about from one to another in turn. Perseus seized their prized accessories and returned them only after they had told him where to find the Nymphs who kept the miraculous wallet, winged sandals, and helmet of Hades. The magical helmet made whoever wore it invisible. When Perseus had obtained these articles, Hermes added the curved sword with which he had slain Argus, and Athene gave him a shield of polished brass.

Thus accoutered, Perseus sought the abode of the Gorgons and, looking in the mirror of his brazen shield in order not to be affected by the petrifying glance of Medusa, he cut off her head and put it in his wallet. The two other Gorgons pursued him for revenge, but he escaped in his invisibility.

As he was returning to Seriphos, Perseus saw a beautiful girl chained to a rock by the seashore. This was **Andromeda.** Her mother **Cassiopea,** who after death was made a constellation, had boasted that she was more beautiful than the Nereids, and Poseidon, to punish her, had sent a sea monster to lay waste her husband's kingdom of Ethiopia. **Cepheus,** the king, learned that the only way in which he could save his kingdom was to sacrifice his daughter to the monster, and under protest he finally had Andromeda chained to the rock where Perseus saw her.

Perseus rescued her, after turning the sea monster into stone by causing it to look on the head of Medusa, and then he claimed Andromeda's hand. Cepheus consented, but he had previously promised Andromeda to **Phineus,** who arrived at the crucial moment to claim his rights. After a fight, Perseus turned Phineus and his followers into stone and carried off Andromeda.

When Perseus and Andromeda reached Seriphos, they found that the king was about to force Danae to marry him against her will. It was no difficult matter for Perseus to turn Polydectes to stone with Medusa's head, a trick that he followed by placing the good Dictys on the vacant throne. Then the three, Perseus, Andromeda, and Danae, set out to return to King Acrisius. This unfortunate king, however, still seeking to avoid his decreed fate, had left Argos and gone to Larissa. At Larissa, Perseus, in his search for him, entered the athletic games, and during the contests hurled a discus an extraordinary distance. It fell on the foot of Acrisius and caused his death. Thus was the oracle fulfilled, and the Greek belief expressed that man can never avoid his determined fate.

Perseus became king of Argos, but as he preferred the town of Tiryns, he traded towns with Megapenthes, the king of Tiryns. Thereafter he settled down and raised a family consisting of Gorgophone, Alcaeus, Electryon, Mestor, Sthenelus, and **Perses,** from the last of whom the Persian kings claimed descent.

In English literature Andromeda has been more popular than Perseus; but the Elizabethan playwright, George Chapman, retold the entire story in a long poem called *Andromeda Liberata,* in which, according to Douglas Bush, Perseus is made to represent the Earl of Somerset and Andromeda the Countess of Essex, whom the earl figuratively rescues from "the ravenous multitude," a representation that gives undeserved virtue to both the earl and the countess. In the *Epithalamion* (189–190), which celebrates his own wedding, Spenser, wishing to describe the transfixing quality of the spiritual beauty of his bride, writes that if one could gaze on it direct, he would

> . . . stand astonisht lyke to those which red
> Medusaes mazeful hed,

and the Dauphin in Shakespeare's *Henry V* (3. 7. 21–24), ecstatically praising his horse's mettle, exclaims,

> It is a beast for Perseus: he is pure air and fire; and the
> dull elements of earth and water never appear in him . . . ,

lines in which the vain prince seems to have confused Perseus with Bellerophon. Robert Browning describes Andromeda's plight in *Pauline* (636–641), though here the symbolism is vague, if indeed the passage is not merely a description of a picture of Andromeda that Browning knew. Among the other Victorians, William Morris, Charles Kingsley, and Gerard Manley Hopkins all wrote poems about the story. Morris retells it at length in *The Doom of King Acrisius,* and Kingsley in *Andromeda.* For Hopkins, however, in his difficult sonnet *Andromeda,* the girl is possibly a symbol of the church awaiting rescue in the second coming of the Christ. In our time Louis MacNeice makes of Perseus with the Gorgon's head a symbol of the power of friends in their own mortality to remind a man of the relentless passage of time that petrifies all human values:

> Ever to meet me comes, in sun or dull,
> The gay hero swinging the Gorgon's head
> And I am left, with the dull drumming of the sun,
>   suspended and dead. . . .[3]

PETASUS (pĕt′*à*·sŭs) is the winged cap of HERMES.

[3] From "Perseus," by Louis MacNeice, in his *Poems, 1925–1940.* Copyright, 1940, by Random House, Inc. Reprinted by permission of the publisher.

PHAEA (fē′à), a wild boar of Crommyon, was killed by THESEUS.

PHAEACIANS (fē·ā′shȧnz) were a seafaring people who befriended ODYSSEUS.

PHAEDRA (fē′drȧ) was a wife of Theseus and the betrayer of her stepson Hippolytus. See THESEUS.

PHAETHON (fā′ė·thȯn) was Apollo's foolish son who insisted on driving the chariot of the sun for one day. See APOLLO.

PHANTASTUS (făn·tăs′tŭs) is a god of dreams. See HADES.

PHEGEUS (fē′jōōs), whose daughter married Alcmaeon, had him killed for deserting her, and Alcmaeon's death ended the long chain of events that began with Zeus's abduction of Europa and led to the founding and the eventual destruction of THEBES.

PHILEMON (fĭ·lē′mȯn) and Baucis were an aged couple whose charity and piety were signally honored by ZEUS.

PHILOCTETES (fĭl′ŏk·tē′tēz) or his father **Poeas** helped to put Heracles out of his misery by lighting the funeral pyre of that great hero, and received from him, in return, his famous bow and poisoned arrows. Philoctetes was regarded as the greatest archer in Greece when he joined the expedition against the Trojans. On the way to Troy, he and his companions landed on a small island to offer sacrifice to an obscure goddess, and Philoctetes was bitten by a snake or scratched by the point of one of his own arrows. Whatever the cause of his wound, it did not heal, and the stench of it became so terrible and his cries of pain so depressing that his companions marooned him on the island of Lemnos.

For nearly ten years he existed alone on the island, enduring the torment of his wound and struggling to control his anger and despair. But in the last year of the Trojan War the Greeks captured the Trojan prophet Helenus, who told them that they could not win until they had obtained, among other things, the bow and arrows of Heracles. The crafty Odysseus and Neoptolemus or Diomedes (accounts differ as to Odysseus' companion) were sent to get the bow and arrows. In *Philoctetes,* a tragedy by Sophocles, Odysseus tries to persuade Neoptolemus to trick Philoctetes into giving up the bow and arrows, but Neoptolemus refuses to do so. The conflict is resolved by the deified Heracles, who appears to Philoctetes and tells him that it is his destiny to fight at Troy. When Philoctetes arrived at the Grecian camp, he was cured of his wound by Machaon, a son of Asclepius, and the first victim of his arrows was Paris of Troy.

In his rare appearances in English literature Philoctetes has been a symbol of lonely suffering. Thomas Russell in the eighteenth century imagined Philoctetes' years of exile in *Suppos'd to Be Written on Lemnos:*

> On this lone Isle, whose rugged rocks affright
> The cautious pilot, ten revolving years
> Great Paean's Son, unwonted erst to tears,
> Wept o'er his wound: alike each rolling light
> Of heaven he watch'd, and blam'd its lingering flight,
> By day the sea-mew screaming round his cave
> Drove slumber from his eyes, the chiding wave,
> And savage howlings chas'd his dreams by night.
>
> Hope still was his: in each low breeze, that sigh'd
> Thro' his rude grot, he heard a coming oar,
> In each white cloud a coming sail he spied;
> Nor seldom listened to the fancied roar
> Of Oeta's torrents, or the hoarser tide
> That parts fam'd Trachis from th' Euboic shore.

Trachis lies at the foot of Mount Oeta, the peak where Philoctetes or his father lighted the funeral pyre of Heracles. Russell mistakenly calls Philoctetes' father Paean, probably because of the variant Latin spelling "Paeas" for "Poeas."

The Philoctetes of Lord de Tabley's nineteenth-century play of that name is an exemplar not only of pagan fortitude but also of Christian forgiveness. Sophocles would have been astonished to see Philoctetes forgiving Odysseus. Edmund Wilson in our own time has used the myth of Philoctetes as a symbol of what he considers to be the plight of the artist or, at least, of some artists. In *The Wound and the Bow* he develops "the idea that genius and disease, like strength and mutilation, may be inextricably bound up together."

PHILOMELA (fĭl′ŏ·mē′lȧ), or **Philomena**, and **Procne** were the daughters of **Pandion.** They avenged the crime of their mutual husband, King **Tereus,** with one of the most terrible acts recorded in classical mythology. Tereus had first married Procne, who had been offered to him by Pandion as a reward for his assistance in a war that Pandion fought against King Labdacus of Thebes. After their son **Itys,** or **Itylus,** was born, Tereus grew tired of Procne. He therefore cut out her tongue and imprisoned her in a cage in a forest. Telling Philomela that her sister was dead, he persuaded her to marry him.

Procne, however, wove the story of her plight into a tapestry and sent it to Philomela. Then the two sisters took their vengeance on Tereus by killing and cooking Itys and serving him to Tereus at dinner. When Tereus discovered that he had eaten his own son, he set out in pursuit of the two sisters. The gods, horrified by the affair, changed Philomela into a nightingale, Procne into a swallow, and Tereus into a hawk or lapwing, so that symbolically the pursuit still continues.

The Latin poets sometimes reversed the role of the two sisters; some accounts specify Philomela as the sister who lost her tongue and thus explain the fact that the nightingale at some seasons is silent. Chaucer prefers this version in the partial account of the myth that he gives in *The Legend of Good Women* (2228–2393), an account that makes its moral point that men are not always to be trusted and that stops short of telling what subsequently happened to Itys.

The story was so interesting to Elizabethan poets and their successors that by the eighteenth century the musical cry of Philomela had become a thoroughly worn cliché, and it was restored to poetic use only by a renewed insight that occurred among nineteenth- and twentieth-century poets. The Elizabethan poet, Sir Philip Sidney, for example, makes a rather typical use of the myth when in a short song (*The Nightingale*) he compares the nightingale's experience in love with his own:

> The nightingale, as soon as April bringeth
> Unto her rested sense a perfect waking,
> While late bare earth, proud of new clothing, springeth,
> Sings out her woes. . . .

Edmund Spenser in *Virgils Gnat* (401–403), alluding to many Greek myths, remembers

> . . . those two *Pandionian* maides,
> Calling on *Itis, Itis* euermore,
> Whom wretched boy they slew with guiltie blades.

Shakespeare makes the story one of the elements in his bloody tragedy *Titus Andronicus,* in which Titus' daughter Lavinia is raped and mutilated by the lustful sons of the empress Tamora. In *Il Penseroso* (56–62) John Milton, wishing to be rid of vain deluding joys, calls for silence unbroken

> 'Less *Philomel* will deign a Song,
> In her sweetest, saddest plight,
> Smoothing the rugged brow of night,
> While *Cynthia* checks her Dragon yoke,
> Gently o're th'accustom'd Oke;
> Sweet Bird that shunn'st the noise of folly,
> Most musical, most Melancholy!

Whereafter for two centuries the name of Philomela was good for an ounce of unfortunate love and fine bird music wherever it was thrust in.

It is remarkable that John Keats, as full of classical lore as he was, and as moved by the song of a nightingale, should ignore the myth altogether in *Ode to a Nightingale.* To him the bird is but a "light-winged Dryad of the trees" that

> Singest of summer in full-throated ease,

references that relieve the bird of all its mythical sorrow and give it instead a free spiritual blissfulness.

Matthew Arnold in *Philomela,* however, hears in the bird's song again its classic sadness:

> O wanderer from a Grecian shore,
> Still, after many years, in distant lands,
> Still nourishing in thy bewilder'd brain
> That wild, unquench'd, deep-sunken, old-world pain—
> Say, will it never heal?
> And can this fragrant lawn
> With its cool trees, and night,
> And the sweet, tranquil Thames,
> And moonshine, and the dew,
> To thy rack'd heart and brain
> Afford no balm?
> Dost thou tonight behold,
> Here, through the moonlight on this English grass,
> The unfriendly palace in the Thracian wild?
> Dost thou again peruse
> With hot cheeks and sear'd eyes
> The too clear web, and thy dumb sister's shame?

Arnold concludes that the song expresses

> Eternal passion!
> Eternal pain!

as much in his own day as in the day of its origin. Thus, because he found the emotional center of the myth, he was able to give it poetic life again.

Swinburne, striving for the kind of realization that Arnold had been able to achieve, puts into his poem *Itylus* an echo of the myth itself but does not approach the intensity of Arnold's feeling. *Itylus* is occupied with Philomela's reproach to Procne for seeming to forget

> The woven web that was plain to follow,
> The small slain body, the flowerlike face,

and concludes,

> Thou hast forgotten, O summer swallow,
> But the world shall end when I forget.

If the tragic feeling is weaker in *Itylus,* it is almost entirely missing in Oscar Wilde's *The Burden of Itys,* where

> . . . that throbbing throat which once I heard
> On starlit hills of flower-starred Arcady

gives Wilde the occasion to review, as Spenser had done, a great many Greek myths. But Wilde lacks the poetic finesse of Spenser, and he seems frequently to be drawing on Keats for his effects.

As remarkable in its way as Keats's ignoring of the myth is the revivification of it that T. S. Eliot accomplishes in two poems, *Sweeney among the Nightingales* and *The Waste Land.* The myth provides a poignant irony in the context of both poems. In the first, a seduction is going on in a cheap dive, probably to be followed by a murder, while outside

> The nightingales are singing near
> The Convent of the Sacred Heart,

> And sang within the bloody wood
> When Agamemnon cried aloud,
> And let their liquid siftings fall
> To stain the stiff dishonoured shroud.[4]

Here the nightingales form one of Eliot's favorite points of reference, the theme of the conversion of meaningful suffering into significance and beauty. The modern cheap vulgarity of Sweeney's behavior in toying with sensuality is ironically contrasted with the classically tragic but now lovely suffering of Philomela. (For further comment on these lines see Agamemnon under ATREUS and Oedipus under THEBES.)

The theme is given fuller expression in the second section of *The Waste Land, A Game of Chess* (98–103). Here the neurotic lady, who is for the moment the poem's protagonist, sits uncomprehendingly before a mantel above which a picture shows

> As though a window gave upon the sylvan scene
> The change of Philomel, by the barbarous king
> So rudely forced; yet there the nightingale
> Filled all the desert with inviolable voice
> And still she cried, and still the world pursues,
> "Jug Jug" to dirty ears.[5]

The lady, like the other inhabitants of the waste land in which she lives, has failed to grasp what the myth makes clear, that refusal for high moral reasons to submit to sensuality may lead to a tragic fate, but that the tragedy itself may lead to a higher kind of existence and to an inviolability of spirit; whereas the

[4] From "Sweeney among the Nightingales," by T. S. Eliot, in his *Collected Poems, 1909–1935*. Copyright, 1934, 1936, by Harcourt, Brace and Company. Reprinted with their permission.

[5] From "The Waste Land," by T. S. Eliot, in his *Collected Poems, 1909–1935*. Copyright, 1934, 1936, by Harcourt, Brace and Company. Reprinted with their permission.

indulgence of sensuality with no other aim than self-gratification leads to a neurotic and meaningless existence. The idea is given a brief echo in *The Fire Sermon* (203–206), the third section of the poem. After a mocking account of the dalliance of Sweeney and Mrs. Porter, the poem continues:

> Twit twit twit
> Jug jug jug jug jug jug
> So rudely forc'd.
> Tereu[6]

lines that might appear meaningless if the final word did not make clear that they represent the song of the nightingale. In Elizabethan times the word "jug" was used to indicate the note of a bird's song, and the word "tereu" is not only a shortened form of King Tereus' name but a word that the Elizabethan writer, George Gascoigne, in his poem, *The Complaynt of Philomene,* identified as a trill in the song of the nightingale. Thus again Eliot makes the myth provide an ironic contrast between Philomela's agony because of Tereus' lust and the easy submission of Mrs. Porter to Sweeney.

PHILOMENA (fĭl'ō·mē'na̤) is another name for PHILOMELA.

PHINEUS (fĭ'nūs) was (1) Andromeda's first fiancé who was turned to stone by PERSEUS; (2) a man of many troubles who was aided by the ARGONAUTS.

PHLEGETHON (flĕg'ē·thŏn), or Pyriphlegethon, is a river of HADES.

PHLEGYAS (flĕj'ĭ·a̤s) was the father of IXION.

PHOBOS (fō'bŏs) is an attendant of his father ARES.

PHOEBE (fē'bē), whose name is often given to Artemis, was the first moon goddess and the grandmother of ARTEMIS.

---

[6] From "The Waste Land," by T. S. Eliot, in his *Collected Poems, 1909–1935.* Copyright, 1934, 1936, by Harcourt, Brace and Company. Reprinted with their permission.

PHOEBUS (fē′bŭs) is a name of APOLLO.

PHOENIX (fē′nĭks). (1) Phoenix, a brother of Cadmus, gave up the search for their sister Europa and settled at last in a land that was thereafter called Phoenicia. See **THEBES**. (2) The Phoenix is a miraculous bird of wonderful red and gold plumage that inhabits an earthly paradise in Arabia where it sits on or near a specially reserved tree. Only one of the species is supposed to be alive at any one time, but this single Phoenix lives to an extraordinary age; according to some accounts, five hundred years, and according to others, a thousand or more. At the end of its life span, the Phoenix builds itself a nest of spice and aromatic woods, settles on it, and sets fire to it. From the ashes of this• fire arises a new Phoenix. Some say that the new bird then takes up the remains of the old bird and carries them to the temple of the sun at **Heliopolis** in Egypt, where it either buries them or sacrifices them on the high altar. But others say that it is the same bird that arises from the ashes of the fire, regenerated by the fire which it created, and that this bird then makes a pilgrimage to Heliopolis. In either event, the bird is supposed to be visible to mortals only while it is on its flight to and from Heliopolis.

The early Egyptians were first to see in the myth a symbol of immortality. To them the life cycle of the Phoenix symbolized the life cycle of the sun, which dies every day at sunset and is reborn every morning; consequently they held that the bird was sacred to the sun. Other people interpreted the myth as a more general symbol for the regeneration of life after death, and this is the interpretation usually given it.

The symbolic bird naturally appealed to Christians because of the parallel between its rebirth and the resurrection of the Christ. The Phoenix thus became a favorite early Christian symbol. It is used to this end in *The Phoenix,* one of the few poems in

Old English that have survived. The bird also appears in a poem of Shakespeare's, *The Phoenix and the Turtle,* the meaning of which is obscure; but a much more typical Shakespearian use of the symbol is the remark of Sebastian in *The Tempest* (3. 3. 21–24):

> Now I will believe
> That there are unicorns; that in Arabia
> There is one tree, the phoenix' throne; one phoenix
> At this hour reigning there.

Sebastian has just seen a vision of strange shapes sent by Prospero, the magician, and his credulity has been considerably enlarged by the experience, as the quoted lines indicate.

A typically metaphysical use of the symbol appears in *The Canonization,* where John Donne, expressing the mystic unity that love has made of him and his mistress, writes:

> The Phoenix ridle hath more wit
> By us, we two being one, are it.

To Milton, the bird's remarkable flight to Egypt seems an apt simile for the flight of the angel Raphael from Heaven to Eden in *Paradise Lost* (5. 272–274); sent to warn Adam, Raphael as he flies downward looks like

> A *Phoenix,* gaz'd by all, as that sole Bird
> When to enshrine his reliques in the Sun's
> Bright Temple, to *Aegyptian Theb's* he flies.

Milton obviously is following a variant that locates the temple at Thebes rather than at Heliopolis.

In our own time the Phoenix was a personal symbol for the poet and novelist D. H. Lawrence, and his posthumous papers are appropriately entitled *Phoenix*. Maurice Cramer's novel, *Phoenix at East Hadley,* published in 1941, suggests in a light mood what might happen to a quiet Massachusetts town if three Phoenixes took up residence there.

PHOLUS (fō′lŭs), who guarded the wine of the Centaurs, provoked a battle by giving Heracles a drink. See CEN-TAURS.

PHORCYS (fôr′sĭs) is one of the SEA GODS.

PHOSPHOR (fŏs′fôr), the morning star, is a son of EOS.

PHRIXUS (frĭk′sûs) rode on the golden-fleeced ram to Colchis. See ARGONAUTS.

PIERIA (pī·ĭr′ĭ·à) is a spring on the slopes of Mount Olympus, near which were born the MUSES.

PIERIDES (pī·ĕr′ĭ·dēz) are the MUSES.

PILLARS, or Gates, **OF HERACLES** (hĕr′à·klēz) are two mountains which face each other across the strait where the Mediterranean Sea meets the great river of Oceanus, now called the Atlantic Ocean. These mountains, one of which is now called the Rock of Gibraltar, were raised by HERACLES.

PIPLEA (pĭp·lē′à) was loved by Daphnis, who was saved from death by HERACLES.

PIRENE (pī·rē′nē) was a famous spring at Corinth near which Pegasus was bridled by BELLEROPHON.

PIRITHOUS (pī·rĭth′ō·ûs) was a close friend of THESEUS.

PISCES (pĭs′ēz), the Fish, is a constellation and a sign of the ZODIAC.

PITYS (pĭt′ĭs) was a Nymph whom Pan loved. When she fled from him, she was transformed into the pine tree, which thereafter was sacred to PAN.

PLEIADS (plē′yădz), or **PLEIADES** (plē′yà·dēz), are always running away from ORION.

PLUTON (ploō'tŏn), or **PLUTO** (ploō'tō), is another name of the god HADES.

PLUTUS (ploō'tŭs) is a god of wealth frequently confused with the god Pluto, or HADES.

PODALIRIUS (pō'dȧ·lĭr'ĭ·ŭs), a son of Asclepius, was a Greek leader in the TROJAN WAR.

PODARGE (pŏ·där'jē) is one of the Harpies. See SEA GODS.

POEAS (pē'ȧs) was the father of PHILOCTETES.

POLLUX (pŏl'ŭks) is the Roman name of Polydeuces, the twin brother of CASTOR.

POLYBOTES (pŏl'ĭ·bō'tēz) was one of the GIANTS.

POLYBUS (pŏl'ĭ·bŭs) was foster father of Oedipus, king of THEBES.

POLYDAMNA (pŏl'ĭ·dăm'nȧ), queen of Egypt, entertained Helen of Troy. See TROJAN WAR.

POLYDECTES (pŏl'ĭ·dĕk'tēz), who tried to force Danae to marry him, was turned to stone by PERSEUS.

POLYDEUCES (pŏl'ĭ·dū'sēz) was the twin brother of CASTOR.

POLYDORUS (pŏl'ĭ·dôr·ŭs) was (1) the son of Cadmus, founder of THEBES; (2) one of the Epigoni (see THEBES); (3) a young Trojan prince (see AENEAS).

POLYHYMNIA (pŏl'ĭ·hĭm'nĭ·ȧ), or **POLYMNIA** (pŏ·lĭm'nĭ·ȧ), is the Muse of sacred song and oratory. See MUSES.

POLYNICES (pŏl'ĭ·nĭ'sēz) and Eteocles, sons of Oedipus, vied for the kingship of THEBES.

POLYPHEMUS (pŏl'ĭ·fē'mŭs) was the Cyclops who loved Galatea and was blinded by Odysseus. See GALATEA, ODYSSEUS.

POLYPHONTES (pŏl'ĭ·fŏn'tēz) helped Eteocles defend THEBES.

POLYXENA (pŏ·lĭk'sĕ·nȧ), a Trojan princess, was sacrificed on

309

the grave of Achilles at the demand of Achilles' ghost. See TRO-
JAN WAR.

POMONA (pô·mō′nȧ), the Roman goddess of fruit trees, is the
mistress of VERTUMNUS.

PONTUS (pŏn′tûs) is one of the SEA GODS.

PORPHYRION (pôr·fîr′ĭ·ȯn) was one of the GIANTS.

PORTUNUS (pôr·tū′nûs), the Roman god of harbors, is identified with Palaemon. See SEA GODS.

POSEIDON (pȯ·sī′dȯn) is the chief Olympian god of the sea.
See SEA GODS.

POTHOS (pō′thȯs), the god of longing, is an attendant of
EROS.

PRIAM (prī′ăm), or **PRIAMUS** (prī′ȧ·mûs), was king of Troy
at the time of the TROJAN WAR.

PRIAPUS (prī·ā′pûs), or **Lutinus,** a god of fertility in nature
and man, is the son of Aphrodite or Chione, the Titaness, by
Dionysus or Zeus. He is a guardian of all who cultivate the soil
and a friend and protector, as well, of travelers, shepherds, and
mariners. Statues of him were erected in gardens to increase
the fertility of the soil and to ward off thieves. On these, short
humorous poems, Priapea, were often carved. Eighty of the
poems were collected in the time of Augustus. The narrator in
Chaucer's *Parliament of Fowls* (253–259) remembers:

> The God Priapus saw I, as I wente,
> Withinne the temple in sovereyn place stonde.

Priapus "with his company" is in the procession of deities and
animals in Shelley's *Witch of Atlas* (41–88). Swinburne's *Dolores*
("Our Lady of Pain") is the "daughter of Death and Priapus"
(53). D. H. Lawrence wrote a *Hymn to Priapus,* and Mr. Apollinax, the foreigner, in the poem that bears his name, reminds
T. S. Eliot of

> . . . Priapus in the shrubbery
> Gaping at the lady in the swing.[7]

PROCNE (prŏk′nē) was the sister of PHILOMELA.

PROCRIS (prō′krĭs) was the wife of Cephalus, who was carried off by EOS.

PROCRUSTES (prȯ·krŭs′tēz) had a way of making all his guests fit his guest bed. He was made to fit it also by THESEUS.

PROETUS (prē′tûs) tried to bring about the death of BEL- LEROPHON.

PROMACHOS (prŏm′ȧ·kŏs) (1) is a surname of ATHENE; (2) was one of the Epigoni (see THEBES).

PROMETHEUS (prȯ·mē′thūs) was the son of the Titan, **Iapetus,** and either the goddess Themis, who later married Zeus, or the Oceanid Clymene. By a rather doubtful etymology, his name was commonly taken to mean "forethought," and with his brother **Epimetheus,** or "afterthought," he was credited with a substantial part in the creation of mankind. Though accounts vary widely in detail, they all agree that Prometheus gave fire to mankind against the will of Zeus, and that for this act he was severely punished.

When the world was first organized out of Chaos, it was ruled by Uranus, the sky. Uranus was overthrown by his son Cronus, and for ages he and his fellow Titans were supreme. Finally Zeus and the other Olympian children of Cronus challenged their father's might, and a great war ensued between the Titans and the Olympians. In this struggle Prometheus had the fore- thought to side with Zeus against his own kind, since the Olym- pians were destined by fate to win, and therefore Prometheus and his brother were not cast into Tartarus with other defeated Titans.

[7] From "Mr. Apollinax," by T. S. Eliot, in his *Collected Poems, 1909–1935.* Copyright, 1934, 1936, by Harcourt, Brace and Company. Reprinted with their permission.

Instead, he and Epimetheus were charged with the creation of the animals and of mankind. Epimetheus gave his chief attention to shaping animals and endowing them with their various natures. Prometheus, however, took earth and shaped it with water; he gave to man the form of the gods themselves, so that man, of all the animals, alone stands upright and is always able to look at the heavens, whereas his animal kindred gaze downward at the earth. Meantime Epimetheus had been so generous in endowing animals with faculties such as strength and swiftness and courage that there appeared to be little left for man. Prometheus therefore determined to endow man with the use of fire, the sacred property of the Olympian gods. With the aid of Athene he obtained it, probably by lighting a torch at the chariot of the sun. The gift was a magnificent one, for it enabled man to warm his house against the inclemency of the weather, to cook his food, to shape utensils and weapons out of metal, and in many ways to bring about his own advancement. In fact, it put man so far above the animals and so close to the gods themselves that the gods were alarmed, and a great debate ensued on Mount Olympus as to the proper portion of mankind in the world.

Prometheus was by now in disfavor with Zeus, but he was ordered to decide what portion of a sacrificial bull was due to man and what to the gods. Still determined to favor man, he wrapped the edible parts in the hide and concealed them with useless entrails, and at the same time wrapped the skeleton in fat so that it appeared to be rich. When Zeus was asked to choose between these two portions, he was not taken in by the stratagem; but he chose the skeleton and the fat, thus leaving the better portion to man. Then, as a punishment, he deprived man of the use of fire. Prometheus, however, stole the fire again from heaven in a hollow reed and gave it back to man. Whereupon Zeus determined to punish both the race of man and its creator and friend, Prometheus, in more terrible ways.

As a punishment for man, he ordered Hephaestus to construct the first woman. According to this cynical myth, Hephaestus built a creature named **Pandora,** whom the various gods and goddesses then endowed with suitably dangerous qualities; Athene gave her womanly skill in handicrafts, Aphrodite gave her beauty, and Hermes gave her guile. Then, when she was fatally complete, Hermes led her down to Epimetheus to begin her work of causing the downfall of mankind, an occasion aptly remembered by Milton in *Paradise Lost* (4. 713–719) when he wished to describe the fatal glamour of Eve, who was, he says,

> . . . in naked beauty more adorn'd,
> More lovely then *Pandora,* whom the Gods
> Endowd with all thir gifts, and O too like
> In sad event, when to the unwiser Son
> Of *Japhet* brought by *Hermes,* she ensnar'd
> Mankind with her faire looks, to be aveng'd
> On him who had stole *Joves* authentic fire.

(Here Japhet is Iapetus.) The first woman met with the same success that has been hereditary in her beautiful descendants ever since; she at once caught the eye of Epimetheus who, ignoring his brother's warning (a trait also hereditary in his descendants), made her his wife.

Pandora had brought with her as a gift a magic box into which the gods had put multifarious woes from all of which blissful mankind was at that early time wholly free. Epimetheus was warned not to open the box. Some stories say that it belonged to Epimetheus and contained the ills which had not been distributed in the creation of man and that Pandora was warned against opening it. In any event, the box was opened, and immediately out flew all the grievous things it contained, pain and sickness, envy and anger, sorrow and despair. Hope alone was kept in, so that it might still remain to man, although the nineteenth-century poet, Dante Gabriel Rossetti, in his poem *Pandora,* asks a pertinent question even about hope:

> What of the end? These beat their wings at will,
> The ill-born things, the good things turned to ill,—
> Powers of the impassioned hours prohibited.
> Aye, clench the casket now! Whither they go
> Thou mayst not dare to think: nor canst thou know
> If Hope still pent there be alive or dead.

Thus did Zeus penalize man for the possession of fire, and thus did the Greeks symbolize their adherence to the timeless masculine conviction that all man's troubles begin with woman.

For Prometheus Zeus provided a cruel fate. He had Hephaestus chain the Titan to a crag in the Caucasus mountains, where every day an eagle or a vulture visited him and ate out his liver, which grew back daily. At this point again there are variables in the myth. One story says that Prometheus had received from his mother Themis information that Zeus would have a son who would overthrow him. Because Zeus knew that Prometheus had this information, he did not cast the Titan into Tartarus, and he would have freed him if Prometheus had been willing to tell what he knew. Prometheus' prophetic gift, however, told him also that a descendant of Zeus in the thirteenth generation would free him, and he therefore preferred to await this rescue. It came in the person of Heracles, who shot the hungry eagle and broke the confining chains to free the Titan, in return for which Prometheus told Heracles where to find Atlas and the garden of the Hesperides.

According to another story, Prometheus seems to have divulged to Zeus, who was about to make love to Thetis, the vital information that Thetis' son was destined to be greater than his father. Zeus therefore decreed that Thetis should marry a mortal; she did so, and her son Achilles fulfilled the prophecy by becoming much greater than his father Peleus. Prometheus was released for saving Zeus from disaster. He also received immortality from Chiron, the Centaur, who, in trying to make peace between Heracles and the other Centaurs, was wounded with a poisoned arrow; the agony was so great that he offered to give his immortality to Prometheus so that he might die of his wound. This arrangement was permitted, and Prometheus joined the gods on Olympus.

As a champion of mankind against the ruling forces of the universe, Prometheus has always had a great attraction for poets, especially for Romantic poets. Beginning with the ancient Greek dramatist, Aeschylus, who seems to have written two plays about him, *Prometheus Bound* and *Prometheus Unbound,* the second of which has been lost in the passage of time, Prometheus has been the subject of many symbolic poems.

His more idealistic values are ignored by Jonathan Swift, who accuses him in *Prometheus* of stealing the golden chain that hung from the throne of Zeus and who uses this story to belabor an eighteenth-century Irish patentee named Wood:

> Say, who is to be understood
> By that old thief Prometheus? WOOD.
> For Jove, it is not hard to guess him;
> I mean his m[ajesty], God bless him.

Swift says that Prometheus substituted a brass chain for the golden one, and it is clear that in this poem Swift himself, stealing from his own sovereign, has replaced the gold of the myth with both brass and irony.

315

Byron gives Prometheus more his due in a poem to which he gave the Titan's name:

> Thy godlike crime was to be kind,
> To render with thy precepts less
> The sum of human wretchedness,
> And strengthen Man with his own mind.

Here the poet follows the common idea that the fire which Prometheus stole for man was intellectual and not physical. He adds, generalizing his symbol:

> Like thee, Man is in part divine,
> A troubled stream from a pure source;
> And Man in portions can foresee
> His own funereal destiny;

but like Prometheus, man does not give in, and thus (says Byron) he makes of his own death a victory.

Shelley, too, in the best known of all the English poetic uses of the myth, represents the idealistic symbolic value of Prometheus' resistance to Zeus. In *Prometheus Unbound*, a poetic drama inspired in part by Aeschylus, he identifies Zeus with the principle of evil in the world, and the old Titan, Saturn, with good. Prometheus he sees as a regenerative power able to assist mankind in returning to the state of early innocence. Shelley describes Prometheus as refusing to yield to Zeus the secret that would prevent his overthrow, so that Zeus makes the fatal error of marrying Thetis and is deposed by Demogorgon, who leads him down to dwell in Tartarus. Hercules, who typifies strength, frees Prometheus, and the world returns to an ideal state. The poem ends with a speech by Demogorgon, a character introduced into the myth by Shelley:

To suffer woes which Hope thinks infinite;
To forgive wrongs darker than death or night;
    To defy Power, which seems omnipotent;
To love, and bear; to hope till Hope creates
From its own wreck the thing it contemplates;
    Neither to change, nor falter, nor repent;
This, like thy glory, Titan, is to be
Good, great and joyous, beautiful and free;
This is alone Life, Joy, Empire, and Victory.

To Longfellow, Prometheus seems a good symbol of the poet. In his poem *Prometheus, or The Poet's Forethought* he writes:

All is but a symbol painted
    Of the Poet, Prophet, Seer;
Only those are crowned and sainted
Who with grief have been acquainted,
    Making nations nobler, freer.

Although he wonders whether all the work of poets has been in vain in this unyielding world, he decides that it has not; and he concludes that the poets must continue to hold their torches on high. In *Epimetheus, or The Poet's Afterthought,* he expresses puzzlement that the gods created Pandora so lovely and so destructive, and relief that she did at least save hope for the world.

Prometheus provided a similar inspiration for James Russell Lowell, and for Robert Bridges he offered the opportunity to see, somewhat dimly in spite of two thousand years of hindsight, the coming of Christianity as the overthrow of Zeus. The state of the world in recent decades, however, has not encouraged poets to use a myth that foresees so clearly an end to woe.

PROSERPINA (prŏ·sĕr′pĭ·nȧ) is a Roman name of Persephone, the daughter of Demeter and the wife of Hades. See EARTH GODDESSES, HADES.

317

PROTESILAUS (prŏ·tĕs'ĭ·lā'ŭs) was the first Greek to land on the Trojan shore and the first to die in the TROJAN WAR.

PROTEUS (prō'tĭ·ŭs) is the shepherd of Poseidon's herd of seals. He can change his shape at will, and he is skilled in prophecy. See SEA GODS.

PSYCHE (sī'kē), the personification of the human soul, married the god of love, EROS.

PSYCHOPOMPOS (sī'kŏ·pŏm'pŏs) is another name for HERMES.

PYGMALION (pĭg·mā'lĭ·ŏn) was a mythical sculptor of enormously good fortune. A scorner of women and of lascivious living, according to Ovid (*Metamorphoses* 10), he lived apart from the daily life of Cyprus, his native isle. One day he carved out of ivory a statue of a woman so beautiful and so perfect that he fell in love with it. As his ardor grew greater he began to wish earnestly that the statue had life, and at last he went to the temple of Aphrodite and prayed to the goddess to grant his wish. Aphrodite was moved by his prayer and caused the statue to come to life. Pygmalion was naturally overjoyed and made this extraordinary woman his wife. The result of their union was a son named **Paphos,** whose name the Cyprians gave to their city as a memorial of Aphrodite's miracle.

Pygmalion's experience has appealed to many poets. Some of them, congenitally of the opinion that women are as fair and as unyielding as ivory, see in it the symbol of their frustration. One of them whose name has not come down to us but whose poem, *The Tale of Pigmalion,* survives in *Tottel's Miscellany,* a famous Elizabethan anthology, recounts the story to his mistress in order to conclude pointedly,

> Since that this ymage dum enflamde so wyse a man:
> My dere, alas since I you loue, what wonder is it than?

A later Elizabethan, John Marston, takes a somewhat more worldly view of the story in his poem, *The Metamorphosis of Pygmalion's Image.* According to his version, Pygmalion made such violent love to the statue that Aphrodite's act was less of a miracle. "Tut," he writes,

> . . . women will relent
> Whenas they find such moving blandishment.

And in his sonnet prefatory to this poem he promises his mistress

> Then when thy kindnes grants me such sweet blisse,
> Ile gladly write thy Metamorphosis.

As might be expected, William Morris expands the myth of Pygmalion to considerable length in *The Earthly Paradise,* his long collection of mythical stories in poetic form, but he has little to add to the story except length. On the other hand, Thomas Lovell Beddoes' *Pygmalion,* as Douglas Bush points out, makes the sculptor a symbol of the artist who lives remote from the world about him. The artist is frustrated by his experience with the world, and Beddoes' modifications show this; in his version Pygmalion's prayer is unanswered until he dies, and then the statue comes to life.

The best-known modern use of the myth is Bernard Shaw's play *Pygmalion.* In this play the statue is represented by a Cockney girl of the lowest social caste, and Pygmalion is a learned professor of phonetics. The girl is in effect transformed into an elegant lady and an equal of high-born snobs when she is taught to speak upper-class English. Thus the giving of life to an inanimate figure is ironic in the play, and Shaw turns his parallel of the myth into a witty satire on snobbery.

PYGMIES (pĭg′mēz) attacked Heracles, who wrapped them up in his lion's skin. See **HERACLES.**

PYLADES (pĭl′à·dēz) was the faithful friend of Orestes. See ATREUS.

PYRAMUS (pĭr′à·mŭs) and **Thisbe** were two lovers in ancient Babylon during the reign of Queen Semiramis. Their story was not originally a classical myth, but it became closely associated with classical mythology when Ovid incorporated it in his *Metamorphoses,* a series of tales of transformations. The two lovers lived in adjoining houses but were forbidden by their parents to see each other. With an independence familiar to readers of romances, they contrived to make love in spite of their parents and held converse through a chink in the wall that separated their two dwellings. At last they agreed to run away together, and they arranged to meet outside the city at the tomb of King **Ninus.** Thisbe arrived first; and while she waited, a lioness, fresh from a kill, approached and frightened her into fleeing for refuge in such haste that she dropped her veil. The lioness drank at a near-by spring and tossed with its bloody mouth the veil that Thisbe had dropped.

When Pyramus arrived, the lioness had left, but Thisbe had not dared to return from her refuge. Seeing the bloody veil, Pyramus hastily concluded that a wild beast had slain Thisbe and eaten her, bones, gristle, and all. After blaming himself in lover's fashion for having brought so unkind a fate on her, he killed himself with his sword. Thisbe, when she returned, found this incontrovertible evidence of Pyramus' death, and after an appropriate lover's speech, she also killed herself, first praying that her ashes and those of Pyramus be mingled in the funeral obsequies. In the meantime the mingled blood of the two lovers, soaking into the ground, caused the berries of a near-by mulberry tree to turn purple, though previously they had been white.

Ovid's version of this myth has been retold countless times.

Chaucer relates it in medieval style in *The Legend of Good Women* (921–923) as an example of "A man that can in love been trewe and kynde" and of a woman who "dar and can as wel as he." Doubtless the best-known later rendition is Shakespeare's burlesque of the story in the last act of *A Midsummer-Night's Dream*. In this small play within the play, pathos is made bathos by Bottom, Quince, and the other low comic characters. To spare the ladies' feelings, Bottom suggests that the prologue say (3. 1. 19–23)

> We will do no harm with our swords, and that Pyramus is not kill'd indeed; and for the more better assurance, tell them that I Pyramus am not Pyramus, but Bottom the weaver.

Bottom and his fellows manage to personify even the separating wall and the moonlight, and they make each moment of feeling so explicit that Hippolyta, watching them, is moved to exclaim,

> This is the silliest stuff that ever I heard
> (5. 1. 213).

PYRIPHLEGETHON (pĭr'ĭ·flĕg'ĕ·thŏn), or Phlegethon, is a river of HADES.

PYRRHA (pĭr'à) was the wife of DEUCALION.

PYRRHUS (pĭr'ŭs), who was also called Neoptolemus, was the son of Achilles. He fought in the TROJAN WAR.

PYTHIA (pĭth'ĭ·à) is a name of Apollo's priestess at Delphi. See ORACLES.

PYTHIUS (pĭth'ĭ·ŭs) is a name given to Apollo in reference to his killing the Python. See APOLLO.

PYTHON (pī'thŏn), a son of the earth goddess Gaea, was a great serpent who guarded the Delphic oracle until he was killed by Apollo. See ORACLES.

PYTHONESS (pī'thŏ·nĕs) is a name of Apollo's priestess at Delphi. See ORACLES.

Q

QUIRINAL (kwĭr′ĭ·nᴀl) is one of the seven hills of later ROME.
QUIRINALIA (kwĭr′ĭ·nā′lĭ·ᴀ) was a festival in honor of Romulus.
See ROME.
QUIRINUS (kwĭ·rĭ′nŭs) is the name under which Romulus was
deified as a minor god of war. See ARES, ROME.

R

REMUS (rē′mŭs) was the brother of Romulus, founder of
ROME.
RHADAMANTHUS (răd′ᴀ·măn′thŭs), a son of Zeus and Europa,
became a judge in HADES.
RHEA (rē′ᴀ) was the Titan earth goddess. See EARTH GOD-
DESSES.
RHEA SILVIA (rē′ᴀ sĭl′vĭ·ᴀ) was the mother of Remus and
Romulus. See ROME.
RHOETUS (rē′tŭs) was one of the GIANTS.
ROME, or **ROMA,** the capital of the Roman empire and
civilization, was founded by Romulus, according to mythology,
on a date that corresponds to April 21, 753 B.C. on the Christian
calendar. According to tradition, also, the city was built on seven
hills, and consequently it is often referred to as the City of the

Seven Hills; but the seven hills on which the ancient city was built are not the seven that became famous in later times, chiefly because the ancient Romans subdivided several of the larger hills in their system. The seven hills of the earliest city were **Palatium, Cermalus, Velia, Oppius, Cispius, Fagutal,** and **Sucusa.**

The Palatium and the Cermalus were both peaks of the **Palatine** hill of later fame; the Velia was the saddle ridge that connected the Palatine with the **Esquiline;** the Oppius and Cispius were both spurs of the Esquiline; the Fagutal was the highest part of the Oppius; and the Sucusa was a spur of the **Caelian** hill. In the much larger city of a later day, the famous hills include the Palatine, Esquiline, and Caelian hills already mentioned, and the **Aventine, Capitoline, Viminal,** and **Quirinal** hills.

The Romans maintained that before their capital city was founded, the area was dominated by the town of **Alba Longa** that had been founded by Aeneas' son, Ascanius, and ruled over ever since by his descendants. One of these, King **Numitor,** was deposed by his younger brother, **Amulius,** who also arranged to have Numitor's son killed on a hunt and then forced Numitor's daughter, **Rhea Silvia,** to become a Vestal Virgin. Rhea Silvia, however, was visited by Mars, and as a result had twin boys, **Romulus** and **Remus.** This annoyed Amulius, who put the lady in prison and the two boys into a basket which he had thrown into the **Tiber** River.

The basket floated along to the Palatine Hill, where it came to rest. There a she-wolf took care of the boys and suckled them. They were rescued and adopted by one of the king's shepherds named **Faustulus.** One day when they had grown to youth, the twins and some of their fellow shepherds quarreled with the shepherds of Numitor, and in the ensuing fray Remus was taken prisoner and afterward brought before Numitor, who recognized

323

him as his grandson because of Remus' bearing. Faustulus, who had long suspected the relationship, now confirmed it. Romulus joined Remus in his grandfather's house, and the three of them plotted to restore the throne of Numitor, a project that they at length successfully completed, slaying Amulius in the process.

Romulus and Remus now decided to found a city of their own, to which one of them was to give his name. Since they were twins, this intention led to trouble. They chose the Palatine Hill as the site for the new city, and Romulus set out to define the locations of the walls by driving a plowshare with a bullock along the lines. Remus, to show his contempt for these walls, leaped over them in mockery, and Romulus in a fit of anger killed him. Thus Romulus was free to name the city after himself, and he called it Roma.

Romulus now set out to build up the population of his city. He had his own group of followers, and some of the Alba Longans had moved with him, but the population was small Romulus therefore declared the city a refuge for slaves and homicides and anyone else who cared to live there, a device that brought a great many men to Rome, but very few women. He then invited the neighboring towns to send women in marriage, but they declined for reasons that are not hard to imagine. As a stratagem, Romulus invited the same towns to a celebration in Rome. A large number of the Sabine tribes came, bringing their wives and families, according to the custom of the time. At an appropriate moment, the Romans seized the daughters and made off with them into the city, where they settled down to married life.

This act, famous as the rape of the **Sabine Women**, brought war on the city. The Romans were generally successful in defending themselves until attacked by an army under the Sabine king,

Titus Tatius. The capable generalship of this king brought the Sabines to the very walls of Rome, and at the critical moment, the city was betrayed to them from within by one of their women named **Tarpeia,** after whom in later days was named the famous **Tarpeian Rock** from which condemned criminals were cast down to their destruction. In the battle that followed, the day was saved for the Romans partly by the intercession of Jupiter in response to a prayer of Romulus; partly by an accident that befell a Sabine leader named Mettius Curtius, who fell into a mire and had to be rescued; but chiefly by the Sabine women whom the Romans had stolen, who rushed between the combatants to make peace.

The Sabines now agreed to join the new city and to add to it by settlements on adjoining hills, over all of which, however, Romulus was to be sole king. Romulus subsequently ruled in comparative peace for nearly forty years, during which time he founded, according to the myth, most of the Roman institutions such as the Senate, the Patrician and Plebeian classes, the system of patrons and clients, and the army. One day while reviewing the army on the **Campus Martius,** or Field of Mars, a large training ground, Romulus was seized up into heaven in the midst of a great thunderstorm. Later, however, he appeared to a Roman named Julius Paterculus and predicted the future greatness of Rome. He warned his people to become proficient in arms so that they might live up to their destiny, and he directed that he be worshiped as **Quirinus,** a lesser Mars. Although some suspected that Romulus had been killed by the Senators in the darkness of the storm, most accepted the story of the miraculous seizure into heaven, and consequently Romulus was considered to be a god. A religious festival called the **Quirinalia** was established in his honor.

The famous statue that represents Romulus and Remus being

suckled by the she-wolf has become emblematic of the city of Rome.

ROMULUS (rŏm′ū·lŭs) was the founder of ROME.

RUTULIANS (rōō·tōō′lĭ·ȧnz) were a people of Italy who fought against AENEAS.

S

SABINE (sā′bĭn) **WOMEN** were stolen from their families by the Romans in the early days of ROME.

SABRINA (sȧ·brī′nȧ) is a river Nymph invented by Milton. See NYMPHS, SEA GODS.

SAGITTARIUS (săj′ĭ·tā′rĭ·ŭs), the Archer, is a constellation and a sign of the ZODIAC.

SALMACIS (săl′mȧ·sĭs) was the Nymph whose union with Hermaphroditus produced the first hermaphrodite. See HERMES.

SAMOTHRACE (săm′ō·thrās), an island in the northern part of the Aegean Sea, was famous in ancient times for its religious mysteries. The **Cabiri,** deities whose nature and worship were kept so secret that nothing definite is known of them, were sometimes called Samothracian gods because of the celebration of their mysteries on the island. In the third poem of *Hugh Selwyn Mauberley,* in which Ezra Pound contrasts the gimcrack present with the beauty of the past, he observes that the Christian mystery is inferior to that of Samothrace. Exploration of the ancient ruins of the island recovered a statue which has become famous as the Victory of Samothrace. It is in the Louvre at Paris.

SARPEDON (sär·pē′dŏn) fought valiantly against the Greeks in the TROJAN WAR.

SATURN (săt′ûrn), or **SATURNUS** (sȧ·tûr′nŭs), is a Roman name for CRONUS.

SATURNALIA (săt·ûr·nā′lĭ·ȧ) was a harvest celebration in honor of Saturn, the Roman CRONUS.

SATYRS (sā′tîrz), or **SATYRI** (sā′tĭr·ī), are wood gods, followers of PAN and DIONYSUS.

SCAEAN (sē′ȧn) **GATES** were the chief entrance to Troy. See TROJAN WAR.

SCAMANDER (skȧ·măn′dĕr) was a river of Troy. See TROJAN WAR.

SCHERIA (skē′rĭ·ȧ) was the land of the Phaeacians. See ODYSSEUS.

SCHOENEUS (skē′nĭ·ŭs) was the father of ATALANTA OF BOEOTIA.

SCIRON (sī′rŏn) was a robber who kicked travelers into the sea. He suffered the same fate at the hands (or feet) of THESEUS.

SCORPIO (skôr′pĭ·ō), the Scorpion, is a constellation and a sign of the ZODIAC.

SCYLLA (sĭl′ȧ), a sea Nymph, was transformed into a monster, and thereafter she preyed on the ships that sailed through the Sicilian straits. See SEA GODS, ODYSSEUS.

SCYROS (sī′rŏs) is the Aegean island to which Theseus retired. He died and was buried there, but his bones were later removed to the Theseum in Athens. Scyros is also the place where Thetis hid her son Achilles, disguised as a girl, to save him from his fated death at Troy. See THESEUS, TROJAN WAR.

SEA GODS. The first sea god was **Oceanus,** a Titan. After the great war in the heavens, he did not lose his place to an Olympian, as most of the Titans did. He retained his power partly because he declined to fight against the younger gods and partly because his domain was remote from that of Poseidon, the Olympian who became the god of the sea. Oceanus rules the mighty river that flows in a circle around the edge of the world and forms the boundary of earth, heaven, and Hades. He is mysterious, powerful, but kindly.

He usually appears (as he does in Ben Jonson's *Masque of Blackness*) with his head horned and garlanded with seaweed. Sometimes he rides on a seahorse and sometimes in a chariot beside his wife **Tethys,** by whom he is the father of the **Oceanids,** the Nymphs of the ocean, and all the river gods. Spenser says (*Faerie Queene*, 6. Prologue. 7), "So from the Ocean all riuers spring." Oceanus and Tethys took care of Hera when she was a child and sheltered her when the Olympians were at war with the Titans.

This royal pair has an honored place in the marriage procession of the Thames and the Medway in *The Faerie Queene* (4. 11. 18):

> Next came the aged Ocean, and his Dame,
> Old *Tethys,* th' eldest two of all the rest.

At Whitehall in 1610 the Queen of England played the part of Tethys in *Tethys' Festival,* a masque by Samuel Daniel; and in Milton's *Comus* (866–869) the Spirit invokes the river Nymph Sabrina:

> Listen and appear to us
> In name of great *Oceanus,*
>
> .   .   .   .   .   .
>
> And *Tethys* grave majestick pace.

Keats in *Hyperion* presents Oceanus as the only one of the Titans who understands and accepts their defeat at the hands of the younger gods. His speech to his fellows (2. 173–243) is the

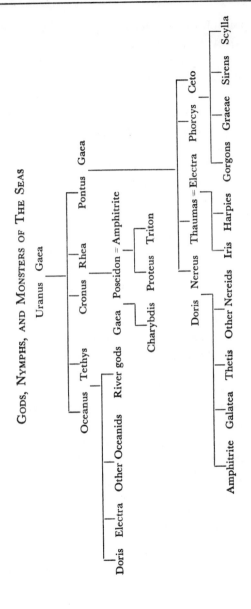

GODS, NYMPHS, AND MONSTERS OF THE SEAS

central expression of the theme of progress, which is the philosophical basis of the poem.

Poseidon, or **Neptune,** is the Olympian god of the sea, the one who was feared and worshiped by the seafaring Greeks and, to a lesser extent, by the land-loving Romans. After the defeat of the Titans, the sons of Cronus—Zeus, Hades, and Poseidon— divided the universe by lot. Zeus became god of the heavens and earth, Hades of the underworld, and Poseidon of the ocean. Poseidon is the supreme sea god, but the Greeks apparently conceived of him as active only in the waters on which they sailed, the Mediterranean and the Euxine Sea (now the Black Sea). Unnavigated waters were still ruled by Oceanus and **Pontus,** another Titan as old as Oceanus but much more shadowy, memorable only because of his children, who will be described later.

With his wife **Amphitrite,** a daughter of Nereus, Poseidon lives in a golden palace at the bottom of the sea. His chariot, entirely of gold, is drawn by horses with brass hooves and golden manes, and the ocean waters grow calm as he approaches. His symbol of kingship is the trident, a three-pronged spear, and the dolphin is sacred to him. He is a strong and moody spirit, with great power on land as well as at sea, for he is also the lord of inland waterways and therefore one of the gods of fertility. Sometimes in sudden rage he raises a storm on the ocean or strikes the land with his trident and causes an earthquake; yet, in spite of his occasional delight in destruction, he is also a god of birth and a protector of cities. Because he created the horse and became the patron of horse racing, millions of people today are aware of his uncertain temper, now benign and now malignant.

In spite of his strength on sea and land, Poseidon was seldom successful in contests with other gods. When he disputed with Athene for Athens, it was agreed that the one who created the more useful gift for man should possess the city. Poseidon struck a stone with his trident and produced the horse, but Athene invented the olive tree, and the city was awarded to her'. Poseidon also failed in his attempts to win Argos from Hera, Corinth from Helios, and other places from other gods.

The quick anger and terrible destructiveness of the sea are described in several stories of Poseidon's vengeance. Once, because he had disputed the power of Zeus, Poseidon was compelled to work for Laomedon, a king of Troy. For a fixed price Poseidon and Apollo, who also had offended Zeus, built the walls of Troy; and when Laomedon refused to pay them, Poseidon sent a monster who killed so many Trojans that Laomedon finally offered his daughter Hesione as a sacrifice to the god. Hesione was saved by Heracles—as Andromeda was saved by Perseus from another monster sent by Poseidon to ravage the shores of Ethiopia —but Poseidon never lost his enmity for Troy. When the Greeks under Agamemnon attacked the city, Poseidon aided them until they had burnt the topless towers of Ilium to the ground.

On his way home from this victory Odysseus, one of the Greek heroes, was compelled to blind the one-eyed cannibal Polyphemus in order to escape death at his hands; but Polyphemus was a son of Poseidon, and thereafter the god pursued Odysseus with implacable fury and for ten years prevented him from returning to his kingdom of Ithaca. When King Minos of Crete prayed for favor, Poseidon sent him a bull, but the animal was so beautiful that Minos kept it and sacrificed another bull to Poseidon. The god responded to this impiety with a terrible and (for him) rather subtle punishment (see DAEDALUS). Yet Poseidon was as kind to some people as he was cruel to others. He helped Pelops to win Hippodamia, and he gave to Peleus, Achilles' father, the famous talking horses that drew the chariot of Achilles.

Poseidon is a lusty god whose love affairs are almost as

numerous though not so celebrated as those of Zeus. The ancient earth goddess Gaea, the younger earth goddess Demeter, Aphrodite, the Gorgon Medusa, and many Nymphs and mortal girls were his mistresses. Among his illegitimate sons (some of whom were horses) were Amycus, Antaeus, Arion, Orion, Pegasus, and Polyphemus. Most of them inherited from their father great strength and uncertain tempers. Their exploits are related elsewhere in this book.

In Spenser's *Faerie Queene* (3. 11. 40–42) the house of the enchanter Busirane is hung with tapestries depicting all the wars of Cupid, and prominent among them are some of Neptune's love affairs. The marriage procession of the Thames and the Medway in the same poem (4. 11. 11–16) is led by Neptune and Amphitrite, and they are followed by such a crowd of Neptune's sons that Spenser needs five stanzas to list them. Several times he refers to the sacrifices offered to Neptune by those who have returned safely from perilous voyages, and in *Muiopotmos* (305–336) he retells the story of the sea god's contest with Athene.

Among the sons of Neptune, Spenser names **Albion**, sea god of England. This addition to classical mythology is natural enough, for Neptune was the king of islands. The Queen in Shakespeare's *Cymbeline* (3. 1. 19–20) recalls his sovereignty when she describes England

> As Neptune's park, ribbed and paled in
> With rocks unscalable and roaring waters;

but, as the Spirit says in Milton's *Comus* (18–29), Neptune graced "his tributary gods" by allowing them to reign on his islands. Neptune often appears as a character in the masques of the late sixteenth and the early seventeenth centuries; see, for example, Ben Jonson's *Neptune's Triumph* and the masque in the first act of *The Maid's Tragedy* by Beaumont and Fletcher. In *Paradise*

Lost (9. 18–19) Milton speaks of the god's persecution of Odysseus. Yet Poseidon is used most commonly in English literature as the ruler or merely the personification of the ocean. Macbeth's words are typical (*Macbeth*, 2. 2. 60–61):

> Will all great Neptune's ocean wash this blood
> Clean from my hand?

The **dolphins** are Poseidon's favorite fish, probably because a dolphin helped him to win his wife. Amphitrite at first rejected Poseidon and tried to hide from him in the great river of Oceanus, but a dolphin found her and brought her back, and Poseidon in gratitude placed the fish in the heavens as the constellation Delphinus. Dolphins are always represented as friendly and helpful to gods and men. When Hera learned that Leto was with child by Zeus, she commanded that no land give refuge to her rival; but Poseidon sent a dolphin to take Leto to the floating island of Delos, and Zeus or Poseidon anchored the island for her in the Mediterranean (see APOLLO).

The poet and harpist **Arion** (not to be confused with Poseidon's son Arion, the horse, for whom see THEBES) once sailed with a piratical crew who decided to murder him for his money. After singing one last song, Arion leaped overboard, and a dolphin that had been attracted by his music carried him to land. Spenser had this musician play at the marriage of the Thames and the Medway (*Faerie Queene*, 4. 11. 23–24), and Milton may have remembered Arion's story when he asked the dolphins to bring the drowned Lycidas to shore (*Lycidas*, 164):

> And, O ye *Dolphins*, waft the haples youth.

It seems more likely, however, that Milton had in mind the story of **Melicertes**, whose drowned body was brought to Corinth by a dolphin but whose spirit became a patron of sailors and the god of harbors. As T. O. Mabbott has recently pointed out, both youths were drowned, both became genii of the shore, and the parallel would have been complete, as Milton seems to indicate, if the dolphins had brought the body of Lycidas to land. In addition to these myths, there are many later stories of dolphins that saved men from the sea or brought their drowned bodies into harbor. Out of these myths and tales—although again the myth of Melicertes is the closest parallel—William Butler Yeats in *Byzantium* created his symbol of the dolphin that carries the souls of the dead to Paradise, through

> That dolphin-torn, that gong-tormented sea.[1]

Since Melicertes has been mentioned, it will be convenient to discuss him and his mother here, although they are less important than several of the sea gods described hereafter. When Hera learned that Semcle was with child by Zeus, she successfully plotted the girl's death, but Zeus saved the child, the god Dionysus, and put him in the care of Semele's sister **Ino,** who was married to Athamas. Hera drove Athamas mad and caused him to kill his son, Learchus. Ino snatched up the other son, Melicertes, and closely pursued by her husband, leaped from a high cliff into the sea. There she was transformed into the goddess **Leucothea** and Melicertes into the god **Palaemon.**

Leucothea and Palaemon were minor deities who protected seafarers, but the Romans identified Palaemon with **Portunus,** who was the god of harbors, and Leucothea with **Mater Matuta,** who was the goddess of sea travel and especially of the dawn. Milton therefore once mentions Leucothea as the dawn (*Paradise Lost,* 11. 133–136). Usually, however, she and her son are remembered as sea deities, as they are in *Comus* (875–876).

[1] From "Byzantium," by W. B. Yeats, in his *The Winding Stair.* Copyright, 1933, by The Macmillan Company, and used with their permission.

Spenser (*Faerie Queene*, 4. 11. 13), following a confused version
of the story, speaks of

> . . . tragicke *Inoes* sonne, the which became
> A God of seas through his mad mothers blame
> Now hight *Palemon,* and is saylers frend.

For Leucothea's most notable exploit, see ODYSSEUS; and for
another story of Ino and Athamas, see THEBES.

An older but less powerful god than Poseidon is **Nereus,** a
son of the shadowy Pontus and the earth goddess Gaea. He is a
wise and gentle old god who possesses the gift of prophecy, but
his greatest distinction came to him through his wife **Doris,** an
Oceanid, by whom he is the father of the fifty **Nereids,** the
Nymphs of the Mediterranean. One of these is Amphitrite,
and Nereus is thus the father-in-law of Poseidon. In *The Faerie
Queene* (4. 11. 18–19) Nereus' skill in prophecy and his great
virtue are emphasized:

> . . . none more vpright
> Ne more sincere in word and deed profest;
> Most void of guile, most free from fowle despight,
> Doing him selfe, and teaching others to doe right.

Milton pictures Nereus as the kind old god who revives the
drowned **Sabrina** and gives her immortality as the Nymph of
the Severn River (*Comus,* 823–841). The story of course has no
classical authority.

Proteus and **Triton** are both sons of Poseidon by Amphitrite.
Triton, who has a dolphin's tail instead of legs, is the herald
and trumpeter of the seas. His trumpet is a conch shell with
which he can calm the ocean or rouse it into storm. He is his
father's messenger and attendant. Proteus is the keeper of
Poseidon's herd of seals, and he carries a shepherd's crook as

the symbol of his office. He has the power of prophecy but also the power to transform himself into a hundred different shapes, and anyone who wishes to question him about the future must have the strength and courage to hold him fast while he turns, for example, from lion to snake to tree to water to panther to fire.

At noon Proteus often drives his herd of seals ashore and takes a nap on the beach. When **Aristaeus,** the god of beekeeping and a son of Apollo, pursued Eurydice in lust and caused her death (see ORPHEUS), the Nymphs killed his bees to punish him. His mother Cyrene told him that Proteus could help him to recover his bees and she warned him of the sea god's tricks. Aristaeus, finding Proteus asleep, tied him so securely that in spite of his transformations he could not escape. At last he admitted his defeat and told Aristaeus to sacrifice cattle and to return to their bodies after nine days. Aristaeus followed instructions and on the ninth day found swarms of bees in the decayed carcasses. (This folktale, based on the likeness of a certain carrion fly to the bee, is an important part of Samson's riddle in Judges. W. B. Yeats alludes to the story in his poem *Vacillation.*) When Menelaus was stranded in Pharos after the Trojan War, he also caught Proteus and held him fast until the god told him how to return to Greece.

In English literature Triton usually appears as the herald or messenger of Poseidon. At the marriage of the Thames and the Medway in *The Faerie Queene* (4. 11. 12) he marched in front of Neptune and Amphitrite and "his trompet shrill before them blew"; in Milton's *Comus* (872) his symbol is his conch-shell trumpet; and in *Lycidas* (89–94) he is "the Herald of the Sea" who, in Neptune's defense, questions his father's servants about the cause of the death of Lycidas.

The myth of Proteus is richer and more productive. His power to transform himself, and his knowledge, reluctantly revealed to the brave and the persistent, have touched the imaginations both of the relativist who believes that for a hundred men truth has a hundred faces and of the idealist who believes that truth can be discovered behind the countless shifting disguises of mutability. Our adjective "protean" is derived from the god. In *The Faerie Queene* (1. 2. 10) the great deceiver Archimago can take

> As many formes and shapes in seeming wise,
> As euer *Proteus* to himselfe could make,

and Milton in *Comus* (871) calls Proteus "the *Carpathian* wisard" because, according to Virgil, Proteus spent most of his time in the Carpathian Sea between Crete and Rhodes.

Francis Bacon in *The Wisdom of the Ancients* interprets Proteus as a symbol of the primary substance that he thought might be obtained by distilling various materials in alembics, and in *Paradise Lost* (3. 603–605) Milton refers to the philosophers who try to

> . . . call up unbound
> In various shapes old *Proteus* from the Sea,
> Draind through a Limbec to his Native forme.

The unfaithful friend in *Two Gentlemen of Verona* is appropriately named Proteus because he changes his loyalty as rapidly as the sea god changes his shape, and Pope in *The Dunciad* (1. 37–38) speaks of the Cave of Poverty from which the bad poets,

> . . . like *Proteus* long in vain tied down,
> Escape in Monsters, and amaze the town.

Two contemporary poets have made interesting use of the myth. In *Men of My Century Loved Mozart* Archibald MacLeish describes Mozart's music as having power to make men discard their disguises—"All cheats and falsehoods"—and become themselves, and in *Proteus, or the Shapes of Conscience* Rolfe Humphries offers a convincing interpretation of the myth in terms of modern psychology.

Proteus and Triton are often seen together, especially as attendants at any formal appearance of their father Poseidon, but in *Colin Clouts Come Home Againe* (244–248) Spenser writes of both of them as shepherds of the flocks of the ocean:

> . . . the shepheard which hath charge in chief,
> Is *Triton* blowing loud his wreathed horne
>
> . . . . . .
>
> And *Proteus* eke with him does driue his heard.

Critics agree that Wordsworth must have had these lines in mind when he wrote *The World Is Too Much with Us:*

> . . . Great God! I'd rather be
> A Pagan suckled in a creed outworn;
> So might I, standing on this pleasant lea,
> Have glimpses that would make me less forlorn;
> Have sight of Proteus rising from the sea;
> Or hear old Triton blow his wreathèd horn.

Today we think that we have explored the earth pretty thoroughly, but the sea is still mysterious to us. The Greeks and the Romans, who were more ignorant of facts than we are, believed that both the earth and the sea spawned monsters and that fabulous lands existed on the farther side of the great river of Oceanus. Beyond the great river the melancholy **Cimmerians** inhabited a region of continual night; in the north the **Hyperboreans** lived in happiness and endless springtime; in the south dwelt the **Ethiopians,** whose banquets were often attended by the ·gods; and in the west were the **Blessed Islands,** a paradise where heroes enjoyed their immortality. (For another location of this paradise, see Elysian Fields under HADES).

Spenser in *The Teares of the Muses* (256) uses Cimmerian blackness as an image of man's ignorance:

> Darknesse more than *Cymerians* daylie night;

and in *L'Allegro* (10) Milton banishes Melancholy to find her dwelling place "in dark *Cimmerian* desert." *The Song of a Hyperborean* by Thomas Moore represents the delights of a life in eternal springtime, and Milton in *Il Penseroso* (17–21) describes the dark majesty of the Ethiopians. These people were burned black by the terrible heat of the chariot of the sun when Apollo's horses refused to be guided by Phaethon and ran wild in the heavens (see APOLLO). As Ulysses, in Tennyson's poem of that name (63–64), prepares to sail beyond the sunset on his last voyage, his reference to the Blessed Islands is typical:

> It may be we shall touch the Happy Isles,
> And see the great Achilles, whom we knew.

In addition to Nereus, the dim sea god Pontus and his mother Gaea had two other sons, Phorcys and **Thaumas.** These two are just as shadowy as their father, but they begot most of the monsters of the sea. The daughters of Thaumas by **Electra,** an Oceanid, were the charming Iris, goddess of the rainbow, and the hideous **Harpies.** The Harpies had the bodies, wings, and claws of birds but the faces of girls. Sometimes these creatures were conceived of as spirits of the wind; the talking horses of Achilles were the children of the Harpy **Podarge** (which means "fleet foot") and the west wind, Zephyrus. But more often the Harpies were thought of as ravenous, filthy creatures who stole from travelers all the food they could eat and defiled the rest.

In *The Faerie Queene* (2. 12. 36) Spenser calls them "The hellish Harpies, prophets of sad destiny," probably in reference to the doleful prophecies that the Harpy **Celaeno** made to Aeneas; and earlier in the same book (2. 7. 23) this Harpy perches with other birds of ill omen at the gate of Mammon's cave:

> . . . sad *Celeno,* sitting on a clift
> A song of bale and bitter sorrow sings.

In *Comus* (603–605) Milton associates the Harpies with the creatures of Hell, and in *Paradise Regained* (2. 403) the banquet created by Satan vanishes "With sound of Harpies wings, and Talons heard." For other stories about the Harpies see AENEAS and ARGONAUTS.

If his performances in Renaissance masques are excepted— at Elvetham in 1591, for example, in an entertainment presented to Queen Elizabeth, he rose from a pond in the company of Neptune, Oceanus, Nereus, and Glaucus, "with a pinnace, in which three virgins played Scottish jigs"—**Phorcys** is notable in English literature only as Spenser describes him (*Faerie Queene,* 4. 11. 13):

> . . . the father of that fatall brood,
> By whom those old Heroes wonne such fame.

Themselves children of incest, Phorcys and his sister **Ceto** produced more terrifying daughters than the Jukes and the Kallikaks together. They were the parents of the Graeae, the Gorgons, the Sirens, and Scylla.

The **Graeae**, three gray-haired crones who acted as sentries for the Gorgons, were of necessity the first practicers of planned economy: they had one eye and one tooth among them, and they passed these about so that each of them could do a little seeing and chewing. Their sisters, the three **Gorgons,** lived in a cave

far at sea; they were shaped like women, but they had wings
and brazen claws, and snakes for hair. Anyone who looked at
their faces was turned to stone. Two of the Gorgons could not
die, but the third, **Medusa,** was mortal. For her death and the
confusion of the Graeae see PERSEUS.

In classical story the three **Sirens—Parthenope, Ligeia,** and
Leucosia—had the heads of girls and the bodies and wings of
birds, but in the Middle Ages and the Renaissance they were
pictured as girls with fishes' tails. They lived on a treacherous
reef in the sea, and when a ship passed by they sang so enchantingly that the sailors leaped overboard and were drowned, and
the steersman turned toward the reef and wrecked his ship.
According to certain storytellers, these lovely enticers committed
suicide on three separate occasions: once when they lost a singing
contest with the Muses, again when Orpheus defeated them in
song, and finally when the wily Odysseus managed to hear them
sing and yet avoid the penalty. If all these stories are true, the
Sirens were born again each time, for they have never ceased to
sing. Centuries after their last reported suicide, they were haunt-
ing the Rhine, where the Germans renamed them the Lorelei;
and if other reports are veracious, they have not confined their
activities to that river or that section of the world.

Milton is inclined to glorify these ladies as "the celestial
sirens" (*Arcades,* 63; *At a Solemn Music,* 1); in *Comus* (877–881)
Sabrina is invoked by calling not only on the attributes of the
benevolent sea gods but also on

> . . . the Songs of *Sirens* sweet,
> By dead *Parthenope's* dear tomb,
> And fair *Ligea's* golden comb,
> Wherewith she sits on diamond rocks
> Sleeking her soft alluring locks.

Other English poets are more traditional and more strict than

Milton. Since they conceive of all sea maids as girls with fishes' tails, and of all as dangerous, they are likely to call the Sirens simply mermaids, and to attribute to all mermaids the power of seductive song. Thus Chaucer (*Nun's Priest's Tale,* VII. 3270) writes of a lady who "soong murier than the mermayde in the sea"; Spenser describes the mermaids' unsuccessful attempt to entice Sir Guyon by their melodies (*Faerie Queene,* 2. 12. 17, 30–34); Samuel Daniel skillfully arranges for the defeat of the mermaid in *Ulysses and the Siren;* John Donne in his ironic *Song* urges his listeners to teach him, among other impossibilities, "to heare Mermaides singing"; and the hero in T. S. Eliot's *Love Song of J. Alfred Prufrock* (124–125) remembers with regretful irony:

> I have heard the mermaids singing, each to each.

> I do not think that they will sing to me.[2]

In each of these poems, except those of the ordinarily stern Milton, the Sirens are the symbol of physical desire. Only the contemporary poet John Manifold, in *The Sirens,* has suggested that business is sometimes more seductive than sex:

> Odysseus saw the sirens; they were charming,
> Blonde, with snub breasts and little neat posteriors,
> But could not take his mind off the alarming
>
> Weather report, his mutineers in irons,
> The radio failing; it was bloody serious.
> In twenty minutes he forgot the sirens.[3]

[2] From "The Love Song of J. Alfred Prufrock," by T. S. Eliot, in his *Collected Poems, 1909–1935.* Copyright, 1934, 1936, by Harcourt, Brace and Company. Reprinted with their permission.

[3] From "The Sirens," by John Manifold, in his *Selected Verse.* Reprinted with the permission of the publisher, The John Day Company.

For other stories of the Sirens see ORPHEUS and ODYS-
SEUS.

Scylla was the only child of Phorcys and Ceto who had a fair
start in life. She was a pretty and good-tempered sea Nymph
and doubtless would have remained one if a newly created sea
god named **Glaucus** had not fallen in love with her. Glaucus
had been a fisherman, but one day he emptied his net on the
beach, and the fish he had caught, instead of flopping helplessly
about, touched a strange herb that grew there and immediately
leaped back into the sea. Glaucus ate a bit of the herb and at
once felt a passionate desire to jump in the ocean. He did so
and was made immortal. Although he kept his man's body, his
legs became a fish's tail, and seaweed, stones, and mussels always
hung rather untidily about him. He had the gift of prophecy—
Milton (*Comus,* 873) calls him "old sooth-saying *Glaucus"*—and he
was kind to unlucky sailors.

Scylla haughtily rejected Glaucus' advances, and he asked the
enchantress Circe for a love potion. Circe, however, fell in love with
him herself; and when he paid no attention to her, she poisoned
the water of the bay where Scylla bathed, and Scylla was transformed into a monster. From head to waist she remained a
beautiful girl, but below she was disfigured with various ap-
pendages, including six dogs' heads on long necks. Filled with
hatred, she lived in a cave on the straits between Italy and Sicily
and preyed on passing ships.

The myth of Scylla and Glaucus has been interpreted in
several ways by English poets. In *Scillaes Metamorphosis* by the
Elizabethan Thomas Lodge the transformation of Scylla is a
punishment visited on her for scorning the love of Glaucus. A
commoner explanation, which depends entirely on the appearance of Scylla the monster and not on the cause of her transformation, is that she is a symbol of uncontrolled lust. George Sandys

(as Douglas Bush observes), commenting on his translation of Ovid's *Metamorphoses,* says the upper part of Scylla's body "is feigned to retaine a humane figure, and the lower to be bestiall; [which] intimates how man, a divine creature, . . . can neuer so degenerate into a beast, as when he giueth himself over to the loe delights of those baser parts of the body." In the nineteenth century, however, Keats (*Endymion,* 3. 421–472) represents Glaucus as seduced from his pure love of Scylla by the sensual enchantress Circe.

Scylla was not the only peril of the straits between Sicily and Italy. On the other side of the narrow passage was the monster **Charybdis.** A daughter of Poseidon and Gaea, she was an obstreperous girl with a big appetite. Because of some notable display of intemperance, Zeus condemned her to live under a great stone on the straits. Her gluttony caused her to swallow as much water as she could hold and then spew it out again. Mariners who sailed through the straits had to risk the whirlpool of Charybdis or the six ravenous dogs' heads of Scylla. Spenser's description (*Virgils Gnat,* 539–542) of the sailor's dilemma is typical: he must choose between

> . . . greedie *Scilla,* vnder whom there bay
> Manie great bandogs, which her gird about:
>
> .   .   .   .   .   .
>
> And deep *Charybdis* gulphing in and out.

Naturally this dilemma was allegorized into that of the temperate man steering between the two extremes of excess and defect; in *The Faerie Queene* (2. 12. 9) Scylla and Charybdis are described as

> . . . th' ensamples in our sights,
> Of lustfull luxurie and thriftlesse wast.

For other stories about Charybdis and Scylla see ODYSSEUS.

SELENE (sĕ·lē′nē) was the Titan moon goddess. Her name is often given to ARTEMIS.

SEMELE (sĕm′ĕ·lē) was one of the mistresses of Zeus. See DIONYSUS, ZEUS.

SESTOS (sĕs′tŏs) was the home of HERO.

SIBYL OF CUMAE (sĭb′îl kū′mē), or Cumaean Sibyl, who was given the power of prophecy and a thousand years of life by Apollo, guided Aeneas to Hades. See APOLLO, AENEAS.

SIBYLLINE (sĭb′ĭ·lĭn) **BOOKS** were prophetic books written by the Sibyl of Cumae. See APOLLO.

SIDE (sīd′ē) was the first wife of ORION.

SILENI (sĭ·lē′nī) are wood gods, followers of PAN and DIONYSUS.

SILENUS (sī·lē′nûs) is the son or brother of Pan and the tutor and follower of Dionysus. See DIONYSUS, PAN.

SILVER AGE preceded the great flood that drowned all mankind except Pyrrha and DEUCALION.

SIMOIS (sĭm′ō·ĭs) was a river of Troy. See TROJAN WAR.

SINIS (sĭn′ĭs) was a murderer who became the victim of his own trick when he tried to kill THESEUS.

SINON (sī′nŏn) assisted Odysseus with the ruse of the wooden horse, which brought victory to the Greeks in the TROJAN WAR.

SIRENS are three enchantresses whose sweet songs lure sailors to disaster. See SEA GODS, ODYSSEUS, ORPHEUS.

SISYPHUS (sĭs′ĭ·fûs), a king of Corinth, was a famous sinner who suffers a special torment in Hades. He was also the shrewdest of men. He outwitted even **Autolycus,** the thief who could make himself and his loot invisible or cause whatever he had stolen to assume a new shape or color. Autolycus took some of Sisyphus' cattle and changed their appearance so that Sisyphus could not recognize them. When more of his cattle disappeared, Sisyphus exposed the thief by examining all the cattle in Autolycus' herd and identifying his own by a small mark that he had cut in the bottom of their hooves.

Although Greek and Roman writers agree that Sisyphus was a rascal and often accuse him of large but vague crimes, his first mistake seems to have been to tell the truth. He saw Zeus in the form of an eagle carrying off Aegina, and when her grieving father asked help in finding her, Sisyphus told him what he had seen. Thereafter the king of the gods hated Sisyphus, but he succeeded in escaping punishment for many years. Thanatos, the god of death, was sent to take him, but the wily king trapped Thanatos and held him captive until Zeus had him freed by force. Then Thanatos seized his victim, but not before Sisyphus had instructed his wife **Merope** to perform none of the required funeral rites but simply to throw his body out in the street. This impiety so shocked Hades that he told Sisyphus to return to life for a few hours in order to punish his wife. Sisyphus gladly rejoined the living, but he never punished Merope and thus he was able to live to a triumphant and impious old age. In *Virgils Gnat* (390) Spenser says that the sin of Sisyphus was "scorning to the sacred Gods to pray," but perhaps Sisyphus felt that nothing could help him short of a revolution on Olympus. When he died at last, he was thrust into Tartarus. There he must eternally try to roll a big rock to the top of a hill; whenever he gets it near the top, it tumbles down to the bottom again. Many English and American writers have commented on the punishment of Sisyphus. John Dyer's description of it is quoted in the section on famous sinners in HADES.

SLEEP. See Hypnos under HADES.

SOCK is a light thin-soled shoe once worn by actors in Greek and Roman comedy, and therefore a symbol of comedy, as it appears in Milton's *L'Allegro* (131-132):

> Then to the well-trod stage anon,
> If *Jonsons* learned Sock be on.

See Thalia under MUSES.

SOLYMI (sŏl'ĭ·mē) were a race of mighty warriors who fought against BELLEROPHON.

SOMNUS (sŏm'nŭs) is the Roman name of Hypnos, the god of sleep. See HADES.

SOTEIRA (sŏ·tī'rȧ) is a surname of ATHENE.

SPARTA (spär'tȧ) and her husband Lacedaemon both gave their names to the land they ruled, Laconia. See LACEDAEMON.

SPARTAE (spär'tē) were the sons of the serpent's teeth. See THEBES.

SPHINX (sfĭngks) was a monster whose riddle was finally answered by Oedipus, later king of THEBES.

STHENELUS (sthĕn'ė·lŭs) was (1) the father of Eurystheus, who commanded the labors of HERACLES; (2) one of the Epigoni (see THEBES).

STROPHIUS (strō'fĭ·ŭs) was the father of Pylades and the protector of Orestes. See ATREUS.

STYMPHALIAN (stĭm·fā'lĭ·ȧn) **BIRDS** were driven from the vale of Stymphalus by Heracles. They flew to an island in the Black Sea from which they attacked the Argonauts. See ARGONAUTS, HERACLES.

STYX (stĭks) is a river of HADES.

SUCUSA (sû·kū'sȧ) was one of the seven hills of earliest ROME.

SYCHAEUS (sĭ·kē'ŭs) was once the husband of Dido. See AENEAS.

SYLVANS (sĭl'vȧnz), or **SYLVANI** (sĭl·vā'nī), are wood gods, followers of PAN.

SYLVANUS (sĭl·vā'nŭs) is a Roman deity of the woods who was identified with PAN.

347.

SYMPLEGADES (sĭm·plĕg′a·dēz) were two cliffs floating at the entrance to the Black Sea. They imperiled the ARGONAUTS.

SYRINX (sĭr′ĭngks), who gave her name to Pan's pipes, was a Hamadryad loved by PAN.

T

TALARIA (ta·lā′rĭ·a) are the winged sandals of HERMES.

TALUS (tā′lŭs) was (1) the inventor of the saw and a nephew of DAEDALUS; (2) a bronze giant who guarded the island of Crete (see THESEUS).

TANTALUS (tăn′ta·lŭs) was the earliest ancestor of the tragic house of ATREUS.

TARPEIA (tär·pē′ya) was a Sabine woman who tried to betray ROME.

TARPEIAN (tär·pē′yan) **ROCK** was a rock from which condemned criminals were cast to their destruction in the city of ROME.

TARTARUS (tär′ta·rŭs) is the place of punishment in HADES.

TAURUS (tô′rŭs), the Bull, is a constellation and a sign of the ZODIAC.

TAYGETA (tā·ĭj′ĕ·ta) was the mother of LACEDAEMON.

TELAMON (tĕl′a·mŏn) was the father of the greater Aias. See TROJAN WAR.

TELEMACHUS (tĕ·lĕm′a·kŭs) was the son of ODYSSEUS.

TELEPHASSA (tĕl′ē·fă′sa) was the mother of Cadmus. See THEBES.

TELLUS (tĕl′ŭs) was a Roman name of the first earth goddess, Gaea. See EARTH GODDESSES.

TEMPE (tĕm′pē) is a vale in Thessaly through which flows the river PENEUS.

TEREUS (tīr′ōōs), the husband of Procne, deceived Procne's sister, PHILOMELA.

TERPSICHORE (tĕrp·sĭk′ŏ·rē) is the Muse of dancing. See MUSES.

TERRA MATER (tĕr′a mā′tĕr) was a Roman name for the first earth goddess, Gaea. See EARTH GODDESSES.

TETHYS (tē′thĭs) is the wife of Oceanus. See SEA GODS.

THALIA (tha·lī′a) is (1) one of the GRACES; (2) the Muse of comedy and pastoral poetry (see MUSES).

THANATOS (thăn′a·tŏs) is the god of death. See HADES.

THAUMAS (thô′mas) is one of the SEA GODS.

THEA (thē′a) was the mother of Helios, Eos, and Selene, the predecessor of ARTEMIS.

THEBES (thēbz). A whole fabric of myth surrounds the city of Thebes from the day of its foundation by the hero Cadmus until the day of its destruction by the Epigoni, a fabric that provided the matter for some of the great tragedies of Aeschylus and Sophocles. The myth had its beginning in one of the love indiscretions of Zeus. When Zeus, in the form of a bull, swam off with Europa (see ZEUS), the maiden's father, King Agenor, sent his three sons, **Phoenix, Cilix,** and **Cadmus,** to find her, and ordered them not to return without her. Phoenix wandered through a land that later bore his name, Phoenicia, and Cilix through the land that came to be called Cilicia after him. Both were unsuccessful in their quest, and consequently settled down to new lives among strangers.

Cadmus, with his mother, **Telephassa,** set off among the Greek islands and finally reached Thrace, where his mother died. In

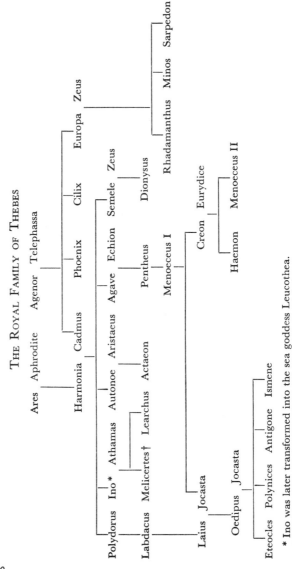

THE ROYAL FAMILY OF THEBES

* Ino was later transformed into the sea goddess Leucothea.
† Melicertes was later transformed into the sea god Palaemon.

350

despair, he consulted the oracle at Delphi and was told to abandon his search. The oracle directed him to follow a cow that he would encounter and to build a city on the spot to which she led him. Cadmus accepted this strange order, and as he left the oracle, he at once saw a cow and followed her. She led him through Boeotia to the plain of Panope where at last, lowing meaningfully, she lay down. Cadmus, having examined the place and observed the mountains around it, decided to sacrifice the fateful cow to Athene, his patroness. He sent his followers for pure water for the ceremony, and they entered a dark wood where they found a pure spring. When they dipped in their vessels, the sound of the water rushing into them aroused a terrible serpent, sacred to Ares or possibly even his offspring, which plunged forth and slew them all. When the men did not return, Cadmus went to look for them. Near the spring he, too, was attacked by the terrible monster. First, aided by Athene, he cast his javelin at it and wounded it in the body. The serpent, writhing in pain, turned back on itself and tried to draw out the javelin with its teeth, but succeeded only in breaking it off. As the snake pursued Cadmus through the wood, he waited his moment and caught it at last with its head near a tree. Hurling his spear full at the monster, he pinned its head to the tree and so killed it.

While Cadmus contemplated his success, he heard a voice, doubtless Athene's, telling him to sow the teeth of the dragon in the ground. Had not Cadmus been suggestible, he would never have followed the cow in the first place; and he now made furrows and planted in them the teeth of his dead enemy. No sooner had he done this than the teeth began to grow. First there appeared spear points, breaking through the soil; next helmets; and finally a tribe of fierce, fully armed men. Cadmus expected them to attack him, but they did not. One story says that they exclaimed to him, "Don't meddle in our civil war," and straightway fell to fighting among themselves. According to another version, Cadmus, at the suggestion of Athene, threw a stone among them and touched off their strife. In any event, the men (who were called **Spartae,** which means "sown men") fought each other violently until all except five were dead. Then one threw away his weapons and invited his fellows to make peace, an offer that they accepted. These five then joined Cadmus in constructing a citadel, and from them the oldest families of Thebes in later times traced their lineage.

But before Cadmus could settle down in peace to found his city, he had to serve Ares for eight years because he had killed the god's serpent. At the end of this period, Ares, fully appeased, gave his and Aphrodite's lovely daughter **Harmonia** to Cadmus in marriage, and Athene made Cadmus king of Thebes. The marriage was celebrated in heaven and attended by all the Olympian gods, and music for the occasion was provided, fittingly, by the Muses themselves, who sang a marriage song. Among the wedding gifts were a *peplos,* or splendid dress, made by Athene, and a necklace wrought by Hephaestus; some say that these gifts were responsible for Cadmus' later misfortunes.

The wedlock of Cadmus and Harmonia was as fertile of children as of myths. The royal pair had four daughters: Agave, Autonoe, Ino, and Semele; and one son: Polydorus. **Agave** married one of the five surviving Spartae, a man named Echion, and their son, **Pentheus,** became king of Thebes after Cadmus. **Autonoe** married Aristaeus and had a son named Actaeon, the story of whose unfortunate encounter with a goddess in deshabille is told under ARTEMIS. **Ino** married **Athamas,** and they had two children. Athamas had previously married a goddess named Nephele, under orders from Hera, and he had had two children by her. When he abandoned her for Ino, Nephele brought a drought on the land, and Ino declared that an oracle demanded the sacrifice of Nephele's children to relieve the drought. The story of the children's rescue is told in the article on the Argonauts. For a time Ino cared for Dionysus, the divine son of her sister Semele, and thus brought on herself the wrath of Hera. Because she hated Athamas for deserting Nephele, and Ino for taking care of one of Zeus's illegitimate children, Hera drove Athamas mad and caused him to turn against Ino. He killed his son Learchus and pursued Ino until she threw herself and their other son, Melicertes, into the sea, where they were changed into sea deities under the names of Leucothea and Palaemon (see SEA GODS).

For Semele was reserved the doubtful privilege of illicit sexual relations with Zeus; her story can be found in the article on that god. Her son, Dionysus, was nursed by Ino, but she and Semele's other sisters, Autonoe and Agave, refused to believe that Zeus was the boy's father. Some years later, however, when Dionysus returned in triumph to Thebes, Agave led the other women in the celebration of his rites; and in a frenzy she killed her son, King Pentheus, when he opposed the worship of the frenzy-inspiring god (see DIONYSUS). When she recovered her senses, she fled to Illyrium.

These fatal misfortunes that fell on their children made Thebes a sad place for Cadmus and Harmonia. Consequently they left the city and went to Illyrium, where they were well received and Cadmus was accepted as king. Even there, however, they could not forget their woes. One day Cadmus, remembering his troubles and blaming them all on his having slain the serpent, exclaimed, "If a serpent's life is so dear to the gods, I wish I were a serpent." His prayer was answered. Harmonia wished to share his fate and was allowed to do so. This miraculous change is referred to by Milton in *Paradise Lost* (9. 503–506) in lines where he describes the attractive air of Satan disguised as a snake:

> . . . pleasing was his shape,
> And lovely, never since of Serpent kind
> Lovelier, not those that in *Illyria* chang'd
> *Hermione* and *Cadmus* . . . ,

though Milton seems to have thought that Cadmus' wife was not Harmonia but Hermione. The incident is also the subject of a song sung by Callicles in Matthew Arnold's long poem, *Empedocles on Etna:*

> There those two live, far in the Illyrian brakes.
> They had stay'd long enough to see,
> In Thebes, the billow of calamity
> Over their own dear children roll'd,
> Curse upon curse, pang upon pang,
> For years, they sitting helpless in their home,
> A grey old man and woman; yet of old
> The Gods had to their marriage come,
> And at the banquet all the Muses sang.
>
> Therefore they did not end their days
> In sight of blood; but were rapt, far away,
> To where the west-wind plays,
> And murmurs of the Adriatic come
> To those untrodden mountain-lawns; and there
> Placed safely in changed forms, the pair
> Wholly forget their first sad life, and home,
> And all that Theban woe, and stray
> For ever through the glens, placid and dumb.

The curse did not leave their line, however, until five generations later when almost all the family were destroyed in the war of the Seven against Thebes.

After the death of Pentheus, the throne of the city passed

through the regencies of **Nycteus** and **Lycus** and of **Amphion** and **Zethus** to Polydorus' son, Labdacus. (The shadowy **Polydorus** should have ruled when Pentheus did, but instead he simply provided a genealogical link between Cadmus and Labdacus.) During this period Thebes owed most to the twin brothers, Amphion and Zethus. These two were sons of Zeus, who had approached their mother, **Antiope,** in the form of a Centaur. When Antiope became pregnant, her father, Nycteus the regent, would not believe her story that Zeus was to blame. She fled to the court of King Epopeus of Sicyon; but Nycteus, before committing suicide because of his shame, demandèd that his wayward daughter be punished, and Lycus compelled Epopeus to return Antiope to Thebes. On the way back she gave birth to twin sons, Amphion and Zethus, in the vicinity of Eleutherae, and left them to be cared for by a herdsman. In Thebes Antiope received such cruel treatment from Lycus and **Dirce,** his wife, that she fled again and this time found temporary safety in the house of the very herdsman who was rearing her youthful twins on the slopes of Mount Cithaeron, though she did not recognize him or them. Soon after, Dirce, who had arrived in the same neighborhood to celebrate the rites of Dionysus, found Antiope. The unrelenting woman ordered Amphion and Zethus to bind Antiope to the horns of a wild bull and allow her to be dragged to death. At this point, however, the herdsman realized the identity of the intended victim and made it known to the boys, who in anger gave Dirce the fate that she had intended for Antiope. Dirce, after her death, was transformed into a fountain.

Antiope and her sons returned to Thebes, and the boys killed or intimidated Lycus, who gave over the regency of the city to them. Their most famous accomplishment was the building of new walls for the city, which had outgrown the smaller enclosure built by Cadmus and the Spartae. Zethus was a man of great physical strength, and as his share of the work he dragged huge stones in for the wall; but Amphion was so greatly skilled in the use of the lyre which Hermes had given him that when he played on it he could persuade equally great stones to move of their own accord to be fitted into the wall, a power that Tennyson made the subject of a somewhat heavily humorous poem called *Amphion*, which contains the following stanza:

> 'T is said he had a tuneful tongue,
>   Such happy intonation,
> Wherever he sat down and sung
>   He left a small plantation;
> Wherever in a lonely grove
>   He set up his forlorn pipes,
> The gouty oak began to move,
>   And flounder into hornpipes.

This is only another of the many Greek myths which show that intellectual skill is the equal, if not the superior, of mere physical strength, and it is a close parallel to the myth that describes the building of Troy's walls by Apollo and Poseidon. In the walls of Thebes, Amphion and Zethus built seven gates, symbolic of the seven strings of the lyre. These gates were later to be attacked by the Seven against Thebes.

Amphion married Niobe, the daughter of Tantalus, and had fourteen children by her. The story of Niobe's pride in these children and how it brought down on her the wrath of Leto and her son and daughter is told under ARTEMIS. On the deaths of Amphion and Zethus, the kingship of Thebes came to **Labdacus.** For him the curse on the house of Cadmus seems to have remitted its effect, because he had a peaceful reign; but the curse returned in full force on his descendants.

Laius, the son of Labdacus, became the next Theban king. He and his wife, **Jocasta,** had a single son, of whom they were informed by an oracle that he would be the death of his father if he grew to manhood. Following an old Greek custom, Laius therefore "exposed" the child; that is, abandoned him on the wild slopes of Mount Cithaeron, expecting him to die of exposure. As was so often the case in Greek myths, the child did not die. Instead, he was found by herdsmen and brought to King **Polybus** and Queen **Periboea** of Corinth. They named the child **Oedipus,** which means "swollen foot," because his feet had been pierced with a spike before he was abandoned; and they raised him as their own son, for they were childless. Shelley's dramatic satire on the matrimonial difficulties of King George IV is called *Oedipus Tyrannus, or Swellfoot the Tyrant.*

When he reached young manhood, Oedipus consulted an oracle to learn, if he could, who his parents were. The oracle told him that he would cause the death of his father and marry his mother. Oedipus, not unnaturally, wished to avoid the fulfilment of this prediction. On the chance that it referred to his foster father and mother, he left Corinth and became a wanderer. Fate, however, was not so easily to be avoided. On a narrow road in the mountains, Oedipus met King Laius, his real father, who was returning from the oracle at Delphi. Neither recognized the other. Oedipus angrily blocked the road, and he would not yield passage to Laius. In the altercation a servant of Laius killed one of Oedipus' horses. In a rage, Oedipus attacked and slew not only the servant but Laius himself. Thus, though Oedipus did not know it, the first half of the oracle was fulfilled.

The second of the oracle's predictions came about in a similarly unexpected way. In Thebes, where Oedipus arrived soon after slaying Laius, he found great distress resulting from the ravages of a monster called the **Sphinx.** This winged monster

357

had the body of a lion and the head and breasts of a woman; she infested one of the highways. Crouching on a rock above the road, she blocked the way of travelers and asked them a riddle. If they could answer it, she permitted them to pass; but if they could not, she killed them by throwing them from her high rock. Oedipus determined to overcome her. When he approached, she asked him her question, "What animal is it that in the morning goes on four feet, at noon on two, and in the evening on three?" Oedipus answered that the animal was man, who in childhood crawls on hands and knees, in manhood walks on two feet, and in old age must use a staff. The Sphinx, her riddle answered correctly, in chagrin threw herself off the high rock and was killed. Much later a statue of the Sphinx was carved in Egypt, and of this enigmatic figure W. H. Auden writes:

> Did it once issue from the carver's hand
> Healthy? Even the earliest conquerors saw
> The face of a sick ape, a bandaged paw,
> A Presence in the hot invaded land.
>
> The lion of a tortured stubborn star,
> It does not like the young, nor love, nor learning:
> Time hurt it like a person; it lies, turning
> A vast behind on shrill America,
>
> And witnesses. The huge hurt face accuses,
> And pardons nothing, least of all success.
> The answers that it utters have no uses
> To those who face akimbo its distress:
> "Do people like me?" No. The slave amuses
> The lion: "Am I to suffer always?" Yes.[1]

See also Caesar's address to the Sphinx in the first act of Bernard Shaw's *Caesar and Cleopatra.*

Returning to Thebes, Oedipus was greeted with considerable gratitude and accepted as king. The Thebans also gave him Queen Jocasta for his wife; and so he came to marry his own mother, although he was ignorant that he was doing so. Oedipus and Jocasta lived together for many years, and had two daughters, Antigone and **Ismene,** and two sons, Eteocles and Polynices. Retribution for their incest finally came, however, in the form of a famine and pestilence that wasted the land. To know the cause of this misfortune, they sent to the oracle and received the answer that it would continue until the man who had killed King Laius should be found. Oedipus therefore sent for **Tiresias,** the blind prophet (see TIRESIAS), and asked him who had killed Laius. Tiresias was at first reluctant to discuss the matter, but on being urged, he revealed that Oedipus himself had committed the crime and that in killing Laius, he had killed his own father.

Both Oedipus and Jocasta were horrified to learn what they had unintentionally done in marrying. Jocasta at once committed suicide, and Oedipus blinded himself. The throne of Thebes was given over to Jocasta's brother **Creon** as regent until Eteocles and Polynices should be old enough to rule. Oedipus desired to leave the kingdom but Creon, acting on instructions from the oracle, refused to let him go. Later Creon changed his mind and exiled Oedipus, who set forth for the second time in his life as a wanderer, this time accompanied by his faithful daughter, **Antigone.** The curse of the House of Cadmus had not, however, reached its end. This first phase of Oedipus' unfortunate life is the subject of Sophocles' great tragedy, *Oedipus Tyrannus,* often called *Oedipus Rex.*

The struggles of **Eteocles** and **Polynices** for the throne of

Thebes set off the last phase of the curse, and this phase, known as the story of the Seven against Thebes, provided the subject matter for a tragedy by Aeschylus that bears that title. The two brothers at first could not agree as to which should be king, until at last they reached the compromise that they would both reign, though in alternate years. Eteocles took the throne first because he was the elder; but at the end of his year of the kingship he refused to turn it over to Polynices and instead expelled him from Thebes.

Polynices betook himself to the court of King **Adrastus** of Sicyon, where he found not only sympathy for his grievance but a fellow exile, **Tydeus,** who hoped for the throne of Argos. The two exiles married the daughters of Adrastus and thus formed an alliance. Plans were formed to attack first Thebes, to reinstate Polynices, and then Argos, to instate Tydeus; and Adrastus raised a large and powerful army for the purpose. Four other heroes joined the expedition to make up the Seven. The four consisted of **Capaneus** of Argos, **Hippomedon** of Argos, **Parthenopaeus** of Arcadia, and **Amphiaraus,** the brother-in-law of Adrastus. Amphiaraus, who was a soothsayer, foresaw that disaster would befall the enterprise and that only Adrastus would survive it, since Polynices, though wronged, had no moral right to invade his native city with an army of foreigners. Consequently, Amphiaraus demurred at joining the campaign; but Adrastus urged him to do so with such vigor that at last the two agreed to leave the decision to Amphiaraus' wife and Adrastus' sister, **Eriphyle.** Polynices bribed Eriphyle by giving her the baleful but beautiful necklace of Harmonia, and she therefore decided in favor of Amphiaraus' participation in the war, though he had told her that he could not return from it alive. As he departed, Amphiaraus cursed his wife and called on his son Alcmaeon to avenge his death.

When the forces of the Seven were gathered for the attack, an oracle was consulted to learn who would be the victor. The oracle stated that whichever side had Oedipus in its camp would win. Polynices thereupon traveled into Attica where the old man and his faithful daughter Antigone had taken refuge, and there he besought Oedipus for his blessing on the attack. Oedipus cursed it instead. Eteocles, hearing of the oracular prophecy, sent Creon to bring back Oedipus by force if necessary, but Oedipus was protected by Theseus of Athens, who drove out Creon and his followers. Oedipus cursed both his faithless sons, declaring that they should each die by the other's hand, and soon thereafter he died himself in the grove sacred to the Eumenides at Colonus, not far from Athens, leaving Antigone to return with her grief to Thebes. The story of this attempt to involve Oedipus in the war and of his refusal and death is the subject of Sophocles' tragedy, *Oedipus at Colonus*. It is interesting to note, also, that T. S. Eliot borrows from Sophocles' tragedy the account of Oedipus' death in the grove and transfers it to Agamemnon in the climax of his famous poem, *Sweeney among the Nightingales:*

> The nightingales are singing near
> The Convent of the Sacred Heart,
>
> And sang within the bloody wood
> When Agamemnon cried aloud,
> And let their liquid siftings fall
> To stain the stiff dishonoured shroud.[2]

Agamemnon was murdered in his bath (see ATREUS), but Eliot borrows for him the death scene of Oedipus, in order to make a

[2] From "Sweeney among the Nightingales," by T. S. Eliot, in his *Collected Poems, 1909–1935.* Copyright, 1934, 1936, by Harcourt, Brace and Company. Reprinted with their permission.

closer connection between the symbolic nightingales and the murdered hero.*

The expedition against Thebes was attended by misfortune from the first. When the heroes reached Nemea, they found that Dionysus, the protective deity of Thebes, had brought a drought on the land; so there was no water to drink. In the midst of this misfortune they met **Hypsipyle,** once queen of Lemnos, who was tending to **Opheltes,** the child of King Lycurgus of Nemea, whose slave she was. Under their persuasion, she led them to a well, but she foolishly left Opheltes on the ground. When they returned to him, they found a snake had killed him in its coils. Tydeus and Capaneus wanted to kill the snake, but Amphiaraus warned them that it had probably been sent as an omen by Zeus; perhaps heedful of Cadmus' experience, they withheld their hands. Amphiaraus renamed the child Archemorus, which means "beginner of death," because his death was the first of many on the ill-fated expedition; and the army then put on a tremendous funeral celebration to soothe his angry parents. The athletic contests at this funeral are reported to be the origin of the **Nemean Games.** (For the earlier life of the child's nurse Hypsipyle see ARGONAUTS.)

When the army arrived at Thebes, an attempt was made to settle the dispute without bloodshed. Tydeus was sent to demand that Eteocles surrender the throne; but Eteocles set an ambush for him, and Tydeus barely escaped with his life, having killed forty-nine of the fifty men sent against him. The siege of the city now began, and its progress was a series of calamities for both sides. Thebes' seven gates were defended by seven heroes within: Eteocles, **Melanippus, Polyphontes, Megareus, Hyper-**

* T.S.E.: "I . . . arbitrarily revised the circumstances of Agamemnon's death because it suited my convenience to do so. I'm surprised that no one has pounced on this. They have pounced on everything else." Conversation with P.R. on May 20, 1947.

bius, **Lasthenes,** and **Menoeceus;** and attacked by the Seven from without. Early in the contest Eteocles consulted the soothsayer Tiresias and was told that Thebes would be successfully defended if a descendant of the Spartae would give himself as a voluntary sacrifice. Accordingly, Menoeceus, a son of Creon, allowed himself to be killed early in the attack.

In one engagement Amphiaraus, after fighting bravely, was forced to flee along a river when Zeus hurled a thunderbolt that opened the ground before his chariot, and he was swallowed up, to be seen no more. Capaneus, in an excess of zeal, declared that he would burst into the city in spite of Zeus himself. While he was scaling the wall on a ladder, Zeus killed him with a thunderbolt for his impiety. His wife, **Evadne,** cast herself on his funeral pyre and died in its flames. The intransigence of Capaneus is attributed by Ezra Pound to his character Mauberley, in *Hugh Selwyn Mauberley,* I. Fighting with his usual reckless courage, Tydeus was fatally wounded. Athene intended to grant him immortality, but when she found him on the battlefield he had yielded to wild anger and was chewing on the head of one of his fallen enemies. The goddess left him to die.

The siege lasted so long and was so indecisive that finally Eteocles and Polynices decided to settle the issue by personal combat. Thus they fulfilled the curse of their father, for each killed the other. Then the two armies joined in combat again, and the invaders were at last forced to flee without even burying their dead. The Seven against Thebes were defeated. Only Adrastus survived, and he only because of the swiftness of his winged horse **Arion,** the son of Poseidon and Demeter.

But the curse on the house of Cadmus had not yet reached its end. Creon now became king of Thebes, and he ordered that the body of Eteocles the patriot be buried with all fitting obsequies but that the body of Polynices the traitor lie unburied.

He promised death to anyone who disobeyed his order, but even this threat could not frighten Antigone, who determined in sisterly piety to bury her brother's body. When Ismene proved too timid to help her, she set out alone and buried Polynices. Caught in the act and condemned by Creon to be buried alive, she declared that she had acted in compliance with laws made by Zeus himself. Creon, however, was adamant, and his sentence was carried out. Creon's son, **Haemon,** Antigone's lover, killed himself in grief for her; and **Eurydice,** wife of Creon, killed herself in grief for Haemon. Thus Creon was pun ʰed for his sternness. The story of Antigone's devotion is embodied in a tragedy by Sophocles that bears her name.

The curse had only one more act to play. In that last act the city of Thebes was destroyed by the sons of the Seven, called the **Epigoni,** which means "offspring." These sons consisted of **Aegialeus,** the son of Adrastus; **Diomedes,** the son of Tydeus; **Promachos,** the son of Parthenopaeus; **Sthenelus,** the son of Capaneus; **Thersander,** the son of Polynices; **Polydorus,** the son of Hippomedon; and **Alcmaeon,** the son of Amphiaraus. Although Alcmaeon's mother Eriphyle had sent Amphiaraus to his death, as he had foretold, the son had not yet carried out his father's command and killed his mother. When the oracle at Delphi ordered him to undertake another expedition against Thebes, this order was reinforced by his mother's persuasion, for she had been bribed again, this time by Thersander, who gave her the *peplos* of Harmonia as his father had given her Harmonia's necklace.

The second expedition against Thebes had the sanction of the gods, and it succeeded completely. Only one of the Epigoni, Aegialeus, was killed. The city was leveled and remained an empty plain for years. Its inhabitants, on the advice of Tiresias, fled to other lands, and Tiresias died in the flight. Alcmaeon returned to Argos and killed his mother, as his father had commanded, though in doing so he incurred the same fate as Orestes (see ATREUS). The Furies drove him mad and pursued him until he fled to Psophis in Arcadia, where he was cleansed of his guilt by King **Phegeus.** He married Phegeus' daughter, **Arsinoe,** and gave her as wedding gifts the fateful *peplos* and necklace of Harmonia, which he had taken from his mother.

King Phegeus' lands, however, now became sterile because of Alcmaeon's presence. The oracle at Delphi, always ready with an answer, told Alcmaeon to travel to a land that had not existed when he committed his crime. Alcmaeon solved this problem by settling on land that was formed by silt in the mouth of the river Achelous. Here he married **Callirhoe,** the daughter of the river god, and she required of him the *peplos* and necklace. Alcmaeon accordingly returned to Psophis and persuaded Phegeus to return the two gifts to him on the pretext that they would restore him to his right mind. When Phegeus learned later that Alcmaeon had deceived him and had given the gifts to Callirhoe, he sent his sons to slay Alcmaeon.

Alcmaeon's death brought to an end the long chain of events that began with the abduction of Europa by Zeus and that destroyed cities and men. As for the *peplos* and necklace, they were at last placed in the temple at Delphi where they could no longer bring mortals under their terrible influence.

THEMIS (thē′mĭs) is the goddess of divine justice and the second wife of ZEUS.

THERSANDER (thĕr·săn′dĕr) was one of the Epigoni. See THEBES.

THERSITES (thĕr·sī′tēz) was a crippled and foul-mouthed Greek who fought in the TROJAN WAR.

THESEUM (thē·sē′ûm) was a temple in Athens that contained the bones of THESEUS.

THESEUS (thē′sōos) was the great hero of the Athenians and one of their early kings. The story of his life is a blend of the historical and the mythical in which the governmental activities of a primitive city ruler merge with the prodigious exploits of a superman. He was born in faraway **Troezen,** the son of **Aethra,** a princess of that place, and of **Aegeus,** who was king of Athens. Before Theseus' birth, his father left Troezen to return to Athens, but at his parting he hid his sword and sandals under a huge stone and directed Aethra to send her son to Athens with them when he became strong enough to lift the stone.

The lifting of this stone was not the first of Theseus' feats of strength. He had been taught to hunt by Chiron, the Centaur who trained other famous heroes such as Asclepius and Achilles, and his proficiency in athletics was such that he was later credited with inventing certain forms of sport. He dared to face even Heracles himself when Heracles appeared in Troezen and was mistaken for a lion because of his lion-skin garb. Thus the day on which Theseus lifted the stone and recovered his father's sword and sandals was the climax of a vigorous youth and the beginning of a heroic manhood.

In traveling to Athens to meet his father, Theseus declined to take the easy way by sea and chose instead to make his hard way through all the perils of the land route. On his way he performed six famous exploits and rid the world of six violent destroyers of men. The first of these was a brigand, **Periphetes** of Epidaurus, whose custom it was to kill with his iron club all travelers who came his way. Theseus killed him. The next was **Sinis,** a man who induced travelers to help him bend down a great pine tree and then unexpectedly released it so that the helpful travelers were catapulted into the air and killed. Theseus, however, released his grasp first, and Sinis was thrown to his own death. In Crommyon, Theseus killed a wild sow named **Phaea** that made dangerous the countryside there. As he walked along a high cliff by the sea, he met a robber named **Sciron** who was fond of forcing travelers to wash his feet near the edge of the cliff. While he was receiving this unwilling service, he customarily pushed the unfortunate foot washers over the cliff into the sea, where a great tortoise ate them. Sciron, however, met his match in Theseus and consequently became food for the tortoise by his own device. At Eleusis, Theseus wrestled with King **Cercyon,** who made a practice of killing all whom he overcame at the sport. When Theseus won, he naturally killed Cercyon.

The last of Theseus' exploits on the road to Athens was his most famous. The giant **Procrustes** had an iron bed on which he made all passers-by lie down. If they were longer than the bed, he accommodatingly lopped them off to size; or if they were too short, he stretched them to fit. With his usual sense of appropriateness, Theseus eliminated the giant on his own bed, and passed on to Athens. Procrustes' bed has been commonly used as a symbol of tyranny and of enforced order. Ben Jonson, for example, in his *Conversations with Drummond of Hawthornden,* "cursed Petrarch for redacting verses to Sonnets, which he said were like that Tirrants bed, where some who were too short were racked, others too long cut short."

Since the trip to Athens had caused the hero to shed the blood of five men and one wild sow, on reaching the city he first felt the need of purifying himself. Later, as he was proceeding to his father's house, his long hair and the strangeness of his garb provoked several workmen to laugh at him for being effeminate, but Theseus put an end to their merriment by throwing their loaded wagon into the air.

When Theseus reached his father's house, he was at first recognized only by **Medea**, the sorceress, who was living with his father. This contriving Asiatic woman, wishing to be rid of the hero for fear that he might diminish her influence with the king, persuaded Aegeus that Theseus would be the cause of trouble in the kingdom and that he should be poisoned. As Theseus accepted the poisoned cup, however, Aegeus recognized his sword and knew that Theseus was his son. Medea, for her plotting, had to flee from Athens.

Theseus was now proclaimed to be the son and heir of Aegeus. He soon had to fight against his uncle **Pallas** who, with his fifty sons, the **Pallantides,** attacked Athens in the hope of obtaining the throne for himself, but Theseus defeated him. He also overcame a great bull that was ravaging the country near Marathon, and sacrificed it to Athene. At this time the people of Athens were required to send each year seven maids and seven youths to Crete to be eaten by the **Minotaur,** a monster with the body of a man and the head of a bull (for details of his strange origin, see DAEDALUS). This penalty had been exacted of the Athenians by King **Minos** to avenge his son, who had been killed in a war between the Athenians and the Cretans in which the latter were victorious. Theseus volunteered and, with the consent of his father, went off to Crete as a member of this group.

The island of Crete was guarded by a great living bronze giant named **Talus,** who either was the last survivor of the Age of Bronze or had been made for King Minos by Hephaestus, the god of craftsmen. Talus patrolled the shores of the island three times a day, and when he found intruders he burned them to death by heating himself red-hot and throwing his arms around them or by tossing them into a fire. In the fifth book of *The Faerie Queene* an iron man named Talus serves Artegall, the knight of justice. Talus allowed the Athenian ship to reach Crete safely, and at the capital city of **Cnossus** Theseus and his companions presented themselves to King Minos as the annual tribute. At this point Theseus offered himself as the first victim, and his action endeared him to Minos' daughter, **Ariadne,** who was present. When Theseus was taken off to confinement until he should be given to the Minotaur, Ariadne found her way to him and offered him her aid in overcoming the monster and in escaping from the island.

The Minotaur was kept in a maze that had been built by Daedalus (see DAEDALUS), and the intricacies of this maze were such that no one could find his way out of it alone. But Ariadne gave Theseus a ball of thread that he unrolled as he went, and when he had slain the Minotaur, he found his way out again by following the thread back to the gate. Taking Ariadne along, Theseus and the other Athenians then set sail on their return trip to Athens. On the way, Theseus abandoned Ariadne on the island of Naxos, some say because he was ordered to do so by the goddess Athene. Whatever the circumstances, the harshness of Ariadne's fate was lessened when the god Dionysus fell in love with her and married her. Theseus had left Athens with black sails on his ship and with the agreement that the ship would return with white sails if he had been successful in killing the Minotaur; but he forgot to make the change of sails, and Aegeus, who had watched every day for the ship, sighting the black sails from afar, threw himself over a cliff into the sea and was killed. Theseus thus became king of Athens on his arrival there.

Theseus brought about a great flourishing of the city. There appears to be historical basis for some of the achievements with which he was credited. He was thought to have united the cities of Attica into a single state, and to have introduced the coinage of money, and in other ways to have organized the city into its greatness. Yet he could not be content, hero that he was and accustomed to a strenuous life, with a peaceful overlordship.

Consequently, he joined in the expedition of the Argonauts with Jason, and he participated in the Calydonian Boar Hunt. Moreover, he joined Heracles in his expedition against the Amazons, the renowned female warriors, and carried off their queen **Hippolyta,** or as is more often said, her sister **Antiope.** In order to rescue Antiope, the Amazons made war against Athens and almost entered the city. But Antiope had fallen in love with Theseus, and while fighting by his side she was killed, though not before she had borne him a son called **Hippolytus.** This boy grew up to be a hunter, a favorite of Artemis and a scorner of Aphrodite, who marked him for destruction.

After the death of Antiope, Theseus indefatigably married **Phaedra,** another daughter of King Minos of Crete. Unfortunately, this lady fell in love with Theseus' son, Hippolytus. When the young man rejected her love, she told Theseus that Hippolytus had made love to her, and Theseus prayed to Poseidon for revenge. Poseidon caused a sea monster to frighten the horses drawing Hippolytus' chariot, and Hippolytus was killed in the ensuing wreck. His innocence, however, became known to Theseus, and Phaedra, who had given him two sons, Acamas and Demophoon, killed herself. According to some stories, Artemis persuaded the great physician Asclepius to restore Hippolytus to life, and Zeus killed Asclepius for this act of impiety.

About this time, **Pirithous,** king of the **Lapiths,** decided to test Theseus' character. He stole some of Theseus' cattle, and as Theseus was about to engage him in a fight, Pirithous was struck with admiration for the hero. The same feeling for Pirithous touched Theseus, and the two united in a firm contract of friendliness. Theseus attended the marriage of Pirithous and **Hippodamia.** At this wedding the Centaurs also attended; all became drunk, and one attempted to violate the bride. With Theseus' help, Pirithous and his other friends routed the Centaurs.

When Hippodamia died, Pirithous and Theseus decided to find themselves other wives who should be daughters of Zeus himself. First, for Theseus, they kidnaped Helen of Lacedaemon, later to become famous as Helen of Troy, and made off with her. Then they went down to Hades to attempt the kidnaping of Persephone for Pirithous, but Hades himself caught them and imprisoned them, some accounts say by fastening Pirithous to the fiery wheel with his father Ixion. (Pirithous was the son of either the daring and impious Ixion or Zeus.) Theseus was later rescued by Heracles, and he returned to Athens. He found that during his absence Menestheus had become king with so much continuing popular support that supplanting him appeared impossible. Helen, too, had been rescued by her brothers Castor and Polydeuces. Thus without his kingdom or his prospective wife, Theseus retired to Scyros, where he had lands. He was well received by **Lycomedes,** the king of the island, but later he fell in a mysterious manner over a cliff into the sea and was killed. There were some who thought that Lycomedes was responsible; in any event, the career of the Athenian hero came to a close as dramatically as it had begun. Theseus' bones were later removed to Athens, where they were placed in a temple called the **Theseum** and made the subject of religious ceremonies.

For the Athenians, Theseus represented all that they could admire in a man—vigor, strength, bravery, intelligence, and a keen desire for the active and adventurous life. So closely did they identify their native spirit with him that centuries after his death, at the battle of Marathon when the fate of the city lay in the balance, they thought they saw the figure of Theseus fighting with them against the Persians.

Of Theseus, Nicholas Grimald writes epigrammatically but inaccurately in *Of Friendship*,

Down Theseus went to hell, Pirith, his frend, to finde:
O that the wives in these our dayes, were to their mates so kind.

The marriage of Theseus to Hippolyta, the queen of the Amazons, is the chief event of Shakespeare's *Midsummer-Night's Dream,* though in this play Theseus is much more of a Renaissance nobleman than an early Athenian; and in *Two Gentlemen of Verona* (4. 4. 172–173) Julia, disguised in boy's clothes, professes to have acted a "lamentable part":

Madam, 'twas Ariadne, passioning
For Theseus' perjury and unjust flight.

This is one of Shakespeare's many ironies that depend on the Elizabethan custom of having young boys play women's parts. Here, on the Elizabethan stage, a boy playing the part of a girl who has disguised herself as a boy speaks of having taken the part of a girl in a play. The theme of Ariadne's desertion is perhaps the favorite poetic reference to Theseus, and echoes of it are to be found in Christina Rossetti's *Ariadne to Theseus,* as well as in later poems. In *Sweeney Erect* T. S. Eliot remembers the desertion:

Display me Aeolus above
Reviewing the insurgent gales
Which tangle Ariadne's hair
And swell with haste the perjured sails,[3]

lines that provide an ironic contrast to the animal quality of the love affair that he is about to describe. In *Casino* Auden compares modern life to the maze from which Theseus escaped by means of Ariadne's device:

[3] From "Sweeney Erect," by T. S. Eliot, in his *Collected Poems, 1909–1935.* Copyright, 1934, 1936, by Harcourt, Brace and Company. Reprinted with their permission.

> The labyrinth is safe but endless, and broken
> Is Ariadne's thread.[4]

Phaedra's involvement with Hippolytus has been the subject of tragedies by the Greek Euripides and the Roman Seneca.

THESSALY (thĕs′à·lē) was in the northeast section of ancient Greece. Its mountains included Olympus, Pelion, and Ossa. Through it flowed the river Peneus, creating the famous vale of Tempe, and its chief plain was a grain-producing area. In ancient myths Thessaly figures as the home of the Centaurs and the Lapiths, among others, and it was famous for its magicians.

THETIS (thē′tĭs), a Nereid, was the wife of Peleus and the mother of Achilles. See PELEUS, TROJAN WAR.

THISBE (thĭz′bē) was the lover of PYRAMUS.

THRACE (thrās), the birthplace of Orpheus, was the region north of Greece. The Hebrus was its principal river and Rhodope its principal mountain range. The Thracians aided the Trojans in their war against the Greeks.

THRINACIA (thrĭ·nā′shà) was the island of the cattle of the sun. See ODYSSEUS.

THYESTES (thī·ĕs′tēz) was the brother of ATREUS.

THYRSUS (thĭr′sûs), a staff tipped with a pine cone, is a symbol of DIONYSUS.

TIBER (tī′bĕr) is the river of ROME.

TIRESIAS (tī·rē′sĭ·às), the famous Theban prophet, was descended on his father's side from one of the Spartae, the five sons of the dragon's teeth who helped Cadmus found Thebes; his mother was the Nymph **Chariclo.** One day on Mount Cithaeron he saw two snakes mating and killed the female. At once he became a woman. Sometime later he saw another pair of snakes mating; this time he killed the male and was turned into a man again.

[4] From "Casino," by W. H. Auden, in *The Collected Poetry of W. H. Auden.* Copyright, 1945, by W. H. Auden. Reprinted with the permission of Random House, Inc.

This unique experience made Tiresias the only person who could settle an argument that had arisen between Zeus and Hera. Zeus said that women get more pleasure from sex than men do, and Hera maintained that the opposite is true. When they called on Tiresias for his expert opinion, he declared that a woman has nine times as much pleasure as a man. The queen of the gods became so angry that she blinded Tiresias, but Zeus made it easier for him to endure this infirmity by giving him the power of prophecy and promising him an extremely long life. According to Hesiod, he lived for seven generations.

Another myth accounts for Tiresias' blindness and prophetic powers by relating that he once surprised Athene bathing, as Actaeon had surprised Artemis, and that the goddess blinded him but granted him the gift of foreknowledge. The blind seer, such as Tiresias, and the blind poet, such as Homer, are familiar figures in primitive societies. Unable to work or fight beside his fellows, the blind man spends most of his time with his own thoughts; his leisure and his introspection produce visions and works of the imagination.

In the course of his long life Tiresias foresaw much evil and some good. He prophesied the future greatness of Heracles in the childhood of that great hero. When King Pentheus of Thebes forbade the newly introduced worship of Dionysus, Tiresias told him that Dionysus was a true god; but Pentheus refused to listen and thus brought about his own death. Reluctantly Tiresias revealed that King Oedipus of Thebes had killed his father and married his mother. When the Seven attacked Thebes, Tiresias foresaw that the city might be saved by the sacrifice of a descendant of the Spartae. Menoeceus, a son of Creon, allowed himself to be killed, and the siege of the Seven failed. Later Thebes was again attacked, this time by the Epigoni, the sons of the Seven. Knowing that the city was fated to fall, Tiresias urged the Thebans to put the besiegers off guard by pretending to negotiate for peace and then to flee from the city secretly at night.

His advice was taken and many Thebans escaped, but Tiresias died on the journey. In Hades he still retained his prophetic power, and the enchantress Circe sent Odysseus to Hades to consult Tiresias about the dangers that would face him on his journey from Aeaea to Ithaca. (For a detailed account of the events mentioned in this paragraph see the articles on Heracles, Thebes, and Odysseus.)

In *The Strayed Reveller* by Matthew Arnold, the youth who has drunk of Circe's enchanted cup sees a vision of Tiresias

> Sitting, staff in hand,
> On the warm, grassy
> Asopus' bank,
> His robe drawn over
> His old, sightless head,
> Revolving inly
> The doom of Thebes.

Tiresias in Tennyson's dramatic monologue of that name is engaged in prophesying that Thebes will be saved from the Seven, who are at the city gates, if a descendant of the Spartae will give his life—a prophecy that is to be followed by Menoeceus' sacrifice of himself. Tennyson accepts the myth that Tiresias was blinded and given the gift of foreknowledge by the goddess Athene, whom he saw naked, and the prophet describes this experience in the course of the monologue.

Swinburne alludes to the same myth in his poem *Tiresias,* in which he imagines the old man at the grave of Antigone, filled with sad thoughts about the house of Cadmus but firmly convinced that joy, love, truth, and freedom will finally prevail. In the second part of the piece the poet, looking at the prophet, observes that the face is "not of Tiresias"; instead it is the face of Dante and some other Italians. In this poem Tiresias' habit of becoming other people is confusing, and his fervent hopes for the future make him seem remote from the old Greek soothsayer.

In T. S. Eliot's *The Waste Land* Tiresias, although only a spectator of one scene, is, according to a note of Eliot's, "the most important personage in the poem, uniting all the rest." His importance seems to come from his gift of foresight and from his experience of both femaleness and maleness (218–219):

> . . . Tiresias, though blind, throbbing between two lives,
> Old man with wrinkled female breasts,[5]

in witnessing the weary and casual surrender of the typist to "the young man carbuncular," understands the joyless lust and foresees the spiritual death of a whole generation.

TISIPHONE (tĭ·sĭf′ŏ·nē) is one of the three FURIES.

TITANS (tī′tănz), or **TITANES** (tī·tăn′ēz), or **TITANI** (tī·tăn′ī). The Titans were the children of Uranus, the sky, and Gaea, the earth. Although their number varies in different accounts, the theory gradually developed that there were twelve of them, as there are twelve of the Olympian gods. The Titans were gigantic figures that personified the many forces of nature, some of them constructive, but most of them destructive. The significance of some of their names has survived:

Cronus	the harvester
Rhea	the earth
Oceanus	the river of Ocean
Tethys	the nourisher or nurse
Hyperion	the wanderer on high, the sun
Thea	the divine one
Phoebe	the bright one
Themis	justice or law
Mnemosyne	memory
Iapetus	the hurler or wounder

[5] From "The Waste Land," by T. S. Eliot, in his *Collected Poems, 1909–1935.* Copyright, 1934, 1936, by Harcourt, Brace and Company. Reprinted with their permission.

Others were **Coeus; Creus; Ophion,** a great serpent; and **Eurynome,** a great ruler. Fourteen are here accounted for. Classical lists vary from the two, Cronus and Iapetus, mentioned by Homer, to the thirteen named by Hesiod.

Uranus and Gaea, the parents of the Titans, had other children also. The three Cyclopes were reputed to be theirs, though in the *Odyssey* Homer names Poseidon as the father of the best-known Cyclops, Polyphemus. The **Hecatoncheires,** hundred-handed monsters named **Acgaeon** (or **Briareus**), **Cottus,** and **Gyges,** were certainly children of Uranus and Gaea. The Cyclopes seem to represent the violence of the thunderstorm and the volcano, and the Hecatoncheires to embody the terrors of the stormy sea. No wonder that Uranus became nervous about the hundred-handed monsters and thrust them down into Tartarus, the great depth in Hades that always served as a catchall for those unwanted by the ruling gods. This act, however, alienated the affections of Gaea, who urged her other children, the Titans, to revolt.

Cronus led the revolution, destroyed his father, and became master of the world, though a tradition to which Milton refers in *Paradise Lost* (10. 582–583) says that Ophion and Eurynome

> . . . had first the rule
> Of high *Olympus*

and had also to be displaced. See CRONUS for an account of his revolt and long rule. The Titans under Cronus were finally attacked and defeated by Cronus' children, the Olympians, led by Zeus. See ZEUS for the story of that heavenly warfare.

Zeus cast most of the Titans except Oceanus, Tethys, Themis, Mnemosyne, Prometheus, and Epimetheus into Tartarus. In the battle between the Olympians and the Titans, Oceanus and his wife Tethys took no part, and under Zeus they continued to rule the great river of Ocean (see SEA GODS). Themis, too, must not have fought against Zeus, for he chose her for his second wife; and Mnemosyne also had his favor, for she became by him the mother of the Muses. Prometheus and Epimetheus, the sons of Iapetus, actively sided with Zeus and thus were saved from Tartarus; but Prometheus because of his kindness to man later endured a fate equally terrible. For his life and his brother's, see PROMETHEUS.

Of all the Titans, Hyperion, the sun god, has been perhaps the best known to English poets. For him, see APOLLO; for Rhea, see EARTH GODDESSES; for Mnemosyne, see MUSES; for Phoebe and Thea, see ARTEMIS; for Themis, see ZEUS.

TITHONUS (tǐ·thō′nŭs) was the most famous lover of EOS.

TITUS TATIUS (tī′tŭs tā′shǐ·ŭs) led the Sabines against ROME.

TITYUS (tǐt′ǐ·ŭs), a Giant, insulted Leto, and was killed by her children, Artemis and APOLLO.

TMOLUS (tě·mō′lŭs) judged the music contest between Pan and APOLLO.

TRIPTOLEMUS (trǐp·tǒl′ě·mŭs), a priest of Demeter, traveled about the world teaching men the art of planting. See EARTH GODDESSES.

TRITOGENEIA (trǐt′ō·jě·nī′à) is another name of ATHENE.

TRITON (trī′tŏn) is the trumpeter and the messenger of Poseidon. See SEA GODS.

TRITONIA (trī·tō′nǐ·à) is a surname of ATHENE.

TROEZEN (trē′zěn), a city of Peloponnesus about forty miles southwest of Athens by sea, was the birthplace of THESEUS.

TROILUS (troi′lŭs), a prince of Troy, was one of the minor heroes in the TROJAN WAR.

TROJAN WAR. A thousand years or so before the birth of Christ the Greeks made war on the Trojans, a people who inhabited a section of Asia Minor near the Hellespont. The war was probably the result of trade rivalry; the Greek strategy apparently

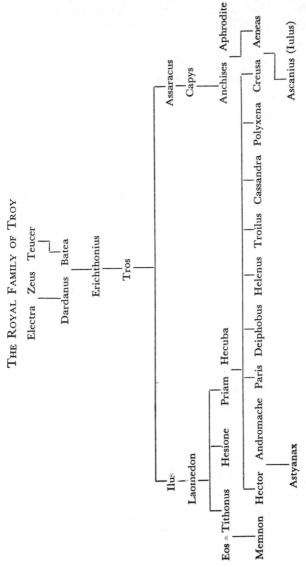

The Royal Family of Troy

379

consisted of blockading the Trojan fortress city, and the economic and military exhaustion of the Trojans seems finally to have given the victory to the Greeks. As soon as the war was over, the Greeks began to turn history into legend, and of all their stories none is richer than that of the Trojan War. Its events

THE FAMILY OF PELEUS, ACHILLES, AND AIAS

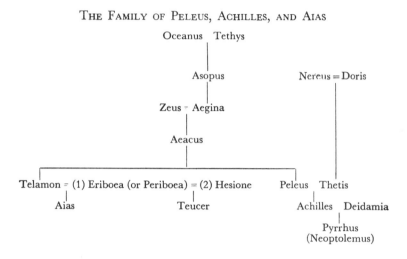

and its consequences provided the material for the three classical epics, Homer's *Iliad* and *Odyssey* and Virgil's *Aeneid;* for plays by the three great tragedians, Aeschylus, Sophocles, and Euripides; and for scores of tales and commentaries in Greek and Latin.

The cause of the war, according to the poets, was not trade rivalry between Greeks and Trojans but personal rivalry between three powerful goddesses. When **Peleus,** a mortal hero, married the Nereid **Thetis,** all the gods and goddesses were invited to the wedding except Eris, the goddess of discord. Angered by this social slight, Eris threw into the midst of the happy party a

golden apple inscribed "For the fairest." Naturally, all the goddesses claimed the apple, but finally the rivalry narrowed to
Hera, Athene, and Aphrodite. These three demanded that Zeus
choose the most beautiful, but the king of the gods knew better
than to judge a beauty contest in which the candidates were his
wife and two of his daughters. He referred them to **Paris,** a
Trojan prince who, because his mother dreamed that she had
been delivered of a firebrand when he was born, had been left
to die on Mount Ida; but he had been suckled by a she-bear,
brought up by shepherds, and now kept sheep on Mount **Ida** and
enjoyed the favors of a lovely Nymph named Oenone.

The goddesses appeared before Paris dressed in their most
gorgeous attire, and each one offered him a bribe in accordance
with her nature. Hera promised him royal dominion, Athene
prowess in war, and Aphrodite the most beautiful woman in the
world for his wife. Although this point is never made by the
storytellers, Paris may simply have chosen the most beautiful
goddess in spite of the delights and dangers attendant on his
choice. Whatever his motives were, he awarded the golden
apple to Aphrodite, the goddess of beauty. Spenser says (*Faerie
Queene,* 2. 7. 55):

> . . . partiall *Paris* dempt it *Venus* dew,
> And had of her, faire *Helen* for his meed,
> That many noble *Greekes* and *Troians* made to bleed.

The most beautiful woman in the world was **Helen,** the wife
of King **Menelaus** of Sparta, and Helen's story is full of the
tragic irony of divine ordination of human destiny. Helen's
mother **Leda,** the wife of the Spartan king **Tyndareus,** found
favor in the eyes of Zeus, and he visited her one day in the
guise of a swan. Leda produced two eggs: from the first were
hatched her immortal daughter and son by Zeus, Helen and

Polydeuces, or Pollux; and from the second her mortal daughter and son by Tyndareus, **Clytemnestra** and Castor. (For the exploits of the two boys see CASTOR.) In English poetry the mating of Leda and Zeus is described in every key from Spenser's luxurious stanza in *The Faerie Queene* (3. 11. 32):

> Then was he turnd into a snowy Swan,
> To win faire *Leda* to his louely trade:
> O wondrous skill, and sweet wit of the man,
> That her in daffadillies sleeping made,
> From scorching heat her daintie limbes to shade:
> Whiles the proud Bird ruffing his fethers wyde,
> And brushing his faire brest, did her inuade;
> She slept, yet twixt her eyelids closely spyde,
> How towards her he rusht, and smiled at his pryde

to Sir John Falstaff's sly comment (*Merry Wives of Windsor*, 5. 5. 7–9): "You were also, Jupiter, a swan for the love of Leda. O omnipotent Love! how near the god drew to the complexion of a goose!" But the most effective use of the myth is made by W. B. Yeats in *Leda and the Swan*. Having described the strange coupling of the woman and the divine bird, Yeats writes:

> A shudder in the loins engenders there
> The broken wall, the burning roof and tower
> And Agamemnon dead.
>   Being so caught up,
> So mastered by the brute blood of the air,
> Did she put on his knowledge with his power
> Before the indifferent beak could let her drop?[6]

Zeus, while about his pleasure, knew the great and terrible events in which Leda's children would take part, for which they would

[6] From "Leda and the Swan," by W. B. Yeats, in his *The Tower*. Copyright, 1928, by The Macmillan Company and used with their permission.

in a sense be responsible: Helen, whose abduction by Paris would be the immediate cause of the Trojan War and the fall of Troy, and Clytemnestra, whose hatred of her husband **Agamemnon** would lead her to murder him after he returned in triumph from this war (see ATREUS). Yeats leaves us to wonder whether Leda for an instant shared the god's knowledge. Zeus not only foresaw but ordained the Trojan War; he believed that the human population of the world should be reduced.

Even as a child Helen was so lovely that she was kidnaped by Theseus and had to be rescued by her brothers Castor and Polydeuces, and as she grew up she became so beautiful that every bachelor king in Greece wished to marry her. Because the rivalry was so intense, **Odysseus** of Ithaca wisely proposed that he and all the other suitors swear to support the husband whom Helen chose and to avenge any wrong done him because of his marriage. This agreement was made, and Helen chose Menelaus, whose brother Agamemnon was already the husband of her sister Clytemnestra. Well pleased with Helen's marriage, Tyndareus resigned the crown of Sparta to Menelaus.

Helen and Menelaus lived happily together and had a daughter whom they named **Hermione.** But Helen was the most beautiful woman in the world, and after Paris awarded the golden apple to Aphrodite the goddess kept her promise and led him to Sparta. There he was entertained in friendly fashion by Menelaus and Helen until Menelaus was called away on business. Because custom and religion demanded that host and guest deal honorably with each other, Menelaus did not fear to leave Paris with Helen; but when he was gone, Aphrodite caused Helen to give her love to Paris and the two lovers set sail for **Troy.**

As soon as Menelaus discovered that his wife was gone, he called on the kings of Greece to fulfill their promise and avenge the wrong done to him because of his marriage. All the heroes responded except Odysseus and **Achilles.** Although Odysseus had proposed the oath that bound him to support Menelaus, he now had a wife and an infant son whom he was loth to leave. He therefore pretended to be mad; and when messengers arrived to urge him to join the expedition, they found him plowing the seashore and sowing it with salt. To test him the messengers laid his infant son in front of the plow. Odysseus stopped plowing, admitted his ruse, and reluctantly joined the army.

He was then given the job of finding Achilles and persuading him to fight. Achilles, the son of Peleus and Thetis, was destined to live a long undistinguished life or to win glory and die young in the siege of Troy. While he was still a baby his immortal mother tried to make him invulnerable to weapons by dipping him in the River Styx in Hades, but she held him by one heel, and the arrow that finally killed him struck him in that place. Today any man's unhideable weakness is still described as his Achilles' heel. Achilles was trained in the arts of peace and war by Chiron the Centaur, who was also the tutor of such heroes as Asclepius and Jason. Thetis was determined to save her son from any death, no matter how glorious, and when she heard of the preparations against Troy she sent Achilles to the island of **Scyros** to live disguised as a girl among the daughters of King **Lycomedes.** Achilles fell in love with **Deidamia,** one of Lycomedes' daughters, and they had a son named **Pyrrhus,** who was afterward called **Neoptolemus** ("the recruit") because he joined the Greek forces late in the war.

The army, however, needed Achilles because the prophet **Calchas** had said that without him the Greeks could not defeat the Trojans. Odysseus, learning that Achilles was on Scyros, disguised himself as a peddler and offered Lycomedes' daughters a fine collection of dresses and jewels and also a few handsome weapons. Achilles revealed himself by handling the weapons, and Odysseus had no trouble in persuading him to disregard his mother's warnings. Karl Shapiro's poem *Scyros* concerns a man newly drafted into the army, and the title alludes to Achilles' hiding place as a symbol of every man's reluctance to leave civilian life to enter a war.

Under the leadership of Agamemnon, the Greek kings and their followers mobilized at **Aulis,** a town on the eastern coast of Boeotia. The army was huge, and the preparations were elaborate. Seeing a vision of Helen, Marlowe's Faustus asks (*Dr. Faustus,* 13. 112–113),

> Is this the face that launch'd a thousand ships,
> And burnt the topless towers of Ilium?

According to tradition, a thousand vessels were used to transport the expeditionary force to Troy. At Aulis the soothsayer Calchas interpreted a portent. A snake climbed a tree to get at a bird's nest; it devoured the eight young birds and the mother bird that tried to protect them, and then was turned to stone by Zeus. The meaning of this, said Calchas, was that nine years would be fruitlessly consumed by the war but that in the tenth year the Greeks would be victorious.

At length the expedition was ready, but a strong north wind day after day prevented it from sailing. When Calchas was consulted, he declared that the goddess Artemis was angry because Agamemnon, diverting himself while the army assembled, had killed a stag sacred to her. If Agamemnon wished a safe passage to Troy, he must appease the goddess by sacrificing his eldest daughter **Iphigenia.** There was no alternative, and in deep sorrow Agamemnon made his decision. He sent a false message to his wife Clytemnestra that he wished to marry Iphigenia to Achilles before the army sailed for Troy; and when the lovely girl arrived, happily anticipating her wedding with the hero, she was ceremonially put to death. The pathos of this death has been represented many times in English poetry. Walter Savage Landor, for example, in *Iphigeneia and Agamemnon* shows the girl pleading gently for life; yet when the priest's knife was raised

> Then turn'd she where her parent stood, and cried
> "O father! grieve no more: the ships can sail."

In Tennyson's *A Dream of Fair Women,* however, she appears still full of hate for Helen, who she says was the cause of her death:

> My father held his hand upon his face;
>   I, blinded with my tears,
>
> Still strove to speak: my voice was thick with sighs
>   As in a dream. Dimly I could descry
> The stern black-bearded kings with wolfish eyes,
>   Waiting to see me die.
>
> The high masts flicker'd as they lay afloat;
>   The crowds, the temples, waver'd, and the shore;
> The bright death quiver'd at the victim's throat;
>   Touch'd, and I knew no more.

According to Euripides' version of the story, Artemis pitied the girl and, as she was about to be sacrificed, took her away and left a deer in her place. For Iphigenia's further adventures and for the effect of her sacrifice on the relations between Clytemnestra and Agamemnon see ATREUS.

Iphigenia and her mother were only the first of thousands of women who suffered because of the Trojan War. An oracle had predicted that the first Greek to land on the hostile shore should be the first to die; to land first therefore became a point of honor. The honor fell to **Protesilaus,** who had left behind him in Greece a bride of only one day, **Laodamia.** The oracle was fulfilled, and when the news reached Laodamia, she was inconsolable. In her grief the gods took pity on her, and granted her urgent prayer that Protesilaus might return to her from death for three hours. When the time was up, she joined her husband in Hades by committing suicide. Wordsworth tells this story in *Laodamia,* an overmoralized poem but nevertheless his best excursion into classic myth.

After landing and establishing themselves on the windy plains of Troy between the rivers **Simois** and **Scamander** (the second was sometimes called **Xanthus** after the god who inhabited it), the Greeks spent nine years in subduing minor cities and besieging without success the capital and fortress city of Troy, or **Ilion** (from which the title of Homer's epic, the *Iliad*). Besides Agamemnon, the commander in chief, and Menelaus, the celebrated cuckold, the leaders in war and council in the Grecian camp were Achilles, Odysseus, **Diomedes,** the two **Aiasès,** or **Ajaxes, Nestor, Machaon, Podalirius,** and Calchas. Diomedes, king of Argos, was almost the equal of Achilles and the greater Aias in warfare, and of Odysseus in wisdom. As a favorite of Athene, he was successful in battle and respected in council; he assisted Odysseus in several of the clever exploits that helped to bring about the fall of Troy.

The greater Aias, the son of King **Telamon** of Salamis, was usually called Telamonian Aias to distinguish him from his lesser namesake, the son of King **Oileus** of the Locrians. Telamonian Aias was a stupid man, but he had unshakable courage and great skill in battle. In the *Essay on Criticism* (370–371) Pope describes the sort of verse which he considers appropriate to this warrior:

> When Ajax strives some rock's vast weight to throw,
> The line too labours, and the words move slow.

Unfortunately, Aias was as proud as he was slow witted, and his pride caused his tragic death. The lesser Aias was a brave man with bad manners; he was disliked by the gods and by Homer, who told his story. Nestor, the king of Pylos, was sixty years old at the beginning of the war. He was full of good advice and rather too fond of reminiscence, though the stories he remembered were almost always interesting. Machaon and Podalirius were sons of Asclepius who inherited their father's skill in medicine and therefore were able to save many Greek heroes from death.

Odysseus was a great warrior, but he was chiefly valued for his shrewdness and piety. He became equally famous for his exploits in the war and for his adventures on his long journey home, which are related in a separate article under his name. The chief Grecian hero was Achilles, and he had all the shortcomings that accompany his sort of greatness. He was an inspiring leader and an invincible fighter, passionate and tender in his loyalties; but he was also self-centered, moody, quick to take offense, and a great nurser of grudges. While these brave Greeks competed with the Trojans and with one another, the crippled and ugly-minded **Thersites** delighted in every misfortune and tried to turn each noble action to ridicule. He is best represented for English readers in Shakespeare's *Troilus and Cressida*.

The Trojans had a magnificently fortified city and a number of capable defenders. King **Priam,** or **Priamus,** was an old man when the war began, but his wife **Hecuba** had borne him many strong sons, among whom were **Hector,** Paris, **Troilus, Deiphobus,** and **Helenus;** and three daughters, **Cassandra, Creusa,** and **Polyxena.** One of Priam's chief councilors was **Antenor,** who urged from the first that Helen be returned to Menelaus but whose advice was disregarded. **Aeneas,** a son of Anchises and the goddess Aphrodite, married Princess Creusa and distinguished himself not only in the defence of Troy but also in his later adventures, which ended in his founding the Roman race and which are told in a separate article under his name. The most important allies of the Trojans were **Sarpedon,** a son of Zeus; his companion **Glaucus; Memnon,** king of Ethiopia; and **Penthesilia,** queen of the Amazons.

Of Priam's sons, Paris won the name of **Alexander** (which means "champion") when he lived among shepherds, but he was really a cowardly man who was more concerned with Helen than he was with the war. On the battlefield he was as apt to run away as he was to fight. Troilus, Deiphobus, and Helenus all fought bravely, but Troilus was soon killed and Helenus (who had the gift of prophecy) was finally captured by the Greeks and forced to reveal the obstacles to their victory. The chief Trojan champion was Prince Hector, a brilliant and chivalrous fighter and a loving husband and father. At his moment of greatest crisis he was moved equally by his duty to maintain his honor on the battlefield and by his love for his wife **Andromache** and his infant son **Astyanax.**

The events that Homer relates in the *Iliad* occurred in tne tenth year of the indecisive siege of Troy. In one of their raids on a minor Trojan stronghold the Greeks had captured two girls, **Chryseis** and **Briseis.** The first was awarded to Agamemnon and the second to Achilles. Chryseis, however, was the daughter of **Chryses,** a priest of Apollo. When Agamemnon refused to release her, Chryses prayed to Apollo for vengeance, and the god sent a pestilence among the Greeks. When the plague was at its height, Achilles called a conference of the Greek leaders and said that they must either appease Apollo or give up the war. The prophet Calchas, after begging the protection of Achilles, declared that Chryseis must be returned to her father. Agamemnon was forced to agree, but he insisted that Briseis, who had been awarded to Achilles, must then be given to him. Although he had become fond of the girl, Achilles yielded to the order of the commander in chief; but he announced that hereafter he and his Myrmidons would take no part in the fighting. (For the meaning of the name of Achilles' followers see the account of Aeacus under ZEUS.)

Fate had decreed that the Greeks would win if they persisted, but several of the gods used their power to protect their favorites and even to influence the outcome of the war. Aphrodite of course favored the Trojans, and she enlisted the help of her lover Ares, the god of battle. Athene and Hera championed the Greeks. Poseidon aided the Greeks because he and Apollo had built the walls of Troy but had received no payment from Laomedon, Priam's father. Apollo, more forgiving in this instance, simply protected his favorites. Zeus preferred the Trojans, but he tried to remain neutral to avoid trouble with his wife.

The Nereid Thetis, however, angered by Agamemnon's treatment of her son, came to Olympus and begged Zeus to assist the Trojans so that the insult to Achilles might be avenged. Zeus allowed himself to be persuaded, and he sent a false dream to Agamemnon that promised him victory. Agamemnon addressed the troops and, in an effort to inspire them to great deeds, spoke so movingly of home and peace that the common soldiers, under the leadership of Thersites, demanded that they give up the siege. Nestor and Odysseus, however, managed to quell the revolt, and the next day the Greeks attacked in force.

Sitting above the battle on the walls of Troy, Priam and his advisors looked at Helen, who sat with them, and said in their hearts that it was right that men should fight and die for her. Suddenly the fighting was stopped by Paris, who challenged any Grecian champion to single combat. A truce was declared, Menelaus accepted the challenge, and for a time it looked as if the war might be brought to a sensible conclusion by a fight between the two men most concerned. While the armies watched, Paris threw his spear, but Menelaus turned it aside with his shield. Menelaus' spear only ripped the tunic of Paris, and the two champions drew their swords. At the first exchange Menelaus broke his sword, but in the next instant he grabbed Paris by the helmet and was dragging him toward the Greek side when Aphrodite cut the chin strap of the helmet, wrapped Paris in a cloud, and carried him off to Helen's bedroom.

Agamemnon, addressing the armies, argued that Menelaus had won and that Helen should be returned to him. The Trojans all agreed, and the war would have ended there if Athene, urged on by the implacable Hera, had not persuaded a foolish Trojan named **Pandarus** to shoot an arrow at Menelaus. It wounded him only slightly, but because of this treacherous breaking of the truce the battle was resumed.

Many Greeks fought well, but Diomedes seemed invincible. He killed Pandarus with his spear and then felled Aeneas with a great stone. Aphrodite tried to protect her son Aeneas, but Diomedes, knowing that she was a cowardly goddess, dared to wound her in the hand, and she fled, weeping, to Olympus. Aeneas' life was saved by Apollo, who carried him to Artemis and Leto to be healed. Cheated of this victory, Diomedes sought out Hector but found that the war god Ares was fighting beside the Trojan champion. Diomedes called for an orderly retreat, but Athene, seeing his plight, stood beside him and urged him to strike the war god himself. Athene guided his spear and it wounded Ares in the belly. The blustering but cowardly god screamed like a stuck pig and rushed off to Olympus to complain to Zeus, but Zeus told him to stop whining.

As Diomedes raged about the field and the Trojans retreated, Hector returned to the city to urge the women and old men to pray for victory. On the wall he met Andromache and Astyanax.

"My dear," she said, "stay here with us. Do not make our boy an orphan and me a widow." Deeply touched, Hector admitted (as he never had before) that he expected death for himself and defeat for Troy. But his greatest fear was that harm would come to Andromache and Astyanax. He took the boy in his arms and prayed to Zeus, "May men sometime say of my son that he is greater than his father." To Andromache he said, "I must do my part until my time comes." Then he returned to the battle and fought so brilliantly that the Greeks, until then victorious, were driven back almost to their ships.

That night the Greeks built a wall to protect their ships, and Agamemnon was so disheartened that he was ready to give up the war; but Nestor pointed out that Agamemnon alone was responsible for the defeat because he had insulted Achilles. Agamemnon admitted that he had been foolish, and he sent Odysseus and Telamonian Aias to take Briseis back to Achilles, to offer his apologies, and to urge Achilles to fight again. No one could have asked for a fuller confession of fault or a handsomer apology, but Achilles, still filled with black anger, refused to be reconciled with Agamemnon. He was sailing for home, he said, and he advised all the other Greeks to do likewise.

The next day the Greeks fought with desperate courage, and for a time a ruse of Hera's brought them success. Knowing that Zeus was helping the Trojans, she used every queenly art to make herself beautiful and then offered herself to Zeus. Surprised and delighted, the king of the gods enjoyed his wife and then fell into a deep sleep. While he slept Telamonian Aias beat down Hector, and although Hector was rescued by Aeneas, the Trojans had to retreat. At this point Zeus awoke, snarled at Hera for her trickery, and ordered Poseidon, who was helping the Greeks, to leave the battlefield. Apollo then revived the wounded

Hector, and the Trojans drove the Greeks before them and breached the wall that protected the ships.

Not even this disaster touched the heart of Achilles, but his retainer and friend **Patroclus** (the relation between them was so close and so intense that it may have been homosexual) asked to wear Achilles' armor and to lead the Myrmidons into the fight. A Greek ship burst into flame as he spoke, and Achilles gave his permission but cautioned Patroclus to do no more than defend the ships. The appearance of a man dressed in Achilles' armor and followed by the Myrmidons rallied the Greeks, and they soon drove the Trojans away from the ships.

Patroclus seemed Achilles himself on the battlefield. The lesser Trojans fled before him, and when he encountered Sarpedon, a son of Zeus, he gave him a mortal wound (for Sarpedon's burial see Thanatos under HADES). Then he met Hector. The Trojan hero killed him, stripped from him the armor of Achilles, put it on, and returned to the fight. Aias and Menelaus managed to save the body of Patroclus, but otherwise the victory belonged to the Trojans.

When Achilles learned of the death of Patroclus, he was overwhelmed with grief. Only his desire for revenge seemed to keep him alive. His mother Thetis came to comfort him and to make one last effort to avert his destiny. She reminded him that he was fated to die soon after Hector, but he answered, "I will accept death when I have avenged the death of Patroclus." At the request of Thetis, the god Hephaestus built a new magnificent suit of armor, and at dawn the goddess brought it to her son's tent.

Agamemnon and Achilles were formally reconciled, and Agamemnon in a gracious speech blamed their disagreement on Ate, the goddess of infatuation. As Achilles drove his chariot toward Troy, one of his immortal horses, which had been given to his father by Poseidon, spoke and warned him of his approaching death; but Achilles was undisturbed. The Trojans fought bravely but futilely; Achilles slew all who opposed him. The gods still fought with one another, although they knew how the battle would end. Finally the Trojans retreated, and the **Scaean Gates,** the chief entrance to Ilion, were thrown open to receive them.

Hector stood alone to meet the victorious Achilles. His mother and father shouted from the walls and begged him to take refuge in the city, but he refused. The general fighting was over, and the Greeks watched from the field and the Trojans from the walls as Achilles approached Hector. But the Trojan's courage failed, and he ran three times around the city with Achilles in pursuit. At last he stood, and threw his spear, but it rebounded harmlessly from the magic shield of Achilles. He realized then that his time had come to die, and he drew his sword and rushed at his enemy. Since Hector wore Achilles' old armor, Achilles knew its weakness, and he thrust his spear through Hector's throat. As a final humiliation to the Trojans, he stripped Hector's body, tied it to his chariot, and dragged it around and around the city.

Zeus was angered by Achilles' treatment of the corpse of his enemy, and he sent word to King Priam that he should go to Achilles and ask for Hector's body. Hermes guided the old man to Achilles' tent. There Priam kissed the hands of the Greek, and said, "Remember your father, who is perhaps as old and as wretched as I am, but remember that I am more pitiable than he, for I have stretched out my hands in entreaty to the killer of my son." Achilles was moved to pity and admiration, and he ordered that Hector's body be given to King Priam. For nine days the Trojans lamented the death of their hero, and on the tenth day they lighted his funeral pyre.

Homer's *Iliad* ends with the funeral of Hector, but the siege of

Troy dragged on. Achilles met and killed two of Troy's principal allies. One was Penthesilia, queen of the Amazons, a warlike race of women whose right breasts were cut off so that they would have the free movement of their fighting right arms. The Amazons were dangerous warriors, and as beautiful as they were brave; when Achilles had killed Penthesilia he wept for her beauty. The foul-mouthed Thersites chose this moment to make jokes, and Achilles killed him, but nobody was sorry. In Spenser's *Faerie Queene* (5. 5. 6–17) Artegall, knight of justice, defeats the Amazonian queen Radigund; but when he unlaces her helmet he is so struck by her beauty that he allows her to make him captive, and he remains her thrall until he is released by his warlike fiancée Britomart.

Achilles' other victim was Memnon, the king of Ethiopia, a son of Tithonus and Eos, the goddess of the dawn. That the allies of Troy came from as far east or south as Ethiopia and as far north as the kingdom of the Amazons indicates that the Trojan War was a world conflict. When Memnon fell, his mother Eos in great sorrow carried his body back to Ethiopia, and at Thebes in Egypt a miraculous monument was erected to him (see EOS).

Shortly after his victory over Memnon, Achilles himself died from an arrow wound in his vulnerable heel. Ironically, the arrow was shot by Paris, the lion in love and the dastard in war. According to one story, Achilles had fallen in love with the Trojan princess Polyxena, and he was killed when he kept a tryst with her in the temple of Apollo. After Troy fell, the ghost of Achilles demanded that Polyxena be sacrificed on his grave. Achilles was given a magnificent funeral, and then his arms were claimed by Telamonian Aias and Odysseus. Athene presided over a solemn meeting of the Greek army at which Trojan prisoners testified that Odysseus rather than Aias had done more harm to Troy. The army therefore voted that Achilles' arms should be awarded to Odysseus. This was a triumph for Odysseus but a disgrace for the brave and stupid Aias, who could not accept this blow to his pride. Filled with anger, he determined to murder Agamemnon and Menelaus; but as he approached their tents, Athene touched him with madness and he attacked a flock of sheep, believing them to be his enemies. When the madness left him and he saw the slaughtered sheep lying about the field, he was overcome with shame and committed suicide. Sophocles describes this tragic death in his play *Aias*.

Now the Greeks had lost two of their greatest heroes, and the Trojans, although their best fighters were also dead, were still protected by the walls of Ilion. At this point, the Greeks captured the Trojan prince Helenus, who had the gift of prophecy. He revealed that the Greeks could win the war if they would fulfill three conditions: first, Achilles' son Neoptolemus must join their army; second, they must have the bows and arrows of Heracles; and third, they must remove from Troy the Palladium, a statue of Athene which guaranteed security to the city that possessed it (see ATHENE).

Odysseus, the Greek strategist, made the necessary arrangements. He sailed to Scyros and persuaded Neoptolemus to join the army by offering him his father's armor. It was a more difficult job to obtain the bow and arrows of Heracles, for they belonged to Philoctetes, a great archer who had joined the expedition against Troy but who had been wounded on the way and marooned on the island of Lemnos because Odysseus and his other companions could not stand the smell of his wound and his cries of pain. For more than nine years Philoctetes, whose wound had never healed, had existed in pain on Lemnos and cursed the companions who had deserted him. Nevertheless Odysseus, with the aid of Neoptolemus or Diomedes (accounts vary as to who was his helper), succeeded in persuading Philoctetes to come to Troy. There his wound was healed by Machaon, the son of Asclepius, and Philoctetes fought skillfully for the Greeks. For a fuller account of this archer see **PHILOCTETES.**

The first victim of Philoctetes' arrows was Paris. Dying of the wound, Paris asked his men to carry him to Oenone, the Nymph of Mount Ida whom he had deserted when Aphrodite promised him Helen. Oenone, although she had made him promise to return to her when he was wounded, refused to save him because of his unfaithfulness; but when he was dead she killed herself (for further details see Oenone under NYMPHS). The third exploit, the stealing of the Palladium from Ilion, was carried out by Odysseus and Diomedes, some say with the help of Helen.

Even though Odysseus had fulfilled the three conditions necessary to a Grecian victory, Troy continued to hold out. Odysseus finally proposed that they abandon the siege and try to win the city by a trick. On his orders a **wooden horse** was built big enough to accommodate in its hollow belly Odysseus and a picked group of warriors. One morning the Trojan watchers were astonished because a huge wooden horse stood before the Scaean Gates, and the Greek camp was empty and every ship was gone. In the abandoned camp the Trojans found a Greek named **Sinon,** a pitiful wretch who swore that he had escaped the night before from his cruel countrymen, who had intended to sacrifice him to Athene in order to appease her anger because of the theft of the Palladium from Troy. He also said that the wooden horse was a Greek offering to Athene and that the Greeks hoped the Trojans would destroy it and thus bring the wrath of the goddess on Ilion. If the Trojans took the horse into the city, Sinon said, they would win the favor of Athene.

It was a plausible story, and only two Trojans disbelieved it. One was the prophetic princess Cassandra, to whom no one ever listened; the other was a priest of Poseidon named **Laocoön**. He said that he feared the Greeks even when they bore gifts, a remark that has since become proverbial; but as he spoke, two terrible snakes came out of the sea and strangled him and his two sons. Since Laocoön was a priest of Poseidon and his destroyers came from the sea, the Trojans drew the obvious inference that Laocoön was wrong. The serpents' attack on the priest and his sons is the subject of a famous sculpture now in the Vatican at Rome, and in *Childe Harold* (4. 160) Byron describes Laocoön's death:

> . . . Vain
> The struggle; vain, against the coiling strain
> And gripe, and deepening of the dragon's grasp,
> The old man's clench; the long envenom'd chain
> Rivets the living links, the enormous asp
> Enforces pang on pang, and stifles gasp on gasp.

The Trojans pulled the wooden horse inside the city, and for the first time in ten years they failed to post a guard as the entire city celebrated the end of the war. When the last revelers had gone drunk to bed, Sinon opened the trap door in the wooden horse, and Odysseus and his warriors hurried to open the gates of the city. The Greek fleet of course had gone only far enough away to hide its sails from Trojan watchers; in the dark the fleet returned, and the entire Greek army entered the city.

The rest was butchery. The well-organized Greeks set fire to various parts of the city and then proceeded to exterminate the Trojans. Some were slaughtered in their beds; some seized their weapons and fought desperately for a time; but before the night was over the city was burned to the ground, and all the Trojan heroes except one had been killed. The surviving hero was Aeneas, who fought until he saw that the cause was lost, and then tried to save his family and retainers. His wife Creusa was lost, but with the aid of his mother Aphrodite, Aeneas led out of the carnage his aged father, his son, and a few followers.

Cassandra tried to take refuge in the temple of Athene, but she was dragged from the sacred building and raped by the lesser Aias, who on his way home was finally punished for this and other crimes. His ship was wrecked, but with the aid of Poseidon he managed to swim to shore, and there he boasted that he had saved his life in spite of the gods. Poseidon smashed the big rock he stood on, and he was drowned. Priam and Hecuba sought the protection of Zeus's temple, but Neoptolemus, Achilles' son, found them there and killed the aged king. In *Hamlet* (2. 2. 472–541) the First Player and Hamlet, quoting from a play about Dido, describe Priam's death and Hecuba's tears.

When day came, the only Trojan survivors were a handful of weeping women and children. Queen Hecuba, with her sons and her husband dead and her city destroyed, was a figure of heroic sorrow. Hamlet, comparing his own real grief for his murdered father with the First Player's artistic assumption of sorrow for the Trojan queen, asks himself (2. 2. 585–586),

> What's Hecuba to him, or he to Hecuba,
> That he should weep for her?

In *Antic Hay* Aldous Huxley lets his characters dance in a smart cabaret to the latest jazz tune: "What's he to Hecuba? Nothing at all." This ironic recollection of Hamlet's words that contrasts the cheapness of the present with the tragic dignity of the past may have been suggested to Huxley by what T. S. Eliot in *The Waste Land* (128–130) calls

> . . . that Shakespeherian Rag—
> It's so elegant
> So intelligent.[7]

[7] From "The Waste Land," by T. S. Eliot, in his *Collected Poems, 1909–1935*. Copyright, 1934, 1936, by Harcourt, Brace and Company. Reprinted with their permission.

Achilles' ghost claimed the life of Hecuba's daughter Polyxena, and she was put to death on his grave. Andromache, the wife of Hector, became the slave of Neoptolemus, and her little son Astyanax, for whom Hector had prayed that he might be a greater man than his father, was thrown from the wall of Troy to his death. Cassandra, whom Apollo graced with the gift of foresight and then cursed (because she would not love him) with the terrible sentence that no man should believe her prophecies, became the slave of Agamemnon. For his death and hers see ATREUS.

Helen, the lovely cause of all this woe, was returned to her husband Menelaus, who accepted her without question. The ship of this royal pair was driven from its course by adverse winds and touched on Cyprus, Phoenicia, and Egypt before Menelaus captured and held the sea god Proteus and forced him to reveal the proper course to steer for home. In Egypt Queen **Polydamna** gave Helen a magic drink called **Nepenthe** which had the power to banish sad recollections (Milton mentions this draught in *Comus,* 675–677); and apparently Menelaus and Helen lived happily together after their return to Sparta. Few were inclined to blame Helen for what had happened. Indeed, a Greek poet named Stesichorus, having been blinded for speaking ill of Helen, invented in his *Palinode* a myth that excused Helen entirely. According to this story, Paris carried her off by force but lost her to the king of Egypt, who kept her safe until Menelaus came to claim her after the war. Meantime a phantom of Helen accompanied Paris to Troy, and it was for this phantom that the war was fought. Most poets did not accept Stesichorus' invention but thought of Helen as the hapless possessor of fatal beauty. Spenser describes her thus in *The Faerie Queen* (3. 9. 35):

> Faire *Helene,* flowre of beautie excellent,
> And girlond of the mighty Conquerours,

That madest many Ladies deare lament
The heuie losse of their braue Paramours,
Which they far off beheld from *Troian* toures,
And saw the fieldes of faire *Scamander* strowne
With carcases of noble warrioures,
Whose fruitless liues were vnder furrow sowne,
And *Xanthus* sandy bankes with bloud all ouerflowne.

Thomas Nashe in a song in *Summers Last Will and Testament,* showing the power of death over human beings, chooses as his most poignant symbol the extinguishing of Helen's radiance:

Beauty is but a flowre,
Which wrinckles will deuoure,
Brightnesse falls from the ayre,
Queenes haue died yong and faire,
Dust hath closde Helens eye.

And Poe's *To Helen* owes its classical imagery to Helen of Troy, even though she is not the Helen of his poem.

It is true that Helen seems as powerless to understand as to avert the disasters caused by her loveliness; and she is sometimes represented, as in Ovid's *Heroides,* as a personification of lust, a shallow courtesan who delights in the death of the heroes and in the final destruction of Troy. Men have usually taken her seriously, either as a girl of innocent and fatal charm or as a heartless courtesan; but Dorothy Parker produced this gay quatrain (*Words of Comfort to Be Scratched on a Mirror*):

Helen of Troy had a wandering glance;
Sappho's restriction was only the sky;
Ninon was ever the chatter of France;
But oh, what a good girl am I![8]

[8] "Words of Comfort to Be Scratched on a Mirror," by Dorothy Parker, in her *Enough Rope.* Copyright, 1926, by Boni & Liveright. Reprinted with the permission of The Viking Press.

Rupert Brooke in *Menelaus and Helen* adds a footnote to Helen's history:

> So far the poet. How should he behold
>   That journey home, the long connubial years?
> He does not tell you how white Helen ·bears
> Child on legitimate child, becomes a scold,
> Haggard with virtue. Menelaus bold
>   Waxed garrulous, and sacked a hundred Troys
>   'Twixt noon and supper. And her golden voice
> Got shrill as he grew deafer. And both were old.
> Often he wonders why on earth he went
>   Troyward, or why poor Paris ever came.
> Oft she weeps, gummy-eyed and impotent;
>   Her dry shanks twitch at Paris' mumbled name.
> So Menelaus nagged; and Helen cried;
> And Paris slept on by Scamander side.[9]

In the Middle Ages and the Renaissance the significance of the Trojan War for English poets was strongly colored by two medieval legends. The first of these, as recorded in Geoffrey of Monmouth's Latin *History of the Kings of Britain,* Layamon's Middle-English *Brut,* and elsewhere, maintains that the first king of Britain was **Brutus,** or **Brut,** a great-grandson of the Trojan Aeneas. The English therefore, when they described the Trojan War, favored the Trojans as much as possible.

The second legend concerns the love affair of Troilus and Criseyde, which was added to the story of the Trojan War by Benoît de Sainte-Maure in *Le Roman de Troie* (1160), and repeated by Guido delle Colonne in his *Historia Trojana* (1287). In *Il Filostrato* (1341–1346) the Italian writer Boccaccio added Troilus' wooing and winning of Criseyde (Benoît's episode begins with the separation of the lovers) and made the story com-

[9] "Menelaus and Helen," II, by Rupert Brooke, in *The Collected Poems of Rupert Brooke.* Copyright, 1915, by Dodd, Mead & Company. Reprinted with the permission of Dodd, Mead & Company.

plete in itself. In Boccaccio's tale the fall of Troy becomes a background for the tragic love affair. The English poet Chaucer, making some use of the earlier versions but relying chiefly on Boccaccio, wrote in *Troilus and Criseyde* a subtle, witty, and touching account of a doomed love.

In this tale the Trojan prince Troilus (in the classical account an unimportant son of Priam who was killed early in the war) falls desperately in love with Criseyde, the daughter of the prophet Calchas who, in this version, is a Trojan who deserts to the Greeks because he foresees the fall of Troy. Pandarus, the Trojan who in Homer's *Iliad* is distinguished only for his foolish breaking of the truce after the duel between Menelaus and Paris, in Chaucer's story is responsible for bringing the lovers together. As Criseyde's uncle and Troilus' friend, he is the kindly ironist whose irony is finally turned on himself, for he stakes his life on the faithfulness of Criseyde. Almost as soon as she yields to Troilus, Criseyde's father Calchas arranges that Antenor, who has been captured by the Greeks, shall be exchanged for his daughter, and she is compelled to leave her lover. They vow eternal faithfulness, but in the Greek camp Criseyde finds her heart turning toward Diomedes, and finally she gives her favors to him. Troilus and Diomedes fight one inconclusive duel, and later Troilus is killed by Achilles.

Chaucer shows Criseyde as a faithless woman, but he understands her so well and pities her so much that he is finally driven to say (5. 1093–1099):

> Ne me ne list this sely womman chyde
> Forther than the storye wol devyse.
> Hire name, allas! is punysshed so wide,
> That for hire gilt it oughte ynough suffise.
> And if I myghte excuse hire any wise,
> For she so sory was for hire untrouthe,
> Iwis, I wolde excuse hire yet for routhe.

Later poets were less kind. The Scot, Robert Henryson, in the *Testament of Cresseid* shows her as a whore soon deserted by Diomedes and finally deprived of her beauty and stricken with leprosy. In the final scene she sits by the road with her beggar's cup and Troilus, riding by, tosses her a coin. He does not recognize her nor she him; but when she learns who has befriended her, she sends him a ring that he once gave her and then she dies. In the Elizabethan Age her name is so debased that Pistol in *Henry V* (2. 1. 80) represents the popular opinion when he describes the whore Doll Tearsheet as a "lazar kite of Cressid's kind."

Working with this degraded tradition, Shakespeare wrote his bitter play *Troilus and Cressida*. The evil-tongued Thersites is a revealing chorus. Of the war he says, "All the argument is a whore and a cuckold. . . . Now, the dry suppeago on the subject, and war and lechery confound all!" (2. 3. 78–82). And the argument is not one whore but two: Cressida as well as Helen. Although Cressida, as she leaves Troilus, promises prettily to be true to him, Ulysses, when he first sees her at the Greek camp, recognizes her for what she is (4. 5. 54–57):

> Fie, fie upon her!
> There's language in her eye, her cheek, her lip;
> Nay, her foot speaks. Her wanton spirits look out
> At every joint and motive of her body.

Pandarus is reduced to his lowest possible denominator. He says (3. 2. 208–212) that if Cressida and Troilus prove false,

> let all pitiful goers-between be call'd to the world's end
> after my name; call them all Pandars. Let all constant men
> be Troiluses, all false women Cressids, and all brokers-
> between Panders! Say 'Amen.'

Most of the other characters are equally degraded. Troilus is a soft fool, Achilles is an unscrupulous fighter, and Ajax is "Mars his idiot" (2. 1. 59). Thersites makes the common Elizabethan pun when he says (2. 1. 70), ". . . whomsoever you take him to be, he is Ajax [that is, a jakes or outhouse]." Sir John Harington cracks this joke in the title of his famous book on privies, *The Metamorphosis of Ajax*. In Shakespeare's play very few characters retain the heroic stature that Homer gives them.

TROY was conquered by Greece in the TROJAN WAR.

TURNUS (tûr′nŭs) fought against AENEAS.

TYCHE (tī′kē) is the goddess of fortune. See FATE.

TYDEUS (tī′dūs) was one of the Seven against THEBES.

TYNDARIUS (tĭn‧dā′rĭ‧ŭs) was Leda's husband. See TROJAN WAR.

TYPHOEUS (tī‧fē′ŭs) is TYPHON.

TYPHON (tī′fŏn), or **Typhoeus,** was a monster with a hundred dragon heads, fiery eyes, and a loud voice. He was made especially for causing trouble in the world, and he carried out his mission with terrible success. His father was Tartarus, the great abyss at the very bottom of Hades, and his mother was Gaea, the earth, who brought him into the world to fight against Zeus when that newly powerful god had just overcome the Titans and was, in the opinion of Gaea, mistreating them by confining some of them in Tartarus. Typhon made war against Zeus in the most violent manner, throwing against the Olympian everything that came to hand, even mountains. According to a late story, Zeus at first was terrified and he and the other gods and goddesses fled to Egypt, where they disguised themselves as animals, Artemis as a cat, Hera as a cow, Aphrodite and Eros as fish, and so on. Later Zeus returned to Greece, struck Typhon with a thunderbolt, and confined the monster in Tartarus, where his struggles to escape still cause earthquakes.

Not all of Typhon's troublemaking was direct. He married **Echidna,** a monstrous creature half-woman and half-snake, and by her sired a family of children who would have seemed hopeless even to modern child psychologists. One of them was the Chimaera whom Bellerophon slew; another was the Sphinx whom Oedipus overcame; third and fourth were the Nemean Lion and the Lernean Hydra whom Heracles killed. Typhon was also the father of Cerberus, the three-headed dog who guards the realm of Hades, and (according to some stories) of all the fierce, destructive winds.

Typhon appears in Egyptian mythology, where he is credited with being the brother of the benevolent Osiris, whom he murdered, and for whose wife Isis he made almost as much trouble as he caused for Zeus.

The many loud and dangerous heads of Typhon seemed to Dryden an apt figure for the multiheaded mob that deposed King Charles I. In *Astraea Redux* (37–40), a poem celebrating the restoration of this king's son, Charles II, Dryden describes the action of the rabble against the king as having been like the occasion

> . . . when the bold Typhoeus scal'd the sky
> And forc'd great Jove from his own heaven to fly,
> (What king, what crown from treason's reach is free,
> If Jove and heaven can violated be?).

TYRRHENIAN (tǐ·rē′nǐ·ǎn) **SEA.** See MEDITERRANEAN SEA.

ULYSSES (ū·lǐs′ēz) is the Roman name for ODYSSEUS.
URANIA (ū·rā′nǐ·à) is the Muse of astronomy. See MUSES.

URANUS (ū′rȧ·nŭs), the sky, was the son and husband of the earth goddess Gaea, and the first ruler of the universe. By Gaea he was the father of many creatures, including the Titans, the Cyclopes, and the Hecatoncheires. The Titan Cronus, urged on by Gaea, attacked and castrated Uranus, and succeeded him as supreme ruler. See CRONUS, EARTH GODDESSES, TITANS.

VELIA (vē′lĭ·ȧ) was one of the Seven Hills of earliest ROME.
VENUS (vē′nŭs) is the Roman name of APHRODITE.
VERTUMNUS (vėr·tŭm′nŭs), whose name means "the changing one," is a minor Roman god who is connected chiefly with the crops of the changing seasons and with the plants' transformation from blossom into fruit. Sacrifices were made to him of garlands of budding flowers and the first fruits of the garden. He fell in love with **Pomona,** the Roman goddess of fruit trees, but she had refused many suitors and for a long time refused Vertumnus also. Milton (*Paradise Lost,* 9. 394–395), describing the innocence of Eve before the fall, says,

> Likeliest she seemd, *Pomona* when she fled
> *Vertumnus* . . . .

The god, using his power to change his shape, approached Pomona in many guises; but nothing he did or said pleased her until he assumed the form of an old woman and eloquently pled his cause. At the climax of the speech he appeared in his own person as a handsome young man, and Pomona at last accepted him as her lover.

VESPER (věs′pẽr) is the Roman name of the evening star, HESPERUS.

VESTA (věs′tȧ) is the Roman name of the goddess of the hearth, HESTIA.

VESTAL VIRGINS were priestesses of the temple of Vesta at Rome. See HESTIA.

VIMINAL (vĭm′ĭ·nȧl) is one of the seven hills of later ROME.

VIRGO (vĭr′gō), the Virgin, is a constellation and a sign of the ZODIAC.

VOLUPTAS (vȯ·lŭp′tȧs), the goddess of pleasure, is the daughter of Psyche and EROS.

VULCAN (vŭl′kȧn) is a Roman name of HEPHAESTUS.

WINDS. The four winds are brothers: the north wind, **Boreas,** or **Aquilo;** the west wind, **Zephyrus,** or **Favonius;** the south wind, **Notus,** or **Auster;** and the east wind, **Eurus.** Their king **Aeolus,** who is also called **Hippotades,** lives a gay life on the island of **Aeolia** where he carouses perpetually with his six sons and six daughters. He keeps the winds imprisoned in a cave and releases them at his pleasure, at the command of a god, and sometimes at the request of a mortal. He once gave Odysseus the storm winds in a bag to assure the safe return of Odysseus' ship to Ithaca; and at the urging of Juno he sent the winds to wreck Aeneas' fleet, which was saved by Neptune. In *Lycidas* (97) when Triton seeks the cause of Lycidas' drowning, sage Hippotades replies that "not a blast was from his dungeon stray'd," and T. S. **Eliot in**

Sweeney Erect writes of Aeolus "Reviewing the insurgent gales." In imitation of Pindar, the famous Greek writer of odes, Thomas Gray invokes the Aeolian lyre (*The Progress of Poesy,* 1), a stringed instrument on which the winds produce musical tones.

The parents of the winds are usually said to be Astraeus or Aeolus and Eos, the goddess of the dawn, but according to one story all the winds but Zephyrus and Notus are the sons of Typhon, the terrible monster created by Gaea, the ancient earth goddess, to fight against the Olympians. This myth is the basis of an amusing poem called *The Weather of Olympus* by the contemporary poet Robert Graves:

> Zeus was once overheard to shout at Hera:
> "You hate it, do you? Well, I hate it worse—
> Boreas all May, Sirocco all the Summer.
> Hell take this whole impossible Universe!"
>
> A scholiast explains this warm rejoinder
> Which seems too manlike for Olympic use,
> By noting that the snake-tailed Chthonian winds
> Were answerable to Fate alone, not Zeus.[1]

("Chthonian" means "of the earth.")

Most of the stories about the winds are of Boreas and Zephyrus, the fiercest and the gentlest. Boreas fell in love with **Orithyia,** but the match was opposed by her father, the king of Athens. One day when Orithyia was playing with her sisters on the bank of a river, Boreas roared down and carried her away. Donne refers to this story in *Elegy 16.* Zephyrus, at the bidding of Eros, gently transported Psyche from the mountain top where she awaited her fate to the valley where Eros made love to her. Zephyrus is also

---

[1] "The Weather of Olympus," by Robert Graves, in his *Poems, 1938–1945.* Reprinted with the permission of the publisher, Creative Age Press, Inc.

the lover of Chloris, or Flora, the goddess of spring. **Chaucer** (*Canterbury Tales*, I. 5–7) wrote of the time

> Whan Zephirus eek with his sweete breeth
> Inspired hath in every holt and heeth
> The tendre croppes,

and countless other poets have related Zephyrus to the spring-time and any time of gentle weather. In Spenser's *Prothalamion* (1–4), for example,

> Calme was the day, and through the trembling ayre,
> Sweete breathing *Zephyrus* did softly play
> A gentle spirit, that lightly did delay
> Hot *Titans* beames. . . .

And Sappho, in Herrick's *The Apron of Flowers,* bringing home spring flowers in her apron,

> . . . lookt as she'd been got with child
> By young *Favonius.*

WOODEN HORSE was the device invented by Odysseus that brought victory to the Greeks in the TROJAN WAR.

XANTHUS (zăn′thûs) is the god of the Scamander river of **Troy.** See TROJAN WAR.

Z

ZEPHYRUS (zĕf′îr·ûs) is the west wind. See WINDS.

ZETES (zē′tēz) was one of the ARGONAUTS.

ZETHUS (zē′thûs) and his twin brother Amphion were regents of THEBES.

ZEUS (zo͞os), or **Jupiter,** or **Jove,** is the son of Cronus and Rhea, and the supreme power of all the Olympian gods. Cronus, having been told that he would be supplanted by one of his children, swallowed each of them at its birth. By the time Zeus was born, Rhea was tired of losing offspring to her husband's digestive tract; so she gave Cronus a stone wrapped like a child and hid Zeus in the island of Crete on Mount Ida. There he was fed by the milk of a goat named **Amalthea,** while Rhea's servants, the Curetes, made a continual clatter with their weapons to prevent Cronus from hearing the young god's crying.

Zeus is said to have grown up in a single year. When he reached maturity, he turned to his grandmother Gaea for aid, and together they succeeded in making Cronus disgorge his five other children—Hades, Poseidon, Demeter, Hestia, and Hera. He also disgorged the stone he had swallowed in the mistaken idea that it was Zeus, and this Zeus placed at Delphi where it became a sacred treasure (see Omphalus under ORACLES). Zeus then with the support of his brother and sister gods overthrew his father and replaced him in control of the world. This usurpation led to a war with the other Titans, most of whom opposed Zeus (see TITANS). The Titans established themselves on Mount **Othrys,** and the gods of course held Mount Olympus. The war was waged inconclusively for a long time, until Zeus again turned

THE GODS OF OLYMPUS
(The names of the chief Olympian deities are italicized.)

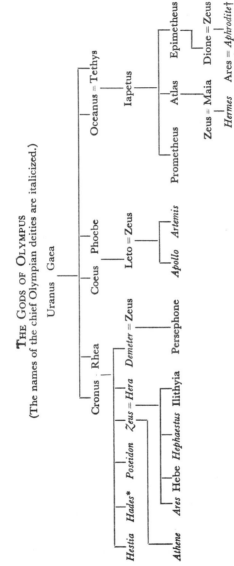

* Hades is customarily omitted in lists of the chief Olympian gods because he spends no time on Mount Olympus, but this is a confusing distinction. The Olympian gods are a family, and Hades is one of the family's most important members.

† According to Hesiod, Aphrodite rose from the foam of the sea where the bits of Uranus' genitals fell when he was mutilated by Cronus.

to his grandmother Gaea for help. She advised him to liberate her sons the Cyclopes and the Hecatoncheires whom Uranus, her husband, had imprisoned in Tartarus. The Cyclopes produced a secret weapon for Zeus, the thunderbolt, which thereafter remained his chief destructive force, and the hundred-handed Hecatoncheires lent their enormous strength. As a result, the Titans were defeated; in their ruin some were destroyed and some imprisoned underground.

Zeus thus became the ruler of the world, but he was soon faced with another danger in the form of an insurrection led by Gaea, who turned against him because of his treatment of the Titans. Gaea created a terrible monster called Typhon, who very nearly overcame the gods but was at last defeated by Zeus's thunderbolt. Then Gaea stirred up her sons the Giants to attack the Olympians, but the gods with the help of Heracles subdued them also, and peace was again established. Zeus then created order in the universe. First he accepted his brother and sister gods as part of his divine government. He and his brothers divided the universe by lot; Poseidon became the ruler of the seas, and Hades of the underworld. The others Zeus took with him into the Olympian household, where they assisted or advised him when necessary and fostered projects among men.

Having gained control of the world of gods and men, Zeus's next preoccupation was to raise a family. He first married **Metis,** whose name means "cleverness," but he was informed by fate that Metis would bear him a child who would be more powerful than he. Fearing a fate like his own father's, he swallowed Metis when she became pregnant. Soon after, he was overcome with a terrible headache. Hephaestus at his request split open Zeus's head, and out of the opening there sprang a goddess in full splendor with a loud battle cry. This was Pallas Athene, the goddess of war and of wisdom, who became one of Zeus's favorites.

Zeus's second wife was **Themis,** the goddess of divine justice. She bore him six children—the three Fates and the three Horae or Hours. But apparently Zeus had always favored Hera, his sister, and at last he married her; they became the parents of Ares, the god of war, Hephaestus, the god of fire, Hebe, the goddess of youth, and (some say) Ilithyia, the goddess of childbirth. Zeus's lust was as great as his power, and his marriages never accounted for much of his sex life. In his affairs with other goddesses and with human girls he became the father of a great number of distinguished children. By the goddess Leto, he had Apollo and Artemis; by Mnemosyne, the Muses; by Demeter, Persephone; by Dione (according to one story), Aphrodite; and by Maia, Hermes.

Of Zeus's illicit affairs, all of which enraged Hera, the best known were with Nymphs or human beings. Because of Hera's jealousy, and for other reasons too, Zeus often approached his paramours in disguise. One to whom he appeared as an eagle was **Aegina,** the daughter of a river god named **Asopus.** Zeus surreptitiously flew off with this young lady, but his abduction of her was seen by Sisyphus, the king of Corinth, who suffers eternally for not keeping the secret (see HADES). Aegina bore Zeus a son named **Aeacus,** and the small island on which the birth occurred was named after Aegina. Hera, in jealousy, sent a plague to the island and destroyed most of its inhabitants. Aeacus, by then the island's king, called on Zeus for aid, and Zeus changed a number of ants into human beings to repopulate the island, for which reason the people were afterward known as **Myrmidons,** which means "of the ant." Aeacus was the father of Peleus and the grandfather of Achilles; after his death he became one of the three judges in Hades.

Another young lady whom Zeus loved was **Alcmene,** his own great-granddaughter by a previous affair. She was the granddaughter of Perseus and Andromeda and the wife of **Amphitryon.**

Zeus fell in love with her and, on the night when Amphitryon was to return from war, appeared to her as her own husband and, to prolong his pleasure, made the night three times its usual length. In the *Epithalamion* (328) Spenser asks that his wedding night may be

> Lyke as when Ioue with fayre Alcmena lay . . . .

Later in the same night the real Amphitryon returned to his wife. From this affair twin sons were born: Heracles, the son of Zeus, and **Iphicles,** the son of Amphitryon. The central situation, the appearance of two connubially inclined Amphitryons in a single evening, has always appealed to writers of sophisticated comedy. The Roman Plautus made a play of it, and later both Molière, the French playwright, and John Dryden followed suit. A few years ago this myth appeared on Broadway under the title *Amphitryon 38,* the thirty-eighth version of the story, by a Frenchman, Jean Giraudoux.

By a girl named Antiope Zeus had two sons out of wedlock. Their names were Amphion and Zethus, and they rebuilt the walls of the city of Thebes, Zethus by lifting and carrying stones and Amphion by charming them into position with the music of his lyre (see THEBES). By Callisto, a Nymph of the train of Artemis, Zeus became the father of a son named Arcas and thereby the cause of two constellations and (according to some stories) a whole tribe of Greeks. For this story see ARTEMIS. Milton alludes to both Antiope and Callisto in *Paradise Regained* (2. 184–187) where he has Satan accuse Belial, another fallen angel, of having sought in other guises,

> In Wood or Grove by mossie Fountain side,
> In Valley or Green Meadow to way-lay
> Some beauty rare, *Calisto, Clymene,*
> *Daphne,* or *Semele, Antiopa.* . . .

One of the best known of Zeus's love involvements was with a princess named **Danae**, the daughter of King Acrisius of Argos. An oracle foretold to King Acrisius that his daughter's son would destroy him. After giving thought to the matter, Acrisius shut Danae inside a brass prison; but brass was not proof against the desires of Zeus, who visited Danae in the form of a shower of gold. The result of this unusual metallurgy was Danae's son, Perseus. Danae's adventure has been one of the favorite stories of English poets. Spenser in *The Faerie Queene* (3. 11. 31) describes many of Zeus's love encounters as tapestries in the House of Busyrane, an enchanter who for Spenser symbolizes illicit love. Of Zeus and Danae, Spenser writes,

> . . . into a golden showre
> Him selfe he chaung'd faire *Danaë* to vew,
> And through the roofe of her strong brasen towre
> Did raine into her lap an hony dew,
> The whiles her foolish garde, that little knew
> Of such deceipt, kept th'yron dore fast bard,
> And watcht, that none should enter nor issew;
> Vaine was the watch, and bootlesse all the ward,
> Whenas the God to golden hew him selfe transfard.

In the 1860's, William Morris retold the story at length and with full imaginative detail in a poem called *The Doom of King Acrisius* in *The Earthly Paradise,* and Tennyson made of it a distinguished metaphor in one of the songs added to his long poem, *The Princess,* in 1853:

> Now lies the Earth all Danaë to the stars,
> And all thy heart lies open unto me.

It is also alluded to by the contemporary poet W. H. Auden in the speech of Herod in *For the Time Being.*

By **Electra**, the Pleiad, Zeus had one of the most important of his extramarital sons. This son was Dardanus, founder of the royal house of Troy. One of the main reasons for Hera's unremitting enmity for the Trojans was this unfaithful act by Zeus. To **Europa,** the daughter of Agenor, king of Tyre, Zeus appeared as a snow-white bull who played so gently before her and her companions that she was tempted at last to sit on his back, whereupon the bull arose and swam off with her into the sea to the island of Crete, where he made love to her. From Crete, Europa went ultimately to the mainland of Europe, a continent that still bears her name. The amour produced for Zeus three sons, Minos, Rhadamanthus, and Sarpedon. This myth is frequently used in English poetry. Europa's ride is one of the subjects of Busyrane's tapestries in *The Faerie Queene* (3. 11. 30), and Spenser also describes the scene more fully in *Muiopotmos* (277–288), where Arachne wove the story to show

how *Ioue* did abuse
Europa like a Bull, and on his backe
Her through the sea did beare; so liuely seene,
That it true Sea, and true Bull ye would weene.

She seem'd still backe vnto the land to looke,
And her play-fellowes aide to call, and feare
The dashing of the waues, that vp she tooke
Her daintie feete, and garments gathered neare:
But (Lord) how she in euerie member shooke,
When as the land she saw no more appeare,
But a wilde wildernes of waters deepe:
Then gan she greatly to lament and weepe.

In later times, Walter Savage Landor in his poem *Europa and Her Mother* gave a full account, in rather stilted terms, of Europa's departure on her unorthodox voyage.

Zeus appeared to **Io** in his own form, but he became aware that his attentions to this girl were about to be discovered by

Hera. He therefore transformed Io into a heifer. Hera, arriving on the scene, asked the origin of the beast; and when Zeus swore that he had just created it, she begged it of him. Zeus could hardly refuse so small a gift without disclosing his guilty secret; so he turned poor Io over to Hera, who put her under the guard of **Argus,** the watchman with a hundred eyes, some of which were always awake. Io was rescued by Hermes, who sang and told stories until all the eyes of Argus were asleep, and then killed him. Hera put Argus' eyes into the tail of the peacock, but she did not abandon her jealousy. She sent a gadfly to sting Io, who wandered in torment over half the classical world. The **Ionian Sea,** which lies off the west coast of the Greek peninsula, was named for her; and she crossed to the east at the **Bosphorus,** "the ford of the cow." Arriving at last in Egypt, she bore a son named **Epaphos.** Robert Bridges gives a colorful recounting of this myth in *Prometheus the Firegiver* (1883) where Prometheus prophesies to Inachus what will happen to his daughter Io.

The story of Zeus's love affair with Leda, which is one of the most important myths, is related in the article on the Trojan War. Another mistress of Zeus was **Semele,** who was the daughter of Cadmus and Harmonia. Since Harmonia was the daughter of Ares and Aphrodite, and since Ares and perhaps Aphrodite were Zeus's children, in this affair Zeus was again adventuring within his own family. To Semele, Zeus appeared as himself, though without his full splendor. Hera, by way of revenge, persuaded Semele to insist on seeing the god in his glory, and he reluctantly consented. The sight was so overwhelming that mortal Semele fell to the ground in ashes, though not before Zeus had rescued their unborn son, Dionysus.

The most questionable of Zeus's love affairs was with a handsome youth named **Ganymedes,** who was the son of King Tros of Troy and his wife Callirhoe. Zeus saw this young man on the slopes of Mount Ida, and in the form of an eagle he seized him and carried him off to Olympus to be his paramour and cup-bearer, in the latter of which functions he replaced Hebe, the earlier holder of the office. This scandalous behavior of Zeus did not escape his wife nor English poets. The former appears to have been able to accept it without comment, but the latter have frequently alluded to it publicly. Christopher Marlowe, in *Hero and Leander* (1. 148–149), a poem not noted for constraint in its treatment of passions, describes the affair of Ganymedes as one of the pictures in the glass floor of the temple of Venus at Sestos:

> Jove slyly stealing from his sister's bed
> To dally with Idalian Ganymed.

The nineteenth-century poet, Robert Lytton, devotes an entire poem to the love affair, and in Sonnet 11 of *In Time of War* W. H. Auden alludes to the myth.

To understand the Greek idea of Zeus, one must turn away from the myths of his licentious private life, for Zeus to the Greeks represented a personage of great and compelling dignity, the upholder of justice and the punisher of wrong, and the controller of the natural order, of the coming of day and night and the seasons. He was the overlord of Olympus who made the other gods as subject to his wishes as were mere mortals. It was to this majestic power that the great temple at Olympia was erected, with its statue of the god forty feet high, made of ivory and gold by the renowned sculptor Phidias. In Zeus's honor the **Olympic Games** were celebrated every fourth year at the stadium in Olympia; all other occupations, even war, were laid aside while the athletes competed. The oldest oracle in Greece was Zeus's oracle at Dodona in Epirus, where the god made known his will by rustling the leaves of the oak trees (see ORACLES).

419

The respectable character of this regal Zeus is perhaps best illustrated by the story of **Philemon** and **Baucis**, an aged couple who dwelt in poverty on the outskirts of a village. Zeus and Hermes, traveling in human disguise through the country, sought hospitality at many houses and were refused; but Philemon and Baucis welcomed them, though they were strangers, and gave them the best that their house had to offer. As a reward Zeus offered them the fulfillment of their most cherished desire. Philemon and Baucis asked that neither of them should survive the other, and by way of granting their wish, Zeus transformed their house into a temple and made them its custodians. At the end of their lives, he changed both of them into trees growing by the temple, so that they could continue in each other's company. Thus did Zeus reward piety and fitting charity.

One must recognize a duality of character in the chief of all the gods. On the one hand, there is the philandering Zeus whose amours have been one of the favorite subjects for poets even down to our own day. On the other hand, there is the Zeus who, second only to fate, represents supreme power in the universe; he is the wielder of the thunderbolt and the source of order and justice among men and gods. How the two characters of Zeus, conflicting as they are, came into existence is a question for an oracle to answer. Plato blamed the disreputable Zeus on the poets such as Homer, who, Plato said, told lies about the gods, for which reason he decided to expel poets from his ideal republic. Whatever the justice of Plato's accusation, Homer's successors in English have continued to tell his kind of story.

ZODIAC (zō′dĭ·ăk) means "relating to animals," and it was applied by ancient astronomers to an area of the celestial sphere because the constellations that fill this area were named after animals and were supposed partly to outline them in configuration. If one imagines the celestial sphere as enclosing the earth at its center, then one can also imagine that it would have coordinates such as a north and south pole and an equator similar to the earth's which would be located immediately outward from the earth's. Thus the north-south pole of the earth, extended to intersect the celestial sphere, would become the north-south pole of the sphere; and the earth's equator would be a circle concentric with and in the same plane as the equator of the celestial sphere.

With these coordinates in mind, one can visualize the Ecliptic also, for it is the path of the sun moving in its annual course. As every one knows, the sun follows an annual course that moves from south to north and back to south again, bringing summer with it and leaving winter behind. This path is a circle on the celestial sphere concentric with the celestial equator, but intersecting it at an angle; and it is called the Ecliptic.

The Zodiac is a band 16 degrees in width, whose center line is the Ecliptic. It was imagined to be 16 degrees in width in order that it might include the paths of the five planets (Mercury, Venus, Mars, Jupiter, and Saturn) known to the ancients, as well as the path of the sun; and it was subdivided into twelve arcs of 30 degrees each in such a way that a major constellation was included in the area of each arc.

The sun in moving along its path from summer to winter each year, passes through each of these twelve areas of the Zodiac, and so also do the five planets. Beginning at the point where the sun's path crosses the sphere's equator going from south to north, and following around the Zodiac in order, the twelve areas, or "celestial houses," are:

Aries	.... the Ram	**Cancer**	...... the Crab
Taurus	...... the Bull	**Leo**	.... the Lion
Gemini	...... the Twins	**Virgo**	.... the Virgin

Libra .... the Scales	**Capricornus** ... the Goat
Scorpio .... the Scorpion	**Aquarius** ..... the Water-Bearer
Sagittarius .... the Archer	**Pisces** .... the Fish

Each of these houses gets its name from the constellation that it includes, and each is commonly represented by the appropriate figure derived from the mythological origin of the constellation. The Ram is the golden-fleeced one that carried off Phrixus and Helle (see ARGONAUTS); the Bull is the form in which Zeus made love to Europa (see ZEUS) and which he afterward placed in the heavens as a constellation; the Twins are Castor and Polydeuces (see CASTOR); the Crab is the one dispatched by Hera to bite the toes of Heracles while he was fighting the Lernean Hydra; later Hera placed this crab among the stars (see HERACLES); the Lion is the Nemean monster slain by Heracles (see HERACLES); the Virgin is Astraea, the goddess of human justice, who fled the earth when the Iron Age came; and the Scales belong to her and are the symbol of her justice (see ASTRAEA); the Scorpion was summoned by Artemis to bite Orion, the huntsman, when he tried to rape the goddess (see ORION); the Archer is Chiron the Centaur (see CEN-TAURS); the Goat is the nanny named Amalthea whose milk fed the infant Zeus (see ZEUS); the Water-Bearer is the young boy Ganymedes, the gods' cupbearer, whom Zeus snatched up from among mortals (see ZEUS); and the Fish are the two forms that Aphrodite and Eros assumed to hide from Typhon in Egypt (see TYPHON).

The Zodiac was first invented by the Babylonians, but its use spread ultimately over the classical world of ancient times, and it was the chief means of telling calendar time. Later astronomical discoveries, chiefly that of Copernicus, which revealed that the earth moves around the sun (instead of the sun around the earth) and that even the *apparent* path of the sun should be an ellipse instead of the true circle which the Zodiac represented, caused the Zodiac to be abandoned by the astronomers before it was abandoned by the poets. Chaucer uses it in his treatise, *The Astrolabe,* which describes the operation of a mechanical device for indicating planetary movements; and in the *Prologue* to *The Canterbury Tales* to indicate the season of the year:

> Whan that Aprille with his shoures soote
> The droghte of March hath perced to the roote,
>
> . . . . . .
>
> . . . and the yonge sonne
> Hath in the Ram his halve cours yronne . . . .

Spenser, in the second of the two cantos of *Mutabilitie* that are appended to *The Faerie Queene* (7. 7. 32–43), gives a symbolic description of the months riding by in procession each on or with the appropriate figure from the Zodiac, March astride a ram, April on a bull, and so on.

In Shakespeare's *Twelfth Night* (1. 3. 144–147) Sir Andrew Aguecheek asks,

> Shall we set about some revels?

and Sir Toby Belch replies:

> What shall we do else? Were we not born under Taurus?

by which he means that they were born in April, or in astrological language, under the sign of Taurus. According to astrological medicine, Taurus ruled conditions of the throat and neck, and Sir Toby is inferring that revelry means drinking and is therefore appropriate to this sign of the Zodiac and to people born under its influence.

A fine poetic use of the Zodiac is to be found in *Paradise Lost*

(10. 671–679) where the angels of Heaven, obeying the commands of the Almighty to make the world less comfortable after the fall of man, arrange for the heat of summer and the cold of winter to replace the equable climate of Eden:

> . . . Som say the Sun
> Was bid turn Reines from th' Equinoctial Rode
> Like distant breadth to *Taurus* with the Seav'n
> *Atlantick* Sisters, and the *Spartan* Twins
> Up to the *Tropic* Crab; thence down amaine
> By *Leo* and the *Virgin* and the *Scales*,
> As deep as *Capricorne*, to bring in change
> Of Seasons to each Clime; else had the Spring
> Perpetual smil'd on Earth with vernant Flours. . . .

LITERARY REFERENCES

LITERARY
REFERENCES

A

Acis and Galatea (Gay), 166

Adonais (Shelley), 72

Aeneid (Virgil), 14–15, 17, 21, 32, 55, 68, 163, 175, 380

Aeschylus, 316, 380
  Agamemnon, 90, 93, 98, 99
  Choephoroe, 90, 98, 99
  Eumenides, 47, 90, 94, 99
  Prometheus Bound, 315
  Prometheus Unbound, 315
  Seven against Thebes, 349, 360

Agamemnon (Aeschylus), 90, 93, 98, 99

Age of Bronze, The (Byron), 131

Ah, Sunflower (Blake), 46

Aias (Sophocles), 396

Alcestis (Euripides), 24–25

Alcibiades (Plato), 129

Aldington, Richard
  Lemures, 216

Amaryllis (Robinson), 54

Amoretti (Spenser), 265, 276

Amphion (Tennyson), 356

Amphitryon (Dryden), 415

Amphitryon 38 (Giraudoux), 415

Amphitryon (Molière), 415

Amphitryon (Plautus), 415

Anatomy of Melancholy, The (Burton), 271

Andromeda (Hopkins), 297

Andromeda (Kingsley), 297

Andromeda Liberata (Chapman), 296

Anonymous
  Beowulf, 10
  Phoenix, The, 306–307
  Priapea, 310
  Tale of Pigmalion, The, 318

Another Actaeon (Bishop), 72

Antic Hay (Huxley), 399

Antigone (Sophocles), 349, 364

Antony and Cleopatra (Shakespeare), 163, 205

Apollo and the Fates (Browning), 158

Apparition of His Mistress Calling Him to Elizium, The (Herrick), 181

Appeasement of Demeter, The (Meredith), 144

Appointment in Samarra (O'Hara), 159

Apron of Flowers, The (Herrick), 410

Arcades (Milton), 52, 141, 217, 341

Arcadia (Sannazaro), 51

Arcadia (Sidney), 51

Areopagitic Oration (Isocrates), 56

Areopagitica (Milton), 56

Arethusa (Shelley), 4, 244

Ariadne to Theseus (C. Rossetti), 372

Aristotle
  Poetics, The, 136

Arnold, Matthew
  Bacchanalia: or, The New Age, 138

427

Jonson, Ben (*cont.*)
    Catiline, 37
    Conversations with Drummond of Hawthornden, 367
    Epitaph on Solomon Pavy, 157
    Masque of Blackness, 328
    Neptune's Triumph, 332
    Oberon, 288
    "Queene and Huntress," 75, 213
Joyce, James
    Portrait of the Artist as a Young Man, A, 129
    Ulysses, 216, 267
Julius Caesar (Shakespeare), 56, 57, 160, 181

K

Keats, John, 129
    Endymion, 1, 4, 73–74, 117, 138, 152–153, 184, 244, 273, 275, 287, 344
    Hyperion, 48, 121, 275, 328–330
    I Stood Tip-Toe upon a Little Hill, 239, 283
    Lamia, 210
    Ode on a Grecian Urn, 100
    Ode on Melancholy, 172, 182
    Ode to a Nightingale, 137–138, 181–182, 302, 303
    Ode to Psyche, 153
    On an Engraved Gem of Leander, 212
    On First Looking into Chapman's Homer, 39
King Lear (Shakespeare), 158, 160
Kingsley, Charles
    Andromeda, 297
Knight's Tale, The (Chaucer), 55, 122, 160

L

L'Allegro (Milton), 10, 170, 184, 278, 339, 346–347
Lamia (Keats), 210
Landor, Walter Savage
    Dirce, 176
    Dryope, 245
    Europa and Her Mother, 417
    Iphigenia and Agamemnon, 386
Laodamia (Wordsworth), 387
Last Poems XXIV (Housman), 219
Last Oracle, The (Swinburne), 49
Laus Veneris (Swinburne), 34
Lawrence, D. H.
    Hymn to Priapus, 310
    Phoenix, 307–308
Layamon
    Brut, 402
Leander (M. Cowley), 212–213
Leda and the Swan (Yeats), 382
Legend of Good Women, The (Chaucer), 18, 24, 60–61, 66, 181, 300–301, 321
Lemures (Aldington), 216
Life and Death of Jason, The (Morris), 67, 277
Locksley Hall (Tennyson), 274
Lodge, Thomas
    Rosalind, 51, 165–166
    Scillaes Metamorphosis, 343
Longfellow, Henry Wadsworth
    Epimetheus, or the Poet's Afterthought, 317
    Prometheus, or the Poet's Forethought, 317
Lotos Eaters, The (Tennyson), 251
Love of Alcestis, The (Morris), 26
Love Song of J. Alfred Prufrock, The (Eliot), 342
"Love Still Has Something of the Sea" (Sedley), 150